A Practical Guide to TPM 2.0

Using the Trusted Platform Module in the New Age of Security

Will Arthur

David Challener

With Kenneth Goldman

Managing Director: Welmoed Spahr
Associate Publisher: Jeffrey Pepper
Lead Editors: Steve Weiss (Apress); Patrick Hauke (Intel)
Coordinating Editor: Melissa Maldonado
Cover Designer: Anna Ishchenko

Distributed to the book trade worldwide by Springer Science+Business Media New York, 233 Spring Street, 6th Floor, New York, NY 10013. Phone 1-800-SPRINGER, fax (201) 348-4505, e-mail orders-ny@springer-sbm.com, or visit www.springeronline.com.

For information on translations, please e-mail rights@apress.com, or visit www.apress.com.

About ApressOpen

What Is ApressOpen?

- ApressOpen is an open access book program that publishes high-quality technical and business information.

- ApressOpen eBooks are available for global, free, noncommercial use.

- ApressOpen eBooks are available in PDF, ePub, and Mobi formats.

- The user friendly ApressOpen free eBook license is presented on the copyright page of this book.

I dedicate my portions of this work to my wife Ruth, and sons Tim and Stephen — D. Challener

To pastor Jon MacKinney and Intel managers Linda Zavaleta and Jody Pfotenhauer, who encouraged me to pursue an engineering degree at an age when many men start thinking about retirement. To John Pennington and Monty Wiseman: for support and mentoring. To my wife, Tammy, and daughters, Casey, Megan, and Rachel: for your patience and support as I've ridden this high-tech roller coaster for the past 30 years. Most of all to Jesus Christ, my ultimate source of security. — Will Arthur

Contents at a Glance

Contents

About the Authors

Will Arthur is a senior staff firmware engineer in the Datacenter Engineering Group for Intel Corporation. He leads the development of authenticated code modules (ACMs) for the server version of Intel Trusted Execution Technology (TXT). As an active participant in the Trusted Computing Group's TPM and TSS working groups, he wrote the TCG TPM 2.0 System API and TPM 2.0 TAB and Resource Manager specifications, developed the TCG versions of the code that implements those specifications, and reviewed and edited the TPM 2.0 specification for readability and accuracy. Will has over 30 years of experience in low-level embedded firmware and software, the last 19 of those years with Intel. Will earned a BSCS in computer science from Arizona State University.

David Challener has been working on Trusted Computing since it started over a dozen years ago. He is currently co-chair of the TPM Working Group, and in the past has been chair of the TSS workgroup and on the TCG technical committee and Board of Directors. He has contributed to a number of other TCG specifications as well. He has a PhD in applied mathematics from the University of Illinois and currently works at The Johns Hopkins University Applied Physics Laboratory.

About the Technical Reviewers

Justin D. "Ozzie" Osborn is the chief scientist of the Commercial Device Operations Group at The Johns Hopkins University Applied Physics Laboratory. He has almost a decade of experience in software reverse engineering and embedded software development. He has worked on several projects that involved developing TPM software and performing vulnerability analyses of TPM solutions.

Monty Wiseman is a security architect in Intel's Data Center Group (DCG). His current projects include architecture for TCG, Intel's TXT technologies, Boot Guard, and other security initiatives. Monty has participated in and chaired the TCG PC Client working group and Security Evaluation working group for TPM 1.2. He participates in the TPM and other TCG workgroups and is Intel's representative on the TCG Technical Committee. Monty has 20 years of experience in desktop, network, and mainframe environments and has held security-related and other engineering positions at Novell, Fujitsu, and Control Data. He has been developing hardware and software for computers ranging from mainframes to microcomputers since 1975.

Acknowledgments

The authors gratefully acknowledge the contributions, edits, and suggestions from our external and internal reviewers:

- Ken Goldman wrote many of the chapters and ruthlessly reviewed the text for technical errors.

- Emily Ratliff and Jon Geater contributed their expertise and knowledge to the ARM and AMD sections of Chapter 22. Bill Futrall also contributed text to Chapter 22.

- Paul England, David Wooten, and Ari Singer helped us understand the specification.

- Paul England helped us understand Microsoft interfaces to the TPM.

- Monty Wiseman, Justin Osborn, Alex Eydelberg, Bill Futral, Jim Greene, and Lisa Raykowski did technical reviews.

- Patrick Hauke of Intel provided moral support and guidance throughout this process.

- We would also like to recognize the many direct and indirect contributions of the TSS and TPM WG members.

Introduction

"Seminal!"

"Riveting! I couldn't put it down until the last page."

"I'm exhausted from reading this book! It kept me up three nights in a row. Where's my Ambien when I need it?"

"The suspense was killing me. I just *had* to read it straight through!"

Although these responses to our book would be gratifying, it's doubtful that any book on digital security will ever garner this type of reaction. Digital security is the computer equivalent of disaster insurance. Few people care very much about it or give it much thought, and everyone hates paying for it ... until a catastrophe hits. Then we are either really glad we had it or really sad that we didn't have enough of it or didn't have it at all.

We may sound like Chicken Little crying the "the sky is falling, the sky is falling," but mark our words: a digital security catastrophe is headed your way. We could quote a plethora of statistics about the rising occurrence of digital security threats, but you've probably heard them, and, quite frankly, you don't care, or at least you don't care enough. It's questionable whether any preaching on our part will make you care enough until you're personally impacted by such a calamity, but we'll try anyway.

When your reputation is tarnished, your finances are impacted, your identity is stolen, your physical well-being is threatened, your company's reputation and finances are harmed, and, quite possibly, your country is overthrown, then you'll wake up to the need for cyber security. But it might be too late then. Like people living in a flood zone, the question isn't whether the flood is coming, but rather when the disaster will hit and whether you'll be prepared for it. The time to buy digital-security flood insurance is now! Don't wait until the flood hits.

A Practical Guide to TPM 2.0 can be part of your digital-security insurance policy. The TPM was designed as one of the core building blocks for digital security solutions. The November 2013 "Report to the President: Immediate Opportunities for Strengthening the Nation's Cybersecurity" recommends "the universal adoption of the Trusted Platform Module (TPM), an industry-standard microchip designed to provide basic security-related functions, primarily involving encryption keys, including for phones and tablets. Computers and devices that incorporate a TPM are able to create cryptographic keys and encrypt them so they can be decrypted only by the TPM. A TPM provides this limited but fundamental set of capabilities that higher layers of cybersecurity can then leverage. Today, TPMs are present in many laptop and desktop personal computers. They're used by enterprises for tasks like secure disk encryption, but they have yet to be incorporated to any significant extent in smartphones, game consoles, televisions, in-car computer systems, and other computerized devices and industrial control systems. This needs to happen for such devices to be trustworthy constituents of the increasingly interconnected device ecosystem."

Our passion in writing this book is to empower and excite a rising generation of IT managers, security architects, systems programmers, application developers, and average users to use the TPM as the bedrock of increasingly sophisticated security solutions that will stem the rising tide of threats that are being aimed at us, our employers, and our civil institutions. Furthermore, the TPM is just plain cool. How many engineers, as children, played with simple cryptography for fun? The ability to send an encrypted message to a friend appeals to the secretive part of our human nature—the same part that enjoyed playing spy games when we were young. And besides being fun, there's something inherently, morally right about protecting people's assets from being stolen.

The TPM 2.0 technology can accomplish this. We believe in this technology and hope to make believers of you, our readers, as well. Our hope is that you'll get as excited about this technology as we are and "go out and do wonderful things" with it, to paraphrase Robert Noyce, one of Intel's founders.

Why a Book?

Technical specifications are typically poor user manuals, and TPM 2.0 is no exception. One reader of the specification claimed it was "security through incomprehensibility." Although the specification attempts to describe the functionality as clearly as possible, its prime objective is to describe how a TPM should work, not how it should be used. It's written for implementers of TPMs, not for application writers using TPMs.

Also, for better or for worse, the detailed operations of the TPM commands are specified in C source code. The structures are defined with various keywords and decorations that permit the Word document to be parsed into a C header file. Microsoft agreed with TCG that the source code in the specification would have an open source license and could be used to implement a TPM. However, although C can describe actions very precisely, even the best code isn't as readable as text. One of the major purposes of this book is to interpret the specification into language that is more understandable to average software developers, especially those who need to understand the low-level details of the specification.

Many readers don't need to understand the detailed operation of the TPM and just want to know how to use the various functions. These readers expect TSS (the TCG software stack) middleware to handle the low-level details. They're interested in how to use the new TPM features to accomplish innovative security functions. Thus, this book is just as concerned with describing how the TPM can be used as it is with explaining how it works. Throughout the book, as features are described, use cases for those features are interwoven. The use cases aren't complete—they describe what the TPM 2.0 specification writers were thinking about when those features were designed, but the specification is so rich that it should be possible to implement many things beyond these use cases.

Audience

In writing this book, we're trying to reach a broad audience of readers: low-level embedded system developers, driver developers, application developers, security architects, engineering managers, and even non-technical users of security applications. We hope to encourage the broadest possible adoption and use of TPMs.

Non-technical readers will want to focus on the introductory material, including the history of the TPM (Chapter 1), basic security concepts (Chapter 2), and existing applications that use TPMs (Chapter 4). Visionaries who know what they want to accomplish but aren't themselves programmers will also benefit from reading these chapters, because knowing the basic ways in which TPMs can be used may provide inspiration for new use cases.

Engineering managers, depending on their needs and technical expertise, can go as deep as they need to or want to. We hope that executives will read the book, see the possibilities provided by TPMs, and subsequently fund TPM-related projects. When they realize, for example, that it's possible for an IT organization to cryptographically identify all of its machines before allowing them onto a network, that true random number generators are available to help seed OSs' "get random number" functions, and that weaker passwords can be made stronger using the anti-dictionary-attack protections inherent in the TPM design, they may decide (and we hope they will) to make these features easily available to everyday people.

Security architects definitely need to understand the functions provided by TPM 2.0 and, depending on the applications being developed, dive deep into how the TPM works in order to understand the security guarantees provided. Linking disparate machines or different functions to provide trusted software and networks should be possible using TPM functionality as security architects get creative. Commercial availability of this capability is long overdue.

Application developers, both architects and implementers, are a significant focus of this book. These readers need to understand the TPM from a high-level viewpoint and will be especially interested in the use cases. TPM 2.0 is feature rich, and the use cases we describe will hopefully inspire creativity in developing and inventing security applications. Developers have to know the basics of symmetric and asymmetric keys and hashes in developing their applications—not the bit-by-bit computations, which are done in the TPM or support software—but rather the types of guarantees that can be obtained by using the TPM correctly.

We also want the book to be useful to embedded system developers, middle ware developers, and programmers integrating TCG technology into operating systems and boot code. The TPM now exposes more general-purpose cryptographic functions, which are useful when a crypto library isn't available due to either resource constraints or licensing issues. We hope that low-level developers will find that this book goes as deep as they need it to and that it serves as a critical tool in interpreting the specification. Toward this end, diagrams and working code examples are used to help clarify many concepts. We expect that embedded systems will increasingly use TPMs as the cost of the technology is reduced (making cryptographic computations cheap to integrate into embedded software) and as attacks on embedded software become more active.

Roadmap

If you're new to security or need a refresher, Chapter 2 gives an overview of the security concepts required to understand the book. This chapter provides high-level knowledge of cryptography: we explain symmetric and asymmetric keys, secure hash algorithms, and how a message authentication code (MAC) can be used as a symmetric key digital signature. This chapter doesn't delve into the underlying math used to implement cryptographic algorithms; this isn't intended as a general-purpose security or cryptography textbook, because there is no need for most TPM 2.0 developers to possess that depth of knowledge.

Chapter 3 presents a high-level tutorial on TPM 2.0 and the design rationale behind it. It begins with applications and use cases enabled by TPM 1.2, all of which are also available in TPM 2.0, and then continues by describing the new capabilities that are available with the TPM 2.0 specification. This chapter should help you understand why people are excited about the technology and want to use it in their applications and environments.

Chapter 4 describes existing applications that use TPMs (currently, mostly 1.2). We assume that many of these applications will be ported to TPM 2.0. Some are open source, some are demonstration code written by academics to demonstrate what the TPM can do, some are applications that have been around a long time and that can be linked to use TPM features, and some are generally available applications written specifically to take advantage of the TPM's capabilities.

Chapter 5 provides a high-level orientation to the TPM 2.0 specification, offers pointers to critical parts of the specification, and explores some best practices for using the specification.

Chapter 6 describes the setup and use of the execution environments available for running TPM 2.0 code examples.

Chapter 7 discusses the trusted software stack (TSS). This is presented early in the book because succeeding code examples use various layers of the TSS.

Chapter 8 begins the deep dive into TPM 2.0 functionality with a description of TPM 2.0 entities: keys, data blobs, and NV indices.

Chapter 9 discusses hierarchies.

Chapter 10 covers keys.

Chapter 11 discusses NV indexes.

Chapter 12 explores PCRs and attestation.

Chapter 13 is one of the most in-depth chapters and is crucial if you're developing low-level code or architecting systems that make extensive use of sessions and authorizations.

Chapter 14 discusses enhanced authorization.

Chapter 15 explains key management.

Chapter 16 describes the TPM's auditing capabilities.

Chapter 17 examines decryption and encryption sessions and how to set them up.

Chapter 18 describes object, sequence, and session context management and the basic functionality of a resource manager.

Chapter 19 discusses TPM startup, initialization, and provisioning. In typical usage, these occur before keys and sessions are used, but knowledge of TPM entities and sessions is a prerequisite to understanding TPM initialization and provisioning. This is why we include this chapter after the previous three chapters.

Chapter 20 presents best practices for debugging TPM 2.0 applications.

Chapter 21 examines high-level applications that could use TPM 2.0 functionality.

Chapter 22 discusses platform-level security technologies that incorporate TPM 2.0 devices into their security solutions.

Assumptions

Although this is a technology book, we have tried to assume as little about our readers as possible. Code examples use C, and a working knowledge of C is useful. However, most of the concepts stand alone, and much of the book should be comprehensible to non-programmers. Security concepts are explained at a high level, and every attempt is made to make them understandable.

Some knowledge of the TPM 1.2 and 2.0 specifications is definitely beneficial but not required. We encourage you to download the TPM 2.0 specifications from www.trustedcomputinggroup.org so that you can refer to them as you read the book.

CHAPTER 1

■ ■ ■

History of the TPM

A Trusted Platform Module, also known as a TPM, is a cryptographic coprocessor that is present on most commercial PCs and servers. In terms of being present in computers, TPMs are nearly ubiquitous, but until recently they've been mostly invisible to users due to lack of compelling applications that use them. That situation is rapidly changing. With the recent awarding of Federal Information Processing Standards (FIPS) certification to various TPM designs, and recommendations from the President's Council of Advisors that the United States government begin using TPMs to defend the nation's computers, the TPM has become a strategic asset for computer owners to defend their cryptographic assets. It is still true that very few people know enough about TPMs to use them in an advantageous manner, a situation that motivated the writing of this book. This chapter introduces you to TPMs, starting with TPM 1.1b, and describes the history of TPM 2.0's predecessors.

Why a TPM?

In the 1990s, it became increasingly obvious to people in the computer industry that the Internet was going to change the way personal computers were connected, and that commerce was going to move toward this environment. This immediately led to a realization that there was a need for increased security in personal computers. When PCs were first designed, little thought was given to their security, so the hardware did not support it. Additionally, software was designed without any thought to security—ease of use was the main driving force in software development.

The computer engineers who got together to develop the first TPMs—and who were part of what came to be known as the Trusted Computing Group (TCG)—were trying to reverse this trend and create a hardware anchor for PC system security on which secure systems could be built. Cost pressures dictated that any such solution had to be very cheap. The result was a hardware TPM chip intended to be physically attached to the motherboard of a PC. The TPM command set was architected to provide all functions necessary for its security use cases, detailed in Chapter 3; but anything not absolutely necessary was moved off chip to software, to keep the cost down. As a result, the specification was hard to read, because it wasn't obvious how commands were to be used when a lot of the logic was left to software. This started a trend in unreadability that has continued through all the updates to the specification.

Hardware security is not an easy topic to begin with, and it doesn't help to have a specification that is hard to understand. A good starting place to understand this technology is the history of its development.

History of Development of the TPM Specification from 1.1b to 1.2

The first widely deployed TPM was TPM 1.1b, which was released in 2003. Even at this early date, the basic functions of a TPM were available. These included key generation (limited to RSA keys), storage, secure authorization, and device-health attestation. Basic functionality to help guarantee privacy was available through the use of anonymous identity keys, based on certificates that could be provided with the TPM; owner authorization was required to create those identity keys. A new network entity called a *privacy certificate authority (CA)* was invented to provide a means to prove that a key generated in the TPM came from a real TPM without identifying which TPM it came from.

Areas of dynamic memory inside the TPM, called Platform Configuration Registers (PCRs), were reserved to maintain the integrity of a system's boot-sequence measurements. PCRs, together with identity keys, could be used to attest to the health of the system's boot sequence. This began the building of a secure architecture based on the TPM anchor, one of the key aims of the TCG.

One specific non-goal of the TCG was making the TPM design immune to physical attacks. Although such capabilities are possible, it was decided to leave physical protections to the manufacturers as an area where they could differentiate. Any software attacks are within scope for TPM-based security, however.

In a manner similar to smart-card chips attached to the motherboard, IBM PCs were the first to use TPMs (similar security coprocessors had been used in mainframe computers for decades). HP and Dell soon followed suit in their PCs, and by 2005 it was difficult to find a commercial PC that did not have a TPM.

One drawback of TPM 1.1b was incompatibilities at the hardware level. TPM vendors had slightly different interfaces, requiring different drivers, and package pinouts were not standardized. TPM 1.2 was developed from 2005–2009 and went through several releases. Its initial improvements over 1.1b included a standard software interface and a mostly standard package pinout.

The TCG realized that although TPM 1.1b protected keys against attackers who did not know a key's authorization password, there was no protection against an attacker trying one password after another in an attempt to guess a correct password. Attackers who do this usually try passwords from a dictionary of common passwords; this is known as a *dictionary attack*. The TPM 1.2 specification required that TPMs have protection against dictionary attacks.

Privacy groups complained about the lack of implementations of privacy CAs. This led to the inclusion in TPM 1.2 of new commands for a second method of anonymizing keys to help address this concerns—direct anonymous attestation (DAA)—and a method of delegating key authorization and administrative (owner-authorized) functions.

It turned out that shipping a machine with a certificate for its TPM's endorsement keys on the hard disk was in many case impractical, because IT organizations often erased the hard disk when they received it and installed their own software load. When they did so, the certificate was deleted. In order to provide a solution, a small amount of nonvolatile RAM (usually about 2KB) was added in TPM 1.2; it had specialized access controls along with a small number of monotonic counters.

The 1.1b specification had a means of copying migratable keys from one TPM to another TPM in case a machine died or needed to be upgraded. This process required the approval of the key owner and the TPM owner. It was designed with the assumption that an IT administrator would be the TPM owner and the user would be the key owner. But in 1.2, the user needed to be able to use the TPM owner authorization to mitigate dictionary attacks and create NVRAM, which made this design impractical. Therefore, in 1.2, another technique was designed to let users create keys that could only be migrated by a designated third party. Such keys could be certified to this effect and hence were called Certified Migratable Keys (CMKs).

Signing keys are often used to sign contracts, and having a timestamp of when the signing takes place is useful. The TCG considered putting a clock into the TPM, but the problem was that the TPM loses power whenever the PC is turned off. Although putting a battery in the TPM is possible, it is unlikely that the increased function would be worth the higher cost. Therefore the TPM was given the ability to synchronize an internal timer with an external clock and then to sign with the value of the internal timer. As an example, this combination could be used to determine when a contract was signed. This functionality also lets the TPM be used to distinguish how much time elapsed between two signature operations performed by the TPM.

No changes were made to existing application programming interfaces in 1.2, which preserved binary compatibility of software written to the 1.1b specification. A side effect was that the TPM 1.2 specification became even more complex, because special cases had to be used to maintain compatibility.

Before TPMs became ubiquitous, security coprocessors such as smart cards were used by some applications to store keys to identify users and keys to encrypt data at rest. TPMs are well equipped to take over this task. But they can do much more: because the security coprocessor is integrated onto the system's motherboard in the form of a TPM, it has additional uses (such as device identification) that are detailed in Chapter 3.

TPM 1.2 was deployed on most x86-based client PCs from 2005 on, began to appear on servers around 2008, and eventually appeared on most servers. Just having hardware does nothing, however—software needs to use it. In order to make use of the TPM hardware, Microsoft supplied a Windows driver, and IBM open sourced a Linux driver. Software began to be deployed, as described in Chapter 4.

How TPM 2.0 Developed from TPM 1.2

In early 2000, when the TCG was faced with the choice of a hash algorithm, it had two choices: MD5, which was most widely deployed; and SHA-1, which was stronger and was deployed widely, although not as widely as MD5. SHA-1 was the strongest commercial algorithm at the time and could feasibly be used in a small, cheap package. This was a fortunate choice, because MD5 weaknesses became apparent shortly afterward.

Around 2005, cryptographers published the first significant attack on the SHA-1 digest algorithm. The TPM 1.2 architecture relied heavily on the SHA-1 algorithm and had hard-coded SHA-1 everywhere. Although an analysis of the attack showed that it did not apply to the ways SHA-1 was used in the TPM, a common axiom in cryptography is that cryptographic algorithms only become weaker over time, never stronger. The TCG immediately began work on a TPM 2.0 specification that would be agile with respect to digest algorithms. That is, the specification would not hard-code SHA-1 or any other algorithm, but rather would incorporate an algorithm identifier that would permit design of a TPM using any algorithm without changing the specification. With this change (and other changes allowing all cryptographic algorithms to be agile), the TCG hoped the new specification could be the last major TPM specification to be released.

The original mandate of the TPM 2.0 Work Group within the TCG was only that: digest agility. However, even a cursory look at the TPM 2.0 specification shows that it's far more than TPM 1.2 plus an algorithm identifier. How did that happen?

TPM 1.1b had carefully crafted structures so that serialized versions (the structures translated into byte streams) were compact enough to be encrypted with a 2,048-bit RSA key in a single encryption. That meant there were only 2,048 bits (256 bytes) to work with. No symmetric encryption algorithms were required in the design, which kept the cost down and avoided problems when exporting designs that could do bulk symmetric encryption. RSA was the only required asymmetric algorithm, and performance required that structures be encrypted in one operation.

TPM 2.0 had to provide for digests that were larger than SHA-1's 20 bytes, so it was clear the existing structures were too large. An RSA key could not directly encrypt the serialized structures in one operation. Using multiple operations to encrypt the structures in blocks was impractical, because RSA operations are slow. Increasing the size of the RSA key would mean using key sizes that were not widely used in the industry and would also increase the cost, change the key structures, and slow the chip. Instead, the TPM Work Group decided the specification had to use the common practice of encrypting a symmetric key with the asymmetric key and the data with the symmetric key. Symmetric key operations are well suited for encrypting large byte streams, because they are much faster than asymmetric operations. Symmetric key encryption thus removed the barrier on the size of structures. This freed the specification developers to use their creativity to architect several functions that were distinct from TPM 1.2.

It is said that the best designs come about when the architects make a design and then, having learned all the problems they will encounter, throw away the first design and start over with a second. TPM 2.0 gave the architects the opportunity to do this. However, they still had to make sure that the opportunities for software development that were enabled by the TPM 1.2 design were not lost with the new architecture.

History of TPM 2.0 Specification Development

The specification made slow but steady progress for several years, with features being debated, added, and deleted. David Grawrock of Intel was the chair of the specification committee; under his leadership, the group selected the major features of the design and settled on a basic feature set and high-order design. At this point, the committee decided to change all the structures to allow for algorithm independence in the specification— this is called *algorithm agility*. All the authentication techniques were unified with a technique originally called *generalized authorization* and now called *enhanced authorization* (EA). This increased the flexibility of authorization while simultaneously reducing the cost of the implementation and reducing the cognitive difficulty of understanding the specification. All objects and entities use the same authentication techniques. Many discussions took place regarding the problems created by having algorithm flexibility while still allowing a user to determine precisely what algorithms were used, both by a given key and also to protect the key, so the overall security of any key held by the TPM could be determined.

When Grawrock left the chairmanship due to changing responsibilities at Intel, Microsoft contributed a full-time editor, David Wooten, and HP took over the chairmanship. It was decided at this point that the specification should be compilable, which drove Wooten to create an emulator while writing the specification. A compilable specification has the advantage of much-reduced ambiguity: if there is doubt about how the specification is supposed to work, it can be compiled into an authoritative emulator. Additionally, the generalized authentication structure was moved from Polish notation (such as used in a TI calculator) to Reverse Polish notation (such as used in an HP calculator), which made implementing the specification easier (but made understanding the specification harder). The committee decided to add multiple key hierarchies to accommodate different user roles.

Wooten worked tirelessly to develop an implementation of the specification and provided strong leadership that drove the specification to its current feature set. When HP's Graeme Proudler stepped down from the chairmanship, David Challener of Johns Hopkins Applied Physics Laboratory formed a joint chairmanship first with Julian Hammersly of AMD, and later with Ari Singer of DMI. Kenneth Goldman (of IBM) took over the editorship from David Wooten after the first release, reprising a role he held for many years with the TPM 1.2 specification.

As new members joined the group over the years and began trying to understand the specification, some of them, notably Will Arthur and Kenneth Goldman, dove deep into the specification line by line. They submitted many bug and readability fixes to the TPM Work Group, and most of those resulted in changes to the specification that enhanced its consistency and readability. Even with these changes, it still is not easy reading, which led to the original impetus for this book.

Summary

The TPM specification has been developed twice. The first time, it developed from 1.1b to 1.2, evolving to incorporate capabilities as they came to be known to the specification committee. This feature-creep form of evolution made the final specification very complicated. In the second generation, TPM 2.0, after the cryptographic weaknesses of SHA-1 caused the need for a change, the architecture was redesigned from scratch—resulting in a much more integrated and unified design. The next chapter introduces the cryptographic concepts that will be used throughout the rest of the book. A good high-level understanding of these is imperative for you to understand TPM 2.0.

CHAPTER 2

■ ■ ■

Basic Security Concepts

This chapter provides an overview of security concepts and their application to the TPM. It is not important that you understand the underlying mathematics of those concepts, so they will not be described. Instead, the chapter discusses the behavior of the various cryptographic algorithms so you can understand how they are used in the TPM 2.0 specification.

Security experts can skip this chapter. If you have less or somewhat rusty knowledge, you are advised to skim it to refresh your memory or learn how basic cryptographic concepts are used in TPMs. If you have little or no TPM knowledge, this chapter is a must read.

All the cryptographic algorithms included in TPM 2.0 are based on public standards that have been extensively reviewed. Creating custom algorithms that are cryptographically strong has generally proven to be very difficult. Many years of cryptanalysis must be performed before an algorithm is considered strong by the community, and only algorithms that have met that criteria are approved for use in the TPM by the Trusted Computing Group (TCG). This chapter describes three types of these algorithms: hash algorithms used mostly for integrity, symmetric-encryption algorithms used mostly for confidentiality, and asymmetric-encryption algorithms used mostly for digital signatures and key management. Specifically, we explore secure hash algorithms the Advanced Encryption Standard (AES); and two asymmetric standards, RSA and elliptic curve cryptography (ECC). But before considering the actual algorithms, you need to know what they are used to defend against.

The chapter begins with a description of the two attack classes: brute force and cryptanalysis. It then defines some fundamental concepts: messages, secrecy, integrity, authentication, and authorization, along with two higher-layer concepts, anti-replay and nonrepudiation. It finishes with a listing of the cryptographic algorithm classes used in the TPM.

For the most part, these are general security principles. They are used throughout the TPM design, and a description of their specific application to TPM 2.0 will be given as they are used throughout the book. In the few cases where the TPM uses cryptography in a less common way, or where the specification introduces a new cryptographic term, we explain it here. (The *extend* operation is an example of both cases: it's a general security concept that has been applied in a new way in TPMs.)

Everything done in a TPM is related in some way to mitigating cryptographic attacks.

Cryptographic Attacks

Cryptography is all about preventing attackers from doing malicious things. Security systems that use cryptography are designed to prevent bad people from having their way with your data, impersonating you, or changing documents without being detected. These attackers may attempt to compromise the security of a cryptographic design in two basic ways: either by deeply understanding the mathematics of the algorithms and protocols and using that knowledge to look for and exploit a flaw in the design, or by using brute force.

If you use well-vetted algorithms and protocols, and use them the way they were designed to be used, your design will *probably* be immune to the first type of attacks. That is why you need to take care to use accepted algorithms and protocols in your design. In a brute-force attack, the attacker tries every possible key, input, or password, trying to guess the secrets used to protect the design.

Brute Force

Cryptographers don't like to claim that anything is impossible. Rather, they say something is "computationally infeasible," meaning it would take an impractical amount of time to attack the cryptography by trying every combination. For the Data Encryption Standard (DES), 2^{56} possible keys could be used. This number is large: 72,057,594,037,927,936. Although breaking the DES algorithm might seem to be computationally infeasible, in 1998, a machine was developed that did exactly that.[1]

Passwords are also often attacked using brute force—first dictionary words are tried, then combinations of words and numbers, and even special characters. Attackers may even try Klingon words or words from the Harry Potter books or *The Lord of the Rings*! RainbowCrack (`www.project-rainbowcrack.com/`) is a well-known program used to crack even fairly long passwords using brute force.

A cryptographic algorithm is well designed if the strength of the algorithm is not dependent on keeping the algorithm secret. The algorithm is infeasible to break if this is true and if it is infeasible to guess the algorithm secret, commonly called a *key*. Defending against brute force attacks is about picking key sizes so large that it is infeasible to try them all, or reducing the number of attacks that can be performed in a period of time.

TCG assumes that all the algorithms it approves are well designed. This may not be true. Because the specification is not wedded to a particular algorithm, if one is found to be weak at some point in the future, then instead of the specification having to be rewritten, just that algorithm can be removed from the list of approved algorithms.

The strength of an algorithm that is well designed is measured by its immunity to mathematical attacks. The strength of an implementation depends on both the type of algorithm and the size of the key used.

---

[1]`http://en.wikipedia.org/wiki/Data_Encryption_Standard#Chronology`.

Calculating the Strength of Algorithms by Type

Symmetric algorithms are used for traditional encryption, where the same key is used for encryption and decryption. For a well-designed symmetric algorithm, the strength of the cryptographic algorithm should depend exponentially on the size of the key used. Thus if a key is only 4 bits long, there are 2^4 or 16 possible keys. A brute-force attacker who tried all 16 keys would break the encryption; but on average the attacker would have to try only half of them, or 8 keys, before finding the correct key. Because the numbers get large quickly via exponentiation, the strength of algorithms is generally quoted in bits. A well-designed symmetric algorithm has a strength equal to the number of bits in its key. In a TPM, the symmetric algorithms usually have key sizes of 128, 192, or 256 bits.

A *secure hash algorithm* is sort of like an algorithm that encrypts but cannot decrypt. This may sound non-useful, but it has a number of very interesting uses. A secure hash algorithm always produces the same size output, independent of the input. A wonderful property of a secure hash algorithm is that given the input, you always get the same output; but given just the output, you can't calculate the input. The strength of such an algorithm can be calculated two ways:

- The number of tries that would have to be attempted to guarantee finding an input that produces a given hash output. For a well-designed hash algorithm, this is assumed to be the size of the output in bits.

- The number of tries that would have to be attempted to have a 50% chance of finding two inputs with exactly the same output. For a well-designed hash algorithm, this is half the size of the output in bits.[2]

Depending on how the secure hash is used, either can be correct; but because cryptographers tend to be P3 people (Paid Professional Paranoids), the latter is generally used for the strength of a well-designed secure hash algorithm.

Asymmetric algorithms are strange at first introduction: The encryption algorithm is different from the decryption algorithm, and the two use different keys, which together form a public and private key pair. There are two asymmetric algorithms you should be concerned about and that are described later in this chapter: RSA (named after its inventors, Rivest, Shamir, and Adleman) and Elliptic Curve Cryptography (ECC).

For asymmetric algorithms, it is difficult to calculate strength corresponding to a particular key size. For RSA, there are tables you can consult. Those tables say that 2048 bits in an RSA asymmetric key corresponds to 112 bits in a symmetric key; 3,076 bits corresponds to 128 bits; and 15,360 bits corresponds to 256 bits of key strength. For ECC, the strength is considered to be half the number of bits of its key's size. Therefore, a 256-bit ECC key is the same strength as a 128-bit symmetric key, and a 384-bit ECC key corresponds to a 192-bit symmetric key.

---

[2]This kind of attack is generally called a *birthday attack*, because of an old party trick. If there are 23 (which is close to the square root of 365) people in a room, the chances of 2 of them having the same birthday is 50%. If there are substantially more people in the room, the probability rises accordingly. If there are 40 people, the probability is almost 90%.

If brute-force attacks are infeasible due to a large key size, the attacker may seek to analyze the mathematics of the cryptographic algorithm or protocol with the hope of finding a shortcut.

Attacks on the Algorithm Itself

Cryptographic algorithm design is a bit of an art. The mathematics are based on how hard it is to solve a particular type of problem, and that difficulty in turn is based on current knowledge. It's very difficult to design an algorithm against which no attacks can ever be mounted.

An attack on the SHA-1 hash algorithm[3] was one of the motivations for moving from TPM 1.2 to TPM 2.0. Under normal circumstances, a brute-force birthday attack on SHA-1 would take about 2^{80} calculations, with a cryptographic strength of 80. The attack, which was based on a weakness in the underlying mathematics, successfully reduced the number of calculations required for a successful attack to 2^{63}—a cryptographic strength of 63. TPM 1.2 used SHA-1 throughout the design. With 56-bit DES encryption defeated by brute-strength attacks in 1998, it was clear that 63 bits was not enough for the industry. For that reason, TPM 2.0 removed this dependency on the SHA-1 algorithm. To defend against such an attack ever happening again, the specification was made *algorithm agile*—algorithms can be added to or subtracted from the specification without requiring that the entire specification be rewritten.

To summarize, in order to be secure, cryptographic algorithms must not have the following vulnerabilities:

- *Weaknesses in algorithms*: You can avoid weak algorithms by using well-vetted, internationally accepted, widely reviewed standards.

- *Brute-force attacks*: By choosing large key sizes and by allowing the end user to pick the key size they wish to use, you can avoid this vulnerability. Today 128 bits is generally considered a safe value for symmetric algorithms, but some researchers and security agencies insist on 192 bits.

Now that you've seen the attacks you're defending against, we can discuss the basic cryptography constructs used in the TPM specification. Let's begin with some definitions.

Security Definitions

Several concepts are important for understanding the TPM architecture and cryptographic concepts. People often equate security solely with secrecy: the inability of an attacker to decode a secret message. Although secrecy is certainly important, there is much more to security. It's easiest to understand these concepts by considering an

---

[3]Xiaoyun Wang, Yiqun Lisa Yin, and Hongbo Yu, "Finding Collisions in the Full SHA-1," *Advances in Cryptology–CRYPTO 2005*.

example. Because electronic business was a big motivator in the design of the TPM, the following example comes from e-business.

An electronic order is transmitted from a buyer to a seller. The seller and buyer may want to keep details (credit card numbers, for example) of the purchase secret. However, they may also want to ensure that the order really came from the buyer, not an attacker; that the order went only to the seller; that the order wasn't altered in transit (for example, by changing the amount charged); and that it was sent exactly once, not blocked or sent multiple times. Finally, the seller may wish to verify that the buyer is permitted by their company to buy the item and to spend the total amount of the purchase order. All these aspects are the problems that cryptography and security protocols attempt to solve.

Based on this example, we can describe several commonly used security terms and concepts, and then explain how they can be used to provide the various aspect of security.

- *Message*: An array of bytes sent between two parties.

- *Secrecy*: A means of preventing an unauthorized observer of a message from determining its contents.

- *Shared secret*: A value that is known to two parties. The secret can be as simple as a password, or it can be an encryption key both parties know.

- *Integrity*: An indication that a message has not been altered during storage or transmission.

- *Authentication*: A means of indicating that a message can be tied to the creator, so the recipient can verify that only the creator could have sent the message.

- *Authorization*: Proof that the user is permitted to perform an operation.

- *Anti-replay*: A means of preventing an attacker from reusing a valid message.

- *Nonrepudiation*: A means of preventing the sender of a message from claiming that they did not send the message.

Let's consider how each of these security concepts fits into the electronic purchase order example. The message is the number of items ordered and any confidential customer information, such as a credit card number. Integrity ensures that the order has not been altered in transit—for instance, from 3 items to 300 items. Authentication proves that the order came from the buyer. Authorization checks that the buyer is permitted to purchase the items on behalf of their company. Anti-replay prevents the attacker from sending the buyer's message again to purchase three items multiple times. And nonrepudiation means the buyer can't claim they never ordered the items.

To provide these security guarantees, designers of a security system have a toolbox of cryptographic functions that have been developed, analyzed, and standardized. Some items are fundamental mathematical building blocks, such as the SHA-256 secure hash algorithm or the RSA asymmetric-key encryption calculation. Other items, such as digital signatures, build on these fundamentals by using the RSA algorithm. These cryptographic functions are described next.

Cryptographic Families

Trust us, there's no math in this section. We won't be describing prime number algorithms and elliptic curves. But it's important to understand some cryptographic operations and how they relate to the basic security principles you've already seen.

A secure hash algorithm is used to provide integrity. It can be combined with a shared-secret signing key in an HMAC algorithm to ensure authentication. HMAC is in turn the basis for a cryptographic ticket and key-derivation functions. A shared secret provides secrecy when used in symmetric-key encryption. A nonce provides anti-replay protection. An asymmetric key used as a signing key offers nonrepudiation. The TPM also uses an asymmetric key for secrecy in some protocols. All these concepts are described in the following sections.

Secure Hash (or Digest)

Most computer science students are familiar with hashes; simple hashes are used to speed searches. A more advanced form of a hash is a checksum that is used to detect random errors in data. But cryptographers are concerned with malicious attackers trying to break a system, so they need a secure cryptographic hash with very specific properties.

A cryptographic hash, like its much simpler cousins, takes a message of any length and compresses it to a hash of fixed length. For example, a SHA-256 hash is 256 bits or 32 bytes. For security purposes, the important properties of a secure hash are as follows:

- It's infeasible, given a message, to construct another message with the same hash.

- It's infeasible to construct two messages with the same hash.

- It's infeasible to derive the message given its hash.

As an example, you can observe that even a very small change in a message causes a large change in the digest produced by the hash. For example, using SHA-1, the message "Hello" hashes to:

`fedd18797811a4af659678ea5db618f8dc91480b`

The message "hello" with the first character changed to lowercase hashes to:

`aa5916ae7fd159a18b1b72ea905c757207e26689`

The TPM 2.0 specification allows for a number of different types of hash algorithms—SHA-1, SHA-256, and SHA-384 are just some of them. Typically, TPMs implement only a few of the allowed hashes. One problem that vexed the developers for a long time was how to integrate multiple hash algorithms (which are used to maintain integrity) if one of those hash algorithms was later broken. This is harder than it sounds, because usually hash algorithms themselves are used to provide integrity to reports, and if the hash algorithm can't be trusted, how can you trust a report of which hash algorithm is being used? The design that was chosen managed to avoid this problem: tags are used throughout the design in data elements that identify the hash algorithms used.

In the TPM, a secure hash is a building block for other operations, such as hash-extend operations, HMACs, tickets, asymmetric-key digital signatures, and key-derivation functions, all described next.

Hash Extend

The term *extend* is not a common cryptographic term, but this operation is used throughout the TPM. An extend operation consists of the following:

1. Start with an existing value, A.

2. Concatenate another value, B (the value to be extended) to it, creating the message, A || B.

3. Hash the resulting message to create a new hash, hash(A || B).

4. This new hash replaces the original value, A.

The whole process can be summarized as: A ← hash (original A || B).

As an example, using SHA-1, extending the digest of the message 'abc' to an initial value of all zero yields this result:

```
ccd5bd41458de644ac34a2478b58ff819bef5acf
```

The extend value that results from a series of extend operations effectively records a history of the messages extended into it. Because of the properties of a secure hash, it is infeasible to back up to a previous value. Thus, once a message is extended, there is no "undo" to go backward—to reverse the calculation and erase past history. However, the actual size of the value, such as 32 bytes for the SHA-256 hash algorithm, never changes, no matter how many messages are extended. The fixed length of an extend value coupled with its ability to record a virtually unlimited history of extend operations is critical in the memory-constrained TPM.

Extend is used to update platform configuration register (PCR) values. A PCR is a TPM register holding a hash value. The values extended into the PCR can represent the platform state. Suppose the PCR indicates an untrusted state, but an attacker wants to change the PCR to a trusted value. To do this, the attacker would have to construct another message, starting with the current PCR value, whose resulting hash was a trusted value. The properties of a secure hash dictate that this is infeasible.

Extend is also used in TPM audit logs. The audit logs record TPM commands and responses. Because of the extend properties, an item cannot be removed from the log once it has been added, and the size of the log in the TPM remains constant no matter how many commands are audited.

In addition, extend is used in creating policies that represent how a TPM can be authenticated. This is described in the chapter on extended authorization.

Hashes are also used in a simpler form of authorization, which was also used in the TPM 1.1 and TPM 1.2, called an HMAC.

HMAC: Message Authentication Code

An HMAC is a keyed hash. That is, it performs a secure-hash operation but mixes in a shared secret key, the HMAC key. Because of the properties of a secure hash, given a message, only a party with knowledge of the HMAC key can calculate the result. Applying a key to a message in this way is known as "HMACing" the message.

TPM 1.2 used HMACs throughout to prove to the TPM that the user knew a TPM entity's authorization data, which was used as the HMAC key. TPM 2.0 can also authorize entities this way. The HMAC key is a shared secret between the TPM and the caller. As an example, a TPM object, such as a signing key, may have an associated authorization value that is known to both the TPM and an authorized user of the key. The user constructs a TPM command to use the object and calculates an HMAC over the command message using an HMAC key that is derived in part from the object's authorization value. The TPM receives the command message and performs the same HMAC operation using the same HMAC key. If the results are the same, the TPM knows the command has not been altered (integrity) and that the caller knew the object's HMAC key, which in turn means the caller knew the authorization value. Thus the caller was authorized.

The TPM also uses HMAC for integrity of structures that may at times be stored externally—in other words, proof that an attacker has not altered a value. Here, the HMAC key is a secret known only to the TPM, not shared with any party outside the TPM. When the TPM outputs a value to be stored for later use, it includes an HMAC using its secret. When the value is later input, the TPM verifies the HMAC to detect any external alteration of the value. Essentially, the HMAC key is a shared secret between the TPM and itself across a time interval: from the time the value is stored externally to the time the value is input to the TPM. One example of this use of HMACs is an authentication ticket. The TPM uses these tickets to prove to itself that it did an operation by producing an HMAC of a digest of the result of the operation, using an internal secret that only it knows.

HMACs can also be used to derive keys, using something called a key derivation function.

KDF: Key Derivation Function

A manufacturer might want to ship a TPM with certificates for multiple key sizes for multiple algorithms. But a TPM has a limited amount of space to store these keys. Further, many TPM protocols require more than one secret. For example, one secret may be required to symmetrically encrypt a message, and a second may be used to HMAC the result. In order to reduce the cost of manufacturing a TPM, the TPM has the ability to create multiple keys from a single secret. This secret is called a *seed*, and the algorithm used to derive multiple secrets from this seed is called a *key derivation function* (KDF). The TPM can use KDFs to derive both symmetric and asymmetric keys.

Because, as explained earlier, encryption doesn't provide integrity, the usual pattern is to encrypt with a symmetric key and then HMAC with an HMAC key. The question that arises is, "Does this mean there must be two shared secrets?" Not usually. The design pattern is to share one secret, a seed. From this one seed, a KDF is used to derive a symmetric encryption key and an HMAC key.

The TPM uses an HMAC as a KDF based on an algorithm specified by NIST in Special Publication 800-108. In a typical case, it HMACs some varying data using the seed as the HMAC key to derive the keys. The varying data always includes a string of bytes describing the application of the keys. This ensures that, when the same seed is used for different applications, different keys are used. This satisfies a basic crypto rule: never use the same key for two different applications. The other data also includes values unique to the operation. If you need two keys with the same description, you must use different unique values to guarantee that unique keys are created.

Authentication or Authorization Ticket

A *ticket* is a data structure that contains an HMAC that was calculated over some data. The ticket allows the TPM to validate at a later time that some operation was performed by the TPM. The HMAC asserts that some operation has been previously performed correctly and need not be performed again. In practice, the data is often not the actual message, which may be too large to fit in the ticket, but a digest of the message. The TPM uses tickets when it splits cryptographic operations into multiple operations with respect to time. Here, the HMAC key used to generate the HMAC is not a shared secret, but a secret known only to the TPM.

For example, the TPM uses a ticket when it calculates a hash over a message that it will later sign. It produces a ticket that says, "I calculated this hash and I assert that it is a hash that I will sign." It signs the ticket by producing an HMAC using a secret only the TPM knows. Later, the HMAC is presented along with the ticket. The ticket is verified using the same secret HMAC key. Because only the TPM knows the HMAC key, it knows the ticket was produced by the TPM (authenticity) and that it has not been altered (integrity).

The TPM can do something similar when storing data outside the TPM. It can encrypt that data with a secret only it knows and then decrypt it again when loading it back inside the TPM. In this case, a symmetric key is used for encryption.

Symmetric-Encryption Key

A *symmetric-encryption key* is a key used with a symmetric-encryption algorithm. Symmetric algorithms use the same key for both encryption and decryption. (An HMAC key is also a symmetric key, but it's used for signing, not encryption.)

A typical symmetric-key algorithm is the Advanced Encryption Standard (AES). Other algorithms are supported by the specification, including Camellia and SM4; but because they all work pretty much the same, all of this book's examples use AES. The TPM uses symmetric-key encryption in three different ways:

- *Keeping TPM data secret from all observers*: The symmetric key isn't shared outside the TPM. It's generated by and known only to the TPM. For example, when a key is cached (offloaded) from the TPM in order to free memory for other TPM operations, the TPM encrypts the key using symmetric encryption. This symmetric key is known only to the TPM.

- *Encrypting communications to and from the TPM*: Here, the symmetric key is generated based on a secret agreed on by the sender and the TPM. Then parameters are passed to the TPM encrypted, and the results are returned encrypted from the TPM to the user.

- *Using the TPM as a cryptographic coprocessor*: Because the TPM knows how to encrypt things using symmetric keys, you can use the TPM to do that. You can load a key into the TPM and then ask the TPM to encrypt data with that key. TPMs usually aren't very fast at doing this, so this is typically only done for a small amount of data, but it can prevent an application programmer from having to use a cryptographic library for some programs. When specified as optional by the platform-specific TPM specifications, it's likely that TPM vendors and/or platform manufacturers will exclude symmetric encryption and decryption commands, because a hardware device that can do bulk symmetric-key operations can be subject to export (or perhaps import) restrictions or licensing.

Symmetric-key encryption is a little more complicated than just picking an algorithm and a key. You also need to select a mode of encryption. Different modes are used in different protocols.

Symmetric-Key Modes

Typical symmetric-key encryption algorithms like AES work on blocks of data. Two problems must be solved when using block-mode encryption:

- If blocks are simply encrypted with the key, the same block will always produce the same result. This is called *electronic codebook (ECB)* mode. If a bitmap picture is encrypted using ECB, all that happens is that the colors are changed.[4] Obviously this isn't useful if the data being encrypted is large.

  To counter this, the TPM supports several other modes: cipher-block chaining (CBC), cipher-feedback (CFB), output-feedback (OFB), and counter (CTR). All these modes have the property that if the same block is encrypted more than once in the same message, the result is different each time.

- Some modes, like CBC, require that the output be an exact multiple of the block size of the underlying algorithm. If the input isn't a multiple of the block size (which is usually 128 bits or 16 bytes), it is padded to make this true. When this input is encrypted, the output is larger than the initial data by the size of the padding. For applications where the output can be a different size than the input (such as offloading a key), this isn't a problem; but it's inappropriate when the input and output must be the same size (such as when you're encrypting a TPM command).

---

[4]http://en.wikipedia.org/wiki/Block_cipher_mode_of_operation.

16

In this second case, you can use CFB or CTR mode. In CFB mode, a symmetric key encrypts an initialization vector, with the result being used as the initialization vector for the next block. In CTR mode, the symmetric key is used to encrypt incrementing counter values. In both modes, the resulting byte stream is XORed with the input to produce the output. As many bytes of the stream as necessary are used, and extra bytes are discarded, so the output is the same size as the input.

A property of CFB and CTR modes (actually a property of XOR) is that flipping a bit in the encrypted stream flips exactly the same bit in the decrypted stream. The attacker may not know the message but can certainly alter it. An attacker can flip a bit in a message encrypted using CBC mode as well, but more bits will change in the decrypted data.

This leads to an important (and often missed) point. Encryption provides secrecy, but it does not provide integrity or authenticity. To ensure those latter properties, the TPM uses an HMAC on the encrypted data. It does not depend on the decrypted data "looking funny" to detect alteration. Indeed, by calculating the HMAC of the encrypted message first, the TPM will not even attempt to decrypt it unless it is first determined that the message's integrity is intact and that it is authentic.

Additionally, encryption does not provide evidence that the message was produced recently. That is done with a nonce.

Nonce

A *nonce* is a number that is used only once in a cryptographic operation. It provides protection against a replay attack. In order to guarantee that a message hasn't been replayed, the recipient generates the nonce and sends it to the sender. The sender includes that nonce in the message. Because the sender presumably has no way of knowing what nonce the recipient will choose, they can't replay a message that was prepared earlier. But of course, you must take care that a previously prepared message can't just be minimally modified. When sending commands to a TPM and receiving the results back, nonces provide proof to the user that the results of the command were sent by the TPM.

In a typical TPM use, the nonce is included in the calculation of the HMAC of a command message. After an operation using the message is complete, the TPM changes the nonce. If the caller attempts to replay the message which had an HMAC that used the previous nonce, the TPM will attempt to verify the HMAC of the replayed message using the new nonce, and this verification will fail.

For many applications, a nonce can simply be a number that increments at each use and is large enough to never wrap around. However, this would require the TPM to keep track of the last-used value. Instead, the TPM takes advantage of its random-number generator. It uses random numbers as its nonces, and it uses large enough values (for example, 20 bytes) that the odds of a repeat are nil.

Asymmetric Keys

Asymmetric keys are used by asymmetric algorithms for digital identities and key management. They are actually a key pair: a private key known only to one party and a public key known to everyone. Asymmetric keys make use of mathematical *one-way* functions. These functions have the property that calculating the public key from the private key is relatively easy computationally, but calculating the private key from the public key is computationally infeasible.

You all have window seats in The Restaurant at the End of the Universe

—Mullen 2011

If the owner of the private key uses it to encrypt some data (and the key is large enough), everyone can use the public key to decrypt the data, but everyone will know that only the holder of the private key could have encrypted that data. This is called *signing* the data. There are some complications to using this securely—the data that is signed should be in a particular format called a *signing scheme*, but the TPM ensures sure that the correct format is used.

If someone wants to share data (usually a symmetric key) with the owner of a private key in a secure way, they can provide the data to the owner by encrypting it with the owner's public key. Then they can be certain that only the owner will be able to recover the shared data by using the owner's private key. This is done in different ways depending on the type of asymmetric algorithm, but we skip these deep mathematical details here.

RSA Asymmetric-Key Algorithm

RSA is a well-known asymmetric-key algorithm. It uses the factoring of large numbers into large primes as its one-way function. RSA has an interesting property: If the private key is first applied to a message and then the public key is applied to the result, the original message is obtained. Alternatively, if the public key is applied to a message and then the private key is applied to the result, again the original message is obtained.

Thus, RSA can be used for both encryption and digital signatures. In encryption and decryption, the public key is used to encrypt data, and the private key is used to decrypt data. For digital signatures, the private key is used to digitally sign, and the public key is used to verify signatures.

RSA for Key Encryption

To encrypt using the asymmetric keys, you apply the recipient's public key, which is known to you because it's public, to the message. The holder of the private key can apply their key to recover the message. It is secret from everyone else because the private key is, well, private.

In practice, messages are not typically encrypted directly with an asymmetric key. The data size is limited, based on the size of the key. Breaking up the message into smaller pieces is possible but impractical because asymmetric-key operations are typically very slow.

The usual pattern is to encrypt a symmetric key with the asymmetric public key, send the encrypted symmetric key to the recipient, and then encrypt the message with that symmetric key. The recipient decrypts the symmetric key using their private key and then decrypts the message with the much faster symmetric-key algorithm.

RSA for Digital Signatures

A digital signature is similar to an HMAC but has additional properties. To create an asymmetric-key digital signature, the signer applies their private key to a message. The verifier applies the public key to the signature to recover and verify the message.

A digital signature permits the recipient to know that a message has integrity and is authentic, qualities that an HMAC also possesses. An asymmetric-key digital signature goes further:

- Because the verification key is public, multiple parties can verify the signature. With an HMAC, the verification key is a shared secret, and only a holder of the shared secret can verify the message.

- Because a private key is used to generate the signature, only the sender (the holder of the private key) could have generated the signature, and the recipient can prove it to a third party. With an HMAC, a shared secret is used, and both the sender and the recipient know the shared secret. The recipient can verify that the signature was generated by the sender, but the recipient can't prove this to a third party, because, for all the third party knows, the recipient could also have generated the signature.

As with asymmetric-key encryption, the digital signature isn't typically applied directly to the message, because the message would be limited based on the key size.

The usual pattern is to digest the message and apply the private key to the smaller digest. The verifier applies the public key to the signature to recover the signed digest and compares that digest to one calculated from the message. This works because it is infeasible for an attacker to construct a second message with the same digest.

RSA is not the only asymmetric-key algorithm. Elliptic curve cryptography (ECC) is gaining popularity and is included in the latest specification.

ECC Asymmetric-Key Algorithm

ECC is another type of asymmetric mathematics that is used for cryptography. Unlike RSA, which uses an easily understood mathematical operation—factoring a product of two large primes—ECC uses more difficult mathematical concepts based on elliptic curves over a finite field. We will not describe the mathematics but instead describe how it is used. Just like every other asymmetric algorithm, ECC has a private and public key pair. The public key can be used to verify something signed with the private key, and the private key can be used to decrypt data that was encrypted using the public key.

For equivalent strength, ECC keys are much smaller than RSA keys. The strength of an ECC key is half the key size, so a 256-bit ECC key has 128 bits of strength. A similarly strong RSA key is 3,076 bits long. Smaller key sizes use fewer resources and perform faster. For encryption, a procedure known as *Elliptic Curve Diffie-Hellman (ECDH)* is used with ECC. For signing, *Elliptic Curve Digital Signature Algorithm (ECDSA)* is used.

ECDH Asymmetric-Key Algorithm to Use Elliptic Curves to Pass Keys

When using ECC to encrypt/decrypt asymmetrically, you use the ECDH algorithm. The main difference between ECC and RSA for encryption/decryption is that the process of using an ECDH key takes two steps, whereas RSA takes only one. When encrypting a symmetric key with a TPM-based RSA key, you use the TPM RSA's public key to encrypt it. When encrypting a symmetric key with a TPM-based ECDH key, two steps are required: Generate (in software) another ECDH key; and then use the private key of the newly generated ECDH key and the public portion of the TPM ECDH key to generate a new ephemeral random number, which is input to a KDF to generate a symmetric key. To put this more succinctly, with RSA you can supply the symmetric key to be encrypted, but with ECDH the process generates the symmetric key.

To recover the symmetric key, the public portion of the software-generated ECDH key is given to the TPM. It uses it together with the private portion of its own ECDH key to regenerate the ephemeral random number, which it inputs into a KDF internally to regenerate the symmetric key.

ECDSA Asymmetric-Key Algorithm to Use Elliptic Curves for Signatures

ECDSA is used as an algorithm with ECC to produce signatures. Just as with RSA, in ECDSA the private key is used to sign and the public key is used to verify the signature. The main difference (other than the mathematical steps used) is that when using an ECC key, because it's much smaller than an RSA key, you have to ensure that the hash of the message you're signing isn't too big. The ECDSA signature signs only n bits of the hash, where n is the size of the key. (This is also true of RSA; but RSA keys sizes are typically >=1,024 bits and hash sizes top out at 512 bits, so this is never a problem.)

Whereas with RSA you can typically sign a message with any hash algorithm, with ECC you typically use a hash algorithm that matches the size of the key: SHA-256 for ECC-256 and SHA-384 for ECC-384. If you used SHA-512 (which produces 512-bit hashes) with an ECC-384 key, ECDSA would sign only the first 384 bits of the hash. You can sign smaller hashes without any problem, of course, so an ECC 384-bit key could be used to sign SHA-384, SHA-256, or SHA-1 (160 bits) hashes.

One problem with all signing protocols is that the recipient of the signature needs to be assured that the public key they use to verify the signature really belongs to the owner of the private key who signed it. This is handled with public key certificates.

Public Key Certification

Certification is part of an asymmetric-key protocol and solves the following problem: How do you trust the public key? After all, it accomplishes nothing to verify a digital signature with a public key if you don't know whose public key you're using. Secrecy won't be preserved if you encrypt a message with the attacker's public key. Establishing trust in a TPM public key includes knowing that the key really came from whom it was supposed to come from—in this case, a TPM.

The solution is to create a digital certificate. A certificate includes the public part of the key being certified plus attributes of that key. The certificate is then signed by a certificate authority (CA) key. It's possible that the CA public key is in turn certified by another CA key, forming a hierarchy (a certificate *chain*). At some point, this certificate chain terminates at a root certificate. The root public key must be conveyed to a verifier out of band and is declared trusted without cryptographic proof.

The X.509 standard[5] describes a widely used certificate format. The TPM, as a limited-resource device, neither creates nor consumes X.509 certificates. The TCG Infrastructure work group does specify some X.509 certificate formats, and the TPM typically stores them. This storage is simply for provisioning convenience, pairing a certificate with its key, not to achieve any security goal.

In the TPM space, there are several certification processes:

- The TPM vendor and platform manufacturer may provision the TPM with TPM vendor and platform endorsement keys (EKs) and corresponding certificates before shipment to the end user. The TPM vendor certificate asserts, "This endorsement key is resident on an authentic TPM manufactured by me." The platform manufacturer certificate asserts, "This key is resident on a TPM that is part of my platform, and this platform supports certain TPM features." These certificates typically use X.509 format.

- If the TPM keys (and their corresponding certificates) just described exist as signing keys, they can be used to certify other keys as being resident on the TPM and having certain properties. The TPM 2.0 specification provides commands to create certificates. These TPM-generated certificates do not use X.509, which is too complex for the limited on-chip resources of the TPM.

Essentially, digital certificates rest on the integrity of the CA. The CA is considered to be a neutral party that can be trusted by two parties: the parties that create the certificates and those that use them. A CA's functioning is similar to an escrow agent that mediates fund transfers in a real-estate transaction. If the CA is worthy of trust, all is good. If not, all bets are off.

When a TPM manufacturer produces a certificate for a TPM, the manufacturer faces a quandary. What algorithm should be used for the key? The manufacturer doesn't know if the end user will want RSA-2048, ECC2-56, ECC-384, or some other algorithm. And it also needs to know what hash algorithm and symmetric algorithm should be used in the creation of the key. To solve this problem, the TPM is designed to allow the creation of many keys derived from a single large random number, using a key-derivation function, as described earlier. You see in the chapter on hierarchies how this is used to provide many certificates for multiple algorithms without using up space in the TPM.

---

[5]www.ietf.org/rfc/rfc2459.txt.

Summary

By examining a sample use case, you've seen all the major security operations and concepts that are used in the rest of the book to explain the creation and use of the TPM. This isn't surprising, because the TPM was designed with use cases in mind, and one of the major ones was e-commerce. By starting with the attacks cryptographic operations need to defend against, you saw why cryptographic algorithms are chosen from well-vetted internationally recognized algorithms and how key strengths are chosen. You reviewed the concepts of confidentiality, integrity, electronic identity, and nonrepudiation and how they relate to the standard classes of algorithms: symmetric, asymmetric, hash, and HMAC. Finally, you learned about some specific new features in the TPM specification that use those algorithms: extend, tickets, and certificates. You're ready to consider all the use cases the TPM was design to solve.

CHAPTER 3

■ ■ ■

Quick Tutorial on TPM 2.0

This chapter describes the major uses of TPM capabilities. The use cases for which TPM 1.2 was designed still pertain to TPM 2.0, so we begin by exploring those use cases and the designed functionality that enables them. Then we move to new aspects of the TPM 2.0 design and the use cases enabled by those capabilities.

As noted in Chapter 1, the rise of the Internet and the corresponding increase in security problems, particularly in the area of e-business, were the main driving forces for designing TPMs. A hardware-based standardized security solution became imperative. At the same time, due to the lack of a legacy solution, security researchers were presented with a golden opportunity to design a new security system from the ground up. It has long been a dream of security architects to not merely patch problems that existed in earlier designs, but also provide a security anchor on which new architectures can be built.

The TPM 1.2 specification was the Trusted Computing Group's (TPG's) first attempt to solve this problem and was aimed at addressing the following major issues in the industry:

- *Identification of devices*: Prior to the release of the TPM specification, devices were mostly identified by MAC addresses or IP addresses—not security identifiers.

- *Secure generation of keys*: Having a hardware random-number generator is a big advantage when creating keys. A number of security solutions have been broken due to poor key generation.

- *Secure storage of keys*: Keeping good keys secure, particularly from software attacks, is a big advantage that the TPM design brings to a device.

- *NVRAM storage*: When an IT organization acquires a new device, it often wipes the hard disk and rewrites the disk with the organization's standard load. Having NVRAM allows a TPM to maintain a certificate store.

- *Device health attestation*: Prior to systems having TPMs, IT organizations used software to attest to system health. But if a system was compromised, it might report it was healthy, even when it wasn't.

The TPM 2.0 implementations enable the same features as 1.2, plus several more:

- *Algorithm agility*: Algorithms can be changed without revisiting the specification, should they prove to be cryptographically weaker than expected.

- *Enhanced authorization*: This new capability unifies the way all entities in a TPM are authorized, while extending the TPM's ability to enable authorization policies that allow for multifactor and multiuser authentication. Additional management functions are also included.

- *Quick key loading*: Loading keys into a TPM used to take a relatively long time. They now can be loaded quickly, using symmetric rather than asymmetric encryption.

- *Non-brittle PCRs*: In the past, locking keys to device states caused management problems. Often, when a device state had to go through an authorized state change, keys had to be changed as well. This is no longer the case.

- *Flexible management*: Different kinds of authorization can be separated, allowing for much more flexible management of TPM resources.

- *Identifying resources by name*: Indirect references in the TPM 1.2 design led to security challenges. Those have been fixed by using cryptographically secure names for all TPM resources.

TPM 1.2 was a success, as indicated by the fact that more than 1 billion TPMs using the 1.2 specification have been deployed in computer systems. TPM 2.0 expands on TPM 1.2's legacy. Currently, many vendors are developing implementations for TPM 2.0, and some are shipping them. Microsoft has a TPM 2.0 simulator that can also act as a software implementation of TPM 2.0. Some vendors are in the process of sampling hardware TPMs, and other companies are working on firmware TPMs.

Scenarios for Using TPM 1.2

In general, the TPM 2.0 design can do anything a TPM 1.2 chip can do. Thus, in considering applications that can use a TPM 2.0 chip, it's wise to first examine the applications that were enabled by the TPM 1.2 design.

Identification

The use envisioned for the first embedded security chip was device identification (DeviceID). Smart cards use their keys for this purpose. The private key embedded in the chip identifies the card on which it resides, an authentication password or PIN is used to authenticate a person to the card, and together they form "the thing you have" and "the thing you know" for authentication. Nothing keeps several people from using the same smart card, as long as they all know the PIN. There is also nothing that ties the smart card to a particular machine, which is an advantage when the smart card is used as a proxy for identifying an individual instead of a machine.

By embedding a private key mechanism in a personal computing device, that device can be identified. This is a big advantage for an IT organization, which owns the device and is in control of its software load and security protections. But as computers became more portable with the production of smaller and lighter laptops, the PC itself began to be useful as "the thing you have" in place of a smart card. It turned out that many times, when a smart card was used to authenticate a person to a computer network, the user left the smart card with the device. If one was stolen, both were stolen. As a result, there was no advantage to keeping the two separate.

However, if the password of a key stored in a security chip inside a personal computer was going to be used as a proxy for an individual, it was clear that the key could not reside in a single computer. The key has to be able to exist in multiple machines, because individuals tend to use more than one device. Further, machines are upgraded on average every 3 to 5 years, and keys must move from an old system to a new system in order to make system management possible.

These realizations led to two of the objectives of the original embedded security chips. They needed keys that identified the device—keys that couldn't be moved to different machines. And they needed keys that identified individuals—keys that could be duplicated across a number of machines. In either case, the keys had to be able to be deleted when an old system was disposed of.

What is the identification used for? There are a large number of uses, including these:

- *VPN identifying a machine before granting access to a network*: An IT organization can be certain that only enterprise-owned machines are allowed on the enterprise's network.

- *VPN identifying a user before granting access to a network*: An IT organization can be certain that only authorized personnel are granted access to an enterprise's network.

- *User signing e-mail*: The recipient of an e-mail can know with some certainty who sent the e-mail.

- *User decrypting e-mail sent to them*: This allows for confidentiality of correspondence.

- *User identifying themselves to their bank*: A user can prevent others from logging in to their account.

- *User authorizing a payment*: A user can prevent others from making payments in their name.

- *User logging in remotely to a system*: Only authorized personnel can log in to a remote system.

Encryption

The second use case for a security chip embedded on systems was to provide a means of encrypting keys that were used in turn to encrypt files on the hard drive or to decrypt files that arrived from other systems. Export regulations made putting a bulk encryption/decryption engine in the security chip a nonstarter; but using the chip to store encryption keys was allowed, so that functionality was included. The chip already had to do public/private encryption in order to perform cryptographic signing, so it was inexpensive to add the ability to decrypt a small amount of data containing a key that was encrypted with a public key, if the chip knew the private portion of the key.

Once this basic capability was available, it enabled a number of scenarios such as the following:

- File and folder encryption on a device

- Full disk encryption

- Encryption of passwords for a password manager

- Encryption of files stored remotely

Key Storage

One basic question the designers of the TPM had for possible users was, "How many keys do you think people will want to use with this chip?" If the answer had been "One or two," there would have been sufficient room in the chip to store those keys. However, the answer received was "More than three." Thus cost reasons made it infeasible to store all the keys on the chip, as was done in a smart card. However, the chip is used in PCs, which have hard disks and hence almost unlimited storage for keys—and TPG decided to make use of that fact.

The TPM has access to a self-generated private key, so it can encrypt keys with a public key and then store the resulting blob on the hard disk. This way, the TPM can keep a virtually unlimited number of keys available for use but not waste valuable internal storage. Keys stored on the hard disk can be erased, but they can also be backed up, which seemed to the designers like an acceptable trade-off. Cheap keys associated with a TPM enable a number of scenarios like these:

- *Privacy-sensitive solutions that use different keys to provide only a minimum of information to a requestor*: You don't need a single identity key that includes a user's age, weight, marital status, health conditions, political affiliation, and so on.

- *Different keys for different security levels*: Personal, financial, and business data as well as data that is contractually restricted all require different levels of confidentiality.

- *Different keys for multiple users of the same PC*: Sometimes several people share a computer. If that is the case, they typically don't want to give each other complete access to their files.

- *"Hoteling" of PCs in an office*: Keys are stored on a server and downloaded and used on a PC as required.

Random Number Generator

In order to generate keys, a random number generator (RNG) is necessary, and early PCs generally didn't contain good RNGs. There have been several cases where poor key generation was used to break security protocols. This is true. So the standards body required that a RNG be one of the components of the first TPM.

> *Anyone who considers arithmetical methods of producing random digits is, of course, in a state of sin.*[1]

> —Von Neumann

There are many uses for a good RNG:

- Seeding the OS random number generator
- Generating nonces (random numbers) used in security protocols
- Generating ephemeral (one-time use) keys for file encryption
- Generating long-term use keys (such as keys used for storage)
- Seeding Monte Carlo software routines

NVRAM Storage

A small amount of NVRAM storage that has restricted access-control properties can be very useful in a PC. It can store keys that shouldn't be available when the machine is off, give faster access to data than decryption using public/private key pairs can, and provide a mechanism to pass information back and forth between different parts of a system. NVRAM in TPMs can be configured to control read and write capabilities separately, which means some data can be provided to a user without worrying that it will be erased by accident or malicious intent. Additionally, you can use NVRAM to store keys that are used when the PC doesn't have access to its main storage. This can happen early during the boot cycle or before a self-encrypting drive has been given its password, allowing it to be read.

Having NVRAM provides the following:

- *Storage for root keys for certificate chains*: These are public keys to which everyone should have access—but it's very important that they not be changed.

- *Storage for an endorsement key (EK)*: An EK is stored by the manufacturer and used to decrypt certificates and pass passwords into the TPM during provisioning. In spite of misleading statements made on the Internet, the EK was designed to be privacy sensitive.

- *Storage for a representation of what the state of the machine ought to be*: This is used by some Intel implementations using TPMs and Intel Trusted Execution Technology (TXT), where

---

[1]*Monte Carlo Method* (1951), John von Neumann.

it's called a *launch control policy*. Like the public root key used in Unified Extensible Firmware Interface (UEFI) secure-boot implementations, this is used by the system owner to specify the state they want the machine to be in when it goes through a controlled launch, usually of a hypervisor. The advantage over the UEFI secure-boot method is that with the TPM, the end user has full control over the contents of the NVRAM storage.

- *Storage for decryption keys used before the hard disk is available*: For example, a key used for a self-encrypting drive.

Platform Configuration Registers

One unique thing about a TPM that can't be guaranteed with smart cards is that it's on the motherboard and available before the machine boots. As a result, it can be counted on as a place to store measurements taken during the boot process. Platform Configuration Registers (PCRs) are used for this purpose. They store hashes of measurements taken by external software, and the TPM can later report those measurements by signing them with a specified key. Later in the book, we describe how the registers work; for now, know that they have a one-way characteristic that prevents them from being spoofed. That is, if the registers provide a representation of trusted software that behaves as expected, then all the register values can be trusted.

A clever thing that's done with these registers is to use them as a kind of authentication signal. Just as, for example, a time lock won't allow a bank vault to unlock unless the time is during business hours, you can create a key or other object in a TPM that can't be used unless a PCR (or PCRs) is in a given state. Many interesting scenarios are enabled by this, including these:

- A VPN may not allow a PC access to a network unless it can prove it's running approved IT software.

- A file system may not obtain its encryption key unless its MBR has not been disturbed and the hard disk is on the same system.

Privacy Enablement

The architects of the first TPM were very concerned about privacy. Privacy is of major importance to enterprises, because losing systems or data that contain personally identifiable information (PII) can cause an enormous loss of money. Laws in many states require enterprises to inform people whose private data has been lost; so, for example, if a laptop containing a database of Human Resources data is stolen, the enterprise is required to notify everyone whose data might have been compromised. This can cost millions of dollars. Before the advent of embedded security systems, encryption of private files was nearly impossible on a standard PC because there was no place to put the key. As a result, most encryption solutions either "hid" the key in a place that was easily found by the technically adept, or derived a key from a password. Passwords have a basic problem: if a person can remember it, a computer can figure it out. The best way to prevent this is to have hardware track when too many wrong attempts are made to guess a password and then cause a delay before another attempt is allowed. The TPM specification requires this approach to be implemented, providing an enormous privacy advantage to those who use it.

The second privacy-related problem the architects tried to solve was much harder: providing a means to prove that a key was created and was protected by a TPM without the recipient of that proof knowing which TPM was the creator and protector of the key. Like many problems in computer science, this one was solved with a level of indirection. By making the EK a decryption-only key, as opposed to a signing key, it can't be (directly) used to identify a particular TPM. Instead, a protocol is provided for making *attestation identity keys* (AIKs), which are pseudo-identity keys for the platform. Providing a protocol for using a privacy CA means the EKs can be used to prove that an AIK originated with a TPM without proving which TPM the AIK originated from. Because there can be an unlimited number of AIKs, you can destroy AIKs after creating and using them, or have multiple AIKs for different purposes. For instance, a person can have three different AIKs that prove they're a senior citizen, rich, and live alone, rather than combining all three into one key and exposing extra information when proving one of their properties.

Additionally, some clever cryptographers at Intel, IBM, and HP came up with a protocol called direct anonymous attestation (DAA), which is based on group signatures and provides a very complicated method for proving that a key was created by a TPM without providing information as to which TPM created it. The advantage of this protocol is that it lets the AIK creator choose a variable amount of knowledge they want the privacy CA to have, ranging from perfect anonymity (when a certificate is created, the privacy CA is given proof that an AIK belongs to a TPM, but not which one) to perfect knowledge (the privacy CA knows which EK is associated with an AIK when it's providing a pseudonymous certificate for the AIK). The difference between the two is apparent when a TPM is broken and a particular EK's private key is leaked to the Internet. At this point, a privacy CA can revoke certificates if it knows a certificate it created is associated with that particular EK, but can't do so if it doesn't know.

PCR sensitivity to small changes in design, implementation, and use of PCs makes PCRs for the most part irreversible. That is, knowing a PC's PCR values provides almost no information about how the PC is set up. This is unfortunate for an IT organization that notices a change in PCR values and is trying to figure out why. It does provide privacy to end users, though.

Scenarios for Using Additional TPM 2.0 Capabilities

Lessons learned in the use of TPM 1.2 led to a number of changes in the architecture of TPM 2.0. In particular, the SHA-1 algorithm, on which most 1.2 structures were based, was subjected to cryptographic attacks. As a result, the new design needed to not be catastrophically broken if any one algorithm used in the design become insecure.

Algorithm Agility (New in 2.0)

Beginning in TPM 2.0, the specification allows a lot of flexibility in what algorithms a TPM can use. Instead of having to use SHA-1, a TPM can now use virtually any hash algorithm. SHA 256 will likely be used in most early TPM 2.0 designs. Symmetric algorithms like Advanced Encryption Standard (AES) are also available, and new asymmetric algorithms such as elliptic curve cryptography (ECC) are available in addition to RSA.

The addition of symmetric algorithms (enabled by the weakening of export-control laws) allows keys to be stored off the chip and encrypted with symmetric encryption instead of asymmetric encryption. With this major change to the method of key storage, TPM 2.0 allows any kind of encryption algorithm. This in turn means if another algorithm is weakened by cryptanalysis in the future, the specification won't need to change.

Ideally, the key algorithms should be matched in strength. Table 3-1 lists the key strengths of approved algorithms according to the National Institute of Standards and Technology NIST).[2]

Table 3-1. Approved algorithms

Type	Algorithm	Key strength (bits)
Asymmetric	RSA 1024	80
Asymmetric	RSA 2048	112
Asymmetric	RSA 3072	128
Asymmetric	RSA 16384	256
Asymmetric	ECC 224	112
Asymmetric	ECC 256	128
Asymmetric	ECC 384	192
Asymmetric	ECC 521	260
Symmetric	DES	56
Symmetric	3DES (2 keys)	127
Symmetric	3DES (3 key)	128
Symmetric	AES 128	128
Symmetric	AES 256	256
Hash	SHA-1	65
Hash	SHA 224	112
Hash	SHA 256	128
Hash	SHA 384	192
Hash	SHA 512	256
Hash	SHA-3	Variable

---

[2]NIST, "Recommendation for Key Management – Part 1: General (Revision 3)," Special Publication 800-57, http://csrc.nist.gov/publications/nistpubs/800-57/sp800-57_part1_rev3_general.pdf.

AES is typically used for the symmetric algorithm today. At 128 bits, the two most frequently used asymmetric algorithms are RSA 2048 or ECC 256. RSA 2048 isn't quite as strong as ECC 256 and is much slower. It also takes up a lot more space. However, the patents on RSA have expired, and it's compatible with most software today, so many people still use it. Many people are using RSA 2048 together with SHA-1 and AES-128, even though they're far from a matched set, because they're free and compatible. Most of the examples in this book use both RSA and ECC for encryption and decryption, but SHA 256 is used exclusively for hashing.

SHA-1 has been deprecated by NIST, and it won't be accepted after 2014 for any use for signatures (even though most uses of SHA-1 in TPM 1.2 don't fall prey to the types of attacks that are made possible by current cryptanalysis). The bit strength of SHA-1 is significantly weaker than that of the other algorithms, so there doesn't appear to be any good reason to use it other than backward compatibility.

TCG has announced the families of algorithms that can be supported by publishing a separate list of algorithm IDs that identify algorithms to be used with a TPM. This includes the hash algorithms to be used by the PCRs. This list may change with time.

Algorithm agility enables a number of nice features, including the following

- Using sets of algorithms compatible with legacy applications

- Using sets of algorithms compatible with the US Government's Suite B for Secret

- Using sets of algorithms compatible with the US Government's Suite B for Top Secret

- Using sets of algorithms compatible with other governments' requirements

- Upgrading from SHA-1 to SHA 256 (or other more secure algorithms)

- Changing the algorithms in a TPM without revisiting the specification

Enhanced Authorization (New in 2.0)

The TPM 1.2 specification accrued a number of new facilities over the years. This resulted in a very complicated specification with respect to means and management of authentication. The TPM was managed using either physical presence or owner authorization. Use of the EK was gated by owner authorization. Keys had two authorizations: one for use of the key and one to make duplicates of the key (called *migration* in the TPM 1.2 specification). Additionally, keys could be locked to localities and values stored in PCRs.

Similarly, the NVRAM in TPM 1.2 could be locked to PCRs and particular localities, and to two different authorizations—one for reading and one for writing. But the only way the two authorizations could differ was if one of them were the owner authorization.

Certified migratable keys had the same authorizations as other keys; but to complete the migration, a migration authority had to sign an authorization, and that authorization had to be checked by the TPM. This process also required owner authorization.

Making things even more complicated, the use of certain owner-authorized commands and keys could be delegated to a secondary password. However, the owner of the primary authorization knew those passwords, and delegation used precious NVRAM in the TPM. Even worse, the technique was difficult to understand and, as a result, was never employed to our knowledge.

The 2.0 specification has a completely different take, called *enhanced authorization (EA)*. It uses the following kinds of authorizations:

- *Password (in the clear)*: This was missing in TPM 1.2. In some environments, such as when BIOS has control of a TPM before the OS has launched, the added security obtained by using a hash message authentication code (HMAC) doesn't warrant the extra software cost and complexity of using an HMAC authorization to use the TPM's services.

- *HMAC key (as in 1.2)*: In some cases, particularly when the OS that is being used as an interface to talk with the TPM isn't trusted but the software talking to the TPM *is* trusted, the added cost and complexity of using an HMAC for authorization is warranted. An example is when a TPM is used on a remote system.

- *Signature (for example, via a smart card)*: When an IT employee needs to perform maintenance on a TPM, a smart card is a good way to prevent abuse of an IT organization's privileges. The smart card can be retrieved when an employee leaves a position, and it can't be exposed as easily as a password.

- *Signature with additional data*: The extra data could be, for example, a fingerprint identified via a particular fingerprint reader. This is a particularly useful new feature in EA. For example, a biometric reader can report that a particular person has matched their biometric, or a GPS can report that a machine is in a particular region. This eliminates the TPM having to match fingerprints or understand what GPS coordinates mean.

- *PCR values as a proxy for the state of the system, at least as it booted*: One use of this is to prevent the release of a full-disk encryption key if the system-management module software has been compromised.[3]

---

[3]Yuriy Bulygin, Andrew Furtak, and Oleksandr Bazhaniuk, "A Tale of One Software Bypass of Windows 8 Secure Boot" (presentation, Black Hat 2013), https://www.blackhat.com/us-13/briefings.html#Bulygin.

- *Locality as a proxy for where a particular command came from*: So far this has only been used to indicate whether a command originated from the CPU in response to a special request, as implemented by Intel TXT and AMD in AMD-v. Flicker,[4] a free software application from Carnegie Mellon University, used this approach to provide a small, secure OS that can be triggered when secure operations need to be performed.

- *Time*: Policies can limit the use of a key to certain times. This is like a bank's time lock, which allows the vault to be opened only during business hours.

- *Internal counter values*: An object can be used only when an internal counter is between certain values. This approach is useful to set up a key that can only be used a certain number of times.

- *Value in an NV index*: Use of a key is restricted to when certain bits are set to 1 or 0. This is useful for revoking access to a key.

- *NV index*: Authorization is based on whether the NV index has been written.

- *Physical presence*: This approach requires proof that the user is physically in possession of the platform.

This list isn't complete, but it gives examples of how the new policy authorization scheme can be used. Additionally, you can create more complicated policies by combining these forms of authorization with logical AND or OR operations such as these:

- Mary identifies herself with an HMAC key and a smart card associated with a public key.

- Joe identifies himself with a fingerprint authentication via a particular reader identified by the public key.

- This key can be used by Mary OR Joe.

Policies can be created that are either simple or complex, and all objects or entities of the TPM (including the TPM's hierarchies) can have policies associated with them. EA has enormously extended the possible uses of the TPM, particularly in managing authorizations; yet the net result has been to reduce the amount of code necessary to create a TPM, eliminate the NVRAM that was used for delegation, and eliminate all the previously existing special cases (thus lowering the learning curve for using a TPM).

Clever policy designs can allow virtually any restriction on key use that you can envision, although some (such as restricting use of a document to only one kind of document processor) would be exceptionally difficult, if possible at all.[5] The new EA allows a number of new scenarios, including the following:

---

[4]http://sourceforge.net/p/flickertcb/wiki/Home/.
[5]E.W. Felten, "Understanding Trusted Computing: Will Its Benefits Outweigh Its Drawbacks?" *IEEE Security & Privacy* 1, no. 3 (2003): 60–62.

- Multifactor authentication of resources

- Multiuser authentication of resources

- Resources used only n times

- Resources used only for certain periods of time

- Revocation of use of resources

- Restricting ways resources can be used by different people

Quick Key Loading (new in 2.0)

In the TPM 1.2 specification, when a key was initially loaded, it had to go through a time-consuming private-key decryption using the key's parent's private key. To avoid having to do this multiple times during a session, it was possible to cache loaded keys by encrypting them with a symmetric key that only the TPM knew. During that power cycle, the TPM could reload the key using a symmetric-key operation, which was faster even if the parent no longer resided in the TPM. Once the TPM was turned off, the symmetric key was erased: the next time the key was loaded, it again required a private key operation.

In 2.0, except for the case of a key being imported into a TPM's key structure from outside, keys stored by the TPM using external memory are encrypted using a symmetric-key operation. As a result, the keys are loaded quickly. There is little reason to cache keys out to disk (unless a parent key becomes unavailable), because loading them is usually as fast as recovering them from a cached file.

This quicker loading enables multiple users to use a TPM without noticing a long delay. This in turn makes it easier to design a system on which multiple applications appear to have unfettered access to a TPM.

Non-Brittle PCRs (New in 2.0)

Fragility of PCR values was one of the most annoying problems with the 1.0 family of TPMs. PCR values typically represent the state of the machine, with lower-numbered PCRs representing the process of booting of the system and higher-numbered ones representing events after the kernel has booted. Both keys and data can be locked to certain PCRs having particular values, an action called *sealing*. But if keys or data are locked to a PCR that represents the BIOS of a system, it's tricky to upgrade the BIOS. This is *PCR fragility*. Typically, before a BIOS upgrade was performed on TPM 1.2 systems, all secrets locked to PCR 0, for example (which represents the BIOS), had to be unsealed and then resealed after the upgrade was done. This is both a manageability nightmare and a nuisance to users.

In the TPM 2.0 specification, you can seal things to a PCR value approved by a particular signer instead of to a particular PCR value (although this can still be done if you wish). That is, you can have the TPM release a secret only if PCRs are in a state approved (via a digital signature) by a particular authority.

In typical usage, an IT organization may approve BIOS versions for PCs and then provide signatures of the PCRs that would result from approved BIOS versions being installed on PC clients. Values that formerly could be recovered in only one of those states become recoverable in any of them.

This is done via the TPM2_PolicyAuthorize command, which you can also use many other ways. It's a general-purpose way of making any policy flexible.

This new capability enables a number of different use cases, such as these:

- Locking resources to be used on machines that have any BIOS signed by the OEM

- Locking resources to be used on machines that have any kernels signed by an OEM

- Locking resources to be used on machines that have any set of values for PCRs that are approved by the IT organization

Flexible Management (New in 2.0)

In the 1.0 family of TPM specifications, only two authentications existed in a TPM at a time: the owner authorization and the storage root key (SRK) authorization. Because the SRK authorization was usually the well-known secret (20 bytes of 0s), the owner authorization was used for many purposes:

- To reset the dictionary-attack counter

- To reset the TPM back to factory settings

- To prevent the SRK from having its password changed by someone who knew the well-known secret

- To provide privacy to the end user by preventing creation of AIKs except by the owner of the TPM

- To avoid NVRAM wearout in the TPM by preventing creation and deletion of NVRAM indexes except by those who knew the owner authorization

The problem with giving the same authorization to so many different roles is that it becomes very difficult to manage those roles independently. You might want to delegate some of those roles to different people. For example, privacy controls like those used to restrict creation of AIKs are very different from controls used to reset the dictionary-attack counter or manage SRK authorization.

In the TPM 1.2 family, you could delegate the owner-authorization role to different entities using the Delegate commands in the TPM, but those commands were fairly complicated and used up valuable NVRAM space. We know of no applications that actually used them.

An additional problem with TPM 1.2–enabled systems was that the TPM couldn't be guaranteed to be enabled and active (meaning the TPM couldn't be used). So, many OEMs were unwilling to create software that relied on the TPM to do cryptographic things such as setting up VPNs during the boot process or verifying BIOS software before installation. This inhibited use of the TPM. In TPM 2.0, the OEM can rely on the platform hierarchy always being enabled.

In the TPM 2.0 family, the roles represented by the various uses of the TPM 1.2 owner authorization are separated in the specification itself. This is done by giving them different authorizations and policies, and also by having different hierarchies in the TPM. One is the dictionary-attack logic, which has its own password for resetting the dictionary-attack counter. The others are covered by several hierarchies in TPM 2.0:

- *Standard storage hierarchy*: Replicates the TPM 1.0 family SRK for the most part

- *Platform hierarchy*: Used by the BIOS and System Management Mode (SMM), *not* by the end user

- *Endorsement hierarchy or privacy hierarchy*: Prevents someone from using the TPM for attestation without the approval of the device's owner

- *Null hierarchy*: Uses the TPM as a cryptographic coprocessor

Each hierarchy (except the null hierarchy) has its own authorization password and authorization policy. The dictionary-attack logic also has an associated policy. All Entities on the TPM with an authorization value also have an associated authorization policy.

Identifying Resources by Name (New in 2.0)

In the TPM 1.2 specification, resources were identified by handle instead of by a cryptographically bound name. As a result, if two resources had the same authorization, and the low-level software could be tricked into changing the handle identifying the resource, it was possible to fool a user into authorizing a different action than they thought they were authorizing.[6]

In TPM 2.0, resources are identified by their name, which is cryptographically bound to them, thus eliminating this attack. Additionally, you can use a TPM key to sign the name, thus providing evidence that the name is correct. Because the name includes the key's policy, this signature can be used as evidence to prove what means are possible for authorizing use of a key. The chapter on enhanced authorization describes this in detail. If the key can be duplicated, this signature can also be used to provide a "birth certificate" for the key, proving which TPM was used to create the key.

---

[6]Sigrid Gürgens of Fraunhofer SIT found this attack.

Summary

This chapter has described at a high level the use cases enabled by TPM 1.2 and 2.0. The capabilities of TPM 1.2 are the basis for trusted computing—an anchor for secure generation, use, and storage of keys and for storage and attestation of a PC's health status. TPM 2.0 enhanced this functionality by adding sophisticated management and authorization capabilities, as well as algorithm agility that prevents new cryptographic attacks from breaking the specification.

The next chapter examines applications and SDKs that take advantage of those capabilities to solving existing problems. These include solutions for securing data at rest, like BitLocker and TrueCrypt; for PC health attestation and device identification, like Wave Systems, strongSwan and JW Secure; and a number of SDKs you can use to create applications with that functionality.

CHAPTER 4

■ ■ ■

Existing Applications That Use TPMs

Even though more than 1 billion TPMs are deployed in the market, and they exist on almost all commercial PCs and servers, very few people know about them. And many people who do know about TPMs are surprised to discover that many applications are written for them. There are also a large number of ways to easily write applications that take advantage of TPM 1.2 devices. Because TPM 2.0 devices are just beginning to appear on the market, it's perhaps not surprising that not as many applications can use TPM 2.0 directly. The purpose of this book is to enable you to write programs that take advantage of all the features of TPM 2.0, both basic and advanced.

This chapter starts by looking at the various application interfaces that are used by programs to interface with the TPM hardware. Then you examine a number of applications that already use TPMs. Perhaps the most interesting part of the chapter—and one we hope you will help make out of date—is a short list of types of programs that should use TPMs but don't.

We follow up with some considerations that any programmer using a TPM must take into account, and a description of how some existing programs have handled them.

Application Interfaces Used to Talk to TPMs

A number of different types of applications have been written already for use with TPM 1.2 and 2.0. These can be classified by the programming interface they use:

- Proprietary applications written directly to the TPM (available for both 1.2 and 2.0).

- Legacy applications that use a middleware interface to talk with the TPM, specifically Public-Key Cryptography Standard (PKCS) #11 and Microsoft Cryptographic Application Programming Interface (CAPI). When PKCS #11 stacks are available for TPM 2.0, they work with it as well. They are available for TPM 1.2 in all operating systems. Beginning with Windows 8, Microsoft has made its cryptographic interfaces able to use both TPM 1.2 and TPM 2.0.

- Applications that use the TCG Software Stack (TSS) interface to talk with the TPM (multiple proprietary TSSs are available from IBM, Infineon, and NCP; an open source TSS code named TrouSerS is also available for multiple OSs). These are 1.2 implementations. TSS 2.0 is in development.

- Applications that use Java interfaces to talk with the TPM. So far, only 1.2 implementations that interface between Java code and the TPM exist, but 2.0 versions should soon appear. Mobile devices, especially those running the Android OS, use Java interfaces.

- Applications that use the Microsoft TPM Base Services (TBS) library: These can be used with either TPM 1.2 or TPM 2.0. Some functions work with either. Those that use new capabilities of the TPM 2.0 only work with it.

- Microsoft TSS.net works with TPM 2.0 and comes with a TPM 2.0 emulator! TSS.net is not compatible with the TCG standards, and only currently works on Microsoft products.

The first applications to use the TPM were proprietary applications that were shipped with the machines that had the first versions of TPMs. These included IBM's password manager and file and folder encryption, which used the TPM to store encryption keys. Dell, HP, and Infineon have their own varieties of these applications. Generally speaking, they work well, but are intended to focus on very specific usage models.

The next type of applications that use TPMs use it through cryptographic service providers (CSPs). There are two main kinds: those that use CAPI and those that use the RSA Corporation's PKCS #11. Any application written to use either of these APIs for cryptographic services can use a TPM via a standard means of pointing those cryptographic services to the TPM. Fortunately, most software that uses cryptography uses one of these two services, for good reason. Cryptographic services are notoriously difficult to program correctly, particularly if the programmer is worried about weak implementations that may be vulnerable to attacks such as side-channel attacks.[1] The best practice is to rely on experts to write those cryptographic services. Additionally, those cryptographic services may be certified by NIST as providing validated services that behave as expected, and hence can be used in government institutions.

Both of these APIs contain hooks that allow other cryptographic services to be substituted for those done in software by the service. This lets software take advantage of a hardware interface that provides protection against software attacks by implementing cryptographic services in a separate memory space. Such CSPs are available for Windows for both CAPI and PKCS. These implementations are available from Security Innovation, Wave Systems, Infineon, and Lenovo for a fee. They're often bundled with computers from major manufacturers. Infineon's CSP is noteworthy in that it can find applications on the machine that can use its services and give the user the opportunity to use the

---

[1]Side-channel attacks occur when the time or power it takes to perform a calculation can give hints to an attacker about what key is being used.

TPM with them. In other OSs, such as Linux, BSD, MAC OS, and Solaris, PKCS #11 implementations allow the substitution of TPM functions for public-key generation and random-number creation; these are available for free. Additionally, some companies, such as Charismathics, have made middleware suites that can use the TPM to provide cryptographic services.

The problem with using legacy interfaces (PKCS #11 and MS CAPI) is that they only utilize basic services available with a TPM, such as key generation and signing. Advanced applications that use the TPM's ability to attest to the health of the machine or allow controlled migration of keys without exposing them in the clear aren't available using these middleware solutions. As a result, TSS was created. An open source implementation called TrouSerS was implemented by IBM and ported to Windows by the University Politecnico di Torino in Italy.[2] Proprietary implementations are also shipped by a number of companies. TSS is currently available for TPM 1.2; an updated specification and implementation are being developed for TPM 2.0.

The TSS library is much more suitable to C programming than Java programming. Therefore, some people at MIT created a Java interface to the TPM. It is available from MIT.[3]

Microsoft, starting with Windows Vista, provides almost direct access to the TPM through a programming interface called TPM Base Services (TBS). The TBS interface accepts TPM-formatted byte streams and returns TPM-formatted responses or errors. Because this is a low-level interface, you're expected to use one of the many libraries that convert high-level-language callable functions to the underlying TPM byte-stream representation.

TBS performs several additional functions. First, it provides multiprocess, multithread access to the TPM by "maintaining" an internal queue of commands submitted. Second, the TPM performs under-the-covers TPM context management by using the TPM context save and load commands. This allows TBS to present each application with a virtual TPM that appears to have essentially unlimited resources like key slots, and ensures that one application cannot interfere with the keys or slots created by another. Third, TPM commands are submitted via a TBS context, and TBS automatically cleans up resources when the context is closed or the process dies.

Windows also layers additional security mechanisms on top of the TPM's administrative controls. The problem addressed is that the use of certain TPM commands can impact the stability or correct operation of the operating system or other applications, but the TPM commands are not properly protected by the TPM's protection mechanisms. For example, most Platform Configuration Registers (PCRs) should be updated only by the trusted computing base, but the TPM does not require special authorization to extend a PCR. In Windows Vista and 7, Windows limited TBS access to administrative applications only. In Windows 8, commands are grouped into three sets:

- *No Access*: Including TPM2_ContextSave and TPM2_ContextLoad

- *Administrative-token processes only*: Including TPM2_PCR_Extend and privacy-sensitive operations

- *Standard-use access*: Creation and use of keys, and so on

---

[2]http://security.polito.it/trusted-computing/trousers-for-windows/.
[3]http://projects.csail.mit.edu/tc/tpmj/.

The set of standard-use and administrative commands can be edited by the operating system administrator. The OS keeps copies of the TPM's authorization values in access-protected entries in the registry. This behavior is described in much more detail in the document *Using the Windows 8 Platform Crypto Provider and Associated TPM Functionality*.[4]

In addition to the low-level TPM access provided by TBS, Windows also exposes a subset of TPM behavior through five much higher-level interfaces.

TPM Administration and WMI

Windows exposes many common TPM administrative tasks through GUI tools and through a scriptable and remote programming interface called Windows Management Instrumentation (WMI). This interface lets an administrator switch on TPMs, clear them, disable them, and so on. It transparently supports both TPM 1.2 and TPM 2.0.

The Platform Crypto Provider

Most Windows programs use cryptography through a set of interfaces called Cryptography Next Generation (CNG). CNG provides a uniform library for performing both software-based and hardware (such as High Security Module) based cryptography. Windows 8 lets you specify the TPM as a key protector for a subset of TPM-supported cryptography by specifying use of the Platform Crypto Provider. The Platform Crypto Provider has been extended to include a few specific TPM-like behaviors, such as quoting and key certification.

Virtual Smart Card

Windows 8 further extracts the TPM to behave like a smart card in any and all cases where a smart card can be used. This includes both enterprise and web logon.

Applications That Use TPMs

Table 4-1 lists applications that are currently available that use the TPM, along with the interface they use and the OS on which they run. All these work with TPM 1.2. Some of them, as noted, also work with TPM 2.0.

---

[4]http://research.microsoft.com/en-us/downloads/74c45746-24ad-4cb7-ba4b-0c6df2f92d5d/.

Table 4-1. *Applications and SDKs That Use TPMs, by Interface and OS*

Application Type	Application Name	Interface	OS
VPN	StrongSwan clients (used in Linux, BSD, Solaris, and so on)	TrouSerS (1.2)	Linux
	Cisco client VPNs.	Wave Systems (MS CAPI)	Windows
		Charismathics (1.2)	
	Microsoft embedded VPN or DirectAccess can directly use either TPM 1.2 or TPM 2.0 in Windows 8.	Microsoft TBS TPM Base Services (1.2 or 2.0)	Windows
	Checkpoint Firewall VPN can use the TPM.	(1.2)	
	TypeSafe (TPM-backed TLS).	jTSS (1.2)	Linux
Attestation	Wave Systems Embassy client/ERAS server package.	TrouSerS (1.2)	Windows
	Wave Systems Endpoint Monitor	TrouSerS (1.2)	Windows
	Strong Swan TNC solution hooked to the TPM with PTS.	(1.2)	Linux
	NCP's Secure VPN GovNet Box (a separate box interposed between a computer and the network that establishes a secure VPN). The software is tested using TPM attestation.	(1.2)	Unknown
	AnyConnect	(1.2)	
	JW Secure has written an application that is Kerberos-like for Windows.	Microsoft TBS TPM Base Services (2.0)	Windows
	Integrity Measurement Architecture.	TrouSerS (1.2)	Linux, Unix-like OSs

(continued)

Table 4-1. (*continued*)

Application Type	Application Name	Interface	OS
	TPM Quote tools (SourceForge)	TrouSerS (1.2)	Linux, Windows
	TrustedGRUB	Direct (1.2)	Linux
	TVE	Trousers(1.2)	Linux
	Tboot	Direct(1.2)	Windows, Linux
	Flicker	Direct / Trousers (1.2)	Windows
Full disk encryption	Microsoft BitLocker	Microsoft TBS TPM Base Services (1.2, 2.0)	Windows
	dm-crypt	Direct (1.2)	Linux, Android
	SecureDoc		
File and folder encryption	Pretty Good Privacy (PGP)	PKCS #11 (1.2)	Windows
	OpenPGP	PKCS #11(1.2)	Linux
E-mail	Thunderbird for encrypted e-mail and signed e-mail	PKCS #11(1.2)	Windows, Linux
	Outlook	MS CAPI(1.2, 2.0)	Windows
Web browsers	Internet Explorer	MS CAPI(1.2, 2.0)	Windows
	Firefox	PKCS #11(1.2)	Windows Linux
	Chrome	PKCS #11(1.2)	Windows Linux
TPM Manager	TPM Manager (SourceForge)	microTSS (1.2)	Linux

As the table demonstrates, many applications use TPMs. There are even some large companies that use them.[5] BitLocker is one of the most widely used of these programs that use extended capabilities of the TPM. Wave Systems Embassy Suite is another. Often, conflicting management software requires multiple TPM programs to be used on the same system.

---

[5]See Ellen Messmer, *Network World* (2010), "PwC Lauds Trusted Platform Module for Strong Authentication," www.networkworld.com/news/2010/091510-trusted-platform-authentication.html.

With a 1.2 TPM, there was a single storage root key (SRK), which had to have an authorization that was shared by all applications using the TPM. Unfortunately, there was not unanimity in how to create the SRK—it could be created without needing any authentication, needing only a well-known secret of 20 bytes of 0, or needing the hash of a well-known secret for its password. Additionally, there was an owner authorization that was somewhat sensitive, because it was used to reset the dictionary attack mechanism as well as reset the TPM or create an attestation key (thought by some to be privacy sensitive).

Unfortunately, the owner authorization was also used to authorize allocation of non-volatile RAM space, which meant applications that needed to allocate nonvolatile RAM space had to know it. But if a different application took ownership of the TPM and set the owner authorization to a random number, protected by a back-end management function, it was unknown even to the end user. Some applications did this. If applications did not know how to coordinate with that back-end management application, they could not function.

The result was that the user was restricted to using a single suite of applications with the TPM, in order to allow all applications to have access to the authorizations they needed. In practice, this meant software that directly used the TPM had to be from the same developer as the management software used to set up the TPM.

This issue was somewhat mitigated when using only PKCS #11 or MS CAPI enabled applications, because they only required that there be a single application for managing the TPM; but they also couldn't use the higher functions of the TPM, such as attestation. This problem seems to be gradually disappearing. For example, Wave Systems software can manage TPMs for attestation and also for BitLocker.

TPM 2.0 still requires some coordination for authorization; but it lets you use multiple SRKs with the TPM, allowing completely separate applications to use the TPM with less coordination.

In researching applications that use the TPM, most of the use cases that come quickly to mind are supported by commercial software. However, some obvious use cases for software that uses a TPM, don't seem to exist in the marketplace.

Applications That Should Use the TPM but Don't

In the past few years, the number of web-based applications has increased. Among them are web-based backup and storage. A large number of companies now offer such services, but as far as we are aware, none of the clients for these services let the user lock the key for the backup service to a TPM. If this were done, it would certainly be nice if the TPM key itself were backed up by duplicating it on multiple machines. This appears to be an opportunity for developers.

Another application that has become more useful recently is remote management. Many companies now offer ways of allowing one computer to "take over" management of another computer. For instance, you can use this functionality to monitor your network remotely or to give troubleshooting advice to remote members of your family. But again, the security models we are familiar with, use passwords to gate the remote access. Although long, hard-to-remember passwords can provide some security, they aren't fun to use. This seems to be an ideal place for TPMs to be used—restricting remote access to machines that have been linked together with public/private keys. There do not appear to be any commercial applications that use the TPM for this—most commercial applications don't even support use of other cryptographic devices, including smart cards, for increased security. This is not due to lack of software development kits for writing such software, because several of these kits exist.

Building Applications for TPM 1.2

When you're building an application that will use a TPM, it is important to first decide if you are going to use the advanced facilities of the TPM beyond those that are exposed by PKCS or MS CAPI. If not, then it makes the most sense to write your application to these interfaces. This way, your application can be used on those machines with and without TPMs. But to use unique TPM features such as attestation, extended authorization, localities, an NVRAM locations, you have no choice but to use one of the custom TPM interfaces.

A number of API libraries are available for writing applications using custom interfaces. TSS 1.2 had a reputation for being hard to learn, so other suites were developed. TPM/J was developed at MIT to provide an object-oriented means of programming to the TPM.[6] Institute for Applied Information Processing and Communication (IAIK), of Graz University also delivered a version of Java integration with the TPM through trustedJava.[7] Sirrix provided a microTSS, an attempt to simplify the TSS specification.[8]

Additionally, command-line tools for the TPM were released by IBM together with a TPM emulator on SourceForge. As a result, it was possible to exercise TPM base commands in batch file.

Microsoft's TBS interface started out as a basic interface with the TPM, but its API is growing, and it may turn into a very nice means of programming TPMs. The biggest news in TBS programming came in Windows 8, where the TBS interface abstracted the difference between TPM 1.2 and TPM 2.0 so that all the APIs work with either chip. This is particularly useful for applications that use only those APIs, but it doesn't (yet) expose the new functions in the TPM 2.0 specification. TSS.net, which Microsoft also released, lets all commands be sent directly to the TPM, although it doesn't, as yet, have a high-level interface for the new TPM 2.0 commands.

TSS.Net and TSS.C++

Windows 8 and TPM 2.0 were released before there were standards for TPM programming. To fill this gap, Microsoft developed and open sourced two libraries that let application programmers develop more complicated TPM-based applications than CNG or virtual smart cards allowed.

TSS.Net and TSS.C++ provide a thin veneer over TPM 2.0 for both managed code (such as C#) and native code (C++) applications. Both libraries allow applications to be built for a real TPM device (on TBS) or a TPM simulator (over a TCP/IP network connection.)

---

[6]http://projects.csail.mit.edu/tc/tpmj/.

[7]http://trustedjava.sourceforge.net/.

[8]http://www.filewatcher.com/p/tpmmanager-0.8.tar.gz.3959086/tpmmanager-0.8/src/microtss/TSS.cpp.html.

Although the TSS.Net and TSS.C++ libraries are low level, the authors have made every effort to make programming the TPM easy. For instance, here is a complete program for obtaining random numbers from the TPM:

```
void GetRandomTbs()
{
    // Create a TpmDevice object and attach it to the TPM. Here you
    // use the Windows TPM Base Services OS interface.
    TpmTbsDevice device;

    if (!device.Connect()) {
        cerr << "Could not connect to the TPM device";
        return;
    }

    // Create a Tpm2 object "on top" of the device.
    Tpm2 tpm(device);

    // Get 20 bytes of random data from
    std::vector<BYTE> rand = tpm.GetRandom(20);

    // Print it out.
    cout << "Random bytes: " << rand << endl;

    return;
}
```

All of these interfaces work, but of course some, such as TBS, are specific to the Windows OS. If you want to write programs that are portable to other OSs, you are better off with one of the others. For TPM 1.2, TSS was the interface with the broadest OS adoption. The next section considers an application that was written using TSS to take advantage of advanced TPM functions.

Wave Systems Embassy Suite

Wave Systems has written software to a TPM-specific interface, rather than to a higher-level interface such as PKCS #11. It needed to be done that way, to take advantage of the TPM's attestation capabilities. Because these capabilities aren't addressed in any other crypto-coprocessor, they aren't available in standard interfaces such as PKCS #11. Wave Systems uses the TCG TSS interface implemented in TrouSerS to talk to the TPM, manage the TPM owner password, create attestation identity keys (AIKs), and attest to those values via a standard called Trusted Network Connect, which communicates back to an administrative server. This server notices when PCR values have changed, and it can send alerts to IT staff when that happens. Some PCRs (like 0, which represents the BIOS firmware) should not change, unless the BIOS of a device has been upgraded, an event that IT should be aware of. TSS 1.2 was available for Windows, Linux, Solaris, BSD, and even the MAC OS. TSS 2.0 will be a good selection for the same reasons, if you want to be able to port your code to other OSs.

TSS 2.0 has been designed specifically with the aim of making programming TPM 2.0 as easy as possible. It is designed in layers so that at the lowest level, direct access to the TPM is still possible. Common design patterns that use a cryptographic coprocessor are made particularly easy to use at the highest application level programming interface. However, there are still some ground rules that every application developer should remember when developing applications that use a TPM.

Rocks to Avoid When Developing TPM Applications

When using the TPM in an application, there are two major pitfalls to avoid. First, the TPM (or another component on the motherboard) may die, or users may upgrade their equipment. If the motherboard is replaced, any keys that are locked to the TPM go away. Second, if data is locked to PCRs (a process called *sealing*), and the things measured into the PCRs are updated, that data is no longer unsealable.

Both of these problems amount to the same thing: management of the keys and data locked to a TPM needs to be carefully considered. An example of how do this well is found in Microsoft's BitLocker application, which first came out with Windows Vista Enterprise.

Microsoft BitLocker

Microsoft gave careful consideration to both of the previously described problems when it created the BitLocker application, originally embedded in the Enterprise edition of Vista. This program was used to do full-disk encryption of the hard disk on which Windows resided. To do this, early in the boot sequence BitLocker obtained a key from the TPM. This key was sealed to PCRs that represented the boot sequence of the computer up to the point where the kernel was loaded into memory. BitLocker could also require the user to enter a password. To enable management of the encryption key used for full-disk encryption, the sealed key was used as a key encrypting key (KEK) and used to encrypt the full-disk encryption key. The actual key used for the full-disk encryption key could be then backed up by also encrypting it using a very long random password. This password could be kept secure elsewhere (for example, on a USB key locked in a safe). This way, if the motherboard was replaced, the TPM died, or the hard disk was moved into a new system, the data stored on it was still accessible.

Additionally, Microsoft gave thought to the problem caused by people upgrading their BIOS. Such an upgrade prevented the TPM from being able to unseal the KEK. Although the random-number backup sufficed for recovery in this case, Microsoft decided it would make more sense for an administrator doing the BIOS upgrade, who already had access to the decrypted data, to have a means to temporarily leave the full-disk encryption key in the clear while the BIOS upgrade was performed and then reseal it to the TPM's new PCR values after the BIOS upgrade. It is important to realize that making things easy for the user at a small cost to security (leaving the drive open for the brief time while a BIOS upgrade was taking place) is usually a good tradeoff. Security that is hard to use is seldom used.

When IBM came out with its first TPM solutions, several years before BitLocker saw the light of day, it also had to keep manageability problems in mind.

IBM File and Folder Encryption

IBM had a similar problem when it allowed storage keys to be used for file and folder encryption to the TPM, and it solved the issue in a similar way. Instead of generating a random number, IBM wanted to let users type the answer to questions in order to recover the disk encryption key; this key was normally encrypted with the KEK, which in turn was protected by the TPM. This can be dangerous, because it may allow an attacker to simply try many answers to these questions in the hope of generating the correct answer and unlocking the drive. IBM's solution to this problem was clever. The company realized that although in normal use the key needed to be available almost immediately, in the case of recovery, it was fine if it took several minutes to recover the data. Therefore IBM performed a hash operation on the answers to the questions over and over again until a few minutes had passed, noted the number of operations, and then used the resulting value as a key to encrypt the file and folder encryption key. It then stored the number of operations and the encrypted blob on the hard disk. In order to decrypt this blob, someone had to spend several minutes for every attempt to answer the questions. This quickly becomes impractical for an attacker, but it costs a user only a few minutes in the case of recovery.

When TPM 2.0 was being designed, the architects had experience with the multitude of problems caused by managing TPMs, so new features were built into 2.0 to help solve these issues. One specific problem that is encountered repeatedly in security software is the need to manage authorizations (passwords). For example, someone changes a password while on a plane or late at night at a hotel, when they aren't connected to the network; then, the next day, they can't remember their password. Or someone working for a corporation quits or (worse yet) dies and leaves important corporate data encrypted on their hard disk without telling anyone their password. IT organizations are assumed to be able to fix problems like this—but it's hard to see how they can. TPM 2.0 enhanced authorization was designed to help fix the issue of managing passwords.

New Manageability Solutions in TPM 2.0

Programs to solve the manageability problem can use the same techniques used with TPM 1.2 devices; but with TPM 2.0, a number of new solutions are available. Loss of a password or authorization is unfortunately a big issue in the industry—in an enterprise, many people forget their passwords or lose their smart cards every day. There's no shame in admitting it: we've all done it.

Generally, setting up a certified key on a TPM takes some effort, but doing this during provisioning time in TPM 2.0 is much easier. If users need their TPMs reprovisioned in the field, this burdens IT staff. Because IT staff are major players in computer purchasing decisions, the architects of the TPM specification needed to solve this problem. The TPM 2.0 design allows management not just of keys (so they can be duplicated on other TPMs), but also of authorizations; this is demonstrated in detail in the chapter on enhanced authorization. For now, suffice it to say that major TPM 2.0 enhancements were designed to solve this problem.

Summary

In this chapter, you have seen that many different software interfaces can be used to take advantage of TPM capabilities, and many currently available applications use TPMs. Some of these only take advantage of standard capabilities such as those in any crypto coprocessor—creating, storing, and using keys. These basic interfaces, such as MS CAPI and PKCS, exist in a large number of applications. Taking advantage of higher-level capabilities, such as those used in attestation software, requires talking to TPM-specific interfaces instead of generic cryptographic interfaces. There are several of those for TPM 1.2 and currently at least two, Microsoft TBS and TCG's TSS, for the TPM 2.0 interface.

Finally, you saw that when creating applications that use a crypto coprocessor such as a TPM, there are rocks to avoid: the cryptographic processor may die, or a motherboard to which it's attached may have to be replaced. Even worse, the only user who knows a password may become unavailable. For the sake of manageability, you need a strategy to recover functionality after such an occurrence. Enhanced authorization, a new feature in TPM 2.0, meets this need; it is explained in chapter 14.

To continue your journey into the TPM 2.0 universe, in the next chapter we kick-start your ability to read and understand the TPM 2.0 specification.

CHAPTER 5

■ ■ ■

Navigating the Specification

The TPM 2.0 specification is not an easy read by any means. Although this is true of most technical specifications, TPM 2.0 presents some unique challenges. The specification is long—1,000 pages at last count—and written in a very concise and formal syntax that often attaches significant functional meaning to what appear to be rather insignificant punctuation marks. Part 2 of the specification was written to be parsed by code-generator tools in order to generate C headers and some marshaling and unmarshalling functions, which explains the emphasis on punctuation marks and the style of the specification's tables. At times, explanations of important concepts are tersely expressed and difficult to find. Although technically correct, these explanations can be hard to follow. And while the single-minded desire for conciseness and avoidance of redundancy at all costs in writing the specification enhances maintainability, it also adversely affects readability. The goal was a specification that was highly maintainable; we think the developers succeeded admirably, perhaps even too well!

On the other hand, from a technical perspective, the specification is very robust; the information you need is there—the challenge is to find it. It's like putting together a really large puzzle; you have all the pieces, but they aren't always where you expect them to be. This chapter aims to help you put the pieces together much faster by passing on some hard-earned lessons that we, the authors, have learned as we have negotiated this terrain. We urge you to keep in mind that the specification is quite logical once you get used to it. You will be assimilated!

To summarize, learning TPM 2.0 isn't a trivial task. But the good news for you is that we intend to give you a huge boost.

This chapter discusses the following:

- The high-level structure of the TPM 2.0 library specification

- Some definitions that are required to understand the specification

- The command schematic tables

- Some details of the data structures

- Table decorations

- Command schematic syntax

- Tips on where to find crucial and commonly used information

- Some other TPM 2.0-related specifications you need to know about

- Our strategies for learning the specification

■ **Note**   This chapter doesn't proceed through the four parts of the specification in sequential order. That might seem logical, but having tried it, we can vouch that it's not the best way for newcomers to understand the specification. In order to jump-start your understanding, we alter the order in a way that we hope enhances the learning process.

TPM 2.0 Library Specification: The Parts

The TPM 2.0 library specification is the most important and base-level specification for TPM 2.0. This specification describes the core TPM 2.0 functionality that is common to all TPM 2.0 implementations.

The library specification consists of four parts:

- *Part 1, Architecture*: This lives up to its name and is the most important part to read in detail. In text form, it describes the TPM operation and much of the rationale behind the design. It also contains many of the practical details of how the TPM operates. For instance, this is the only place that describes how to create sessions, which are used to authorize, audit, and encrypt commands. As such, it describes all variations of session types in great detail.

- *Part 2, Structures*: This presents the data types, structures, and unions that are used by TPM 2.0, and is analogous to a description of data types in a programming guide. Included in the definitions are the error codes returned when commands fail.

- *Part 3, Commands*: This presents the TPM 2.0 commands, which are analogous to function descriptions in a programming guide. It describes the input and output parameters for each of the TPM 2.0 commands and the command-specific error conditions. The actions performed by the command are precisely described by the included C code. This code calls many supporting routines that aren't in Part 3; these routines and their error codes are described in Part 4.

- *Part 4, Supporting Routines:* This section contains the code for the supporting routines called by the code in Part 3 as well as the error codes output by that code. This code explains the guts of the TPM 2.0 operation in excruciating detail. When stepping through the simulator code to understand why a particular error is occurring, you will spend a lot of time here. So, one way or another, you're going to become familiar with significant parts of this code.

Some Definitions

Before we get started, some definitions are in order so that you can better understand the specification. This is a good section to bookmark, because you'll refer to these definitions frequently as you read the specification and the rest of this book. Don't get discouraged if you're unable to completely comprehend these definitions at first; aim for a high-level understanding for the first reading, and then bookmark this section for future referral.

General Definitions

The following definitions pertain to both commands and responses:

- *Authorization*: Proves the right to access some entity in the TPM. TPM 2.0 uses three types of authorizations:
- *Password authorization*: this is a one shot clear text authorization.

  - *HMAC authorization*: Uses a hash message authentication code (HMAC) for the authorization. The HMAC key is derived using a shared secret that is the basis of the authorization.

  - *Policy or enhanced authorization (EA)*: Uses policy assertions that must be satisfied in order to authorize an action on an object. *Policy assertions* are commands that are sent to the TPM before the command being authorized.

  - *Session*: As defined in the TPM 2.0 specification, a "collection of TPM state that changes after each use." Unfortunately, this definition is too general and not very informative. A better understanding of sessions comes from knowing how they are used. Sessions are used for authorizations and per-command actions (encryption, decryption, audit, and a few others) in a session. In the case of HMAC and policy sessions, sessions are created and then used for multiple commands. Password authorizations are a special case of sessions that don't carry any state across multiple commands. The different types and uses of sessions are discussed at length in later chapters; for now it suffices to have a high-level understanding.

- *Handle*: An identifier that uniquely identifies a TPM resource that occupies TPM memory.

- *Byte stream*: On a command, the actual bytes sent to the TPM. On a response, the actual bytes received from the TPM.

- *Canonicalized data*: The command schematics in Part 3 describe the inputs and outputs from the TPM with C structures. These structures are often much larger than the data sent to the TPM. For instance, some structures contain unions consisting of elements of widely varying sizes. For a given instance of one of these unions, only the data required by the particular union element being used when sending the command is sent to the TPM. In addition, all data sent to and received from the TPM is in big-endian byte order. Data that meets these characteristics is canonicalized. The aggregation and ordering of all the canonicalized inputs to a command forms the byte stream sent to the TPM. Response data from the TPM is also in canonicalized format.

- *Unmarshalled data*: Data in its C structure format.

- *Marshalled data*: Data in its canonicalized form—that is, the form sent to or received from the TPM.

Definitions of the Major Fields of the Command Byte Stream

The following items are described in the order in which they appear in the command byte stream:

- *Command header*: A common area for all commands. It consists of the `tag`, `commandSize`, and `commandCode` fields, described next.

  - `tag`: Identifies whether the command contains sessions—that is, whether it contains an authorization area (defined shortly).

  - `commandSize`: The size of the command byte stream, including all fields of the header.

  - `commandCode`: Identifies the TPM command to be executed, and controls the interpretation of the rest of the command byte stream.

- *Handle area*: Contains between zero and three handles as specified by the Part 3 command schematics.

- *Authorization area*: Contains command session data. Multiple sessions can be associated with a single command, so this area can contain the parameters for between zero and three sessions. It contains authorization information, per-command session use modifiers, and some session state information that needs to be communicated between the application and the TPM.

- *Parameter area*: Contains command-specific parameters as described in Part 3 of the specification.

Definitions of the Major Fields of the Response Byte Stream

The following items are described in the order in which they appear in the response byte stream:

- *Response header*: A common area for all responses. It consists of the tag, responseSize, and responseCode fields, as described next:

    - tag: Identifies whether the response contains sessions.

    - responseSize: The size of the response byte stream, including all fields of the header.

    - responseCode: Identifies the whether the TPM command succeeded and, if not, what specific error occurred.

- *Handle area*: Contains between zero and three handles, as specified by the Part 3 response schematics.

- *Parameter area*: Contains the command-specific response parameters, as described in Part 3 of the specification.

- *Authorization area*: Contains response session data. Multiple sessions can be associated with a single command, so this area can contain the parameters for between zero and three sessions. It contains authorization information, per-command session use modifiers, and some session state information that needs to be communicated between the application and the TPM.

Getting Started in Part 3: the Commands

If you're like most programmers, you'll start in Part 3. Seriously, who has time to read a lengthy specification? And after all, the goal is to just "Git 'er done," right? That's typically the mindset of busy engineers, and it's actually a good approach, except that it will quickly bring you face to face with some of the harsh realities of the TPM 2.0 specification. In order to help you over some of the hurdles we've encountered when using the specification, here are a few things you need to know before you delve into Part 3.

The generic byte structure for all TPM 2.0 commands and responses is described in Part 1 in the section titled "Command/Response Structure." The Separators table and Command Structure and Response Structure figures are particularly helpful. We recommend that you place a bookmark at these sections in the specification, because you'll be referring to them often.

To make this discussion a bit more practical, we describe in detail two types of commands—a command without authorizations (TPM2_Startup) and a command with authorizations (TPM2_Create)—and explain some of nuances of the command byte stream. We start with TPM2_Startup, because it's the first command that must be sent to the TPM and is one of the simplest TPM 2.0 commands.

If you look at the Part 3 section that describes the TPM2_Startup command, you see three sections:

- *"General Description"*: Describes the command in text form, details some of the constraints on the inputs, and discusses error conditions.

- *"Command and Response"*: A data schematic for the inputs to the command (Command) and the outputs from the command (Response). We discuss these tables in detail in a moment.

- *"Detailed Actions"*: Contains code and a table of the error conditions that are returned by the command's code (not including the ones sent by the supporting code).

This three-part format is used for all commands. For the purposes of our current topic, we mainly look at the Command and Response tables. For the TPM2_Startup command, these tables are shown in Table 5-1 and Table 5-2.

Table 5-1. *TPM2_Startup Command (Table 5 in Part 3 of the TPM 2.0 Specification)*

Type	Name	Description
TPMI_ST_COMMAND_TAG	Tag	TPM_ST_NO_SESSIONS
UINT32	commandSize	
TPM_CC	commandCode	TPM_CC_Startup {NV}
TPM_SU	startupType	TPM_SU_CLEAR or TPM_SU_STATE

The Type column shows the data type for each field of the command. These types are defined in Part 2 of the specification. The Name column is self-explanatory: it contains the name of the parameter to be passed to or from the TPM. This is also the name of the parameter in the Part 3 source code. The Description column describes the field along with any field-specific requirements. TPM2_Startup has two field-specific requirements: tag must be TPM_ST_NO_SESSIONS, and commandCode must be TPM_CC_Startup. The {NV} is a table decoration that means the command may update nonvolatile memory inside the TPM. (Table decorations are described in the Table Decorations section early in Part 3.)

The format of the first three fields—tag, commandSize, and commandCode—is the same for all commands. These fields form the command header.

Following are explanations of the command fields:

- `tag`: Indicates whether the command has sessions. Because the `TPM2_Startup` command can never take sessions, this tag must always be set to `TPM_ST_NO_SESSIONS`.

- `commandSize`: The size in bytes of the entire command stream sent to the TPM.

- `commandCode`: Indicates which command is being sent. This tells the TPM how to interpret the rest of the command data.

Now notice the line following the command code:

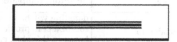

This line indicates that any fields following are in the parameter area. In this case, `startupType` is the only parameter in this area. In general, this area contains fields that configure any command-specific parameters for the command. The meaning of these lines and other table decorations are described in two sections of Part 3: "Table Decorations" and "Handle and Parameter Demarcation." You will want to refer to these two sections frequently when reading Part 3 of the spec.

Table 5-2. *TPM2_Startup Response (Table 6 in Part 3 of the TPM 2.0 Specification)*

Type	Name	Description
TPM_ST	Tag	see clause 6
UINT32	responseSize	
TPM_RC	responseCode	

Following are explanations of the response fields:

- `tag`: Indicates whether the response has sessions. Because this command never has sessions, `tag` is always `TPM_ST_NO_SESSIONS`.

- `responseSize`: The size in bytes of the entire response byte stream.

- `responseCode`: Indicates whether the command passed or failed. `TPM_RC_SUCCESS` indicates passing. Other codes indicate failure.

Notice that `TPM2_Startup` has no return parameters.

Now we'll look at a much more complicated command, `TPM2_Create`. This command is used to create objects such as keys or data objects. Table 5-3 shows its Command table.

Table 5-3. *TPM2_Create Command (Table 19 in Part 3 of the TPM 2.0 Specification)*

Type	Name	Description
TPMI_ST_COMMAND_TAG	Tag	TPM_ST_SESSIONS
UINT32	commandSize	
TPM_CC	commandCode	TPM_CC_Create
TPMI_DH_OBJECT	@parentHandle	handle of parent for new object Auth Index: 1 Auth Role: USER
TPM2B_SENSITIVE_CREATE	inSensitive	the sensitive data
TPM2B_PUBLIC	inPublic	the public template
TPM2B_DATA	outsideInfo	data that will be included in the creation data for this object to provide permanent, verifiable linkage between this object and some object owner data
TPML_PCR_SELECTION	creationPCR	PCR that will be used in creation data

Following are explanations of the command fields:

- tag: In this case, TPM_ST_SESSIONS to indicate that the command must have sessions. Another indication is the @ sign in front of the parentHandle handle name; this means an authorization session is required with this handle. More on that later.

- commandSize: Size of the total byte stream including authorization data.

- commandCode: The command code for this command.

Note this separator. Now things get more interesting; this separator didn't exist the TPM2_Startup command:

This line indicates that the following fields are in the handle area, as described in the "Handle and Parameter Demarcation" section of Part 3. Handles are 32-bit references to various entities in the TPM. parentHandle is the only handle parameter for this command. Commands can take up to two handles in this area.

Notice the @ character in front of parentHandle. This is a table decoration; it means this handle requires that an associated authorization be included in the authorization section. This and other table decorations are described in the "Table Decorations" section early in Part 3.

Also notice the "Auth Index: 1" text in the description. This indicates the ordering of the authorization in the authorization section. In this case, the authorization for the parentHandle must be the first authorization in the authorization section. All commands that take authorizations can take up to three authorizations. When a command has an @ sign in front of one or more handles, the command requires an authorization for each such handle. In this case one authorization is required.

Notice the Auth Role: USER text. This is a further qualification on the authorization, which is described in the chapter on enhanced authorization. Auth roles are analogous to privilege levels in an operating system. They control who can get access to certain entities.

Handles behave differently from parameters in a command: handles aren't used in computing the cpHash, which is a hash of the input parameters. This hash is used in calculating HMACs and, in some cases, policy digests. The purpose of this separation is to allow a resource manager to virtualize the handles in order to swap objects in and out of the TPM, much like a virtual memory manager swaps memory contents between disk drives and memory. Later chapters describe HMACs, policy digests, and the resource manager in detail. For now, it's sufficient to understand that handles and parameters are separated into different fields in the byte stream in order to facilitate some key differences in functionality.

Now you see a line you're familiar with from the Startup command. Again, it indicates the start of the parameter area:

But in this case, because tag is equal to TPM_ST_SESSIONS, indicating that this command requires an authorization session, this separator also indicates where the authorization data is inserted into the command byte stream. This command's authorization area can have between one and three sessions, all of which are inserted here. We describe the authorization area in detail in chapter 13.

This command takes four parameters: insensitive, inPublic, outsideInfo, and creationPCR. Part 2 describes the data structure types for each of these.

Table 5-4 shows the TPM2_Create command's Response table.

Table 5-4. TPM2_Create Response (Table 20 in Part 3 of the TPM 2.0 Specification)

Type	Name	Description
TPM_ST	Tag	see clause 6
UINT32	responseSize	
TPM_RC	responseCode	
TPM2B_PRIVATE	outPrivate	the private portion of the object
TPM2B_PUBLIC	outPublic	the public portion of the created object
TPM2B_CREATION_DATA	creationData	contains a TPMS_CREATION_DATA
TPM2B_DIGEST	creationHash	digest of *creationData* using *nameAlg* of *outPublic*
TPMT_TK_CREATION	creationTicket	ticket used by TPM2_CertifyCreation() to validate that the creation data was produced by the TPM

Following are explanations of the response fields:

- tag, responseSize, and responseCode are as described earlier, except that if the command passes, tag is TPM_RC_SESSIONS to indicate the presence of sessions in the response. There are three cases here:

  - If the command has no sessions, the response will have no sessions. For this command, the tag is always set to TPM_ST_NO_SESSIONS.

  - If the command has sessions and returns success, the response tag is TPM_ST_SESSIONS, indicating that the response, too, has sessions.

  - If the command has sessions but fails, the response tag is TPM_ST_NO_SESSIONS. Failing commands never have sessions or response parameters in their response.

When the following line is present in a response schematic, it indicates the start of the response handle area. In this command, there are no response handles, so this line isn't present:

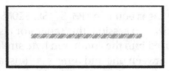

Now you see your old friend the parameter demarcation line:

Unlike for the command data, for the response, this is simply the dividing line for parameters; the authorization area isn't located here, but appears later in the byte stream. This command returns five response parameters: outPrivate, outPublic, creationData, creationHash, and creationTicketNotice.

The response authorization area is tacked on to the last line the in the schematic, after all the parameters. This means the response authorization area is the last area in the response byte stream.

Now that we've described the overall command and response structures, we'll discuss some commonly used data types.

Data Details

If you're writing low-level TPM code, this section is crucial to understand because the majority of your bugs will be in this area. When debugging low-level TPM 2.0 code, you need to understand this section in order to properly decode the byte streams being sent to and received from the TPM. The important data concepts to understand are common data structure constructs, canonicalization of the byte stream, and endianness.

Common Structure Constructs

This section describes some commonly used data structures. A good understanding of these is vital because you will see them often.

TPM2B_XXX Structures

All structures that start with a TPM2B_ prefix are sized-byte buffers. Each sized-byte buffer consists of a size and an array of size bytes. Table 5-5 shows a typical structure of this type.

Table 5-5. *Definition of the TPM2B_DATA Structure (Table 71 in Part 2 of the TPM 2.0 Specification)*

Parameter	Type	Description
size	UINT16	size in octets of the *buffer* field; may be 0
buffer[size]{:sizeof(TPMT_HA)}	BYTE	the buffer area that contains the algorithm ID and the digest

The corresponding C structure looks like this:

```
typedef struct {
    UINT16    size;                       /* size in octets of the buffer field;
                                             may be 0 */
    BYTE      buffer[sizeof(TPMT_HA)];    /* the buffer area that contains the
                                             algorithm ID and
                      the digest */
} TPM2B_DATA;
```

Structure with Union

A union is often contained within a structure and preceded by a union selector. Table 5-6 is an example.

Table 5-6. *Definition of the TPMT_HA Structure (Table 69 in Part 2 of the TPM 2.0 Specification)*

Parameter	Type	Description
hashAlg	+TPMI_ALG_HASH	selector of the hash contained in the *digest* that implies the size of the *digest*
		NOTE The leading "+" on the type indicates that this structure should pass an indication to the unmarshaling function for TPMI_ALG_HASH so that TPM_ALG_NULL will be allowed if a use of a TPMT_HA allows TPM_ALG_NULL.
[hashAlg] digest	TPMU_HA	the digest data

This structure has two elements: hashAlg, which is used as the selector for the digest union. This is indicated by the brackets surrounding hashAlg in front of the digest parameter. In Table 5-6, hashAlg is the selector for the digest union.

The definition of TPM_HA is shown in Table 5-7.

Table 5-7. *Definition of the TPMU_HA Union (Table 68 in Part 2 of the TPM 2.0 Specification)*

Parameter	Type	Selector	Description
sha1 [SHA1_DIGEST_SIZE]	BYTE	TPM_ALG_SHA1	
sha256 [SHA256_DIGEST_SIZE]	BYTE	TPM_ALG_SHA256	
sm3_256 [SM3_256_DIGEST_SIZE]	BYTE	TPM_ALG_SM3_256	
sha384 [SHA384_DIGEST_SIZE]	BYTE	TPM_ALG_SHA384	
sha512 [SHA512_DIGEST_SIZE]	BYTE	TPM_ALG_SHA512	
Null		TPM_ALG_NULL	

In general, in a structure, when there is a parameter A that is enclosed in brackets and is in front of parameter B's name, parameter A is a selector for the type of parameter B. In Table 5-7, if hashAlg is set to TPM_ALG_SHA1, then the union element is sha1 [SHA1_DIGEST_SIZE].

The C code generated by Table 5-6 and Table 5-7 is as follows:

```
typedef struct {
    TPMI_ALG_HASH      hashAlg;
    TPMU_HA            digest;
} TPMT_HA;

typedef union {
    BYTE    sha1 [SHA1_DIGEST_SIZE];         /* TPM_ALG_SHA1 */
    BYTE    sha256 [SHA256_DIGEST_SIZE];     /* TPM_ALG_SHA256 */
    BYTE    sm3_256 [SM3_256_DIGEST_SIZE];   /* TPM_ALG_SM3_256 */
    BYTE    sha384 [SHA384_DIGEST_SIZE];     /* TPM_ALG_SHA384 */
    BYTE    sha512 [SHA512_DIGEST_SIZE];     /* TPM_ALG_SHA512 */
} TPMU_HA;
```

Canonicalization

The data that is sent to the TPM and received from the TPM is minimized to eliminate any unnecessary bytes in the data stream. This guarantees maximum byte-stream transfer rates to the TPM, because TPMs are often connected to rather slow interface buses such as LPC and SPI. This minimized form of data is called *canonical* data and is not equivalent to the C-like data structures described in Part 2 of the specification. This concept is crucial to understand if you're dissecting the data stream.

As an example, look at the MAX_NV_BUFFER_2B structure:

```
typedef struct {
    UINT16    size;
    BYTE      buffer[MAX_NV_BUFFER_SIZE];
} MAX_NV_BUFFER_2B;
```

This structure has a size field and a buffer that is MAX_NV_BUFFER_SIZE bytes long. In the reference implementation, MAX_NV_BUFFER_SIZE is 1,024 bytes. But when this data is sent to the TPM, only the size and the number of bytes specified by the size field are actually sent down the wire. If size equals 10 bytes, only 12 bytes are sent for this structure: 2 for the size field and 10 for the buffer.

In C, unions are used to overlap different types of data structure in a common *union*. The union's size is the size of the largest type included in the union. A TPM 2.0 data structure that includes a union typically includes a selector that tells what type of data is in the union. A canonical representation of the data only contains the selector and the canonical representation of the structure selected from the union. For example, in the TPMT_HA structure, if the selector, hashAlg, is set to TPM_ALG_SHA1, the digest is SHA1_DIGEST_SIZE bytes, which is much shorter than the maximum size of the union.

Endianness

TPM data is always in big-endian format when transmitted to or received from the TPM. This means little-endian CPUs, such as the x86 architecture, must always swap bytes before sending data to the TPM and after receiving data from the TPM.

Part 2: Notation Syntax

The "Notation" section in Part 2 of the specification is very important to understand; we often refer to it when studying the TPM 2.0 data structures. You are highly encouraged to read this entire section of the specification, so we don't repeat all the information here; but we'll touch on a few critical areas (this is another good section to bookmark, because you'll will refer to it often):

- In an enumeration table, a # character specifies the return type when the marshalling of an enumerated value fails: that is, when the passed-in value doesn't match any of the allowed values.

- A $ character specifies that a parameter can be one of a previously defined range of values.

- A + character prefix to a value name in an enumeration means the value is a *conditional type*: it's optional in an enumeration. Whether the optional value is allowed in a particular use of an enumeration is determined by whether the + character is appended to the type specification

- A null parameter in a union definition means the union can be empty.

- If a union member has *no selector*, it means the member is common to all the union types. The no-selector member is a superclass of the members that have selectors.

- { } specifies parameter limits. Read the "Parameter Limits" section for details.

Part 3: Table Decorations

The "Command Modifiers and Table Decorations" section in Part 3 describes the special notation used in the command schematics in Part 3; this is another good area to bookmark. We describe some of the more commonly used ones here, but please refer to the section in the specification for a complete list:

- +: Similar to the notation used in Part 2 for conditional types. When appended to the type, indicates that the null value of the variable can be used.

- @r: When used as a prefix to the name of a handle parameter, indicates that an authorization is required for that handle. This also means the tag for the command must be TPM_ST_SESSIONS.

- +PP, +{PP}: Suffixes to TPM_RH_PLATFORM that indicate an authorization using this handle *is* or *may be*, respectively, required to have physical presence asserted.

- Auth Index: In the description, indicates the number of required handles. (From our viewpoint, this seems redundant. The order of the handles is already indicated by their order in the table.)

- Auth Role: In the description for a required handle, indicates the role of the authorization: USER, ADMIN, or DUP. These roles are described in detail in chapter 13.

Commonly Used Sections of the Specification

Following is a list of some of the most commonly used sections of the specification:

- Command codes are listed in Part 2, in the section "TPM_CC Listing."

- Error codes are found in multiple places:

  - Part 2, "TPM_RC (Response Codes)," lists all the response codes.

  - Part 1, "Response Code Details," shows a flow chart for decoding the error codes. A software decoder application for automating this process is highly advised. After spending months hand-decoding error codes, one of the authors wrote one that he's found extremely useful.

  - Parts 3 and 4 describe the error codes returned by TPM commands and the subroutines called by those commands. A key point with respect to error codes is that Part 3 doesn't describe all the error codes that may be output when a TPM command is executed. The command-specific code in Part 3 calls routines in Part 4, and these also output error codes. This has tripped up many an unwary TPM 2.0 developer.

- The "Table Decorations" and "Handle and Parameter Demarcation" sections near the beginning of Part 3 are very helpful for understanding the Part 3 command tables. Don't overlook these sections!

- To understand the data structures in Part 2, the "Notation" section is very helpful. It describes many of the obscure characters and what they mean. Don't overlook these special characters!

- The various types of sessions and authorizations are described in the "Authorizations and Acknowledgements" section in Part 1. These aren't described to this level anywhere else. It is crucial to know where this section is and refer to it often when decoding command and response byte streams.

- The handle types are described in the "TPM Handles" section of Part 1. Of particular interest is the most significant octet, which describes the type of resource being referred to by the handle. The "TPM_HT (Handle Types)" section in Part 2 describes the various types of handles.

- Names of various entities and how they are derived are described in the "Names" section of Part 1. This is crucial in order to understand how session HMACs and policy digests are created.

- To understand policy session operations, the following sections in Part 1 are very helpful:

    - "Policy Example."

    - "Trial Policy Modification of Policies."

    - "TPM2_PolicySigned(), TPM2_PolicySecret(), and TPM2_PolicyTicket()." This section provides details for these rather complicated policy commands.

How to Find Information in the Specification

You can use a PDF reader to search all four parts of the specification. Sometimes the bit of information you're looking for isn't where you might think it would be. For instance, even though Part 1 isn't normative and isn't targeted at describing structures, it often has the best descriptions of the functionality of certain data structures and their fields.

If you have access to a TPM library header file, you may be able to use the header to find a complete description of how the structure is used. The easiest way to do this is as follows:

1. Find the data structure of interest in the C header file that describes the TPM 2.0 data structures.

2. A well-written instantiation of this header file lists the table number for the structure in comments above the data structure or type. Find this table number in Part 2 of the spec; the descriptive text above the table provides the additional information needed to understand the structure. This is one of the most useful tricks to know.

Strategies for Ramping Up on TPM 2.0

Engineers come in many flavors, so there are many approaches to cracking a specification like TPM 2.0. As authors, we have different personalities and have used different strategies to approach this spec. In this section we describes how we ramped up on TPM 2.0 and what worked best for us. You may pick and choose from one or all three of our approaches or develop your own. We hope our journeys will facilitate yours.

Will

I am the newbie of the bunch. I started working on TPM 2.0 in May 2012. I had worked previously with TPM 1.2 but only with the functionality I needed to know for enabling Intel Trusted Execution Technology (Intel TXT). This means I had never learned about sessions and how they worked in TPM 1.2, and I didn't know much about keys and key management.

As an engineer with product schedules to meet, my goal was to "Get 'er done." I first tried to read through the spec but quickly bogged down in the massive quantities of unfamiliar terms and what was, to me, confusing lingo. So, I started figuring out which TPM 2.0 functions I needed and how to implement them. This led me to Part 3 of the specification as a starting point. As I tried running my coded functions against the simulator, I quickly ran into errors that I couldn't explain, and this caused me to single-step through the simulator. This was when I first understood the difference between the canonical byte stream data that the TPM understands and the C structures used to specify the inputs to TPM 2.0 commands. Painstakingly, I debugged all the functionality needed for a TPM 2.0–enabled TXT prototype in order to meet my scheduled deliverable. In parallel, I began to develop the TSS 2.0 system API code. This required a greater depth of TPM 2.0 knowledge, which came as I simultaneously coded, read the specification, and debugged through the simulator. To be honest, there were still parts of the spec that resisted my attempts at comprehension—my only remedy was telephone consultations with the TPM Working Group chairman, who was extremely helpful in answering my questions about HMAC and policy sessions. As understanding dawned during my consultations with him, we developed some graphical representations of the different types of sessions and how they relate to each other, some of which appear in this book; and thus my idea for this book was born.

After completing much of the TSS system API development work, I had enough knowledge to go back and do a deep dive through the specification; this was largely motivated by the need to prepare training slides for an upcoming TPM 2.0 training session I was slated to present at Intel. For three months, I read the spec from cover to cover, and for the most part, it made sense. This wouldn't have happened if I had tried a deep dive from the very beginning. Here's another tip, which may sound strange: I've found it very effective to read the specification from my Kindle while exercising at the gym. I think the physical exercise keeps me alert; if I did this at my desk, I would be battling to stay awake. And 30 to 45 minutes per day seems to be the right amount of time to make progress, stay alert, and avoid completely overloading my brain.

To summarize my strategy:

- Initially read some of Parts 1, 2, and 3 but struggled to comprehend them. In spite of the difficulties, this initial read helped me get an overview of what's different from TPM 1.2.

- Focused on a bare-bones TPM 2.0 development deliverable by beginning with the Part 3 descriptions of TPM 2.0 functions.

- Developed the TSS system API while reading the spec, developing code, debugging through the simulator, and consulting with an expert more or less in parallel.

- Did a deep dive through the spec by reading 30–45 minutes per day.

Some final pieces of advice: start somewhere, and don't sweat all the details at first. Get a high-level understanding, and then keep digging progressively deeper. And don't be afraid to ask for help when you get stuck. I'm still learning myself.

Ken

I was involved with developing the specification from the start. My input takes the form of advice, rather than a narrative of my own personal experience.

The TPM specification combines the styles of both a user manual (Part 1) and a reference manual (Parts 2 and 3). If you have no prior experience with a TPM, or just TPM 1.2 experience, I recommend reading Part 1, or at least the sections relevant to your application. Even if you don't immediately grasp all its complexities, you will become familiar with the technical jargon and the TPM features and gain some sense of how they fit together.

Once you know what you want to do and have some sense of the command flow, Part 3 gives the details for each command. The description and command and response tables should be sufficient. Users in general won't have to read the code in Parts 3 and 4.

I anticipate that most users won't be constructing command streams. Middleware libraries such as a TPM Software Stack (TSS) normally perform those tasks. If you're writing or needing to debug through such middleware, Part 2 gives the details for each structure, with the names of the structure members, data types, and possible parameters. The platform-specific specification goes further, describing the parameters for a TPM implementation.

Part 4 describes, in C code, the details of TPM operation. Application and middleware developers should rarely have to refer to Part 4.

Dave

I was part of the development of TPM 1.2 and 2.0 from the start. I ramped up by first reading Part 3. It made perfect sense to me, except that it omitted anything about how to actually authorize a command. So for commands that did not require authorization, like TPM2_GetRandom, Part 3 told me everything I need to know: what parameters needed to go where, what size they were, and so on. The first parameter was a bit of a challenge until I realized that it was always likely to be NO_SESSIONS, because I wasn't going to be auditing the TPM2_GetRandom command. The parameters are described in detail in Part 2 and were mostly pretty easy to understand for commands that don't require authorization.

Next I dug into doing simple authorizations using the password session. This was nice because the password session always exists, and I didn't need to do any encryption/ decryption, salting, or auditing of the session. It was just a simple password, which was in the clear. Reading the section "Password Authorizations" in Part 1 explained these easily. I started by changing the basic passwords associated with taking ownership of the TPM.

Next I tackled creating a key. This was a more complicated task, because I needed to understand the unions for defining the algorithms and other parameters associated with the key I was creating. I started with a key that only had a password authorization (as opposed to a policy or HMAC authorization), because it was easier. Basically I created a storage root key (SRK) for the TPM.

Then I tackled policy authorizations. Because I wanted to create a signing key whose password I could change, I created keys locked to the password of an NV index. That meant I had to create an NV index; and I wanted one that couldn't be removed and re-created with a different password, which is what I did. See Chapter 14 later in this book for a description of how I did this.

I wanted to play with types of sessions, so I authorized a key using an HMAC. Then I audited the command. After successfully auditing, I used a decrypt session to pass in the password. Finally I used a salted HMAC session.

Next I did a more complicated policy, using TPM2_PolicyOr and TPM2_PolicyAuthorize. At this point I felt like I had a pretty good handle on how things worked.

Other TPM 2.0 Specifications

Platform specifications augment the library specification to enable the creation of TPM definitions that are platform specific. They list what is mandatory, optional, or excluded; define minimum and maximum values; add initialization and provisioning requirements; and detail the physical interface.

You may need to reference the following platform-specific specifications:

- *TCG PC Client Platform TPM Profile (PTP) Specification*: Defines platform specifics for PCs and server platforms.

- *TPM 2.0 Mobile Reference Architecture*: "[D]efines a reference architecture for the implementation of a TPM in modern mobile platforms using a Protected Environment (section 7). This type of TPM is known as a TPM Mobile" (TPM 2.0 Mobile Reference Architecture).

Summary

Although the climb is steep, you can ramp up on TPM 2.0 much more efficiently with a good overview of the specification and some tips from early explorers. In this chapter we've shared our somewhat hard-earned expertise to assist you. The assimilation process has begun!

The next chapter describes the commonly available execution environments. It prepares you for the code examples that we present in later chapters.

Other TPM 2.0 Specifications

Summary

CHAPTER 6

■ ■ ■

Execution Environment

Future chapters in this book present code examples to illustrate concepts. In order for you to be able to build and run these code examples, this chapter describes how to set up an execution environment and build TPM 2.0 sample applications. An execution environment consists of two things: a TPM and a software stack to communicate with the TPM. You can use a hardware or software TPM to run the code examples. In this chapter you learn how to set up the Microsoft TPM 2.0 simulator, a software implementation of TPM 2.0. For software stacks, currently there are two software API environments for TPM 2.0 programming: Microsoft's TSS.net and TSS 2.0. This chapter demonstrates how to set up both of these environments.

Setting Up the TPM

All TPM 2.0 programming environments require a TPM to run code against. For developers, the TPM that is easiest to use is the Microsoft TPM 2.0 simulator. Of course, you can also use other TPM 2.0 devices, hardware, and firmware, as they become available, to run the code examples. Because communication with a hardware or firmware TPM is platform specific, you must use the correct driver; setting up this driver isn't described here.

Microsoft Simulator

Provided by Microsoft, the Microsoft simulator is a full TPM 2.0 device implemented completely in software. Application code can communicate with the simulator via a sockets interface. This means the simulator can be run on the same system as the application or on a remote system connected via a network.

Two versions of the simulator are available. A binary-only version can be downloaded from: http://research.microsoft.com/en-US/downloads/35116857-e544-4003-8e7b-584182dc6833/default.aspx. For TCG members, the second, and better, option is to obtain the TPM 2.0 simulator source code and build it. The advantage of doing this is that it allows an application developer to step through the simulator itself, which is often quite useful when debugging errors. In either case, the simulator can only run under Windows.

You will first learn how to build the simulator from source code and set it up. Then, for non-TCG members, you will learn how to get the TSS.net or simulator binary and use the simulator executable. Finally, the chapter presents a simple Python program that you can use to test that the simulator is working.

Building the Simulator from Source Code

This option is available only to TCG members, because it requires downloading source code from TCG's web site. Go to the www.trustedcomputinggroup.org web site, click Member Login at top right, click the Groups pull-down at left, select TPMWG under My Groups, and then click Documents. At this point you should be at this web site: https://members.trustedcomputinggroup.org/apps/org/workgroup/tpmwg/documents.php. Find the latest version of the simulator, and download it; it will be called something like TPM 2.0 vX.XX VS Solution.

Building the simulator requires that Visual Studio 2012 or later be installed. Follow the directions in the TPM 2.0 Simulator release notes file to build the simulator.

Setting Up a Binary Version of the Simulator

Download the simulator from http://research.microsoft.com/en-US/downloads/35116857-e544-4003-8e7b-584182dc6833/default.aspx. Unzip the file into the directory of your choice.

Running the Simulator

Search for the simulator binary, simulator.exe, in the install directory, and start it. In some settings, you may need to configure the port numbers that the simulator listens to for commands. You can do this on the simulator command line.

The simulator uses two ports:

- *TPM command port*: Used for sending TPM commands and receiving TPM responses. The default port is 2321; if you need to change this, you can set it on the command line as follows:

  ```
  > simulator <portNum>
  ```

- *Platform command port*: Used for platform commands such as power on/off. The platform command port is always one greater than the TPM command port. For example, the default platform port number is 2322; and if you use the command-line option to set the TPM command port, the platform port is 1 greater than the command-line value.

There are two reasons to use a port other than the default port:

- If the network you're running on is using the default port for some other use

- If you want to run two instances of the simulator on the same machine, in which case you need to run one on a different port

Testing the Simulator

Let's look at three ways to test that the simulator is working: a simple Python script, TSS. net, and the system API test code.

Python Script

To test that the simulator is running correctly, you can use this Python script:

```python
#!/usr/bin/python

import os
import sys
import socket
from socket import socket, AF_INET, SOCK_STREAM

platformSock = socket(AF_INET, SOCK_STREAM)
platformSock.connect(('localhost', 2322))
# Power on the TPM
platformSock.send('\0\0\0\1')

tpmSock = socket(AF_INET, SOCK_STREAM)
tpmSock.connect(('localhost', 2321))
# Send TPM_SEND_COMMAND
tpmSock.send('\x00\x00\x00\x08')
# Send locality
tpmSock.send('\x03')
# Send # of bytes
tpmSock.send('\x00\x00\x00\x0c')
# Send tag
tpmSock.send('\x80\x01')
# Send command size
tpmSock.send('\x00\x00\x00\x0c')
```

```
# Send command code: TPMStartup
tpmSock.send('\x00\x00\x01\x44')
# Send TPM SU
tpmSock.send('\x00\x00')
# Receive the size of the response, the response, and 4 bytes of 0's
reply=tpmSock.recv(18)
for c in reply:
  print "%#x " % ord(c)
```

The script sends the TPM startup command to the TPM. If the startup command works correctly, you should see the following output from the for loop print statement:

```
>>>for c in reply:
...    print "%#x " % ord(c)
...
0x0
0x0
0x0
0xa
0x80
0x1
0x0
0x0
0x0
0xa
0x0
0x0
0x1
0x0
0x0
0x0
0x0
0x0
```

If you're getting this result, the simulator is running correctly.

TSS.net

TSS.net is a C# library of code for communicating with the TPM. Download it from https://tpm2lib.codeplex.com, install it, and run a code example as described shortly.

System API Test Code

Follow the directions in the section "TSS 2.0" for the System API library and test code. If any TPM 2.0 command is successfully sent to the TPM, the simulator is working.

Setting Up the Software Stack

The two software stacks you can use to communicate with the TPM are TSS 2.0 and TSS.net.

TSS 2.0

TSS is a TCG standard for the TCG software stack. TSS 2.0 can be built on (and link to) applications for) Windows and Linux. It consists of five or six layers and is implemented in C code except for a couple of Java layers. The layers at which TPM 2.0 code can be developed are as follows:

- *System API (SAPI)*: The lowest layer in TSS 2.0, which provides software functions for performing all variants of all TPM 2.0 functions. This layer also has tests that you can run against it. It requires detailed knowledge about TPM 2.0.

- *Enhanced System API (ESAPI)*: The next layer in TSS 2.0. It sits directly on top of the SAPI. This layer provides a lot of the glue code for doing encryption and decryption, HMAC sessions, policy sessions, and auditing. It also requires detailed knowledge about TPM 2.0, but it makes session handling much easier.

- *Feature API*: The layer to which most applications should be written. It provides APIs that isolate you from the messiness of the TPM 2.0 specification.

- *Feature API Java*: Layer that sits on top of the C code and performs the translation between C and Java so that Java applications can use TSS.

As of this writing, TSS 2.0 is implemented only at the System API level and includes a linked-in device driver for talking to the simulator. Currently, this code is only available to TCG members at https://github.com/. To access to the code, you must contact the TCG TSS workgroup chair to get permission. Follow the directions in the readme.docx file to install it and run the test code against the simulator.

TSS.net

As noted previously, you can download TSS.net from https://tpm2lib.codeplex.com, and then install it. To understand it, review the file: Using the TSS.Net Library.docx. Unfortunately, this doesn't tell you how to build and run the code examples. The samples\Windows8 directory contains separate directories for sample projects; you can follow these directions for the GetRandom example and then apply those steps to other examples:

1. In Windows Explorer, open the solution file: tss.net\tss.sln.

2. Respond with OK to the prompts for loading the various projects.

3. Select Build > Build Solution.

4. Start the simulator. (See the earlier directions.)

5. Run the GetRandom executable: `tss.net\samples\Windows8\`
   `GetRandom\bin\Debug\GetRandom.exe -tcp 10` (10 is the
   number of random bytes).

You can now run other sample programs in a similar manner. Try them out!

Summary

Now that you have an execution environment (or maybe both of them) set up, you're
ready to run the code samples from the following chapters of the book.

The next chapter describes the TCG Software Stack, TSS. This software stack is
currently being defined and implemented and will be freely available under an open
source license to application programmers. It's used for some of the subsequent code
examples in this book.

CHAPTER 7

■ ■ ■

TPM Software Stack

This book is primarily about TPM 2.0 devices. However, a TPM without software is like a car with a full tank of gas but no driver; it has great potential but isn't going anywhere. This chapter, in preparation for the rest of the book, introduces you to the TPM's "driver"[1], the TPM Software Stack (TSS). A good understanding of this topic will enable you to understand subsequent code examples in this book.

The TSS is a TCG software standard that allows applications to intercept the stack, that is, be written to APIs in the stack at various levels in a portable manner. Applications written to the TSS should work on any system that implements a compliant TSS. This chapter describes the layers of the TSS with a particular focus on the System API and Feature API layers. The other layers are described at a high level.

The Stack: a High-Level View

The TSS consists of the following layers from the highest level of abstraction to the lowest: Feature API (FAPI), Enhanced System API (ESAPI), System API (SAPI), TPM Command Transmission Interface (TCTI), TPM Access Broker (TAB), Resource Manager (RM), and Device Driver.[2]

Most user applications should be written to the FAPI, because it's designed to capture 80% of the common use cases. Writing to this layer is the TPM equivalent of writing in Java, C#, or some other higher-level language.

The next layer down is the ESAPI, which requires a lot of TPM knowledge but provides some session management and support for cryptographic capabilities. This is like writing in C++. At the time of this writing, the ESAPI specification is still a work in progress, so it isn't described in this chapter.

Applications can also be written to the SAPI layer, but this requires much more TPM 2.0 expertise. This is analogous to programming in C instead of a higher-level language. It provides you with access to all the functionality of the TPM but requires a high level of expertise to use.

---

[1]This is not to be confused with an OS device driver.
[2]The device driver isn't officially part of the TCG-defined TSS, but it makes sense to discuss it in this chapter because it's one of the layers in a TPM software stack.

TCTI is the layer used to transmit TPM commands and receive responses. Applications can be written to send binary streams of command data to the TCTI and receive binary data responses from it. This is like programming in assembly.

The TAB controls multiprocess synchronization to the TPM. Basically it allows multiple processes to access the TPM without stomping on each other.

The TPM has very limited on-board storage, so the Resource Manager is used in a manner similar to a PC's virtual memory manager to swap TPM objects and sessions in and out of TPM memory. Both the TAB and the RM are optional components. In highly embedded environments that don't have multiprocessing, these components are neither needed nor, in some cases, desired.

The last component, the device driver, handles the physical transmission of data to and from the TPM. Writing applications to this interface is possible as well and would be like programming in binary.

Figure 7-1 illustrates the TSS software stack. Some points to note:

- Although typically there is only one TPM available to applications, multiple TPMs could be available. Some of these could be software TPMs, such as the Microsoft simulator; others may be accessed remotely over the network—for instance, in the case of remote administration.

- Generally, components from the SAPI on up the stack are per-process components.

- Components below the SAPI are typically per-TPM components.

- Although Figure 7-1 doesn't show it, TCTI may be the interface between the RM and the device driver. In this case, the TCTI appears at multiple layers in the stack.

- At this time, we think the most common implementation will combine the TAB and the RM into a single module.

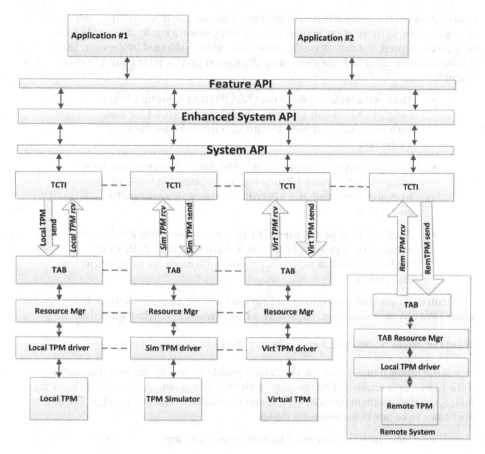

Figure 7-1. TSS diagram

The following sections describe each of the TSS layers.

Feature API

The TSS Feature API (FAPI) was created specifically to make the most-used facilities of the TPM 2.0 easily available to programmers. As such, it does not allow use of all the corner cases that a TPM is capable of doing.

It was designed with the hope that 80% of programs that would eventually use the TPM could be written by using the FAPI without having to resort to using other TSS APIs. It was also designed to minimize the number of calls you have to use and the number of parameters you have to define.

One way this was accomplished was by using a profile file to create default selections so you don't have to select algorithms, key sizes, crypto modes, and signing schemas explicitly when creating and using keys. It's assumed that *users* are normally the ones who wish to select a matched set of algorithms, and you can default to user-selected configurations. In cases where you want to explicitly select a configuration file, you may do this as well, but default configurations are always selected by the user. FAPI implementations ship with pre-created configuration files for most common choices. For example:

- The P_RSA2048SHA1 profile uses RSA 2048-bit asymmetric keys using PKCS1 version 1.5 for a signing scheme, SHA-1 for the hash algorithm, and AES128 with CFB mode for asymmetric encryption.

- The P_RSA2048SHA256 profile uses RSA 2048-bit asymmetric keys using PKCS#1 version 1.5 for a signing scheme, SHA-256 for the hash algorithm, and AES-128 with CFB mode for asymmetric encryption.

- The P_ECCP256 profile uses NIST ECC with prime field 256-bit asymmetric keys using ECDSA as a signing schema, SHA-1 for the hash algorithm, and AES-128 with CFB mode for asymmetric encryption.

Path descriptions are used to identify to the FAPI where to find keys, policies, NV, and other TPM objects and entities. Paths have a basic structure that looks like this:

```
<Profile name> / <Hierarchy> / <Object Ancestor> / key tree
```

If the profile name is omitted, the default profile chosen by the user is assumed. If the hierarchy is omitted, then the storage hierarchy is assumed. The storage hiearchy is H_S, the Endorsement hiearchy is H_E, and the Platform hierarchy is H_P. The object ancestor can be one of the following values:

- SNK: The system ancestor for non-duplicable keys

- SDK: The system ancestor for duplicable keys

- UNK: The user ancestor for non-duplicable keys

- UDK: The user ancestor for duplicable keys

- NV: For NV indexes

- Policy: For instances of policies

The key tree is simply a list of parent and children keys separated by / characters. The path is insensitive to capitalization.

Let's look at some examples. Assuming the user has chosen the configuration file P_RSA2048SHA1, all of the following paths are equivalent:

```
P_RSA2048SHA1/H_S/SNK/myVPNkey
```

```
H_S/SNK/myVPNkey
```

```
SNK/myVPNkey
```

P_RSA2048SHA1/H_S/SNK/MYVPNKEY

H_S/SNK/MYVPNKEY

SNK/MYVPNKEY

An ECC P-256 NIST signing key under a user's backup storage key might be:

P_ECCP256/UDK/backupStorageKey/mySigningKey

The FAPI also has some basic names for default types of entities.

Keys:

- ASYM_STORAGE_KEY: An asymmetric key used to store other keys/data.

- EK: An endorsement key that has a certificate used to prove that it (and, in the process, prove that other keys) belongs to a genuine TPM.

- ASYM_RESTRICTED_SIGNING_KEY: A key like the AIK of 1.2, but that can also sign any external data that doesn't claim to come from the TPM.

- HMAC_KEY: An unrestricted symmetric key. Its main use is as an HMAC key that can be used to sign (HMAC) data that isn't a hash produced by the TPM.

NV:

- NV_MEMORY: Normal NV memory.

- NV_BITFIELD: a 64-bit bitfield.

- NV_COUNTER: A 64-bit counter.

- NV_PCR: A NV_PCR that uses the template hash algorithm.

- NV_TEMP_READ_DISABLE: Can have its readability turned off for a boot cycle.

Standard polies and authentications:

- TSS2_POLICY_NULL: A NULL policy (empty buffer) that can never be satisfied.

- TSS2_AUTH_NULL: A zero-length password, trivially satisfied.

- TSS2_POLICY_AUTHVALUE: Points to the object's authorization data.

- TSS2_POLICY_SECRET_EH: Points to the endorsement hierarchy's authorization data.

- TSS2_POLICY_SECRET_SH: Points to the storage hierarchy's authorization data.

- **TSS2_POLICY_SECRET_PH**: Points to the platform hierarchy's authorization data.

- **TSS2_POLICY_SECRET_DA**: Points to the dictionary attack handle's authorization data.

- **TSS2_POLICY_TRIVIAL**: Points to a policy of all zeroes. This is easy to satisfy because every policy session starts with its policy buffer equal to this policy. This can be used to create an entity that can be trivially satisfied with the FAPI.

All objects created and used by FAPI commands are authorized by a policy. This doesn't mean the authorization value can't be used: it can be used if the policy is TSS2_POLICY_AUTHVALUE. However, under the covers, a password session is never used. And if an authorization value is used, it's always done with a salted HMAC session.

One structure used constantly in the FAPI is TSS2_SIZED_BUFFER. This structure consists of two things: a size and a pointer to a buffer. The size represents the size of the buffer:

```
typedef struct { size_t    size;
               uint8_t   *buffer;
               } TSS2_SIZED_BUFFER;
```

You need to know one more thing before writing a program: at the beginning of your program, you must create a context, which you must destroy when you're done with it.

Let's write an example program that creates a key, uses it to sign "Hello World," and verifies the signature. Follow these steps:

1. Create a context. Tell it to use the local TPM by setting the second parameter to NULL:

   ```
   TSS2_CONTEXT *context;
   Tss2_Context_Intialize(&context, NULL);
   ```

2. Create a signing key using the user's default configuration. Here you explicitly tell it to use the P_RSA2048SHA1 profile instead of the default. By using the UNK, you tell it that it's a user key that is non-duplicable. Name it mySigningKey.

   Using ASYM_RESTRICTED_SIGNING_KEY makes the key a signing key. You also give it a trivially satisfied policy and a password of NULL:

   ```
   Tss2_Key_Create(context, // pass in the context I just created
           "P_RSA2048SHA1/UNK/mySigningKey",  // non-duplicable
   RSA2048
           ASYM_RESTRICTED_SIGNING_KEY,       // signing key
           TSS2_POLICY_TRIVIAL,               // trivially policy
           TSS2_AUTH_NULL);                   // the password is NULL
   ```

3. Use the key to sign "Hello world." First you have to hash "Hello World" with an OpenSSL library call:

```
TSS2_SIZED_BUFFER myHash;
myHash.size=20
myHash.buffer=calloc(20,1);
SHA1("Hello World",sizeof("Hello World"),myHash.buffer);
```

4. The Sign command returns everything necessary to verify the signature. Because you just created this key, the certificate comes back with a certificate that is empty:

```
TSS2_SIZED_BUFFER signature, publicKey,certificate;

Tss2_Key_Sign(context,     // pass in the context
        "P_RSA2048SHA1/UNK/mySigningKey", // the signing key
        &myHash,
        &signature,
        &publicKey,
        &certificate);
```

5. At this point you could save the outputs, but instead let's check them:

```
if (TSS_SUCCESS!=Tss2_Key_Verify(context ,&signature,
    &publicKey,&myHash) )
{
    printf("The command failed signature verification\n");
}
else printf("The command succeeded\n");
```

6. Destroy the buffers that have been allocated, now that you're done with them:

```
free(myHash.buffer);
free(signature.buffer);
free(publicKey.buffer);
/* I don't have to free the certificate buffer, because
it was empty */
Tss2_Context_Finalize(context);
```

It's easy to see that this example cheats a little. In particular, the key doesn't require any type of authorization. Next you will learn what to do if authentication is required.

All FAPI functions assume that keys are authenticated only through policy. If a key is to be authenticated with a password, then the password is assigned to the key, and a policy is created using TPM2_PolicyAuthValue. The predefined TSS2_POLICY_AUTHVALUE does this. However, this leaves you with the bigger question of how to satisfy the policy.

Policy commands come in two flavors. Some policy commands require interaction with the outside world:

- `PolicyPassword`: Asks for a password

- `PolicyAuthValue`: Asks for a password

- `PolicySecret`: Asks for a password

- `PolicyNV`: Asks for a password

- `PolicyOR`: Asks for a selection among choices

- `PolicyAuthorize`: Asks for a selection among authorized choices

- `PolicySigned`: Asks for a signature from a specific device

Other policy commands don't require outside interaction:

- `PolicyPCR`: Checks the values of the TPM's PCRs

- `PolicyLocality`: Checks the locality of the command

- `PolicyCounterTimer`: Checks the counter internal to the TPM

- `PolicyCommandCode`: Checks what command was sent to the TPM

- `PolicyCpHash`: Checks the command and parameters sent to the TPM

- `PolicyNameHash`: Checks the name of the object sent to the TPM

- `PolicyDuplicationSelect`: Checks the target of duplication of a key

- `PolicyNVWritten`: Checks if an NV index has ever been written

Many policies require a mix of the two. If a policy requires one of the authorizations of the second type, it's the responsibility of the FAPI to handle it. If it's an authorization of the first type, then you're responsible for providing to the FAPI the parameters it doesn't have access to.

This is done via a callback mechanism. You must register these callbacks in your program so that FAPI knows what do to if it requires a password, selection, or signature. The three callbacks are defined as follows:

- `TSS2_PolicyAuthCallback`: Used when a password is required

- `TSS2_PolicyBranchSelectionCallback`: Used when the user needs to select from among more than one policy in a `TPolicyOR` or `TPM2_PolicyAuthorize`

- `TSS2_PolicySignatureCallback`: Used when a signature is required to satisfy the policy

The first is easiest. After a context is registered, you have to create a callback function that is used when the FAPI is asked to execute a function that requires interaction with the user asking for a password. In this case, the FAPI sends back to the program the description of the object that needs to be authorized and requests the authorization data. The FAPI takes care of salting and HMACing this authorization data. The user must do two things: create the function that asks the user for their password, and register this function so that the FAPI can call it.

Here is a simple password-handler function:

```
myPasswordHandler (TSS2_CONTEXT        context,
                   void               *userData,
                   char const         *description,
                   TSS2_SIZED_BUFFER  *auth)
{
/* Here the program asks for the password in some application specific
way. It then puts the result into the auth variable. */
return;
}
```

Here is how you register it with the FAPI so it knows to call the function:

```
Tss2_SetPolicyAuthCallback(context, TSS2_PolicyAuthCallback, NULL);
```

Creating and registering the other callbacks is very similar.

At the time of writing this book, the specification for using XML to write a policy for a command has not yet been written, although it's likely to come out in 2014. However, one thing is known: it will be possible for hardware OEMs (for example, a smartcard provider) to provide a library that contains these callback functions. In this case, the callback function will be registered in the policy rather than in the program, so you won't need to provide it. Similarly, software libraries can be used to provide these callback functions in policies. If this is done, you won't have to register any callbacks.

System API

As mentioned earlier, the SAPI layer is the TPM 2.0 equivalent of programming in the C language. SAPI provides access to all the capabilities of TPM 2.0; as is often said in this business when describing low-level interfaces, we give application writers all the rope they need to hang themselves. It's a powerful and sharp tool, and expertise is required to use it properly.

The SAPI specification can be found at www.trustedcomputinggroup.org/developers/software_stack. The design goals of the SAPI specification were the following:

- Provide access to all TPM functionality.

- Be usable across the breadth of possible platforms, from highly embedded, memory-constrained environments to multiprocessor servers. To support small applications, much consideration was given to minimizing, or at least allowing minimization, of the memory footprint of the SAPI library code.

- Within the constraint of providing access to all functionality, make programmers' jobs as easy as possible.

- Support both synchronous and asynchronous calls to the TPM.

- SAPI implementations aren't required to allocate any memory. In most implementations, the caller is responsible to allocate all memory used by the SAPI.

There are four groups of SAPI commands: command context allocation, command preparation, command execution, and command completion. Each of these groups is described in this section. Within the command preparation, execution, and completion groups, there are some utility functions that are used regardless of which TPM 2.0 command in Part 3 of the TPM specification is being called; others are specific to each Part 3 command.

First we will describe each of the four groups of commands at a high level. As these commands are described, we will show code fragments for a very simple code example, a TPM2_GetTestResult command. At the end, we will combine these fragments into a single program to do a TPM2_GetTestResult command using three different methods: one call, asynchronous, and synchronous multi-call. Code examples for SAPI functions that require knowledge of sessions and authorizations and encryption and decryption are deferred until Chapters 13 and 17; the SAPI functions that support these features will only make sense after you understand the features. This chapter ends with a brief description of the test code that is distributed with the System API code.[3]

Command Context Allocation Functions

These functions are used to allocate a SAPI command context data structure, an opaque structure that is used by the implementation to maintain any state data required to execute the TPM 2.0 command.

The Tss2_Sys_GetContextSize function is used to determine how much memory is needed for the SAPI context data structure. The command can return the amount of memory required to support any TPM 2.0 Part 3 command, or the caller can provide a maximum command or response size and the function calculates the context size required to support that.

Tss2_Sys_Initialize is used to initialize a SAPI context. It takes as inputs a pointer to a memory block of sufficient size for the context, the context size returned by Tss2_Sys_GetContextSize, a pointer to a TCTI context (described in the later "TCTI" section) used to define the methods for transmitting commands and receiving responses, and the calling application's required SAPI version information.

---

[3]The code in this SAPI section is working code that is included in the SAPI and test code package. This package is currently shared among TCG members via a GitHub site. TCG members can contact TSS Workgroup members to gain access to it. It is expected that this code will be open sourced before or shortly after this book is published.

■ **Note** One note about the following code: `rval` is shorthand for *return value* and is a 32-bit unsigned integer. This is used repeatedly in upcoming code examples.

Here's a code example for a function that creates and initializes a system context structure.

■ **Note** The function that follows is declared to return a pointer to a `TSS2_SYS_CONTEXT` structure. This structure is defined as follows:

`typedef struct _TSS2_SYS_OPAQUE_CONTEXT_BLOB TSS2_SYS_CONTEXT;`

But the opaque structure is never defined anywhere. This works because `TSS2_SYS_CONTEXT` structures are always referenced by a pointer. Basically, this is a compiler trick that provides an advantage over using `void` pointers: it performs some compile time type checking.

```
//
// Allocates space for and initializes system
// context structure.
//
// Returns:
//    ptr to system context, if successful
//    NULL pointer, if not successful.
//
TSS2_SYS_CONTEXT *InitSysContext(
    UINT16 maxCommandSize,
    TSS2_TCTI_CONTEXT *tctiContext,
    TSS2_ABI_VERSION *abiVersion
)
    UINT32 contextSize;
    TSS2_RC rval;
    TSS2_SYS_CONTEXT *sysContext;

    // Get the size needed for system context structure.
    contextSize = Tss2_Sys_GetContextSize( maxCommandSize );

    // Allocate the space for the system context structure.
    sysContext = malloc( contextSize );
    if( sysContext != 0 )
    {
        // Initialize the system context structure.
        rval = Tss2_Sys_Initialize( sysContext,
                contextSize, tctiContext, abiVersion );
```

```
        if( rval == TSS2_RC_SUCCESS )
            return sysContext;
        else
            return 0;
    }
    else
    {
        return 0;
    }
}
```

The last function in this group is Tss2_Sys_Finalize, which is a placeholder for any functionality that may be required to retire a SAPI context data structure before its allocated memory is freed. Here's an example of how this might be used:

```
void TeardownSysContext( TSS2_SYS_CONTEXT *sysContext )
{
    if( sysContext != 0 )
    {
        Tss2_Sys_Finalize(sysContext);

        free(sysContext);
    }
}
```

■ **Note** In this case, Tss2_Sys_Finalize is a dummy function that does nothing, because the SAPI library code doesn't need it to do anything. Note that the system context memory is freed after the Finalize call.

Command Preparation Functions

As explained in Chapters 13 and 17, HMAC calculation, command parameter encryption, and response parameter decryption often require pre- and post-command processing. The command preparation functions provide the pre-command execution functions that are needed before actually sending the command to the TPM.

In order to calculate the command HMAC and encrypt command parameters, the command parameters must be marshalled. This could be done with special application code, but because the SAPI already contains this functionality, the API designers decided to make this functionality available to the application. This is the purpose of the Tss2_Sys_XXXX_Prepare functions. Because the command parameters are unique for each Part 3 command, there is one of these functions for each TPM command that needs it. The "XXXX" is replaced by the command name; for instance, the Tss2_Sys_XXXX_Prepare function for TPM2_StartAuthSession is Tss2_Sys_StartAuthSession_Prepare. Following is a call to the prepare code for TPM2_GetTestResult:

rval = Tss2_Sys_GetTestResult_Prepare(sysContext);

■ **Note**   The only parameter to this function is a pointer to the system context, because TPM2_GetTestResult has no input parameters.

After the Tss2_Sys_XXXX_Prepare call, the data has been marshalled. To get the marshalled command parameter byte stream, the Tss2_Sys_GetCpParam function is called. This returns the start of the cpBuffer, the marshalled command parameter byte stream, and the length of the cpBuffer. How this is used is described further in Chapters 13 and 17.

Another function that is needed to calculate the command HMAC is Tss2_Sys_GetCommandCode. This function returns the command code bytes in CPU endian order. This function is also used in command post-processing.

The Tss2_Sys_GetDecryptParam and Tss2_Sys_SetDecryptParam functions are used for decrypt sessions, which you learn about in Chapter 17. For now, the Tss2_Sys_GetDecryptParam function returns a pointer to the start of the parameter to be encrypted and the size of the parameter. These two returned values are used by the application when it calls Tss2_Sys_SetDecryptParam to set the encrypted value into the command byte stream.

The Tss2_Sys_SetCmdAuths function is used to set the command authorization areas (also called *sessions*) in the command byte stream. This is explained in detail in Chapter 13, when sessions and authorizations are discussed.

Command Execution Functions

This group of functions actually sends commands to and, receives responses from the TPM. The commands can be sent synchronously or asynchronously. There are two ways to send commands synchronously: via a sequence of three to five function calls; and via a single "does everything" call, the *one-call*. Support for asynchronous vs. asynchronous and one-call vs. a finer-grained multi-call approach arose from the desire to support as many application architectures as possible.

Tss2_Sys_ExecuteAsync is the most basic method of sending a command. It sends the command using the TCTI transmit function and returns as quickly as possible. Here's an example of a call to this function:

rval = Tss2_Sys_ExecuteAsync(sysContext);

Tss2_Sys_ExecuteFinish is the companion function to ExecuteAsync. It calls the TCTI function to receive the response. It takes a command parameter, timeout, that tells it how long to wait for a response. Here's an example that waits 20 msec for a response from the TPM:

rval = Tss2_Sys_ExecuteFinish(sysContext, 20);

Tss2_Sys_Execute is the synchronous method and is the equivalent of calling Tss2_Sys_ExecuteAsync followed by Tss2_Sys_ExecuteFinish with an infinite timeout. Here's an example:

rval = Tss2_Sys_Execute(sysContext);

The last function in the execution group, Tss2_Sys_XXXX, is the *one-call* or "do everything" function. This function assumes that authorizations aren't needed, a simple password authorization is being used, or that authorizations such as HMAC and policy have already been calculated. There is one of these commands for each Part 3 command.[4] As an example, the one-call function for the Tpm2_StartAuthSession command is Tss2_Sys_StartAuthSession. When used with the associated Tss2_Sys_XXXX_Prepare call, the one-call interface can do any type of authorization. An interesting side effect of this is that the command parameters are marshalled twice: once during the Tss2_Sys_XXXX_Prepare call and once during the one-call function call. This was a design compromise because the one-call needed to be capable of being used as a standalone call and paired with the Tss2_Sys_XXXX_Prepare call. Here's an example of the one-call with no command or response authorizations:

rval = Tss2_Sys_GetTestResult(sysContext, 0, &outData, &testResult, 0);

■ **Note**   The function takes a pointer to a system context structure; a pointer to a command authorization's array structure; two output parameters, outData and testResult; and a pointer to a response authorization structure. The parameters that are 0 are the command and response authorization array structures. For this very simple example, these aren't necessary, so NULL pointers are used. Use of these is explained in Chapter 13.

Command Completion Functions

This group of functions enables the command post-processing that is required. This includes response HMAC calculation and response parameter decryption if the session was configured as an encrypt session.

---

[4]Part 3 does describe some hardware-triggered commands. These start with an underscore character and aren't included in the SAPI.

`Tss2_Sys_GetRpBuffer` gets a pointer to and the size of the response parameter byte stream. Knowing these two values enables the caller to calculate the response HMAC and compare it to the HMAC in the response authorization areas.

`Tss2_Sys_GetRspAuths` gets the response authorization areas. These are used to check the response HMACs in order to validate that the response data hasn't been tampered with.

After validating the response data, if the response was sent using an encrypt session, `Tss2_Sys_GetEncryptParam` and `Tss2_Sys_SetEncryptParam` can be used to decrypt the encrypted response parameter and insert the decrypted response parameter into the byte stream prior to unmarshalling the response parameters. These two functions are described in greater detail in Chapter 17 in the discussion of decrypt and encrypt sessions.

After the response parameter has been decrypted, the response byte stream can be unmarshalled. This is done by a call to `Tss2_Sys_XXXX_Complete`. Because each command has different response parameters, there is one of these per Part 3 command.[5] An example of this call is as follows:

```
rval = Tss2_Sys_GetTestResult_Complete( sysContext, &outData, &testResult );
```

You've now seen all the SAPI calls. Some of these are specific to Part 3 commands, and some apply regardless of which Part 3 command is being executed.

Simple Code Example

The next code example, from the SAPI library test code, performs a `TPM2_GetTestResult` command three different ways: one-call, synchronous calls, and asynchronous calls. Comments help delineate the tests of the three different ways:

■ **Note** `CheckPassed()` is a routine that compares the passed-in return value to 0. If they aren't equal, an error has occurred, and the routine prints an error message, cleans up, and exits the test program.

```
void TestGetTestResult()
{
        UINT32 rval;
        TPM2B_MAX_BUFFER      outData;
        TPM_RC                testResult;
        TSS2_SYS_CONTEXT      *systemContext;

        printf( "\nGET TEST RESULT TESTS:\n" );
```

---

[5]Commands that have no response parameters don't have a corresponding `Complete` call.

```
        // Initialize the system context structure.
        systemContext = InitSysContext( 2000, resMgrTctiContext, &abiVersion );
        if( systemContext == 0 )
        {
                Handle failure, cleanup, and exit.
                InitSysContextFailure();
        }
```

Test the one-call API.

```
        //
        // First test the one-call interface.
        //
        rval = Tss2_Sys_GetTestResult( systemContext, 0, &outData, &testResult,
                0 );
        CheckPassed(rval);
```

Test the synchronous, multi-call APIs.

```
        //
        // Now test the synchronous, non-one-call APIs.
        //
        rval = Tss2_Sys_GetTestResult_Prepare( systemContext );
        CheckPassed(rval);
        // Execute the command synchronously.
        rval = Tss2_Sys_Execute( systemContext );
        CheckPassed(rval);

        // Get the command results
        rval = Tss2_Sys_GetTestResult_Complete( systemContext, &outData,
                &testResult );
        CheckPassed(rval);
```

Test the asynchronous, multi-call APIs.

```
        //
        // Now test the asynchronous, non-one-call interface.
        //
        rval = Tss2_Sys_GetTestResult_Prepare( systemContext );
        CheckPassed(rval);
```

```
        // Execute the command asynchronously.
        rval = Tss2_Sys_ExecuteAsync( systemContext );
        CheckPassed(rval);

        // Get the command response. Wait a maximum of 20ms
        // for response.
        rval = Tss2_Sys_ExecuteFinish( systemContext, 20 );
        CheckPassed(rval);

        // Get the command results
        rval = Tss2_Sys_GetTestResult_Complete( systemContext, &outData,
        &testResult );
        CheckPassed(rval);

        // Tear down the system context.
        TeardownSysContext( systemContext );
}
```

System API Test Code

As mentioned, the previous GetTestResult test is included as one of the tests in the SAPI test code. This section briefly describes the structure of the test code and some design features.

Many other tests in this code test various SAPI capabilities. But you should beware that this test suite is by no means comprehensive; there are too many permutations and not enough time for a single developer to write all the tests. These tests were written to provide sanity checks and, in some cases, more detailed tests of targeted functionality.

The test code resides in the Test\tpmclient subdirectory. In this directory, the tpmclient.cpp file contains the test application's initialization and control code as well as all the main test routines. Subdirectories of tpmclient provide support code needed for the tests. The simDriver subdirectory contains a device driver for communicating with the TPM simulator. The resourceMgr subdirectory contains code for a sample RM. And the sample subdirectory contains application-level code that performs the following tasks: maintaining session state information, calculating HMACs, and performing cryptographic functions.

A major design principle of the SAPI test code was to use the TPM itself for all cryptographic functions. No outside libraries such as OpenSSL are used. The reason for this was twofold. First, it increased the test coverage of the SAPI test code by calling TPM cryptographic commands. Second, it allowed the test application to be a stand-alone application with no dependency on outside libraries. And there was a third reason: the developer thought it was kind of a cool thing to do! The SAPI test code can be used as a starting point for developers: find a command you want to use that's called in the test code, and it will give you a significant boost in your code development.

The SAPI test code uses other elements of the TSS stack to perform its tests: the TCTI, TAB, and RM. Because SAPI uses the TCTI to send commands to the TAB, TCTI is described next.

TCTI

You've seen the system API functions, but the question that hasn't been answered yet is how command byte streams are transmitted to the TPM and how the application receives response byte streams from the TPM. The answer is the TPM Command Transmission Interface (TCTI). You saw this briefly in the description of the Tss2_Sys_Initialize call. This call takes a TCTI context structure as one of its inputs. Now we will describe this layer of the stack in detail.

The TCTI context structure tells the SAPI functions how to communicate with the TPM. This structure contains function pointers for the two most important TCTI functions, transmit and receive, as well as less frequently used functions such as cancel, setLocality, and some others described shortly. If an application needs to talk to more than one TPM, it creates multiple TCTI contexts and sets each with the proper function pointers for communicating with each TPM.

The TCTI context structure is a per-process, per-TPM structure that is set up by initialization code. It can be set up at compile time or dynamically when the OS is booted. Some process has to either discover the presence of TPMs (typically a local TPM) or have a priori knowledge of remote TPMs and initialize a TCTI context structure with the proper function pointers for communication. This initialization and discovery process is out of scope of the SAPI and TCTI specification.

The most frequently used and required function pointers, transmit and receive, do what you'd expect them to. Both of them get a pointer to a buffer and a size parameter. The SAPI functions call them when they're ready to send and receive data, and the functions do the right thing.

The cancel function pointer supports a new capability in TPM 2.0: the ability to cancel a TPM command after it's been transmitted to the TPM. This allows a long-running TPM command to be cancelled. For example, key generation can take up to 90 seconds on some TPMs. If a sleep operation is initiated by the OS, this command allows early cancellation of long-running commands so that the system can be quiesced.[6]

The getPollHandles function pointer comes into play when SAPI is using the asynchronous method of sending and receiving responses—that is, the Tss2_Sys_ExecuteAsync and Tss2_Sys_ExecuteFinish functions. This is an OS-specific function that returns the handles that can be used to poll for response-ready conditions.

The last function pointer, finalize, is used to clean up before a TCTI connection is terminated. Actions that are required upon connection termination, if any, are performed by this function.

TCTI can be used at any level in the TPM stack where marshalled byte streams are being transmitted and received. Currently, the thinking is that this occurs at two places: between the SAPI and the TAB, and between the RM and the driver.

---

[6]The cancel capability is specified in the TCG PC Client Platform TPM Profile (PTP) Specification. TPMs that support other platforms may not include the cancel command.

TPM Access Broker (TAB)

The TAB is used to control and synchronize multiprocess access to a single shared TPM. When one process is in the middle of sending a command and receiving a response, no other process is allowed to send commands to or request responses from the TPM. This is the first responsibility of the TAB. Another feature of the TAB is that it prevents processes from accessing TPM sessions, objects, and sequences (hash or event sequences) that they don't own. Ownership is determined by which TCTI connection was used to load the objects, start the sessions, or start the sequences.

The TAB is integrated with the RM into a single module in most implementations. This makes sense because a typical TAB implementation can consist of some simple modifications to the RM.

Resource Manager

The RM acts in a manner similar to the virtual memory manager in an OS. Because TPMs generally have very limited on-board memory, objects, sessions, and sequences need to be swapped from the TPM to and from memory to allow TPM commands to execute. A TPM command can use at most three entity handles and three session handles. All of these need to be in TPM memory for the TPM to execute the command. The job of the RM is to intercept the command byte stream, determine what resources need to be loaded into the TPM, swap out enough room to be able to load the required resources, and load the resources needed. In the case of objects and sequences, because they can have different handles after being reloaded into the TPM, the RM needs to virtualize the handles before returning them to the caller.[7] This is covered in more detail in Chapter 18; for now, this ends the brief introduction to this component.

The RM and TAB are usually combined into one component, the TAB/RM, and as a rule there is one of these per TPM; that's an implementation design decision, but this is typically the way it's done. If, on the other hand, a single TAB/RM is used to provide access to all the TPMs present, then the TAB/RM needs a way to keep track of which handles belong to which TPMs and keep them separated; the means of doing this is outside the scope of the TSS specifications. So, whether the boundary is enforced by different executable code or different tables in the same code module, clear differentiation must be maintained in this layer between entities that belong to different TPMs.

Both the TAB and RM operate in a way that is mostly transparent to the upper layers of the stack, and both layers are optional. Upper layers operate the same with respect to sending and receiving commands and responses, whether they're talking directly to a TPM or through a TAB/RM layer. However, if no TAB/RM is implemented, upper layers of the stack must perform the TAB/RM responsibilities before sending TPM commands, so that those commands can execute properly. Generally, an application executing in a multithreaded or multiprocessing environment implements a TAB/RM to isolate application writers from these low-level details. Single-threaded and highly embedded applications usually don't require the overhead of a TAB/RM layer.

---

[7]For this reason, handles aren't included in authorization calculations. Otherwise, authorizations would fail because the application only sees virtual handles. Names are used instead, and these names aren't affected by virtualization of the handles.

Device Driver

After the FAPI, ESAPI, SAPI, TCTI, TAB, and RM have done their jobs, the last link, the device driver, steps up to the plate. The device driver receives a buffer of command bytes and a buffer length and performs the operations necessary to send those bytes to the TPM. When requested by higher layers in the stack, the driver waits until the TPM is ready with response data and reads that response data and returns it up the stack.

The physical and logical interfaces the driver uses to communicate with the TPM are out of scope of the TPM 2.0 library specification and are defined in the platform-specific specifications. At this time, the choice for TPMs on PCs is either the FIFO[8] or Command Response Buffer (CRB) interface. FIFO is first-in, first-out byte-transmission interface that uses a single hardcoded address for data transmission and reception plus some other addresses for handshaking and status operations. The FIFO interface remained mostly the same for TPM 2.0, with a few small changes. FIFO can operate over serial peripheral interface (SPI) or low pin count (LPC) interface busses.

The CRB interface is new for TPM 2.0. It was designed for TPM implementations that use shared memory buffers to communicate commands and responses.

Summary

This completes the discussion of the TSS layers, which provide a standard API stack for "driving" the TPM. You can intercept this stack at different levels depending on your requirements. These layers, especially FAPI and SAPI, are used in the following chapters, so please refer to this this chapter while studying the code examples.

---

[8]The FIFO interface is mostly identical to the interface used by the TPM Interface Specification (TIS) for TPM 1.2 devices. The TIS specification included much more than the interface, such as the number of PCRs, a minimum set of commands, and so on, so the use of "TIS" has been deprecated for TPM 2.0.

CHAPTER 8

■ ■ ■

TPM Entities

A TPM 2.0 *entity* is an item in the TPM that can be directly referenced with a handle.
The term encompasses more than objects because the specification uses the word *object*
to identify a very specific subset of entities. This can be confusing, so this chapter briefly
describes all of the entity types: permanent entities (hierarchies, the dictionary attack
lockout mechanism, and PCRs); nonvolatile entities (NVRAM indexes), which are similar to
permanent entities; objects (keys and data); and volatile entities (sessions of various types).

   After this introduction, the following chapters discuss each entity and its uses in
more detail. In particular, the next chapter delves into hierarchies, a collection of entities
that are related and managed as a group.

Permanent Entities

A *permanent entity* is one whose handle is defined by the TPM specification and can't be
created or deleted. In TPM 1.2, PCRs and the owner were the only permanent entities; the
storage root key (SRK) did have a fixed handle but wasn't a permanent entity. In TPM 2.0,
there are more: three persistent hierarchies, the ephemeral hierarchy, the dictionary attack
lockout reset, PCRs, reserved handles, the plaintext password authorization session, and
the platform hierarchy NV enable. The following sections discuss each in turn.

Persistent Hierarchies

TPM 2.0 has three persistent hierarchies (platform, storage, and endorsement), each
referenced by a permanent handle: TPM_RH_PLATFORM (0x4000000C), TPM_RH_OWNER
(0x40000001), and TPM_RH_ENDORSEMENT (x4000000B). Permission to use these hierarchies
is granted through authorizations, so each has both an authorization value and a
policy. Either can be changed at the will of the hierarchy's administrator (defined as
anyone who can authorize such a change). The authorization value or policy value may
change, but whenever we refer to, for example, the platform authorization, we mean
the same entity. Persistent hierarchies can never be deleted, but they may be disabled
by the administrator of the platform or the administrator of the hierarchy. These three
hierarchies may have associated chains of keys and data, which can be wiped by clearing
the hierarchy.

The next chapter describes the hierarchies in detail, including each hierarchy's management and use cases. At this point, it's sufficient to understand that the persistent hierarchies are permanent entities. They can't be created or deleted.

Other permanent entities similar to the hierarchies listed here are the ephemeral hierarchy and the dictionary attack lockout reset mechanism.

Ephemeral Hierarchy

TPM 2.0 has an ephemeral hierarchy called the NULL hierarchy, which is also referenced by a permanent handle: TPM_RH_NULL (0x40000007). This hierarchy is utilized when the TPM is being used as a cryptographic coprocessor, as described in Chapter 9. Its authorization value and policy are both always NULL.

Similar to the persistent hierarchies, the ephemeral hierarchy is permanent. It can't be deleted. However, unlike the persistent hierarchies, it's automatically cleared every time the TPM goes through a power cycle. See Chapter 9 for details.

Dictionary Attack Lockout Reset

Similar to the hierarchies is the dictionary attack lockout mechanism, which has the handle TPM_RH_LOCKOUT (0x4000000A). It also has both an authorization and a policy. Like the three persistent hierarchies, these authorizations can be changed at the will of the administrator of this hierarchy. It has no key or object hierarchy. Instead, this mechanism is used to reset the dictionary attack lockout mechanism if it has triggered, or to clear the TPM_RH_OWNER hierarchy. It generally represents the IT administrator of the TPM storage hierarchy.

EXAMPLE: FAILURE COUNT RESET

A TPM is configured to lock out a user for 24 hours after 5 password entry failures. *Lock out* means the user can't successfully authorize any entity that is subject to this dictionary attack protection. The user convinces an IT administrator this this wasn't an attack but rather was just a mistake. The administrator, using lockout authorization, resets the failure count so the user doesn't have to wait for the 24-hour lockout period to expire.

Platform Configuration Registers (PCRs)

The TPM has a number of PCRs, which are accessed using their index. Depending on the platform-specific specification, they can have one or more algorithms. They also have an authentication value and a policy, chosen by the specification (generally NULL), which may be used to change the value stored in the PCR via a PCR extend. Reading the value stored in a PCR doesn't require authentication. The PC Client platform specifies a minimum of 24 PCRs. Only one *bank* (a set of PCRs with the same hash algorithm) is mandatory, programmable to either SHA-1 or SHA-256 at boot time.

Because it's a permanent entity, there is no command to create or delete a PCR; you can only change its attributes or the PCR value. Chapter 12 discusses these permanent entities in detail.

Reserved Handles

Vendor-specific reserved handles may be present in a TPM if a platform-specific specification decides to use them. Such handles are meant to be used by a vendor in the case of a catastrophic security failure of the firmware in the TPM, allowing the TPM to testify to the hash of the software stored in the TPM. At the date of this writing, no reserved handles are specified by any platform specification.

Password Authorization Session

There is one session that is permanent as well, called a password authorization session at handle TPM_RS_PW (0x40000009). A caller uses this handle for plaintext password (as opposed to HMAC) authorization.

Platform NV Enable

The TPM_RH_PLATFORM_NV handle (0x4000000D) controls the platform hierarchy NV enable. When it's clear (disabled), access to any NV index in the platform hierarchy is denied.

NV indexes can belong to either the platform or the storage hierarchy. The storage hierarchy enable controls NV indexes in the storage hierarchy. However, the platform enable doesn't control platform hierarchy NV indexes. That uses is a separate control: platform NV enable. Having two controls permits independent control of the platform hierarchy (for example, keys) and these platform NV indexes.

USE CASE: STORING BOOT PARAMETERS

Platform firmware can use the TPM as a convenient NV space for boot parameters. This space must remain readable even if the TPM platform hierarchy is disabled.

Next let's examine some entities that are similar to permanent entities: nonvolatile indexes, which are nonvolatile but not architecturally defined.

Nonvolatile Indexes

An NVRAM index in a TPM is a nonvolatile entity. There is a certain amount of nonvolatile space in a TPM that a user can configure for storage. When configured, it's given an index and a set of attributes, chosen by the user.

NVRAM indexes aren't considered objects by the TPM specification, because they have more attributes than a standard object. Reading and writing them can be individually controlled. They can be configured as entities that look like PCRs, counters, or bit fields. They can be made into "write once" entities as well. Chapter 11 explains their properties and use cases.

NVRAM indexes have both an associated authorization value and an authorization policy. The authorization value can be changed at the will of the owner of the index, but the policy can't be changed once it's set at the creation of the NVRAM index. NVRAM indexes are associated with a hierarchy when they're created. Hence, when the hierarchy is cleared, the NVRAM indexes associated with that hierarchy are deleted.

Objects are similar to NVRAM in that they belong to a hierarchy and have data and authorization mechanisms, but they have fewer attributes.

Objects

A TPM object is either a key or data. It has a public part and perhaps a private part such as an asymmetric private key, a symmetric key, or encrypted data. Objects belong to a hierarchy. All objects have both associated authorization data and an authorization policy. As with NV indexes, an object's policy can't be changed after it's created.

When an object is used in a command, some commands are considered *administrative* and others are considered *user* commands. At object creation, the user decides which of these commands can be performed with the authorization data and which can exclusively be done with a policy. This comes with a caveat: certain commands can only be done with a policy no matter how the attributes are set at key creation.

Like NVRAM indexes, all objects belong to one of the four hierarchies: platform, storage, endorsement, or NULL. When a hierarchy is cleared, all objects belonging to that hierarchy are also cleared.

Typically, most objects are keys. They're described in detail in the Chapter 10. Using keys or other objects requires the use of a TPM non-persistent entity: the session.

Nonpersistent Entities

A nonpersistent entity never persists through power cycles.[1] Although a nonpersistent entity can be saved (see TPM2_ContextSave), a TPM cryptographic mechanism prevents the saved context from being loaded after a power cycle, thus enforcing volatility. This type of entity has several classes.

Authorization sessions, including HMAC and policy sessions, are perhaps the most widely used, permitting entity authorization, command and response parameter encryption, and command audit. Chapter 13 is devoted to their use.

---

[1]To be precise, it doesn't persist through what the specification refers to as a *TPM Reset* (a reboot). It does persist through a *TPM Restart* (resume from hibernate) or *TPM Resume* (resume from sleep).

Hash and HMAC event sequence entities hold the intermediate results of the typical crypto library "start, update, complete" design pattern. They permit the hashing or HMAC of data blocks that are larger than the TPM command buffer. Chapter 9 describes their application.

In contrast to a nonpersistent entity, a persistent entity persists through power cycles.

Persistent Entities

A *persistent entity* is an object that the owner of a hierarchy has asked to remain resident in the TPM through power cycles. It differs from a permanent entity (which can never be deleted) in that the owner of the hierarchy to which a permanent entity belongs can evict it. A TPM has a limited amount of persistent memory, so you should be sparing in your use of persistent entities. There are, however, some valuable use cases.

USE CASE: VPN KEY ACCESS

A signing key is needed for VPN access early in a boot cycle. At that time, the disk isn't available. The application transfers the key to TPM persistent storage, where it's immediately available for use in early boot cryptographic operations.

USE CASE: PRIMARY KEY OPTIMIZATION

A primary storage key (the equivalent to a TPM 1.2 SRK) is routinely used as the root of a key hierarchy. Key generation is often the most time-consuming cryptographic calculation. After creation, the key is moved to persistent storage to avoid the performance penalty of recalculating the key on every boot cycle.

USE CASE: IDENTITY KEY PROVISIONING

An enterprise provisions a motherboard with a restricted signing key that is fixed to the TPM. The enterprise uses this key to identify the platform. If the motherboard fails and the TPM is thus replaced, this existing key can no longer be loaded. The IT department wishes to provision spare motherboards with new signing keys. Because a motherboard has no disk, the IT department generates the key and moves it to TPM persistent storage. The signing key now travels with the motherboard when it replaces a failed one in a platform.

Usually, primary storage keys (such as an SRK), primary restricted signing keys (such as an attestation identity key [AIK]), and possibly endorsement keys (EK) are the only entities that remain persistent in a TPM. These are discussed in more detail in Chapter 10.

Entity Names

The *Name* of an entity is a TPM 2.0 concept, invented to solve a problem noticed with the TPM 1.2 specification. A paranoid security analyst (and all security analysts are paranoid) noticed that it might be possible for an attacker to intercept data as it was being sent to the TPM. The TPM design had protections against such an attack changing most data that was sent to the TPM. However, the TPM has very few resources, so it allowed a key manager to load and unload keys into the TPM as necessary. After keys were loaded, they were referred to by a handle, a shorthand for the location in memory where the key was loaded. Because the software might not realize that a key manager had been relocating keys in the TPM to free up space, the handle itself wasn't protected against manipulation, and middleware would patch the data that was sent to the TPM to point to the correct handle location.

Normally this wouldn't be a problem. But if someone decided to give the same password to more than one key, then it would be possible for one of those keys to be substituted for another by an attacker, and the attacker could then authorize the wrong key to be used in a command. You might think such an attack would be unlikely, but the people who wrote the TPM specification also tend to be paranoid and decided this was unacceptable behavior. Instead of just warning everyone not to use the same password for multiple keys, they decided to give every entity a unique Name, and that Name is used in the HMAC authorization calculation sent when executing a command that uses that entity. The handle may change, but the name doesn't.

The command parameter stream that is hashed and then HMACed implicitly includes the Name of each entity referred to by handle, even though the command parameters may not include the Name. An attacker can change the handle but can't change the corresponding Name value after it's authorized through the HMAC calculation.

The Name is the entity's unique identifier. Permanent entities (PCRs and hierarchy handles) have handles that never change, so their Name is simply their handle. Other entities (NV indexes and loaded objects) have a calculated name that is essentially a hash of the entity's public data. Both the TPM and caller independently calculate the Name value for use during authorization.

For security, it's extremely important that the Name is calculated and stored when the entity is created. A naïve implementation might offer to help by providing a "handle to Name" function that reads the TPM handle and uses the resulting public area to generate the Name. This would defeat the entire purpose of using the Name in the HMAC calculation, because the result is the Name of the entity currently at the handle, not the Name the authorizer expected.

Following are some examples of how the Name is used.

EXAMPLE: ATTACKER CLEARING A BIT-FIELD NV INDEX

A key owner uses an NV bit-field index in the key's policy, with a set bit 3 revoking the key for a key user. The revoked user / attacker deletes the NV index and re-creates it with the same policy. When the key owner wants to set bit 5, they use the handle-to-Name function to calculate the Name. The key owner uses the result for authorization, and sets bit 5. However, bit 3 is now clear because the TPM initializes bit fields to all bits clear.

If the key owner had properly stored the Name and used it for authorization, the authorization would fail. This would happen because, when the attacker re-created the index, the "written" bit in the public area attributes would go from set to clear, changing the Name on the TPM.

The Name of an NV index is a digest of its public area. An attacker can delete and redefine an index, but unless the public area (the index value, its attributes, and its policy) is the same, the Name will change and the authorization will not verify.

EXAMPLE: ATTACKER READING A SECRET

The user defines an ordinary index intended to hold a secret. The index policy is such that only the user can read the secret. Before the secret is written, an attacker deletes the index and redefines it with a different policy, such that the attacker can also read the secret. The attack fails because the policy change causes the Name to change. When the user tries to write the secret, the authorization fails because the original name was used to calculate the command parameter hash.

The Name of a transient or persistent entity is also a digest of its public area. The public area varies with the type of entity.

USE CASE: PERMITTING A RESOURCE MANAGER TO SECURELY MANAGE TPM KEYS

The user loads a key and receives back a handle for the loaded key. The user authorizes the key with an HMAC of the command parameters, which implicitly includes the Name. Unknown to the user, a resource manager had unloaded the key, and now loads it. Keep in mind, however, that the handle changes. The resource manager replaces the user's handle with the new handle value. The authorization still verifies, because the calculation didn't include the handle (which changed), only the Name (which didn't).

USE CASE: ATTACKER REPLACING A KEY AT THE SAME HANDLE

The user loads a key and receives a handle. The user authorizes that key with an HMAC. However, an attacker replaces the key on the TPM with their own key, and the attacker's key has the same handle. The attack fails because the attacker's key has a different Name, so the HMAC authorization fails.

Summary

The TPM has several types of entities: items that can be referred to by a handle. Permanent entities have a handle that is fixed by the TPM specification. The handle value can't change; nor can such an entity be created or deleted. Its data can be either persistent or volatile. Nonvolatile indexes can be created or deleted at a user-specified handle, and they persist through TPM power cycles. Objects — entities that are attached to a hierarchy — may have a private area and can be volatile or made persistent. When the object is made persistent, it's called a persistent entity.

An entity's Name is its unique identifier. It's used in authorization calculations rather than the entity's handle because the handle may change over time as a resource manager loads and flushes entities.

This chapter has summarized the entity types and provides a road map to the chapters that follow. The details come next, with chapters on hierarchies (permanent entities), keys (objects), NV indexes (persistent entities), PCRs (permanent entities), and sessions (nonpersistent entities).

CHAPTER 9

■ ■ ■

Hierarchies

A *hierarchy* is a collection of entities that are related and managed as a group. Those entities include permanent objects (the hierarchy handles), primary objects at the root of a tree, and other objects such as keys in the tree. NV indexes belong to a hierarchy but aren't in a tree. Entities, other than permanent entities, can be erased as a group.

The cryptographic root of each hierarchy is a *seed*: a large random number that the TPM generates and never exposes outside its secure boundary. The TPM uses the seed to create primary objects such as storage root keys. Those keys form the parent at the top of a hierarchy and are used to encrypt its children. Chapter 15 goes into far more detail about keys.

Each hierarchy also has an associated *proof value*. The proof can be independently generated or derived from the hierarchy seed. The TPM uses the proof value to ensure that a value supplied to the TPM was originally generated by that TPM. Often, the TPM derives an HMAC key from the proof, and HMACs data that the TPM itself generates internally. When the data is later supplied back to the TPM, the HMAC is checked to verify the authenticity of the data.

A hierarchy can be persistent (retained through a reboot) or volatile (erased at reboot). Each hierarchy is targeted at specific use cases: for the platform manufacturer, for the user, for privacy-sensitive applications, and for ephemeral requirements.

Three Persistent Hierarchies

TPM 1.2 has one hierarchy, represented by the owner authorization and storage root key (SRK). There can be only one SRK, always a storage key, which is the lone parent at the base of this single hierarchy. The SRK is generated randomly and can't be reproduced once it's erased. It can't be swapped out of the TPM. Child keys can't be created and wrapped with (encrypted by) the SRK, and these child keys may in turn be storage keys with children of their own. However, the key hierarchy is under the control of the one owner authorization; so, ultimately, TPM 1.2 has only one administrator.

TPM 2.0, on the other hand, expands to three persistent hierarchies (platform, storage, and endorsement) to permit several use cases:

- Using the TPM as a cryptographic coprocessor
- Enabling or disabling parts of the TPM
- Separating privacy-sensitive and -nonsensitive applications

The three hierarchies have some common traits:

- Each has an authorization value and a policy.

- Each has an enable flag.

- Each has a seed from which keys and data objects can be derived. The seed is persistent.

- Each can have primary keys from which descendants can be created.

The primary keys are somewhat analogous to the TPM 1.2 SRK. You could create a single RSA 2048-bit with a SHA-1 primary storage key, which would then be equivalent to the SRK.

However, TPM 2.0 adds more flexibility. First, primary keys aren't limited to storage keys. They can also be asymmetric or symmetric signing keys. Second, there can be more than one (indeed, an unlimited number of) primary keys. This is useful because you might want keys of different types (storage, signing) and of different algorithms (RSA, ECC, SHA-1, SHA-256). Third, because there can be a large number of primary keys, it's impractical to store them all in TPM NV memory. Therefore, unlike the TPM 1.2 SRK, the primary keys are derived from the secret seeds. The process is repeatable: the same seed value and key properties always result in the same key value. Rather than store them all, you can regenerate the keys as needed. Essentially, the seeds are the actual cryptographic roots. A primary key can be swapped out of the TPM, context-saved, and loaded for the duration of a power cycle, to eliminate the time required to regenerate the keys.

Because the hierarchies have independent authorization controls (password and policy), they can naturally have separate administrators. The TCG chose the three hierarchies and their slightly different operations to accommodate different use cases, which are somewhat reflected in their names. They're next described in detail, along with the intended use cases.

Platform Hierarchy

The platform hierarchy is intended to be under the control of the platform manufacturer, represented by the early boot code shipped with the platform.[1] The platform hierarchy is new for TPM 2.0. In TPM 1.2, the platform firmware could not be assured that the TPM was enabled. Thus, platform firmware developers could not include tasks that relied on the TPM.

---

[1]In an x86 PC platform, this early boot code was called BIOS. More recently, it's called UEFI firmware.

USE CASE: UEFI

The platform firmware must verify an RSA digital signature to authenticate software as part of the Unified Extensible Firmware Interface (UEFI) secure boot process. The platform OEM stores a public key, or a digest of a list of trusted public keys, in a TPM NV index. The controls on the index permit only the platform OEM to update it. During boot, the platform firmware uses this trusted public key to verify a signature.

The TPM provides two benefits. First, it provides a secure location to store the public key. Second, it offers the RSA algorithm, so it need not be implemented in software. Here are the steps:

1. TPM_NV_Read

2. TPM2_LoadExternal

3. TPM2_VerifySignature

Unique among the hierarchies, at reboot, the platform hierarchy is enabled, the platform authorization value is set to a zero-length password, and the policy is set to one that can't be satisfied. The intent is that the platform firmware will generate a strong platform authorization value (and optionally install its policy). Unlike the other hierarchies, which may have a human enter an authorization value, the platform authorization is entered by the platform firmware. Therefore, there is no reason to have the authorization persist (and to find a secure place to store it) rather than regenerate it each time.

Because the platform hierarchy has its own enable flag, the platform firmware decides when to enable or disable the hierarchy. The intent is that it should always be enabled and available for use by the platform firmware and the operating system.

Storage Hierarchy

The storage hierarchy is intended to be used by the platform owner: either the enterprise IT department or the end user. The storage hierarchy is equivalent to the TPM 1.2 storage hierarchy. It has an owner policy and an authorization value, both of which persist through reboots. The intent is that they be set and rarely changed.

The hierarchy can be disabled by the owner without affecting the platform hierarchy. This permits the platform software to use the TPM even if the owner disables its hierarchy. In TPM 1.2, turning off the single storage hierarchy disabled the TPM. Similarly, this hierarchy can be cleared (by changing the primary seed and deleting persistent objects) independent of the other hierarchies.

The storage hierarchy is intended for non-privacy-sensitive operations, whereas the endorsement hierarchy, with separate controls, addresses privacy.

Endorsement Hierarchy

The endorsement hierarchy is the privacy-sensitive tree and is the hierarchy of choice when the user has privacy concerns. TPM and platform vendors certify that primary keys in this hierarchy are constrained to an authentic TPM attached to an authentic platform. As with TPM 1.2, a primary key can be an encryption key; and certificates can be created using TPM2_ActivateCredential, equivalent to the TPM 1.2 activate identity command. Unlike with TPM 1.2, a primary key can also be a signing key. Creating and certifying such a key is privacy sensitive because it permits correlation of keys back to a single TPM.

Because the endorsement hierarchy is intended for privacy-sensitive operations, its enable flag, policy, and authorization value are independent of the other hierarchies. They're under the control of a privacy administrator, who may be the end user. A user with privacy concerns can disable the endorsement hierarchy while still using the storage hierarchy for TPM applications and permitting the platform software to use the TPM.

Privacy

Privacy, as used here, means the inability of remote parties receiving TPM digital signatures to *correlate* them—to cryptographically prove that they came from the same TPM. A user can use different signing keys for different applications to make correlation difficult. The attacker's task is to trace these multiple keys back to a single user.

Privacy sensitivity is most applicable to home users who own and control their platform. In an enterprise, the IT department may control the platform completely and weaken the privacy features. This discussion is also concerned mostly with remote correlation—it doesn't consider an attacker who can confiscate a platform.

The requirement for correlation is ensuring that the signing keys came from a single, authentic TPM. If the key can be duplicated on another TPM or is from a software implementation, the signature can't be traced back to a single device.

The TPM vendor generates an endorsement primary seed, generates one or more primary keys from this seed, and then generates certificates for these keys. The certificates attest that the key is from an authentic TPM manufactured by the vendor. The platform manufacturer may create an analogous platform certificate. From primary keys, other keys are in some way certified.

If a primary key is a signing key and directly certifies other signing keys, correlation is simple, because all signatures converge at the same certificate. An attester seeing the certificate chain could prove that the attestation came from an authentic device. Further, the certificate chain can indicate that the key was fixed to that particular TPM. For this reason, primary keys in the endorsement hierarchy are typically encryption keys, not signing keys.

When the primary key is an encryption key, the process to create a descendent key certificate uses a more complicated flow, called *activating* a credential. The certificate authority is referred to as a *privacy CA*, because it's trusted not to leak any correlation between the keys it has certified.

Activating a Credential

The TPM doesn't mandate a credential format, but the intent is something like an X.509 certificate, where a credential provider such as a CA signs a public signing key and a statement about the key's attributes. The credential process in the TCG model has multiple goals:

- The credential provider can be assured of the key attributes it's certifying.

- Receivers of the TPM key signatures can't determine that the multiple keys are resident on the same TPM.

The certificate authority could provide this correlation, but you can assume that this privacy CA would not normally do so.

In TPM 1.2, a key that can be activated is restricted to be an identity key (AIK), which isn't migratable (can't be backed up), is restricted to signing only TPM-generated data, and is always a child of the SRK. In TPM 2.0, all these restrictions have been removed while still achieving both of the previously stated goals.

In this description, recall that a TPM 2.0 key's Name is a digest of its public data. It completely identifies the key. The digest includes the public key and its attributes.

The simplified concept is that the primary key is a decryption key, not a signing key. The CA constructs a certificate and encrypts it with the primary key public key. Only the TPM with the corresponding private key can recover the certificate. See Figure 9-1.

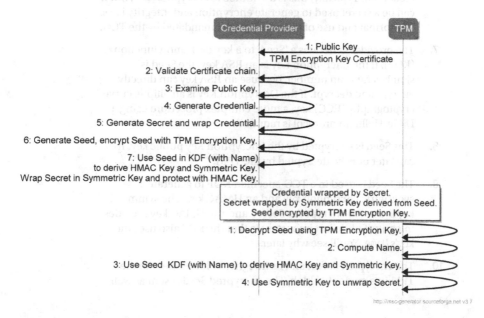

Figure 9-1. *Activating a Credential*

The following happens at the credential provider:

1. The credential provider receives the Key's public area and a certificate for an Encryption Key. The Encryption Key is typically a primary key in the endorsement hierarchy, and its certificate is issued by the TPM and/or platform manufacturer.

2. The credential provider walks the Encryption Key certificate chain back to the issuer's root. Typically, the provider verifies that the Encryption Key is fixed to a known compliant hardware TPM.

3. The provider examines the Key's public area and decides whether to issue a certificate, and what the certificate should say. In a typical case, the provider issues a certificate for a restricted Key that is fixed to the TPM.

4. The requester may have tried to alter the Key's public area attributes. This attack won't be successful. See step 5 in the process that occurs at the TPM.

5. The provider generates a credential for the Key

6. The provider generates a Secret that is used to protect the credential. Typically, this is a symmetric encryption key, but it can be a secret used to generate encryption and integrity keys. The format and use of this secret aren't mandated by the TCG.

7. The provider generates a 'Seed' to a key derivation function (KDF). If the Encryption Key is an RSA key, the Seed is simply a random number, because an RSA key can directly encrypt and decrypt. If the Decryption Key is an elliptic curve cryptography (ECC) key, a more complex procedure using a Diffie-Hellman protocol is required.

8. This Seed is encrypted by the Encryption Key public key. It can later only be decrypted by the TPM.

9. The Seed is used in a TCG-specified KDF to generate a symmetric encryption key and an HMAC key. The symmetric key is used to encrypt the Secret, and the HMAC key provides integrity. Subtle but important is that the KDF also uses the key's Name. You'll see why later.

10. The encrypted Secret and its integrity value are sent to the TPM in a credential blob. The encrypted Seed is sent as well.

If you follow all this, you have the following:

- A credential protected by a Secret

- A Secret encrypted by a key derived from a Seed and the key's Name

- A Seed encrypted by a TPM Encryption Key

These things happen at the TPM:

1. The encrypted Seed is applied against the TPM Encryption Key, and the Seed is recovered. The Seed remains inside the TPM.

2. The TPM computes the loaded key's Name.

3. The Name and the Seed are combined using the same TCG KDF to produce a symmetric encryption key and an HMAC key.

4. The two keys are applied to the protected Secret, checking its integrity and decrypting it.

5. This is where an attack on the key's public area attributes is detected. If the attacker presents a key to the credential provider that is different from the key loaded in the TPM, the Name will differ, and thus the symmetric and HMAC keys will differ, and this step will fail.

6. The TPM returns the Secret.

Outside the TPM, the Secret is applied to the credential in some agreed upon way. This can be as simple as using the Secret as a symmetric decryption key to decrypt the credential.

This protocol assures the credential provider that the credential can only be recovered if:

- The TPM has the private key associated with the Encryption Key certificate.

- The TPM has a key identical to the one presented to the credential provider.

The privacy administrator should control the use of the endorsement key, both as a signing key and in the activate-credential protocol, and thus control its correlation to another TPM key.

Other Privacy Considerations

The TPM owner can clear the storage hierarchy, changing the storage primary seed and effectively erasing all storage hierarchy keys.

The platform owner controls the endorsement hierarchy. The platform owner typically doesn't allow the endorsement primary seed to be changed, because this would render the existing TPM certificates useless, with no way to recover.

The user can create other primary keys in the endorsement hierarchy using a random number in the template. The user can erase these keys by flushing the key from the TPM, deleting external copies, and forgetting the random number. However, these keys do not have a manufacturer certificate.

When keys are used to sign (attest to) certain data, the attestation response structure contains what are possibly privacy-sensitive fields: resetCount (the number of times the TPM has been reset), restartCount (the number of times the TPM has been restarted or resumed), and the firmware version. Although these values don't map directly to a TPM, they can aid in correlation.

To avoid this issue, the values are obfuscated when the signing key isn't in the endorsement or platform hierarchy. The obfuscation is consistent when using the same key so the receiver can detect a change in the values while not seeing the actual values.

USE CASE: DETECTING A REBOOT BETWEEN ATTESTATIONS

An attestation server polls a platform at set intervals, verifying either that the PCRs haven't changed or that the new PCR values are trusted. In TPM 1.2, the platform may have transitioned to an untrusted state and then rebooted back to a trusted state. The server can't detect the reboot.

In TPM 2.0, the attestation data includes boot-count information. Although attestations in the storage hierarchy have the information obfuscated, the server can still tell that a value changed and thus that a reboot occurred.

Here are the steps:

1. Execute the TPM2_Quote command periodically.

2. Each quote returns a TPM2B_ATTEST structure.

3. The quote includes the TPM2B_ATTEST->TPMS_CLOCK_INFO->resetCount value.

4. resetCount is obfuscated with a symmetric key based on the quote key Name.

5. For the same key, the obfuscated resetCount has the same value if resetCount doesn't change.

6. For a different key, the obfuscated resetCount has a different value, preventing correlation.

Separate from the three persistent hierarchies is the one volatile hierarchy, called the NULL hierarchy.

NULL Hierarchy

The NULL hierarchy is analogous to the three persistent hierarchies. It can have primary keys from which descendants can be created. Several properties are different:

- The authorization value is a zero-length password, and the policy is empty (can't be satisfied). These can't be changed.

- It can't be disabled.

- It has a seed from which keys and data objects can be derived. The seed isn't persistent. It and the proof are regenerated with different values on each reboot.

A subtle use case, which the normal end user doesn't see, is that sessions, saved context objects, and sequence objects (digest and HMAC state) are in the NULL hierarchy. This permits them to be voided on reboot, because the seed and proof change. A user typically doesn't change the endorsement hierarchy seed (because it would invalidate certificates), the storage hierarchy seed (because it would invalidate keys with a long lifetime), or the platform hierarchy seed (because the user may not have that capability).

Ephemeral keys are keys that are erased at reboot. An entire hierarchy, primary keys, storage keys, and leaf keys can be constructed in the NULL hierarchy. On reboot, as the seed changes, the entire key hierarchy is cryptographically erased. That is, the wrapped keys may exist on disk, but they can't be loaded.

The TPM can be used as a cryptographic coprocessor, performing cryptographic algorithms on externally generated keys. Keys that have both a public and a private part are loaded in the NULL hierarchy, because they may not become part of a persistent hierarchy.

Cryptographic Primitives

TPM 2.0 can function purely as a cryptographic coprocessor. Although the following applications can be performed using any hierarchy, they're best suited for the NULL hierarchy because it's always enabled and the authorization is always a zero-length password. It's thus always available.

I hesitate to call the TPM a crypto accelerator, because it's likely to be slower than a pure software implementation. However, there are a few niche applications where these features are useful:

- A resource-constrained environment, such as early boot software, may not want to implement complex crypto math.

- In a low-performance application, it may be easier for a developer to use the TPM than to procure commercial software or vet an open source license.

- Applications may deem hardware superior to software.

- Applications could require a certified implementation, assuming the TPM is certified.

The TPM primitives, random numbers, digests, HMAC, and symmetric and asymmetric key operations are described next.

Random Number Generator

The TPM offers a simple interface to a hardware random number generator. It's particularly useful when another source of entropy may not be available. Examples are embedded systems or early in a platform boot cycle.

The TPM can be considered a more trusted source of random numbers than the software generator. See the paper "Ron was wrong, Whit is right"[2] for a discussion of issues resulting from poor software random number generators.

Digest Primitives

TPM 2.0 offers two cryptographic digest primitive APIs. Both are hash agile, permitting the hash algorithm to be specified in the call.

The simpler but less flexible option is TPM2_Hash. The caller inputs the message, and the TPM returns the digest. The message length is limited by the TPM input buffer size, typically 1 or 2 KB. The other API implements the usual start/update/complete pattern using TPM2_HashSequenceStart, TPM2_SequenceUpdate, and TPM2_SequenceComplete.

USE CASE: HASHING A LARGE FILE

In this use case, assume that the TPM input buffer is 2 KB. The user desires to SHA-256 hash a 4 KB file. The user uses the TPM because the SHA-256 algorithm isn't available in software. The user uses the sequence commands because the file is larger than 2 KB.

Here are the steps:

1. TPM2_HashSequenceStart, specifying the SHA-256 algorithm.

2. TPM2_SequenceUpdate two times, with a sequence of 2 KB buffers.

3. TPM2_SequenceComplete to return the result.

This API is similar to that of TPM 1.2, but it has several enhancements:

-   It supports multiple hash algorithms.

-   The start function returns a handle. More than one digest operation can be in progress at a time.

---

[2]Arjen K. Lenstra, James P. Hughes, Maxime Augier, Joppe W. Bos, Thorsten Kleinjung, and Christophe Wachter, "Ron was wrong, Whit is right," *International Association for Cryptologic Research*, 2012, https://eprint.iacr.org/2012/064.pdf.

- The update function isn't restricted to a multiple of 64 bytes.

- The complete function can be more than 64 bytes.

- The complete function can return a ticket, which is used when signing with a restricted key. See the discussion of TPM_GENERATED for details.

USE CASE: TRUSTED BOOT

CRTM software would like to verify a signed software update. Because it's resource constrained, it uses the TPM to digest the update, avoiding the need to implement the digest calculation in the CRTM.

TPM 2.0 offers TPM2_EventSequenceComplete as an alternative to TPM2_SequenceComplete. This command can only terminate a digest process where no algorithm was specified. This null algorithm causes the TPM to calculate digests over the message for all supported algorithms.

The command, an extension of TPM 1.2's TPM_SHA1CompleteExtend, has two enhancements:

- It permits the result of the digest operation to be extended into a PCR. One PCR index is specified, but all PCRs at that index (that is, all banks) are extended with a digest corresponding to that PCR bank's algorithm. Multiple digests are returned, one for each supported algorithm.

- The SHA-1 algorithm is being deprecated in favor of stronger algorithms such as SHA-256. This command, which can do both algorithms simultaneously, permits a staged phase-out of SHA-1, because it can return multiple results and extend multiple PCR banks.

USE CASE: TRUSTED BOOT

TPM2_EventSequenceComplete allows software to measure (digest and extend) software using the TPM. It avoids the need for the measuring software to implement a digest algorithm.

USE CASE: MULTIPLE SIMULTANEOUS TPM DIGEST ALGORITHMS

In one pass, the software can measure into PCR banks for several algorithms. A TPM may be unlikely to support multiple simultaneous PCR banks (multiple sets of PCRs with different algorithms). The current PC Client TPM doesn't require this. But if one ever does, the TPM API supports it.

HMAC Primitives

TPM 2.0 supports HMAC as a primitive, whereas TPM 1.2 offered only the underlying digest API. The HMAC key is a loaded, keyed, hash TPM object. For a restricted key, the key's algorithm must be used. For an unrestricted key, the caller can override the key's algorithm. As with any key, the full complement of authorization methods is available.

As with digests, there are both simple and fully flexible APIs. TPM2_HMAC is the simpler API. You input a key handle, a digest algorithm, and a message, and the TPM returns the HMAC. The other API again implements the usual start/update/complete pattern, using TPM2_HMAC_Start, TPM2_SequenceUpdate, and TPM2_SequenceComplete.

USE CASE: STORING LOGIN PASSWORDS

A typical password file stores salted hashes of passwords. Verification consists of salting and hashing a supplied password and comparing it to the stored value. Because the calculation doesn't include a secret, it's subject to an offline attack on the password file.

This use case uses a TPM-generated HMAC key. The password file stores an HMAC of the salted password. Verification consists of salting and HMACing the supplied password and comparing it to the stored value. Because an offline attacker doesn't have the HMAC key, the attacker can't mount an attack by performing the calculation.

Here are the steps:

1. TPM2_Create, specifying an HMAC key (called a keyedHash object) that can be used with a zero-length, well-known password.

2. TPM2_Load to load the HMAC key, or optionally load and then TPM2_EvictControl to make the key persistent.

3. TPM2_HMAC to calculate an HMAC of the salted password.

RSA Primitives

Two commands offer raw RSA operations: TPM2_RSA_Encrypt and TPM2_RSA_Decrypt. Both operate on a loaded RSA key. Both permit several padding schemes: PKCS#1, OAEP, and no padding. The loaded key's padding can't be overridden. The caller can, however, specify a padding scheme if the key's scheme is null.

TPM2_RSA_Decrypt is the private key operation. The decryption key must be authorized, and padding is validated and removed before the TPM returns the plaintext.

TPM2_RSA_Encrypt is the public key operation. A key and a message must be specified, but no authorization is required for this public key operation. Padding is added before the encryption.

USE CASE: CRTM SIGNATURE VERIFICATION

A platform implements CRTM updates. The design requires that updates be signed, because compromising the CRTM subverts the entire platform. However, the CRTM is constrained in both code and data space. The CRTM would like to use the TPM to verify the signature.

The CRTM uses a hard-coded public key blob in a format ready to be loaded on the TPM. The key has a null padding scheme. The CRTM then uses the TPM2_RSA_Encrypt command to apply the public key to the signature, specifying no padding. Finally, the CRTM does a simply byte compare on the result against a padded digest of the update.

Symmetric Key Primitives

TPM2_EncryptDecrypt permits the TPM to perform symmetric key encryption and decryption. The function operates on a small number of blocks due to the TPM input buffer size. However, the API includes an initialization vector (IV) on input and a chaining value on output, so a larger number of blocks can be operated on in parts.

As with an HMAC key, a restricted key has a fixed mode. The caller can specify the mode when using an unrestricted key.

The key must be a symmetric cipher object. It must be authorized, and the full set of authorization options are available.

Symmetric key encryption is a sensitive subject. Although the TPM isn't very fast, its hardware-protected keys are far more secure than software keys. It thus may be subject to import controls and may draw the attention of government agencies. For this reason, the PC Client platform specifies this command as optional.

Summary

The TPM has three persistent hierarchies. The platform hierarchy is generally used by the platform OEM, as represented by early boot code. The platform OEM can depend on this hierarchy being enabled, even if the end user turns off the other hierarchies. The storage hierarchy is under the control of the user and is used for non-privacy-sensitive operations. The endorsement hierarchy, with its TPM vendor and OEM certificates, is under the control of a privacy administrator and is used for privacy-sensitive operations. The privacy-sensitive credential activation is typically performed in the endorsement hierarchy.

The NULL hierarchy is volatile. Sessions, contexts, and sequence objects are in this hierarchy, but an entire tree of volatile keys and objects can also be created here, ensuring that they're deleted on a power cycle.

Besides its secure storage features, the TPM can be used as a cryptographic coprocessor, performing cryptographic algorithms on externally generated secrets or algorithms for which no secrets are needed. Its capabilities include a random number generator, digest and HMAC algorithms, and symmetric and asymmetric key operations.

CHAPTER 10

Keys

As a security device, the ability of an application to use keys while keeping them safe in a hardware device is the TPM's greatest strength. The TPM can both generate and import externally generated keys. It supports both asymmetric and symmetric keys. Chapter 2 covered the basic principles behind these two key types.

As a memory-constrained device, it acts as a key cache, with the application securely swapping keys in and out as needed. This key cache operation is discussed in the "Key Cache" section.

There are three key hierarchies under the control of different security roles, and each can form trees of keys in a parent-child relationship. Chapter 9 covered the hierarchies and their use cases.

Each key has individual security controls, which can include a password, an enhanced authorization policy, restrictions on duplication to another parent or another TPM, and limits on its use as a signing or decryption key. Keys can be both certified and used to certify other keys. Attributes specific to keys are discussed in the "Key Types and Attributes" section. The details of authorization common to all TPM entities, including password and policy, are deferred to Chapters 13 and 14.

Key Commands

Following is a summary of the TPM commands most often used with keys. It isn't a complete list. See the TPM 2.0 specification, Part 3, for the complete command set and API details. They're used in the descriptions and use cases that follow, as well as in subsequent chapters:

- `TPM2_Create` and `TPM2_CreatePrimary` create all key types from templates.

- `TPM2_Load` (for wrapped private keys) and `TPM2_LoadExternal` (for public keys and possibly plaintext private keys) load keys onto the TPM.

- `TPM2_ContextSave` and `TPM2_ContextLoad` are used to swap keys in and out of the TPM key cache. `TPM2_FlushContext` removes a key from the TPM. `TPM2_EvictControl` can make a loaded key persistent or remove a persistent ley from the TPM. These functions and their applications are explained in detail in Chapter 18.

119

- TPM2_Unseal, TPM2_RSA_Encrypt, and TPM2_RSA_Decrypt use encryption keys.

- TPM2_HMAC, TPM2_HMAC_Start, TPM2_SequenceUpdate, and TPM2_SequenceCompete use symmetric signing keys and the keyed-hash message authentication code (HMAC) algorithm.

- TPM2_Sign is a general-purpose signing command, and TPM2_VerifySignature verifies a digital signature.

- TPM2_Certify, TPM2_Quote, TPM2_GetSessionAuditDigest, and TPM_GetTime are specialized signing commands that sign attestation structures. In particular, TPM2_Certify can be used to have a TPM key sign another key (specifically its Name). Thus, the TPM can be used as a certificate authority, where the issuer key attests to the properties of the subject key.

Key Generator

Arguably, the TPM's greatest strength is its ability to generate a cryptographic key and protect its secret within a hardware boundary. The key generator is based on the TPM's own random number generator and doesn't rely on external sources of randomness. It thus eliminates weaknesses based on weak software random number generators or software with an insufficient source of entropy.

Primary Keys and Seeds

TPM keys can form a hierarchy, with parent keys wrapping their children. Primary keys are the root keys in the hierarchy. They have no parent. Chapter 9 discussed the general concept of hierarchies and their use cases. Their specific application to keys is discussed under "Key Hierarchy."

This section describes, in a linear flow, the creation and destruction of primary keys. In the narrative, the caller is some software that is provisioning the TPM, sending commands and receiving responses, whereas the TPM is the device that processes the commands. Provisioning software (see Chapter 19) typically performs these steps. Although end users may use primary keys, they would not typically be creating them.

Primary keys are created with the aptly named command TPM2_CreatePrimary. If you're familiar with TPM 1.2, you know that it has one key equivalent to the TPM 2.0 primary key: the *storage root key* (SRK), which is persistently stored in the TPM. TPM 2.0 permits an unlimited number of primary keys, which don't need to be persistent. Although you might think the number would be limited by the TPM persistent storage, it's not. Primary seeds, described shortly, permit the expansion.

There were two reasons TPM 1.2 could function with one SRK. First, it had only one algorithm and key size for wrapping keys, RSA-2048. The design of TPM 2.0, of course, permits multiple algorithms and key sizes. Second, TPM 1.2 has only one key hierarchy: the storage hierarchy. TPM 2.0 has three hierarchies, each with at least one root. Chapter 9 discussed the general concept of hierarchies and their use cases.

How can a TPM with limited persistent storage have an unlimited number of root keys? A root can't exist outside the TPM because it has no parent to wrap its secret parts. The answer is the primary seeds.

Each of the three persistent hierarchies has an associated primary seed: the *endorsement primary seed*, the *platform primary seed*, and the *storage primary seed*. These seeds never leave the TPM. They're the secret inputs to key-derivation functions. When the TPM creates a primary key, it uses a primary seed plus a public template. The template includes all the items you would normally expect when specifying a key: the algorithms and key size, its policy, and the type of key (signing, encryption, and so on). The caller can also provide unique data in the template. The unique data is input in the public key area of the template.

The key-derivation function is fixed and repeatable. For the same seed, the same template always produces the same key. By varying the unique data in the template, the caller can create an unlimited number of primary keys. .

When the TPM creates a primary key, it remains on the TPM in volatile memory. The caller now has two choices. A limited number of primary keys can be moved to persistent memory using the TPM2_EvictControl command. Other keys can remain in volatile memory.

If more primary keys are needed than can fit in persistent storage or volatile memory, some can be flushed (from volatile storage) or moved from persistent storage and then flushed. Because the seed is persistent, the key isn't lost forever. If the caller knows the template, which may be completely public, the TPM can re-create the identical key on demand. If the key being regenerated is an RSA key, this process may take a lot of time. If the key is an elliptic curve cryptography (ECC), AES, or HMAC key, the process of creating a primary key is very fast. In most use cases, at least one storage primary key is made persistent in the TPM for the storage hierarchy, to act in a manner similar to the SRK.

How would this work in practice? In TPM 1.2, there was one endorsement key and an associated certificate signed by the TPM vendor. They resided in persistent storage, so that when the final user got a system with a TPM on it, the user also had a certificate stored in the TPM's NVRAM that matched the endorsement key stored in the TPM. In TPM 2.0, there can be many key/certificate pairs—at least one for each algorithm the TPM implements. However, the end user may not want to consume valuable persistent storage for keys and certificates that aren't being used, even if they could fit.

A possible solution, which TPM vendors are expected to implement, is to have the manufacturer use the endorsement seed to generate several endorsement primary keys and certificates using a standard set of algorithms, each with a well-known template. One popular key, say RSA-2048, and its certificate can be moved to persistent storage. The vendor flushes the other keys but retains the certificates.

The TCG Infrastructure work group has defined several such templates for endorsement primary keys. The RSA template uses RSA 2048, SHA-256, and AES-128. The ECC template uses ECC with the NIST P256 curve, SHA-256, and AES-128. Both use the same authorization policy, which requires knowledge of the endorsement hierarchy password. This delegates the key authorization to the endorsement hierarchy administrator. The unique data is empty, a trivial well-known value. The attributes (see "Key Types and Attributes") are fixedTPM and fixedParent true, as expected for an endorsement key that should never be duplicated. userWithAuth and adminWithPolicy are specified so that a policy must always be used, not a password, which is appropriate because the TPM vendor has no way of passing a password to the end user. The key is a *restricted decrypt* key: that is, a storage key.

Suppose the end user desires a different primary key. That user can flush the one that was provisioned with the TPM and generate a new one with their algorithm of choice.

Magic happens now! Because the seed is unchanged and the user creates the primary key using the same template, they get the exact same key that the TPM vendor created. The user can treat the public part as an index into a TPM vendor certificate list. That list could even be on a public server. The user retrieves the certificate and is ready to go. This key-generation repeatability (the same seed and the same template always yield the same key) permits the TPM vendor to generate many keys and certificates during manufacturing, but not have to store them in the limited TPM nonvolatile storage. The end user can regenerate them as needed.

Note that the vendor must generate all needed primary keys and vendor certificates in advance. Because the seed is secret, the vendor would otherwise not be able to determine that a public key value came from the vendor's TPM.

Once a seed is changed, the primary keys can no longer be re-created, and any keys residing in the TPM based on the old seed are flushed. This means any certificates the vendor created also become worthless. Creating a new certificate for a TPM endorsement key (EK) signed by the vendor would be very difficult. Because of this, changing the seed to the endorsement hierarchy is controlled by the platform hierarchy, which in practice means the OEM. This makes it difficult for an end user to change this seed. On the other hand, by simply choosing a random input in the template, the end user can create their own set of endorsement keys that are totally independent of the EKs the vendor produced.

USE CASE: MULTIPLE PRIMARY KEYS

The user has several primary storage keys that serve as the root for a key hierarchy. They can't all fit in persistent storage. If the user creates the keys using well-known templates, they can be re-created as needed.

The TPM commands are as follows:

- TPM2_NV_Read: Reads the well-known template from TPM NV space. The TPM vendor may provision several templates (for example, one for RSA and one for ECC) on the TPM, and these templates match the provisioned key certificates. The user may also have enterprise-wide templates.

- TPM2_CreatePrimary: Specifying the template.

- TPM2_EvictControl: Can optionally be used to make several keys persistent. Especially for RSA keys, this saves the time required to regenerate them. Keys can also remain in volatile memory and be re-created after each power cycle.

USE CASE - CUSTOM PRIMARY KEYS:

The user wishes to create a primary key using a user secret in the template rather than using a well-known template. Again, there are more primary keys than can fit in persistent storage. The user stores the secret in a TPM NV index, with suitable read access control, and retrieves it when needed to re-create the primary key.

The TPM commands are as follows:

- TPM2_NV_Write: Writes and protects a user secret.

- TPM2_NV_Read: Reads the secret using appropriate authorization. The secret is inserted into the key template.

- TPM2_CreatePrimary: Specify the template, which includes a user secret, to generate a custom primary key.

Persistence of Keys

A user calls the TPM2_EvictControl command to move a key from volatile to nonvolatile memory so it can remain loaded (persist) though power cycles. No key needs to be made persistent to be used. Typically, we expect that a small number of primary keys, perhaps one per hierarchy, will be made persistent to improve performance.

Keys in the endorsement, storage, and platform hierarchies, other than primary keys, can also be made persistent. A use case would be early in a boot cycle, when a key is needed before a disk is available. Another use case is a limited-resource platform such as an embedded controller, which may not have any external persistent storage.

No keys in the NULL hierarchy can be made persistent. All are voided at reboot.[1]

Only a limited number of keys can be persistent, but the TPM can handle an unlimited number of keys. The application does this by using the TPM as a key cache.

Key Cache

For keys other than primary keys, the TPM serves as a key cache. That is, the TPM2_Create command creates a key, wraps[2] (encrypts) it with the parent, and returns the wrapped key to the caller. The caller saves the key external to the TPM, perhaps on disk. To use the key, the user must first load it into the TPM under its parent using TPM2_Load. When finished, the caller can free memory using TPM2_FlushContext. This is different from a primary key, which has no parent and remains in the TPM after it's created.

---

[1]Chapter 9 discussed the unique properties of the NULL hierarchy.

[2]Wrapping is a common design pattern for hardware security modules. The wrapping key is an encryption key, sometimes called a *key encrypting key* or *master key*. The TCG calls it a *storage key*. The wrapping key and the wrapped key form a parent-child relationship.

A typical hardware TPM may have five to ten *key slots*: memory areas where a key can be loaded. TPM management middleware is responsible for swapping keys in and out of the cache.

If you read Chapter 13, you may notice that the key *handle* isn't included in the TPM parameters that are authorized. Rather, the key's Name is used. The reason is the key cache and swapping. A platform may have a large number of application keys on disk, perhaps identified by a user's handle. There are many more of these handles than key slots. When a user asks to use a key, the command includes the user's handle. However, when the middleware loads the key, it gets a different handle, related to the TPM key slot rather than the user's handle. The middleware must thus replace the user's handle with the TPM handle. If the authorization included the user's handle, the substitution would cause an authorization failure.

You may now ask, "If the handle can be replaced, then if I have two keys with the same authorization secret, how do I know that the middleware didn't use a different key than the one I wanted?" This was indeed a potential problem in TPM 1.2.

TPM solves this problem by using the key's Name, a digest of the key's public area, in the authorization. The middleware can replace the key handle (which was not authorized) but can't replace the Name (which was authorized).

The root keys (the parents) and the key cache (the children) form a tree of keys. The TPM provides for four of these trees, each with different controlling roles. The trees are called *hierarchies*.

Key Authorization

Although hardware protection of private or symmetric keys alone is a major improvement over software-generated keys, the TPM also offers strong access control. A software key often uses a password for access control, to protect the key. For example, the secret key may be encrypted with a password. This protection is only as strong as the password, and the secret key is vulnerable to an offline hammering attack. That is, once an attacker obtains the encrypted key, extracting the key is reduced to cracking the password. The key owner can't prevent a high-speed attack that tries an unlimited number of passwords. This attack can be parallelized, with many computers trying different passwords simultaneously. The cloud has made this kind of attack very feasible.

The TPM improves on software keys in two respects. First, when the key leaves the TPM (see the "Key Hierarchy" section), it's wrapped (encrypted) with a strong parent key encrypting key. The attacker now has to crack a strong key rather than a weak password. Second, when a key is loaded in the TPM, it's protected by what the specification calls *dictionary attack protection logic*. Each time an attacker fails to crack the key's authorization,[3] this logic logs the failure. After a configurable number of failures, the TPM blocks further attempts for a configurable amount of time. This limits, possibly severely, the speed at which an attacker can try passwords. The rate limiting can make even a weak TPM key password much more time consuming to crack than a strong software key password, where the attack isn't rate limited. Chapter 13 describes password and HMAC authorization in detail.

---

[3]Chapters 13 and 14 discuss the details of TPM authorization.

The TPM provides many access-control mechanisms beyond a simple password. However, it's the hardware protection of the dictionary-attack protection logic that makes a TPM key password resistant to attack.

Key Destruction

Sometimes a key should be destroyed. Perhaps the authorization has been exposed. Perhaps the machine is being repurposed. Keys that are stored in software can never be destroyed, because they may have been copied almost anywhere. But TPM keys have parents or are primary keys.

As described in Chapter 9, there are three persistent hierarchies (endorsement, storage, and platform) plus one volatile hierarchy (the null hierarchy). Each hierarchy has its unique primary seed. Erasing a primary seed prevents re-creation of primary keys in that hierarchy—obviously a drastic and rarely performed action. Erasing the primary keys then prevents their children from being loaded in the TPM. Any key with attributes that prove it can only exist in the TPM is then destroyed.

Key Hierarchy

A hierarchy can be thought of as having parent and child keys, or ancestors and descendants. All parent keys are storage keys, which are encryption keys that can wrap (encrypt) child keys. The storage key thus protects its children, offering secrecy and integrity when the child key is stored outside the secure hardware boundary of the TPM. These storage keys are restricted in their use. They can't be used for general decryption, which could then leak the child's secrets.

The ultimate parent at the top of the hierarchy is a primary key. Children can be storage keys, in which case they can also be parents. Children can also be non-storage keys, in which case they're *leaf keys*: children but never parents.

Key Types and Attributes

Each key has attributes, which are set at creation. They include the following:

- Use, such as signing or encryption
- Overall type, symmetric or asymmetric, and the algorithm
- Restrictions on duplication
- Restrictions on use

Symmetric and Asymmetric Keys Attributes

TPM 2.0 supports a variety of asymmetric algorithms, unlike TPM 1.2, which was fixed to RSA. TPM 2.0 also introduces some entirely new key types.

A symmetric signing key can be used in TPM HMAC commands. TPM 2.0 can do symmetric signing (a MAC) with a key that is never in the clear outside the TPM.

The TPM library specification includes symmetric encryption keys that can be used for general-purpose encryption such as AES. It's uncertain whether TPM vendors will include these functions, due to potential export restrictions. The commands are optional in the PC Client platform specification. Historically, TPM vendors haven't implemented optional TPM features.

Duplication Attributes

Duplication is the process of copying a key from one location in a hierarchy to another. The key can become the child of another parent key. The hierarchy or parent can be on the same or a different TPM. Primary keys can't be duplicated; they're fixed to one hierarchy on one TPM.

A primary use case for duplication is key backups. If a key were locked forever to one TPM, and the TPM or its motherboard failed, the key would be lost permanently. A second use case is the sharing of keys among several devices. For example, a user's signing key may be duplicated among a laptop, tablet, and mobile phone.

TPM 1.2 has a similar process called migration. The term *migration* implies that a key is moved: that is, that it would now exist at the destination location but no longer exist at the source. This implication was incorrect. After migration, the key could exist at both the destination and the source. For that reason, the TPM 2.0 term was changed to the more accurate *duplication*.

TPM 2.0 keys have two attributes that control duplication. At one extreme, a key may be locked to a single parent on a single TPM, and never duplicated. The opposite extreme is a key that may be freely duplicated to another parent on the same or another TPM.

The intermediate case is a key that is locked to a parent but that can be implicitly duplicated if the parent is moved. This case offers the possibility of duplicating an entire branch of a tree. If the parent is duplicated, all children wrapped to that parent are available at the destination, on down through all descendants.

The TPM specification talks of a *duplication root* and a *duplication group*. The root is a key that can be duplicated. The duplication process acts explicitly on that key. The group represents all descendants of that root. The entire duplication group duplicates implicitly when the root duplicates. The children, which aren't explicitly duplicated, remain with their parent. However, as the parent is copied, the children are implicitly copied with it.

The controlling key attributes are defined as follows:

- fixedTPM: A key with this attribute set to true can't be duplicated. Although the name seems to permit duplicating a key from one location in a hierarchy to another within a TPM, this isn't the case.

- fixedParent: A key with this attribute set to true can't be duplicated to (rewrapped to) a different parent. It's locked to always have the same parent.

These two boolean attributes define four combinations.

1. The easiest case to understand is `fixedTPM` true and `fixedParent` false, because it isn't permitted. A key with fixedTPM true can't be duplicated, whereas fixedParent false says it can be moved to a different parent The TPM checks for and doesn't allow this inconsistency.

2. `fixedTPM` true and `fixedParent` true defines an object that can't be duplicated, either explicitly or implicitly.

3. `fixedTPM` false and `fixedParent` true indicates a key that can't be directly duplicated. It's fixed to a parent. However, if an ancestor is duplicated, this key naturally moves with it. That is, it may be in a duplication group, but it isn't the root of a group.

4. `fixedTPM` false and `fixedParent` false indicates a key that can be duplicated. If it's a parent, a duplication root, its children move with it.

The fourth case is perhaps the most interesting, because the key may be a duplication root. For example, it permits backup of a group of keys, called a *duplication group* in the specification. That is, once this parent is duplicated, all descendants are immediately duplicated to the new location without the need to duplicate each child individually. It also simplifies the task of tracking the location of a key. You need only track the parent, not children with `fixedParent` true, which remain with their parent.

Observe also that these children are still wrapped by their original parent. The key being duplicated must have `fixedParent` false. The children can be loaded into the TPM where their parent is loaded, regardless of where their parent was originally loaded. `fixedParent` determines whether a key can be directly duplicated, not whether it can or can't be duplicated by implication when its parent is duplicated. In other words, the child wasn't duplicated through any operation involving the TPM. Once its parent is duplicated, the child can be simply moved to the new location (for example, with a file copy of the wrapped child key) and loaded.

A child can have more than one parent. The duplication process establishes a new parent-child relationship but doesn't destroy the old one.[4] The key is now a child of both the original parent and the new parent. A key can be part of more than one duplication group if more than one of its ancestors has `fixedParent` false. That is, a child key in a tree can have more than one ancestor that is a duplication root. If any root is duplicated, the child is duplicated.

---

[4] It's for this reason that the TPM 1.2 term *migration* was changed to *duplication*. Migration implied that the old parent-child relationship was severed, which isn't true even in TPM 1.2.

The TPM puts a restriction on the relationship between parent and child. A child can only be created with fixedTPM true if:

1. Its parent also has fixedTPM true (the parent can't be explicitly duplicated).

2. Its parent has fixedParent true (the parent can't be implicitly duplicated).

The TPM enforces this restriction back to the primary keys, which are by nature fixed to their TPM.

Restricted Signing Key

A variation on the key attribute sign (a signing key) is the restricted attribute. The use case for a restricted key is signing TPM attestation structures. These structures include Platform Configuration Register (PCR) quotes, a TPM object being certified, a signature over the TPM's time, or a signature over an audit digest. The signature is, of course, over a digest, but the verifier wants assurance that the digest was not simply created externally over bogus values and delivered to the TPM for signing. For example, a quote is a signature over a set of PCR values, but the actual signing process signs a digest. A user could generate a digest of any PCR values and use a nonrestricted key to sign it. The user could then claim that the signature was a quote. However, the relying party would observe that the key was not restricted and thus not trust the claim. A restricted key provides assurance that the signature was over a TPM generated digest.

A restricted signing key can only sign a digest produced by the TPM. This is a generalization of the TPM 1.2 Info keys and attestation identity key (AIKs), which could only sign a TPM internally created structure. For internal TPM data, this assurance is easy, because the TPM created the digest from its internal data at signing time.

However, a restricted key can also sign data supplied to the TPM, as long as the TPM performed the digest using either TPM2_SequenceComplete or TPM2_Hash. Because the digest is later supplied to the TPM for signing, how does the TPM know that it calculated the digest?

The answer is a *ticket*. When the TPM calculates the digest, it produces a ticket that declares that the TPM itself calculated that digest. When the digest is presented to TPM2_Sign, the ticket must accompany it. If not, the restricted key doesn't sign.

So what? How does this restrict what can be signed? If you can digest any external data and obtain a ticket, why would it matter where the digest was calculated?

The answer is a 4-byte magic value called TPM_GENERATED. Each of the attestation structures—the structures the TPM constructs from internal data—begins with this magic number. If the TPM is digesting externally supplied data, it produces a ticket only if the data did *not* begin with the magic number.

The net result is that you can sign almost any externally supplied data with a restricted key. The only data that you can't sign is data beginning with TPM_GENERATED. This prevents you from spoofing TPM attestation structures, which all start with that value.

Restricted Decryption Key

A restricted decryption key is in fact a storage key. This key only decrypts data that has a specific format, including an integrity value over the rest of the structure.

Only these keys can be used as parents to create or load child objects or to activate a credential. These operations place restrictions on the result of the decryption. For example, loading doesn't return the result of the decryption.

An unrestricted key can perform a general-purpose decryption on any supplied data and return the result. If it were permitted to be used as a storage key, it could decrypt and return the private key of a child. If it could be used on sealed data, it would return the data without checking the unseal authorization.

Context Management vs. Loading

Loading a key involves supplying the wrapped (encrypted) key and specifying a loaded parent. The TPM parent key unwraps (decrypts) the child key and holds it in a volatile key slot.

Context management involves *context-saving* a loaded key off the TPM and then *context-loading* it onto the TPM at a later time. When the key is saved, it's wrapped with a symmetric key derived from a hierarchy secret, called a *hierarchy proof*. Upon load, it's unwrapped with the same key. A context-saved key has no parent, but it's connected to a hierarchy.

Why use one or the other? In TPM 1.2, context management was important, because child keys were always wrapped with a parent RSA key. The load operation required a time-consuming RSA decryption. Context-saved keys were wrapped with a symmetric key and thus were much faster. In TPM 2.0, child keys are wrapped with the symmetric key of the parent, even if the parent is itself an asymmetric key. All storage keys have a symmetric secret. Thus, reloading a key using its parent should be as fast as a context load and of course eliminates the context save.

So why ever use context management to load a key? The use case for context-loading keys is when the parent isn't loaded. The key could be a descendent deep down a hierarchy. Loading it could require loading a long chain of ancestors. A parent authorization may require an inconvenient password prompt. A parent authorization may be impossible if, for example, its policy requires a PCR state that has passed.

Specifically, suppose a key is four layers of parent down from a primary key. The first child is loaded under its parent. That parent is no longer needed and can be flushed from the TPM's key cache. Now the next child is loaded, and the process repeats four times until the final leaf key is reached. Once the leaf key is loaded, all its ancestors can be flushed. However, if the leaf key is flushed, the entire process must repeat. The alternative is to context-save the leaf key. Then it can be context-loaded independent of its ancestors. Chapter 18 explains this process in detail.

NULL Hierarchy

In addition to the three persistent hierarchies, the TPM has a NULL hierarchy.[5] This hierarchy has its own unique seed, and both primary and descendent keys can exist in this hierarchy. However, neither the seed nor primary keys can be persistent. A new seed is created on each TPM reset. Thus, keys in this hierarchy are *ephemeral*: they're erased on a reset.

Certification

The TPM can of course act as a certificate authority. In fact, even before you consider unique TPM features such as PCR, authorization policies, audit, and hierarchies, it's valuable simply as a hardware key store. The private signing key is protected by the hardware and a wide range of authorization options, but it can be easily backed up. This widely available and very inexpensive part offers far better protection than a software key.

A third-party certificate authority can also sign a X.509 certificate for a TPM key. For decryption keys, there is a complication due to a typical CA requirement for proof of possession. The certificate requestor must provide evidence to a CA that it possesses the private key. This is typically done by self signing the certificate signing request (CSR).[6]

For decryption keys, the TPM can't simply sign the CSR, because these keys are restricted to decryption and can't sign. The TPM has a workaround (see "Activating a Credential" in Chapter 9), but this requires a nonstandard CA.

Less obvious is that the TPM can certify data located on the device. The TPM offers several commands to support this feature.

TPM2_Certify asserts that an object with a Name is loaded on the TPM. Because the name cryptographically represents the object's public area, a relying party can be assured that the object has an associated private part. The Name also incorporates the key's attributes, including whether it's restricted, fixed to a parent or fixed to a TPM, and the authorization policy.

USE CASE: CERTIFYING A TPM QUOTE KEY

A signing key is used for attestation: for example, to quote (sign) a set of PCR values. The quote is far more useful if the relying party verifying the quote is assured that the signing key is restricted to the TPM, and therefore that the PCR values were actually on the TPM. The party first uses TPM2_Certify to get a certificate over the quote key's public area.

Naturally, the certifying key itself requires a certificate. Eventually, a useful certificate chain leads back to a root. Chapter 19 explains how TPM key certificates are provisioned and how these chains can be validated back to a trusted root key.

---

[5]Chapter 9 discusses the NULL hierarchy.
[6]See, for example the PKCS #10 standard in IETF RFC 2986.

USE CASE: CREATING A CERTIFICATE CHAIN

A signing key is located deep in a key hierarchy. A relying party wants to be assured that all keys in the chain back to a primary key are suitably protected, that all encryption algorithms and key sizes are of sufficient strength. The party uses TPM2_Certify to get a certificate chain that cryptographically signs the public areas of all keys in the chain.

TPM2_Certify signs the entire public area, including a key's policy. This leads to other use cases.

USE CASE: ASSURING THAT A KEY'S AUTHORIZATION REQUIRES A DIGITAL SIGNATURE

A relying party wants assurance that only a restricted role can use a signing key, indicated by a signature with a particular authorizing key. It uses TPM2_Certify to certify a key. It then validates that the policy includes a TPM2_PolicySigned with the public key corresponding to that role.

In this case, the policy need not have a policyRef parameter. The digital signature is over the challenge but not over any additional information specific to the signer.

USE CASE: ASSURING THAT A KEY'S AUTHORIZATION REQUIRES A BIOMETRIC

A relying party can validate that a signing key's policy includes a fingerprint authorization, indicated by a TPM2_PolicySigned with the fingerprint reader's public key and a policyRef parameter referring to a particular user identity.

This case is a variation of the previous case. The fingerprint reader signs not only the challenge but also a policyRef. The digital signature proves both possession of the private key and that the correct user's finger was supplied.[7]

TPM2_NV_Certify serves a similar purpose for an NV defined index. It certifies that the data at an NV index is indeed on the TPM. See Chapter 11 for details on the NV index options.

---

[7]Chapter 14 discusses the details of policies—in particular, the variations of the TPM2_PolicySigned command.

USE CASE: ASSURANCE OF NV DATA

An application is using an NV index as a counter or bit map together with a policy
for a signing key. The index is used to revoke key usage: for example, when a count
is reached or when a bit is set in a bit map. The application wants certainty that the
NV index has been updated and uses TPM_NV_Certify to get a signature over the
NV data.

USE CASE: QUOTE EQUIVALENT FOR AN NV EXTEND INDEX

An application is using a hybrid index as an extend index to effectively create a new
PCR that is authorized, under control of the application. (Using a hybrid extend index
as a PCR is explained in Chapter 11.) The explicit quote command only reports
the standard PCR values. The application can use TPM_NV_Certify to sign the
equivalent of a quote.

As with TPM2_Certify, TPM2_NV_Certify signs the NV index policy. The relying party
can validate the NV index access policy before entrusting the NV index value in another
policy.

Keys Unraveled

TPM keys have many layers of nested structures. For reference, here are several structures
unrolled down to primitive types.

The following is a typical RSA key:

```
TPM2B_PUBLIC

size                 UINT16
publicArea           TPMT_PUBLIC
 type                TPMI_ALG_PUBLIC  = TPM_ALG_RSA
 nameAlg             TPMI_ALG_HASH    = TPM_ALG_SHA256
 objectAttributes    TPMA_OBJECT
 authPolicy          TPM2B_DIGEST
  size               UINT16
  buffer             BYTE
 parameters          TPMU_PUBLIC_PARMS
  rsaDetail          TPMS_RSA_PARMS   = TPM_ALG_RSA
   symmetric         TPMT_SYM_DEF_OBJECT
                     For AES example
   Algorithm         TPMI_ALG_SYM_OBJECT
   keyBits           TPMU_SYM_KEY_BITS->TPMI_AES_KEY_BITS
```

```
        mode                    TPMU_SYM_MODE->TPMI_ALG_SYM_MODE
        details                 TPMU_SYM_DETAILS
      scheme                    TPMT_RSA_SCHEME
        scheme                  TPMI_ALG_RSA_SCHEME     = e.g., TPM_ALG_OAEP
        details                 TPMU_ASYM_SCHEME        = e.g., TPMS_SCHEME_OAEP
        keyBits                 TPMI_RSA_KEY_BITS        = e.g. 2048
        exponent                UINT32                   = default 2^16 + 1
     unique                     TPMU_PUBLIC_ID->TPM2B_PUBLIC_KEY_RSA
       size                     UINT16
       buffer                   BYTE
```

TPMT_SENSITIVE

```
sensitiveType                   TPMI_ALG_PUBLIC          = TPM_ALG_RSA
authValue                       TPM2B_AUTH (TPM2B_DIGEST)
seedValue                       TPM2B_DIGEST
sensitive                       TPMU_SENSITIVE_COMPOSITE,TPM2B_PRIVATE_KEY_RSA
  size                          UINT16
  buffer                        BYTE
```

This is a typical HMAC key:

TPM2B_PUBLIC

```
size                            UINT16
publicArea                      TPMT_PUBLIC
 type                           TPMI_ALG_PUBLIC     = TPM_ALG_KEYEDHASH
 nameAlg                        TPMI_ALG_HASH       = TPM_ALG_SHA256
 objectAttributes               TPMA_OBJECT -> UINT32
 authPolicy                     TPM2B_DIGEST
   size                         UINT16
   buffer                       BYTE
 parameters                     TPMU_PUBLIC_PARMS
  keyedHashDetail               TPMS_KEYEDHASH_PARMS
    scheme                      TPMT_KEYEDHASH_SCHEME
      scheme                    TPM_ALG_HMAC
       details                  TPMU_SCHEME_KEYEDHASH
       hmac                     TPMS_SCHEME_HMAC
        hashAlg                 TPMI_ALG_HASH       = TPM_ALG_SHA256
unique                          TPMU_PUBLIC_ID
  keyedHash                     TPM2B_DIGEST
    size                        UINT16
    buffer                      BYTE
```

```
TPMT_SENSITIVE

sensitiveType           TPMI_ALG_PUBLIC = TPM_ALG_KEYEDHASH
authValue               TPM2B_AUTH
  size                  UINT16
  buffer                BYTE
seedValue               TPM2B_DIGEST
  size                  UINT16
  buffer                BYTE
sensitive               TPMU_SENSITIVE_COMPOSITE
 bits                   TPM2B_SENSITIVE_DATA
  size                  UINT16
  buffer                BYTE
```

And this is a typical ECC key:

```
TPM2B_PUBLIC

size                    UINT16
publicArea              TPMT_PUBLIC
 type                   TPMI_ALG_PUBLIC = TPM_ALG_ECC
 nameAlg                TPMI_ALG_HASH   = TPM_ALG_SHA256
 objectAttributes       TPMA_OBJECT
 authPolicy             TPM2B_DIGEST
  size                  UINT16
  buffer                BYTE
 parameters             TPMU_PUBLIC_PARMS
  eccDetail             TPMS_ECC_PARMS
   symmetric            TPMT_SYM_DEF_OBJECT
            For AES example
    Algorithm           TPMI_ALG_SYM_OBJECT      = TPM_ALG_AES
    keyBits             TPMU_SYM_KEY_BITS->TPMI_AES_KEY_BITS
    mode                TPMU_SYM_MODE->TPMI_ALG_SYM_MODE = TPM_ALG_CBC
    details             TPMU_SYM_DETAILS
   scheme               TPMT_ECC_SCHEME
    scheme              TPMI_ALG_ECC_SCHEME     = TPM_ALG_ECDSA
    details             TPMU_SIG_SCHEME
     ecdsa              TPMS_SCHEME_ECDSA
                        TPMS_SCHEME_SIGHASH
      hashAlg           TPMI_ALG_HASH           = TPM_ALG_SHA256
   curveID              TPMI_ECC_CURVE          = TPM_ECC_NIST_P256
  kdf                   TPMT_KDF_SCHEME
   scheme               TPMI_ALG_KDF            = TPM_ALG_NULL
   details              TPMU_KDF_SCHEME
 unique                 TPMU_PUBLIC_ID
  ecc                   TPMS_ECC_POINT
   x                    TPM2B_ECC_PARAMETER
```

```
      size                UINT16
      buffer                BYTE
   y                        TPM2B_ECC_PARAMETER
      size                  UINT16
      buffer                BYTE


TPMT_SENSITIVE

sensitiveType              TPMI_ALG_PUBLIC = TPM_ALG_ECC
authValue                  TPM2B_AUTH
                           TPM2B_DIGEST
   Size                    UINT16
   Buffer                  BYTE
seedValue                  TPM2B_DIGEST
   size                    UINT16
   buffer                  BYTE
sensitive                  TPMU_SENSITIVE_COMPOSITE
   ecc                     TPM2B_ECC_PARAMETER
      size                 UINT16
      buffer               BYTE
```

Summary

A primary use of a TPM is as a hardware security module to safely store keys. The TPM stores keys on one of four hierarchies. Each hierarchy has primary (root) parent keys and trees of child keys. A parent is an encryption key, and a parent key wraps (encrypts) child keys before they leave the TPM secure boundary.

Keys can be duplicated (wrapped with a different parent), and all children are duplicated when the parent is duplicated. Duplication is subject to restrictions. Some keys are fixed to the TPM; they can't be duplicated. Some are fixed to their parent and so can only be duplicated when the parent is duplicated.

Keys can have use restrictions as well. They can be specified as only signing or only decryption keys, and they can be restricted to only signing or decrypting certain data. Finally, keys can be certified by other TPM keys, and a relying party can validate the public key, the key's attributes, and even its policy.

CHAPTER 11

■ ■ ■

NV Indexes

The TPM requires the use of nonvolatile memory for two general classes of data:

- Data structures defined by the TPM architecture.

- Unstructured data defined by a user or a platform-specific specification

One use of TPM nonvolatile memory is for architecturally defined data, or fields defined in the TPM library specification. This includes hierarchy authorization values, seeds and proofs, and private data that the TPM won't reveal outside its secure boundary. It also includes counters, a clock, and more: nonvolatile data that the caller can read. Nonvolatile memory can also hold structured data made persistent, such as a key.

This section describes a second use of NV memory: unstructured platform or user-defined space. This is sometimes called a *user-defined index*, because the user assigns an index (a handle) to each area and accesses data using the index value.

TPM 1.2 includes user-defined indexes that can hold unstructured data. The user defines the size and attributes of the index. The user can write data without any restriction on the data value. The TPM provides authorization, controlling access to the index via a shared secret keyed-hash message authentication code (HMAC) key, Platform Configuration Register (PCR) values, locality, and physical presence, and provides various read and write locks.

TPM 2.0 expands the 1.2 features in several ways:

- An index can have the state "uninitialized, not yet written." Reads will fail until the index is first written. Further, the index can't be used in a policy. A party relying on a value can be assured that a party with write authority initialized the index and that the data doesn't simply have a default or uninitialized value.

- As with any other protected entity, TPM 2.0 indexes may have either an authorization value or a policy.

- Another entity's policy can include an NV index value. The policy specifies an operation to be performed on all or part of the index value: a comparison to policy data. The operations include equal, not equal, signed, and unsigned comparisons, and a check for bits set or clear.

Another new NV index feature is the data type. It augments the 1.2 unstructured data type (now called *ordinary*) with three others, giving four NV index types:

- Ordinary
- Counter
- Bit field
- Extend

NV Ordinary Index

An ordinary index is like a TPM 1.2 index. It holds unstructured data of arbitrary length. In contrast with counter, bit-field, and extend indexes, there is no restriction on the type of data that can be written.

USE CASE: STORING A SECRET

A platform contains a 20-byte secret that must be available early in a boot cycle. It stores the secret in an NV index. The index attribute TPMA_NV_PPREAD specifies that reads require platform authorization. The platform software, running early in the boot cycle, knows this authorization and so can read the secret. It's trusted not to reveal the secret once it completes its task. Because other software later in the boot cycle or beyond doesn't know the platform authorization, it can't read the secret.

The TPM commands are as follows:

- TPM2_NV_DefineSpace: Create an ordinary index, size = 20 bytes, with platform authorization to read and write
- TPM2_NV_Read: Uses platform authorization

USE CASE: STORING A CERTIFICATE

A platform OEM creates a certificate stating that an endorsement key is fixed to the platform and that the platform was manufactured with certain security guarantees. The OEM stores the certificate in NV during manufacturing. Read access is unrestricted. Write access is restricted by policy to the OEM and is used to update the certificate.

The TPM commands are as follows:

- TPM2_NV_DefineSpace: Create an ordinary index, size of certificate, platform authorization to write, read with authorization value, and a null (zero-length) password

- TPM2_NV_Write: Run with platform authorization

- TPM2_NV_Read: Run with a null password

USE CASE: STORING A COMMON PASSWORD

A user creates a set of keys with an identical policy, authorizing use if a password in the NV authorization field is known. The user permits access to all keys by supplying the correct secret value. The user writes one NV location to change the common password for all keys.

The TPM commands are as follows:

1. TPM2_NV_DefineSpace: ordinary index, size = 0 bytes (the NV data is not used in this use case), common password, policy password to change authorization.

2. Create a common policy: TPM2_PolicySecret with the name of the NV index.

3. TPM2_Create: Creates multiple keys with the common policy. userWithAuth is clear so that a policy is mandatory.

4. TPM2_NV_ChangeAuth: Changes the password for all keys in one operation, using the current password.

USE CASE: STORING A ROOT PUBLIC KEY

The IT administrator places the hash of a public key in NVRAM, which is locked so the user can't write to it. It's used to verify a public key, which is used in turn to verify that signatures are from IT. Or it's the hash of the root public key of the certificate chain.

The TPM commands are as follows:

1. IT creates the signing key and digests the public key.

2. Create a read policy: TPM2_PolicyCommandCode with the command TPM2_NV_Read. This policy allows anyone to read the index essentially without authorization.

3. TPM2_NV_DefineSpace - ordinary index, size = digest size, IT administrator password, password to write, policy to read with the above read policy.

4. TPM2_NV_Write - with the IT admin password, storing the public key digest.

And here's how to verify a signature:

1. TPM2_NV_Read read the public key digest.

2. Validate the public key against the digest.

3. Validate the signature against the public key.

USE CASE: STORING AN HMAC KEY

In the Linux Integrity Measurement Architecture (IMA) Extended Verification Module (EVM), store an HMAC key that is released to the kernel early in the boot and then used by the kernel to verify the extended attributes of files to see that they have been approved for loading or use by the kernel.

The TPM commands are as follows:

- TPM2_NV_DefineSpace - ordinary index, size = HMAC key size, IT administrator password, password to write, policy to read with the above (anyone can read) read policy

- TPM2_NV_Write: With the IT admin password, stores the HMAC key

- TPM2_NV_Read: Reads the HMAC key

NV Counter Index

An *NV counter* is a 64-bit value that can only increment. At the beginning of the first increment command, it's initialized to the largest value that any counter has ever had on the TPM. This includes counter indexes currently defined and counters that were defined in the past but are no longer on the TPM. Thus a counter can never roll back, even by deleting and re-creating the index.

TPM 1.2 users might be familiar with monotonic counters. These NV counters are the equivalent, but the user is free to define none or as many as are needed up to TPM resource limits.

USE CASE: REVOKING ACCESS TO A KEY

A key holder wants to revoke access to a key. The key is created with a policy that says the key can be used (the policy can be satisfied) as long as the counter value is equal to its current value. Incrementing the counter revokes access.

The TPM commands are as follows:

TPM2_NV_DefineSpace: counter index, password of key holder, password to write, and a policy to read. The policy is TPM2_PolicyCommandCode with the command TPM2_PolicyNV. This policy allows anyone to use the index in a policy essentially without authorization.

TPM2_Create: Create a key with userWithAuth clear, requiring a policy to authorize the key. The policy is TPM2_PolicyNV with the NV value equal to all zero.

TPM2_NV_Increment: Revokes authorization to use the key.

NV Bit Field Index

A bit field contains 64 bits, initialized to all bits clear at the beginning of the first write, which can also optionally set bits. A bit (or bits) can then be set but never cleared.

USE CASE: MULTIPLE-USER KEY REVOCATION

A key holder wants to grant and later revoke access to a key for up to 64 users. The key is created with a policy with up to 64 OR terms. Each term combines some authorization specific to each user (a biometric or smart card digital signature, for example) and an assigned bit being clear. The key is revoked for that user by setting the bit in the NV bit field.

The TPM commands are as follows:

TPM2_NV_DefineSpace: bit field index, password of key holder, password to write, and a policy to read. The policy is TPM2_PolicyCommandCode with the command TPM2_PolicyNV. This policy allows anyone to use the index in a policy essentially without authorization.

TPM2_Create: Create a key with userWithAuth clear, requiring a policy to authorize the key. The policy is TPM2_PolicyNV with the operand TPM_EO_BITCLEAR (the bit assigned to the user is clear).

TPM2_NV_SetBits: Setting the bit assigned to the user, thus revoking authorization to use the key.

NV Extend Index

An extend index is defined with a specified hash algorithm, and it's fixed for the lifetime of the index. The data size of the index is based on its hash algorithm. It's initialized to all zero before the first write. The write is an extend operation, similar to that performed on a PCR.

The most likely use case combines an extend and a hybrid index to create flexible PCRs, as discussed in the "Hybrid Index" section. Another general use case is a secure audit log, because any extend operation creates a cryptographic history that can't be reversed.

USE CASE: SECURE AUDIT LOG OF CA KEY USE

A certificate authority wants to log each time its key is used to sign a certificate. It wants to be able to detect whether the log, kept on disk, has been altered. It creates an NV extend index for which it has exclusive write authority through a policy.

Each time the CA signs a new certificate, it logs the certificate and extends a digest of the certificate into the NV index. To validate the log, it walks the log, re-creating the extend value, and compares it to the NV index value. For additional security, it can even get a signature over the NV index value.

The TPM commands are as follows:

- TPM2_NV_DefineSpace: extend index, policy to write by CA, and a policy to read by anyone. The CA signs a certificate, logs the certificate in an audit log, and digests the certificate.

- TPM2_NV_Extend: Adds the digest to the NV audit log. If the certificate is small enough, it can be extended directly. However, it's probably faster to digest outside the TPM and extend just a digest.

Hybrid Index

Yet another new TPM 2.0 feature is the hybrid index. As with a nonhybrid, the NV index metadata (its index handle, size, attributes, policy, and password) are nonvolatile; its data is created in volatile memory. Except for hybrid counters (described later) the index data is only written to NV memory on an orderly shutdown. Any of the four index types (ordinary, counter, bit-field, or extend) can be a hybrid index.

Hybrid indexes may be appropriate when the application expects frequent writes. Because NV technology is often subject to wear out, a TPM may protect itself by refusing to write at a high rate. Volatile memory doesn't have wear-out issues, so a hybrid index can be written as often as required.

Hybrid index data may only be present in volatile memory if the index is deleted before an orderly shutdown. An application could define the index, write data, use the values in a policy, and then delete the index.

USE CASE: ADDITIONAL PCRS

The simplest use case is adding PCRs beyond the number the TPM vendor provides, typically 24 for a PC Client TPM. As with the permanent PCRs, the index persists through power cycles, but the value is reset back to zero. This means PCRs are no longer a scarce resource ("beach front property," in TCG work group slang).

The TPM commands are as follows:

- TPM2_NV_DefineSpace: hybrid extend index, well known
  null password, so that anyone can read and extend

- TPM2_NV_Extend: Now equivalent to TPM2_PCR_Extend

USE CASE: PCRS WITH DIFFERENT ATTRIBUTES

An application requires PCRs, but the standard TPM PCRs have fixed attributes specified by the platform. For example, the operating system may restrict access, the application may want PCR authorization restrictions, the application may need a hash algorithm different from those in effect for the TPM PCRs, or the application might want extends restricted to an extended locality.

The application creates a hybrid extend index with the desired attributes, uses them as PCRs, and then deletes the index when the application terminates. Note that, because the index is a hybrid, the extend doesn't write NV memory, avoiding performance and wear-out issues.

The TPM commands are as follows:

- TPM2_NV_DefineSpace: hybrid extend index, application-specific digest algorithm, application-specific extend policy more restrictive than "anyone can extend."

- TPM2_NV_Extend: as needed by the application.

- TPM2_NV_UndefineSpace: when the application terminates.

These PCRs can have read authorizations: policy authorizations for either read or write different from those of the platform. They can be used in virtual TPMs to record the state of a helper VM inside the vTPM of a VM (see the Virtualization Specification).

USE CASE: VIRTUALIZATION

A VMM creates an NV extend hybrid index for each VM. When the VMM creates a VM, it creates a corresponding PCR using a hybrid extend index. As the VMM starts the VM, it uses introspection to read and measure the VM's boot code, extending the measurements into the VM's PCR.

This requires a single command:

TPM2_NV_DefineSpace: Create a hybrid extend index

Hybrid ordinary, extend, and bit-field indexes are only written to NV memory on an orderly shutdown. Hybrid counters are more complicated because of the restriction that they never roll back or miss an increment operation. This must be ensured even if the shutdown isn't orderly, when the volatile value would be written to NV memory.

To achieve this, the value is written (flushed) to NV memory every so many increments. Thus a hybrid counter may not be solely in volatile memory, even if it's deleted before an orderly shutdown. If an application wants to avoid the flush, or at least determine when it will occur, a get capability command can report the flush period.

The second hybrid counter complication occurs on startup. If the most recent value wasn't flushed to NV (through an orderly shutdown), the count is set to the highest value it could have had without causing a flush. That is, it might skip some counts, but it will never roll back or miss an increment.

NV Access Controls

We previously discussed the major NV attributes: whether it's an ordinary, counter, bit-field, or extend index, and whether it's a hybrid index. An NV index also has unique controls that are different from objects like keys. Perhaps the most interesting is that it can have separate controls for read and write. In particular, each index can be defined to use its policy, its password authorization, or the owner password or authorization, and the attributes can be set independently for read and write.

The TPM supports a set of NV index read and write locks. An index may be write-locked permanently. It can be write- or read-locked until the next TPM reset or restart. An index may be part of one set of indexes that can be locked in one operation (a global lock), again until the next reset or restart.

Finally, many TPM entities are protected by the dictionary-attack protection mechanism. After some number of failed authorization attempts, the TPM rejects authorization until a certain amount of time has passed. An NV index may be protected as well, but an attribute can be set to remove the protection. Removing the protection might be applicable if the authorization password is known to be a strong secret.

NV Written

Each NV index, when first created, has an implied value: not written. In TPM 1.2, an index was always created with all-zero data. A read could not distinguish between all-zero data and a not-yet-written index. In TPM 2.0, not written is a separate state. A policy can specify that the index must or must not be written.

USE CASE: WRITE-ONCE NV INDEX

The creator wants an index that can be written exactly once, perhaps during provisioning. Once written, it can be read by anyone with the correct password.

To implement this, create an OR policy with two terms. The first term permits the NV Write command code only if the index has not been written. The second term permits a read if the index has been written and the password is supplied.

Here are the steps:

1. Create a policy with two terms:

   - TPM2_PolicyCommandCode (TPM2_NV_Write) *AND* TPM2_PolicyNvWritten (writtenSet clear)

   - TPM2_PolicyCommandCode (TPM2_NV_Read) *AND* TPM2_PolicyPassword

2. TPM2_NV_DefineSpace - create an ordinary index, policy to write and read.

NV Index Handle Values

When the user creates an NV index, the user assigns an index value.[1] In TPM 1.2, certain bits had special properties, such as the D bit used for locking. In the TPM 2.0 library specification, there is no index assignment other than an overall handle range, and no bits of the index value have any special meaning. The TPM doesn't enforce any index properties based on the index value. However, platform-specific specifications or a global TCG registry can assign index values.

For example, the TCG registry assigns handle ranges to the TPM manufacturer (specifically, 0 to 0x3fffff), to the platform manufacturer, and for endorsement and platform certificates. It further reserves ranges for platform-specific specifications, such as the PC Client, server, mobile, and embedded platforms. All these assignments are by convention and aren't enforced in any way by (current) TPMs.

USE CASE: STANDARD CERTIFICATES

We expect that the TCG Infrastructure work group will define standard NV indexes for endorsement key certificates. Whereas TPM 1.2 has two such certificates, for the TPM vendor and for the platform OEM, TPM 2.0 can have certificates for multiple key algorithms and even different creation templates.

Although the previous assignments are solely by convention, a TCG work group can also assign NV index values with implicit hardware properties. For example, the TPM may contain special hardware-package pins for general-purpose IO, called GPIO pins in the library and platform specifications. The platform specification determines the properties of the GPIO pins, including the following:

- The number of pins

- The assignment of a pin to an NV index value

- Whether a pin is mandatory or optional

- Whether the pin is fixed as an input or output, or is programmable

- Whether an output is volatile or persistent

- Whether the assignment is fixed by the TPM vendor firmware during manufacturing, or the index must be defined programmatically by the end user using the TPM_NV_DefineSpace command

The NV data is a hardware pin, but the NV metadata is identical to that of other indexes. Thus the GPIO comes with the full range of NV index controls, including an authorization value or policy, read and write controls, and locking features.

---

[1]This is different from starting a session or loading an object, where the TPM assigns the handle.

NV Names

The Name of a TPM entity uniquely (and cryptographically) defines the entity and is used for authorization. For an NV index, it's a hash of the public area, which includes the index (the handle), the attributes (including whether it has been written), the policy, and the size.

TPM2_PolicyNV permits an NV index value to be used in a policy. The policy can be based on a range of logical and arithmetic operations on the index. If the policy were based merely on the NV index value, it would offer little security: an attacker could delete the index and replace it with one with different access controls. For that reason, TPM2_PolicyNV uses the Name.

An example might help. Suppose you create an NV bit-field index that you intend to use for key revocation. The policy for the key includes a TPM2_PolicyNV term that can only be satisfied if the NV bit 0 is clear. The policy for the NV index says only the owner of a private key can write the index (TPM2_PolicySigned). To revoke the key, the owner signs a nonce to satisfy the NV policy and then sets bit 0 (TPM2_NV_SetBits).

Now suppose an attacker tries to remove the key revocation. They can't clear bit 0, because a bit-field index bit can only be set, never cleared. So, the attacker tries something more promising: they delete the index and re-create it with exactly the same Name. This fails because TPM2_PolicySigned fails on an index that has not yet been written. The attacker can't write the index because it can't satisfy the NV index policy TPM2_PolicySigned term.

The attacker makes one final attempt. They delete the index and re-create it with a policy that they can satisfy. They then write the index so that bit 0 is clear and use that index to authorize the key's policy using TPM2_PolicyNV. Because bit 0 is clear, it appears that the policy should succeed. However, the attacker had to change the policy, which causes the Name to change. When the new Name is used in TPM2_PolicyNV, the key's policy evaluation fails.

In summary, the "delete and re-create an index" attack fails because of two TPM features:

- An NV index can't be used in a policy until it has been written.

- The NV index in a policy uses the entire Name (public area), not just the index handle.

USE CASE: WRITE ONCE, READ ALWAYS NV INDEX

The user desires to create an index that they can write exactly once and that can then be read by anyone. An example is provisioning the TPM with a certificate.

The index has two OR terms. The first policy term is satisfied when the index has not been written and the owner supplies the correct password; it permits only the NV write command. The second term is satisfied once the index has been written; it permits only the NV read command.

Another subtle point is that the Name changes when the index is written, because the index public area includes the written attribute.

USE CASE: SECURING A POLICY SECRET

A policy secret permits authorization for a set of objects to be linked to a single secret. For example, a set of keys can have identical policies that authorize the key if an NV index-authorization password is known. The policy would use the NV index Name after it has been written.

■ **Note** TPM2_PolicySecret ties authorization to the NV password. TPM2_PolicyNV ties authorization to the NV data.

If the Name didn't change when the index was written, an attacker could delete the index and create a new one with the same Name but their own secret and thus gain access to keys tied to the secret. The attack doesn't work, because the attacker's index has not been written and thus has a different Name than the one required in the key's policy.

It's assumed here that the NV index policy (part of the Name) prevents the attacker from writing the index. For example, the NV write policy might require authentication with a public key (TPM2_PolicySigned).

■ **Note** Observe that the data value written to NV doesn't matter and serves only to prove that the index creator can write the index. The key policy is tied to the NV password, not the NV data.

The previous use case demonstrates an interesting property. You can create an NV index with a Name that no one else can reproduce. If the Name includes having written set, and the policy is such that only you can write the index, then only you can create that Name. This ensures that a policy points to your NV index, not one that an attacker created.

Further, the same NV index with the same Name can be created on multiple TPMs.

USE CASE DUPLICATING A SET OF KEYS

In the previous use case, the authorization for a set of keys was tied to an NV index password. A user can duplicate a set of keys to another TPM. Then the user can create an NV index with the same Name on that TPM so that the key's policy can be satisfied on the new TPM.

NV Password

A subtlety of the TPM is that a user can't really change an object's password. The TPM2_ObjectChangeAuth command can create an object with the new password, but the original object still exists. The user can delete all existing copies of the object, but the TPM can't enforce this.

This quirk isn't true of an NV index. The index exists only on the TPM. It can never be context-saved or in any way moved off the TPM. Thus, TPM2_NV_ChangeAuth really does change the password.

Separate Commands

The TPM API defines a set of commands dedicated to NV. TPM2_NV_DefineSpace creates an NV index. The caller specifies the NV metadata, including the size for an ordinary index, the policy, attributes, and the password. As explained earlier, a newly created index isn't initialized, or written, yet. It has no data.

The write commands are as follows:

- TPM2_NV_Write writes an ordinary index. Depending on the attributes, partial writes may or may not be permitted.

- TPM2_NV_Increment increments a counter index. Depending on the attributes and the count value, this may cause a write to nonvolatile memory.

- TPM2_NV_Extend extends arbitrary data (not necessarily a hash value) to an extend index.

- TPM2_NV_SetBits sets bits in a bit-field index. It ORs the current value and the input. An input of all zero is legally and useful. It makes the index written and initializes it to all zero.

TPM2_NV_Read reads any index data. A read can only occur after the index has been written at least once. TPM2_NV_ReadPublic reads the index public data. In combination with the session audit feature, a user can get a signature over the public area to prove its properties.

Several commands are dedicated to locking an index. The index attributes determine whether these locks can be set against a particular index:

- TPM2_NV_WriteLock can lock an index, forbidding further writes until the next boot cycle or forever.

- TPM2_NV_GlobalWriteLock can lock a set of indexes, again either forever or until the next boot cycle.

- TPM2_NV_ReadLock locks an index, preventing further reads until the next boot cycle.

TPM2_NV_ChangeAuth changes the index password. TPM2_NV_Certify can create a signature over index data. This command is optional in the PC Client specification. However, a similar result can be obtained by reading the index in an audit session and then getting a signed audit digest.

Summary

TPM 2.0 has four types of NV indexes: ordinary (unstructured data), bit-field, counter, and extend data indexes. An index can be read or written using the standard TPM password and policy controls. Hybrid indexes normally exist in volatile memory, but an orderly shutdown can save them to NV memory. They can avoid performance and wear-out issues. When an index is created, its state is "not written". Its data can't be read or used in a policy until it's written, and the "not written" state itself can be used on a policy.

Basic applications include provisioning with certificates or public keys. More advanced applications use an NV authorization in a policy, permitting it to be shared among entities. A policy referring to a bit-field or counter index value can be used for key revocation. An extend index offers PCR equivalents with different algorithms, authorizations, or lifetimes.

NV indexes have a separate set of commands and unique attributes to control authorization, read and write locking, and dictionary-attack protection.

■ ■ ■

## CHAPTER 12

Platform Configuration Registers

Platform Configuration Registers (PCRs) are one of the essential features of a TPM. Their prime use case is to provide a method to cryptographically record (measure) software state: both the software running on a platform and configuration data used by that software. The PCR update calculation, called an *extend*, is a one-way hash so that measurements can't be removed. These PCRs can then be read to report their state. They can also be signed to return a more secure report, called an *attestation* (or *quote*). PCRs can also be used in an extended authorization policy to restrict the use of other objects.

The TPM never passes judgment on the measurements. Internally, it doesn't know which measurements are good or bad, or more or less secure or trusted. At the time of measurement, TPM PCRs just record values. Security or trust comes later, when an application uses PCR values in an authorization policy, or a remote party asks for a signed attestation (quote) of the values and judges their trustworthiness.

New for TPM 2.0, TPMs no longer hard-code the SHA-1 algorithm for PCRs. The algorithm can be changed. Some implementations include banks of PCRs, with each bank implementing a different algorithm.

A TPM implements a number of PCRs: for example, 24 for a PC TPM. The PCRs are allocated by convention to the various software layers, from early boot code to the operating system and applications. They're also allocated for both the software to be run (often the even-numbered PCRs) and the configuration files that customize the boot process (typically the odd-numbered PCRs.)

PCR Value

The primary use case for a PCR is to represent the platform software state, the history of the critical software (and configurations) that have run on the platform until the present. The TPM initializes all PCRs at power on, typically to either all zeroes or all ones, as specified by the TPM platform specification. The caller can't directly write a PCR value. Rather, a PCR value is changed through what the TPM calls an *extend* operation, as described in Chapter 2. Cryptographically, it is as follows:

```
PCR new value = Digest of (PCR old value || data to extend)
```

In words, it takes the old PCR value and concatenates some data to be extended. The data to be extended is almost always a digest, although the TPM can't enforce this. The TPM digests the result of the concatenation and stores the resulting digest as the new PCR value.

After reboot, a platform begins with trusted software called the *core root of trust measurement (CRTM)*. The CRTM measures (calculate a digest of) the next software to be run and extends that digest into an even PCR. It then extends that software's configuration data into an odd PCR. This software, perhaps a BIOS, in turn measures and extends the next software, perhaps a master boot record. The measurement chain continues through the early OS kernel code and perhaps further. Security-critical configuration files are also measured.

The net result is that the PCR value represents the history of all measurements extended into it. Because of the one-way nature of a secure digest, there is no way to undo a measurement (to extend the PCR back to a desired value).

As a typical example, the PC Client specification allocates the PCRs as shown in Table 12-1.

Table 12-1. *Example PCR Allocation*

PCR Number	Allocation
0	BIOS
1	BIOS configuration
2	Option ROMs
3	Option ROM configuration
4	MBR (master boot record)
5	MBR configuration
6	State transitions and wake events
7	Platform manufacturer specific measurements
8–15	Static operating system
16	Debug
23	Application support

The security of this process depends on the security of the CRTM. The CRTM, being the first software to run, can't be measured or validated. It's a *root of trust*. The platform manufacturer can protect the CRTM from attack by making it immutable, putting it in ROM, or otherwise preventing software updates. Because this precludes bug fixes, an alternate method is to use signed code and have the current CRTM validate the signature before updating itself.

The Linux open source Integrity Measurement Architecture (IMA) integrates boot-time measurements into the kernel. An IMA policy determines which software elements are measured. These typically include libraries and executables run under root privilege during boot, as well as Linux configuration files that determine the boot path. It doesn't typically measure user-level applications.

Number of PCRs

In practice, a TPM contains multiple PCRs. The PC Client platform requires 24 PCRs, and this minimum is expected to be the actual number in PCs. Automotive TPMs may have many more. The platform TPM specification specifies the PCR attributes, and a platform software specification standardizes what measurements go into which PCRs.

The platform specifications may set aside several PCRs for user-level applications. And one PCR (16), the debug PCR, is reserved for testing software. As such, it's resettable without a power cycle.

As described in Chapter 11, TPM 2.0 provides for user-defined NV extend indexes, which are essentially PCRs. They have additional flexibility in that the hash algorithm, password, and policy can be individually set for each index. The metadata (mainly algorithm and authorization) is nonvolatile, whereas the actual data values are likely to be volatile through the use of a hybrid index.

The remainder of this chapter is limited to architecturally defined PCRs.

PCR Commands

PCR commands include the following:

- TPM2_PCR_Extend: Likely to be the most-used PCR command. Extends a digest into a PCR.

- TPM2_PCR_Event: Permits the TPM to do the digest and then extend the digest in one operation. The message is limited to 1,024 bytes.

- TPM_PCR_Read: Reads a PCR, which is useful when validating an event log as described later.

- TPM2_PCR_Reset: Resets a PCR, which is useful for some application-defined PCRs that permit this. Most PCRs can't be reset.

- TPM_PCR_Allocate: Assigns digest algorithms to PCRs. This is likely to be done once at most, if the default algorithm is to be changed.

- TPM2_PCR_SetAuthPolicy: Assigns an authorization policy to a PCR group. It isn't required in the PC Client.

- TPM2_PCR_SetAuthValue: Assigns an authorization value to a PCR group. It isn't required in the PC Client.

PCRs for Authorization

Authorization is a common use for PCRs. An entity can have a policy that prevents it from being used unless specific PCRs have specific values. Chapter 14 explains this in detail. The policy can specify a subset of PCRs and a value for each. Unless the PCRs are in this state, the policy is not satisfied and the entity can't be accessed.

USE CASE: SEALING A HARD DISK ENCRYPTION KEY TO PLATFORM STATE

Full-disk encryption applications are far more secure if a TPM protects the encryption key than if it's stored on the same disk, protected only by a password. First, the TPM hardware has anti-hammering protection (see Chapter 8 for a detailed description of TPM dictionary attack protection), making a brute-force attack on the password impractical. A key protected only by software is far more vulnerable to a weak password. Second, a software key stored on disk is far easier to steal. Take the disk (or a backup of the disk), and you get the key. When a TPM holds the key, the entire platform, or at least the disk and the motherboard, must be stolen.

Sealing permits the key to be protected not only by a password but by a policy. A typical policy locks the key to PCR values (the software state) current at the time of sealing. This assumes that the state at first boot isn't compromised. Any preinstalled malware present at first boot would be measured into the PCRs, and thus the key would be sealed to a compromised software state. A less trusting enterprise might have a standard disk image and seal to PCRs representing that image. These PCR values would be precalculated on a presumably more trusted platform. An even more sophisticated enterprise would use TPM2_PolicyAuthorize, and provide several tickets authorizing a set of trusted PCR values. See Chapter 14 for a detailed description of policy authorize and its application to solve the PCR brittleness problem.

Although a password could also protect the key, there is a security gain even without a TPM key password. An attacker could boot the platform without supplying a TPM key password but could not log in without the OS username and password. The OS security protects the data. The attacker could boot an alternative OS, say from a live DVD or USB stick rather that from the hard drive, to bypass the OS login security. However, this different boot configuration and software would change the PCR values. Because these new PCRs would not match the sealed values, the TPM would not release the decryption key, and the hard drive could not be decrypted.

These are the steps to seal:

1. Construct the policy, a TPM2_PolicyPCR, specifying the PCR values that must be present at the time of the unseal operation.

2. Use either of the following (similar to TPM 1.2 seal)

   - TPM2_GetRandom() to create the symmetric key external to the TPM

   - TPM2_Create(), specifying the symmetric key and the policy to create the sealed object

   - or (new TPM 2.0 alternative)

   - TPM2_Create(), specifying just the policy, to let the TPM create the symmetric key used in the sealed data object

Use the following to unseal:

   - TPM2_Load() to load the object

   - TPM2_PolicyPCR() to satisfy the sealed object policy

   - TPM2_Unseal() to return the symmetric key

USE CASE: VPN KEYS

Similar to the previous use case, a VPN private key can be locked to PCRs. The TPM permits the use of the VPN to connect to the enterprise intranet only if the software is in an approved state.

USE CASE: SECURELY PASSING A PASSWORD FROM THE OS PRESENT TO OS ABSENT ENVIRONMENT

A platform administrator (for example, the IT administrator) wishes to grant the end user permission to change a BIOS setting, perhaps changing the boot order. The BIOS needs the administrator password. The administrator must pass the privileged-access password to the BIOS but doesn't want to reveal the password to the end user.

The administrator seals the password to the PCR state present while the BIOS is running (after a reboot). The admin supplies this sealed password to the user at the OS level. The user can't unseal the password while the OS is running, but the BIOS can unseal and use it after a reboot.

These are the steps at the OS level:

1.   Construct a policy, a TPM2_PolicyPCR specifying that PCR[2] is all zeroes. This PCR will only have this value very early in the boot cycle, when the CRTM passes control to the first part of the BIOS.

2.   Use TPM2_Create(), specifying the password and the policy to create the sealed object. The password is supplied via an encrypted session (see Chapter 17), essentially a secure tunnel into the TPM.

These are the steps at the BIOS level:

3.   Use TPM2_Load() to load the object.

4.   Use TPM2_PolicyPCR() to satisfy the sealed object policy.

5.   Use TPM2_Unseal() to return the secret.

A typical use of PCRs for authorization would be to tie the use of an entity to the platform software state, but other uses are possible. For example, a password can be extended into a PCR, thus unlocking access. When access is no longer desired, the PCR can be reset (if permitted) or just extended with some other value.

PCRs for Attestation

Attestation is a more advanced use case for PCRs. In a non-TPM platform, remote software can't usually determine a platform's software state. If the state is reported through strictly software means, compromised software can simply lie to the remote party.

A TPM attestation offers cryptographic proof of software state. Recall that a measurement can't be undone. A PCR can't be rolled back to a previous value. The attestation is a TPM quote: a number of PCR are hashed, and that hash is signed by a TPM key. If the remote party can validate that the signing key came from an authentic TPM, it can be assured that the PCR digest report has not been altered.

We say this is a more advanced use because it's insufficient to simply validate the signature and the key's certificate. The party has to next validate that the digest of the PCR matches the reported PCR values. This is straightforward.

Next, the party has to read an event log—a log of all software and other states measured, with their hashes—and validate that the event log matches the PCR values. This is still not too hard; it just involves some math.

The TCG Infrastructure Work Group (IWG) and PC Client Work Group specify the details of the event log format. The Platform Trust Services (PTS) specification from the IWG specifies how to report measurements through Trusted Network Connect (TNC). Standardizing the logging and reporting formats permits standard software to parse and validate the log against the attestation (quote).

The Integrity Measurement Architecture (IMA) for Linux specifies an event-log file format. Typical entries looks like this and includes a PCR index, a template hash, a template name, the file hash, and a hint (untrusted) as to the file name:

```
10 88da93c09647269545a6471d86baea9e2fa9603f ima
a218e393729e8ae866f9d377da08ef16e97beab8 /usr/lib/systemd/systemd

10 e8e39d9cb0db6842028a1cab18b838d3e89d0209 ima
d9decd04bf4932026a4687b642f2fb871a9dc776 /usr/lib64/ld2.16.so

10 babcdc3f576c949591cc4a30e92a19317dc4b65a ima
028afcc7efdc253bb69cb82bc5dbbc2b1da2652c /etc/ld.so.cache

10 68549deba6003eab25d4befa2075b18a028bc9a1 ima
df2ad0965c21853874a23189f5cd76f015e348f4 /usr/lib64/libselinux.so.1
```

The hardest part comes next. Through the TPM signed attestation quote, the party knows the platform software state. It now has to decide whether that software state is secure. The party has to match the measurement hashes against a whitelist, potentially requiring cooperation from third-party software providers.

This is the essence of the Trusted Computing concept. PCRs provide a means to trust that a list of software modules indeed reflects the software state of a platform. It doesn't make any value judgments as to whether that software is secure.

USE CASE: QUOTE

A networking device wants to decide whether to let a client platform connect to a network. It wants to know whether the platform is running fully patched software. The device quotes the TPM PCR and validates the result against a whitelist of patched software modules. If the platform is current, it's permitted on the network. If not, it's routed to a patch server but not otherwise permitted network access.

The StrongSwan open source VPN solution can use the TCG TNC standard, combining TPM quotes and a policy to gate access to a VPN.[1]

---

[1]http://wiki.strongswan.org/projects/strongswan/wiki/TrustedNetworkConnect.

The Kaspersky antivirus software end user license agreement (EULA) permits the software to report on the files processed, versions of the software, and more. The license permits use of the TPM, if present, to authenticate the report.[2]

PCR Quote in Detail

It's interesting to examine the quote data in detail. Through this data, the reader can understand the security properties of the quote. A quote's structure—the structure that is hashed and signed—contains these fields:

- *Magic number* TPM_GENERATED: Prevents an attacker from signing arbitrary data with a restricted signing key and claiming later that it was a TPM quote. See Chapter 10 for the interaction between restricted signing keys and TPM_GENERATED.

- *Qualified name of the signing key*: A key could appear strong but be protected by an ancestor with a weaker algorithm. The qualified name represents the entire ancestry of the key.

- *Extra data provided by the caller*: This data is typically an anti-replay nonce, which is proof that the quote is current.

- *TPM firmware version*: Included so that the verifier can decide if it trusts a particular TPM code version.

- *TPM clock state*: The variable resetCount is of particular importance for the next use case. For privacy, the clock information is obfuscated when signing with a key outside the endorsement hierarchy.[3] This isn't an issue, because the attester only wants to detect if resetCount changes, not read its actual value.

- The type of attestation structure (a quote, in this case).

- The selection of PCRs included in the quote.

- A digest of those selected PCRs.

---

[2]http://support.kaspersky.com/8752.
[3]For a detailed explanation of this privacy issue, see the "Other Privacy Considerations" section of Chapter 9.

USE CASE: DETECTING A REBOOT BETWEEN TRANSACTIONS

A platform is performing financial transactions. A monitoring device performs a quote every 15 minutes to detect changes to the platform software state. However, an attacker sneaks in between quotes, reboots into compromised software, performs an unauthorized transaction, and then reboots the platform back to the trusted state. The next quote will show the same trusted PCR values. However, the resetCount change tells the monitoring software that two unexpected reboots occurred.

PCR Attributes

Each PCR comes with several attributes. The attributes are defined in the TPM library specification, but which PCR indexes have which attributes is left to the platform-specific specification. Generally, most PCR indexes are assigned by convention to specific software, but a few are unassigned and open for use by applications.

The PCR Reset attribute indicates whether the PCR can be reset using the TPM2_PCR_Reset command. Typically, the reset value is all zeroes. Most PCRs are not resettable, because this would permit compromised software to set the PCR value to a known good state. Some PCRs are resettable only in a certain locality, corresponding to dynamic root of trust measurement (DRTM) sequences.

The PCR Extend attribute indicates whether the PCR can be extended using the TPM2_PCR_Extend or TPM2_PCR_Event command. Obviously, a PCR that couldn't be extended would be useless, but some can be extended only in some localities.

The PCR Reset attribute via DRTM indicates whether a PCR can be extended through writes directly to the TPM interface, as opposed to the normal TPM command format. These are both platform specific and linked to the particular TPM hardware interface. This attribute typically varies by locality.

All PCRs are reset at reboot when TPM2_Startup is issued with the CLEAR parameter. Most are typically reset to all zeroes, but some can have other values, such as all ones or a value related to the locality at which the startup command was issued.

The No Increment attribute is tied to the TPM2_PolicyPCR command. A policy tied to a PCR is an immediate assertion. The PCR values at the time of the TPM2_PolicyPCR command are extended into the policy session hash. However, a PCR value could change after the immediate assertion, which should normally invalidate the policy session. This invalidation is implemented though a counter that is normally incremented whenever a PCR is changed. The policy session records the value during TPM2_PolicyPCR and then checks it when the session is used. If the count values aren't equal, the TPM knows that a PCR changed, and the policy session use fails.

Note the word *normally* in the previous paragraph. The TPM specification provides the No Increment attribute. PCRs with this attribute, when changed, don't increment the counter and thus don't invalidate policy sessions in use. Most PCRs don't have this attribute, but the PC Client specification assigns it to a debug PCR and a few reserved for applications.

USE CASE: NO INCREMENT ATTRIBUTE PCRS FOR VMS

An application-level PCR may be assigned to measure a virtual machine. This PCR
is reset because the VM is instantiated and extended frequently over the lifetime of
the VM. If each extend invalidated a policy session, the TPM2_PolicyPCR command
would be useless.

USE CASE: NO INCREMENT ATTRIBUTE PCRS FOR AUDIT

An application-level PCR may be assigned to secure an audit log. See Chapter 16
for details on this use case. This PCR is reset when the audit log is initialized and
is extended as the log is updated. If each extend invalidated a policy session, the
TPM2_PolicyPCR command would be useless.

PCR Authorization and Policy

As with other entities, a PCR may have an authorization value or policy. The library
specification permits either to be set per PCR or per group of PCRs.

The PC Client TPM has neither. No authorization is required to access the PCR.
The rationale is that authorization would increase the boot time, which is often an
important parameter.

PCR Algorithms

The first requirement that led to TPM 2.0 was the removal of TPM 1.2's hard-coding of
the SHA-1 hash algorithm. Because PCRs are closely tied to hash algorithms, TPM 2.0
theoretically offers many PCR possibilities through the TPM2_PCR_Allocate command.

The key word is *theoretically*. PCRs can be allocated in banks, with each bank
corresponding to a hash algorithm. The command permits PCRs to be allocated in any
combination, and a PCR can be assigned to more than one bank and have more than
one algorithm. The TPM2_Extend command must now specify not only a PCR index and a
digest but also an algorithm. If no index exists with that algorithm, the extend operation is
ignored.

So, in theory, software would perform multiple measurements, create multiple
digests, and then extend each digest into the appropriate bank. What does the PC Client
specification do in practice?

That specification requires only one bank with all PCRs in it. The bank defaults to
SHA-1 but can be changed to SHA-256. Although a TPM vendor is free to implement more
complicated combinations, we expect most TPMs to be operated as either purely SHA-1
or purely SHA-256. The supporting software knows the TPM's algorithm and measures,
digests, and extends accordingly.

Further, we expect that TPMs won't change algorithms very often. If fact, the most likely scenario is that it's shipped with SHA-256 and remains SHA-256 forever, or that it's shipped with SHA-1 and then updates to SHA-256 once as the support software is simultaneously updated.

Summary

PCRs have two basic uses. Their value may be reported in a signed attestation quote, permitting a relying party to determine the platform software's trust state. They may be used in a policy to authorize the use of other objects based on PCR values. Whereas TPM 1.2 PCRs were hard-coded to use the SHA-1 algorithm, TPM 2.0 PCRs can use other hash algorithms.

CHAPTER 13

■ ■ ■

Authorizations and Sessions

Authorizations and *sessions* are among the most important concepts in TPM 2.0. Authorizations control access to entities in the TPM, providing many of the security guarantees of the TPM. *Sessions* are the vehicle for *authorizations* and maintain state between subsequent commands; additionally, *sessions* configure some per-command attributes such as encryption and decryption of command and response parameters and auditing. This chapter describes sessions as they relate to authorization of actions on entities. Chapters 16 and 17 describe details of the per-command session use modifiers.

Authorizations and sessions represent a large topic, so this chapter will proceed as follows:

1.   You'll learn some new terms specific to sessions and authorizations. You are advised to review the definitions in Chapter 5 as well.

2.   You'll see password, HMAC, and policy authorizations at a high level, along with the security properties of each.

3.   The chapter clarifies the differences and commonalities between sessions and authorizations, as well as some aspects of the specification that can be confusing.

4.   You'll drill down into some aspects of authorizations that apply to all three types of authorizations: password, HMAC, and policy. You will learn about the authorization roles and the authorization area in the command and response byte streams.

5.   You will examine the different types of authorizations in detail, from simplest to most complex: password, HMAC, and policy. After looking at password authorizations, you will see some common aspects of HMAC and policy authorizations, followed by the details of HMAC and policy authorizations.

6.   Finally, all the authorization types are tied together into a combined authorization lifecycle.

This chapter doesn't describe the various policy authorization commands. Nor does it describe decrypt, encrypt, and audit sessions, other than to note that sessions are the vehicle for setting these.

This chapter uses diagrams, logical flows, and working code examples to illustrate how authorizations and sessions work. This material is foundational to understanding TPM 2.0. Get ready for a deep but rewarding dive.

Session-Related Definitions

Before you delve into this subject, you need to clearly understand some new terms. These are in addition to the terms described in Chapter 5; you should refer to those definitions as well as these while reading this chapter:

- *Session creation variations:* These are set at session creation time and last for the lifetime of the session. They determine how the session and HMAC keys are created and how the HMAC is generated. There are two choices here: bound vs. unbound, and salted vs. unsalted. The combination of these two choices results in four session variations. These are discussed in detail later. For now, here are high-level descriptions:

  - Bound sessions essentially "bind" the authorization to some entity's authorization value. This binding is done by including the bind entity's authorization value in the session key generation. This affects all calculations that depend on the session key, including HMAC, policy, encryption, and decryption calculations.

  - An unbound session doesn't use a bind entity's authorization in the session key generation.

  - A salted session adds extra entropy, the *salt*, into the session key generation; similar to bound sessions, this affects all calculations that depend on the session key. The extra entropy is sent to the TPM in encrypted form, the encrypted salt parameter which is passed in to the TPM2_StartAuthSession command.

  - An unsalted session doesn't add entropy in this way.

- *Session use modifiers:* These modify the actions of an HMAC or policy session on a per-command basis. Continue, encrypt, decrypt, and audit are the more commonly used modifiers:

  - *Continue*: If not set, the session is terminated after a successful command.

  - *Decrypt*: Indicates that the first TPM2B command parameter is sent to the TPM in encrypted form.

- *Encrypt*: Causes the first TPM2B response parameter to be returned from the TPM in encrypted form.

- *Audit*: Causes a command using the session to be audited.

Based on an understanding of these terms, I can now describe the different types of sessions.

Password, HMAC, and Policy Sessions: What Are They?

All three types of sessions are a means of authorizing actions and, in the case of HMAC and policy sessions, configuring sessions on a per-command basis. Password sessions are the simplest type of authorization: a clear text password is passed down to the TPM to authorize an action. This has obvious security issues if the TPM is being accessed remotely; the intended use of password sessions is for local access. In the TPM, there is a single, always-available password session that is used to authorize a single TPM command with no state preserved between subsequent uses. Because of this, the password session never needs to be started.

HMAC authorizations are a way of using a simple password in a more secure manner; once the calling application and the TPM agree on the password (at the time the entity is created or its authorization value is modified), there is never a need to communicate the password again. This one-time communication of the password to the TPM can be accomplished in a secure manner: that is, the password can be communicated to the TPM in encrypted form. An HMAC session accomplishes this greater level of security by using the password (authValue, as it's called in the TPM 2.0 specification) as one of the inputs into an HMAC that is calculated on commands and responses. On a command, the calling application calculates the HMAC and inserts it in the command byte stream. When the TPM receives the command byte stream, if the TPM determines that the HMAC is calculated correctly, the action is authorized. On a response, the TPM calculates an HMAC on the response and inserts it into the response byte stream. The caller independently calculates the response HMAC and compares it to the response byte stream's HMAC field. If they match, the response data can be trusted. All this works only if both the calling application and the TPM know and agree on the authValue.

HMAC sessions use two nonces—one from the caller (nonceCaller) and one from the TPM (nonceTPM)—to prevent replay attacks. These nonces factor into the HMAC calculation. Because nonceTPM changes for every command that is sent, and the calling application can, if it wants to, change nonceCaller on every command, an attacker can't replay command byte streams. Replayed command bytes streams that use HMAC authorization will always fail because the nonces will be different on the replay.

HMAC sessions maintain state during the lifetime of the session and can be used to authorize multiple actions on TPM entities. An HMAC session is started using the TPM2_StartAuthSession command. When started, HMAC sessions can be configured as bound vs. unbound and salted vs. unsalted sessions. The combination of these two options results in four variations of HMAC sessions; these four variations determine how the session key and HMACs are calculated.

Policy sessions, otherwise known as *Enhanced Authorization* (EA), are built on top of HMAC sessions and add an extra level of authorization. Whereas HMAC authorizations are based only on an authorization value or password, policy authorizations enhance this with authorizations based on TPM command sequences, TPM state, and external devices such as fingerprint readers, retina scanners, and smart cards, to name a few. Many conditions can be ANDed and ORed together into complex authorization trees, providing unlimited authorization possibilities.

Table 13-1 shows a high-level summary of the various types of authorizations.

Table 13-1. *Comparison of the Three Types of Sessions*

	Password	HMAC	Policy
State/Other Info	No state is maintained between subsequent uses.	State is maintained for the lifetime of the session.	State is maintained for the lifetime of the session. Built on top of HMAC sessions.
Security	The password is in the clear on every command; a snooper could easily grab the password.	Much more secure than a password (especially when sending commands to remote a TPM). Nonces are used to prevent replay attacks.	Enhanced security by allowing complex sequences of commands and internal and external states to authorize. Nonces are used to prevent replay attacks if an HMAC is being used.
Method of Starting	None	TPM2_ StartAuthSession	TPM2_ StartAuthSession
Per-Command Session Modifiers	None	Decrypt, encrypt, audit	Decrypt and encrypt

With that under your belt, let's look at some important nuances in how the specification uses the terms *session* and *authorization*. Pay attention here; understanding these will greatly enhance your ability to read and understand the TPM 2.0 specification as well as the rest of this chapter.

Session and Authorization: Compared and Contrasted

Sessions and authorizations are closely related and sometimes overlapping concepts in the TPM 2.0 specification, but they are not synonymous terms. Sessions are the vehicle for authorizations, but they're also used for purposes other than authorization, in conjunction with authorizations or completely independent of them. For example, sessions used for authorization can also be used to specify per-command modifiers such as encrypt, decrypt, and audit. Sessions can also be used for these per-command modifiers without being simultaneously used for any authorizations at all.

The TPM 2.0 specification itself often overlaps the terms *session* and *authorization*. Here are some examples of this in the specification:

- The *authorization area*[1] in commands is used for both authorizations and sessions. But sessions can be used in ways that have nothing to do with authorization. For instance, they can be used to set up encryption and decryption of command and response parameters and to enable auditing of commands. Sessions that have nothing to do with authorization can be configured for these purposes.

- The TPM_ST_NO_SESSIONS and TPM_ST_SESSIONS tags are used to indicate whether an authorization area is present in a command, an obvious lack of consistency in nomenclature.

- Sessions are started with the TPM2_StartAuthSession command. The name of the command indicates that an authorization is being started, but in fact a session is being started by this command.[2] The session being started might never be used for authorization.

- Another case is password authorizations. Technically these are sessions, but no state is maintained between subsequent commands, and TPM2_StartAuthSession isn't used to start a password "session". A password authorization is a one-shot authorization that applies to only one command.

The reason for noting these aspects is to help you comprehend the specification. Understanding the distinctions between these blurred usages of terms helped me as I was struggling to understand these concepts. As a result, I developed diagrams to help categorize the various types of authorizations, sessions, and session modifiers. Hopefully these will help you, too.

---

[1] A more technically accurate name for this would have been the *sessions area*.
[2] A more technically accurate name for this command would have been TPM2_StartSession.

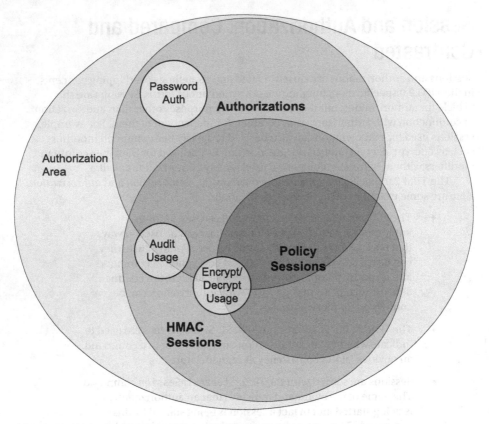

Figure 13-1. *Authorizations and sessions Venn diagram*

The following points are of special note in this diagram:

- Authorizations can be password, HMAC, or policy authorizations.
- Password authorizations can never be used for session use modifiers.

■ **Note**   In Figure 13-1, audit, encrypt, or decrypt are the only session use modifiers shown, but there are others. These three are shown because they're the more commonly used ones.

- HMAC and policy sessions can be used for authorizations but can also be used to set session-use modifiers apart from any authorization. This why the HMAC and policy sessions straddle the authorization circle's boundary.

- The command's authorization area is where all of these authorizations, sessions, and session modifiers are specified.

- Command modifiers can be used in sessions used for authorization as well as those that aren't, which is why the audit, encrypt, and decrypt circles straddle the authorization circle's boundary.

- Sessions that aren't used for authorization can also be in the authorization area of the command and response byte streams.

- Policy sessions can be used for encrypt or decrypt, but not for audit.[3]

- HMAC sessions can be used for encrypt, decrypt, and/or audit.

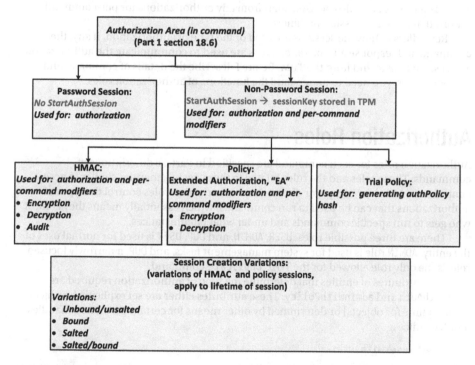

Figure 13-2. Authorizations and sessions block diagram

---

[3]According to the TPM 2.0 specification developers, this was an optimization and not due to any fundamental technical difficulty.

Figure 13-2 illustrates the relationship somewhat differently. Note the following points in this diagram:

- The authorization area can specify the parameters for password, HMAC, or policy sessions. The authorization area is described in detail in the next section.

- Sessions started with the TPM2_StartAuthSession command can be HMAC, policy, or trial policy sessions.

- HMAC sessions can be configured on a per-command basis to be audit, decrypt, and/or encrypt sessions.

- Policy sessions can be configured on a per-command basis to be decrypt and/or encrypt sessions. They cannot be used for audit.

- The four session initialization variations can apply to HMAC, policy, or trial policy sessions.

The important things to remember are that sessions are the vehicle for authorizations but can also be used apart from any authorizations for per-command actions that are set by session modifiers.

Regardless of how the sessions are used or the type of authorization, if any, the command and response authorization areas are used to communicate the authorization and session data to and from the TPM. Before I describe the details of command and response areas, you need to understand the functions of authorization roles.

Authorization Roles

Authorization roles for each command are specified in Part 3's descriptions of commands. These roles and the rules related to them act in a manner similar to access control lists (ACLs) for computer directories. Authorization roles control the types of authorizations that can be used to run commands, which essentially means they control who gets to run specific commands and under what circumstances.

There are three possible roles: USER, ADMIN, and DUP. USER is used for normal uses of the entity, ADMIN role is used for system management tasks, and DUP, a narrowly focused role, is the only role allowed for the TPM2_Duplicate command.

Two attributes of entities that determine the type of authorization required are userWithAuth and adminWithPolicy. These attributes either are set explicitly (at object creation time for objects) or determined by other means for certain permanent handles and NV indices:

- userWithAuth:

  - Set means USER role authorization can be provided by a password, HMAC, or policy session.

  - Clear means USER role authorization must be provided by a policy session.

- `adminWithPolicy`:

  - `Set` means `ADMIN` role authorization must be provided by a policy session.[4]

  - `Clear` means `ADMIN` role authorization can be provided by a password, HMAC, or policy session.

If the authorization role is `ADMIN`:

- For object handles, the required authorization is determined by the object's `adminWithPolicy` attribute, which is set when the object is created.

- For the handles `TPM_RH_OWNER`, `TPM_RH_ENDORSEMENT`, and `TPM_RH_PLATFORM`, the required authorization is as if `adminWithPolicy` is set.

- For NV indices, the required authorization is as if the `adminWithPolicy` attribute was set when the NV index was created.

If authorization role is `USER`:

- For object handles, the required authorization is determined by the object's `userWithAuth` attribute, which is set when the object is created.

- For the handles `TPM_RH_OWNER`, `TPM_RH_ENDORSEMENT`, and `TPM_RH_PLATFORM`, the required authorization is as if `userWithAuth` is set.

- For NV index handles, the required authorization is determined by the following NV index attributes: `TPMA_NV_POLICYWRITE`, `TPMA_NV_POLICYREAD`, `TPMA_NV_AUTHWRITE`, and `TPMA_NV_AUTHREAD`. These attributes are set when the NV index is created.

---

[4]A more accurate name for this attribute would have been `adminOnlyWithPolicy`.

If the authorization role is DUP:

- The authorization must be a policy authorization.

- The DUP role is only used for objects.

If the authorization role is DUP or ADMIN, the command being authorized must be specified in the policy.

Now that you understand roles, let's look at the authorization area.

Command and Response Authorization Area Details

Chapter 5 described the command and response data schematics but purposely left out one important area in commands and responses: the authorization area. This area is where sessions and authorizations are specified in the command and response byte stream, and a detailed discussion was deferred until this chapter.

To make the concepts more practical, this section examines these two areas using the TPM2_NV_Read command. The same general format is followed for authorization areas for all commands that can have authorization areas.

Command Authorization Area

Figure 13-3 shows the TPM2_NV_Read command and response data schematics and the location of the authorization areas in the command. Note that these areas aren't specifically called out in the Part 3 schematics, but they're implied; this is why they're shown in boxes off to the left side of the command and response schematic tables. For all commands that take authorizations, the authorization area for the command is located after the handles area and before the parameters area. The authorization area for the response is located at the end of the response after the response parameters.

Type	Name	Description
TPMI_ST_COMMAND_TAG	Tag	TPM_ST_SESSIONS
UINT32	commandSize	
TPM_CC	commandCode	TPM_CC_NV_Read
TPMI_RH_NV_AUTH	@authHandle	The handle indicating the source of the authorization value Auth Index: 1 Auth Role: USER
TPMI_RH_NV_INDEX	nvIndex	The NV Index to be read Auth Index: None
UINT16	size	Number of octets[5] to read
UINT16	offset	Octet offset into the area This value shall be less than or equal to the size of the nvIndex data.

The box on the left labeled "Authorization Area" points to the rows between commandCode and size.

Type	Name	Description
TPM_ST	Tag	
UINT32	responseSize	
TPM_RC	responseCode	
TPM2B_MAX_NV_BUFFER	data	The data read

The box on the left labeled "Authorization Area" points to the area after responseCode.

Figure 13-3. NV_Read command and response schematic from TPM 2.0 spec, Part 3, and the location of authorization areas. The boxes to the left indicate where the authorization areas are sandwiched in. This is often confusing to new readers of the specification but is very important to grasp.

For any command that can take authorizations, there can be up to three authorization structures in the authorization area. For a successful TPM 2.0 command, the number of authorization structures in the response is always equal to the number of authorization structures in the command. For a TPM 2.0 command that fails, the number of authorization structures in the response is always 0.

---

[5]The term *octet* is used in the TPM specification to denote 8 bits, which is often, although somewhat inaccurately, referred to as a *byte*. Because some computers use *bytes* that have a different number of bits, the TPM 2.0 architects used the term *octet*.

For the command, notice the @ sign in front of authHandle: this means an authorization structure is required to authorize actions on the entity corresponding to the authHandle. Further notation in the description column, "Auth role: USER," indicates the authorization role required.

Command Authorization Structures

The command authorization structure, TPMS_AUTH_COMMAND, is illustrated in Figure 13-4. This shows the details of the command authorization area box from Figure 13-3.

session handle	A four-octet value indicating the session number associated with this data block (TPM_RS_PW for a password authorization)
size field	A two-octet value indicating the number of octets in *nonce*
nonce	If present, an octet array that contains a number chosen by the caller
session attributes	A single octet with bit fields that indicate session usage
size field	A two-octet value indicating the number of octets in *authorization*
authorization	If present, an octet array that contains either an HMAC or a password, depending on the session type

Figure 13-4. Command authorization structure, TPMS_AUTH_COMMAND

Although not strictly part of the authorization structure in the current TPM 2.0 specification, the authorizationSize field in a command is present if the command tag is TPM_ST_SESSION, which indicates that the authorization area is present. This authorizationSize field allows code that is parsing the command to determine how many sessions are in the authorization area and where to find the parameters. The field immediately precedes the authorization area as shown in Figure 13-5.

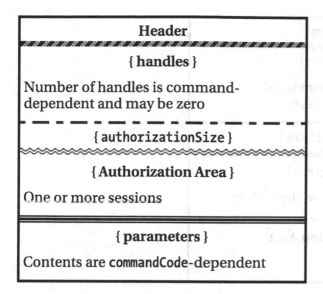

Header

{ handles }

Number of handles is command-
dependent and may be zero

{ authorizationSize }

{ Authorization Area }

One or more sessions

{ parameters }

Contents are **commandCode**-dependent

Figure 13-5. *Command structure showing where the command authorization area(s) are located*

Response Authorization Structures

For a response, the authorization structure, TPMS_AUTH_RESPONSE, is shown in Figure 13-6. This shows the details of the response authorization area box from Figure 13-3.

size field	A two-octet value indicating the number of octets in *nonce* (zero for a password authorization)
nonce	If present, an octet array that contains a number chosen by the TPM
session attributes	A single octet with bit fields that indicate session usage
size field	A two-octet value indicating the number of octets in *acknowledgment*
acknowledgment	If present, an octet array that contains an HMAC

Figure 13-6. *Response authorization structure, TPMS_AUTH_RESPONSE*

The response authorization area is at the very end of the response. To make it easy to find, a parameterSize field, a UINT32, is inserted before the response parameter area for all responses that contain an authorization area. Code that is parsing the response can use the parameterSize field to skip past the response parameters to find the response authorization area. The parameterSize field isn't present when a response doesn't include an authorization area (see Figure 13-7).

```
┌─────────────────────────────────────────┐
│                 Header                    │
│═══════════════════════════════════════════│
│               { handles }                 │
│                                           │
│  Number of handles is command-            │
│  dependent and may be zero                │
│ ─ ─ ─ ─ ─ ─ ─ ─ ─ ─ ─ ─ ─ ─ ─ ─ ─ ─ ─ ─ │
│            { parameterSize }              │
├───────────────────────────────────────────┤
│              { parameters }               │
│                                           │
│  Contents are commandCode-dependent       │
│ ∿∿∿∿∿∿∿∿∿∿∿∿∿∿∿∿∿∿∿∿∿∿∿∿∿∿∿∿∿∿∿∿∿∿∿∿∿∿∿∿ │
│           { Authorization Area}           │
│                                           │
│  One or more sessions                     │
└─────────────────────────────────────────┘
```

Figure 13-7. *Response Structure, showing where the response authorization area(s) and parameterSize fields are located*

Now that you know what the authorization areas look like, let's look at the three types of authorizations in detail.

Password Authorization: The Simplest Authorization

Password authorizations are the simplest authorizations, so I will describe them first. This section presents the password authorization lifecycle: how to create a password authorized entity, how to alter the authorization for an existing entity, and how to use a password authorization to authorize an action.

Password Authorization Lifecycle

A password authorization has a very simple lifecycle: create an entity using a password as the authorization, and then authorize actions on the entity. In more detail, the high-level steps required to create and use a password authorization are as follows:

1. Create an entity that will use an authorization value, or change the authorization value for an existing entity. This step is typically performed once per entity.

2. Authorize actions using the password authorized entity. This step can be performed multiple times for a particular entity and can occur any time after the entity's password has been set, whether by creating the entity or by changing its authorization.

First let's look at step 1, creating an entity to use a password authorization or altering the password for an existing entity.

Creating a Password Authorized Entity

To create an entity, use the following commands: TPM2_CreatePrimary, TPM2_Create, and TPM2_NV_DefineSpace.[6] Each of these has a parameter field for passing in the authValue that will be used to authorize actions on the entity. This authValue can be used either as a simple plaintext password or as an input to an HMAC authorization, but since this section is describing a password session, it just describes its use as a password. HMAC authorizations are described after we finish with passwords.

Here are some more details about the three TPM commands used to create entities:

- TPM2_CreatePrimary is used to create primary objects (objects directly under the primary seed) in a hierarchy. The USER authorization can be a password authorization if the inPublic parameter's userWithAuth attribute is set; this means authorization for actions that require the USER role can be performed by a password or HMAC. The authValue, a password in this case, is passed in by setting the userAuth field of the inSensitive parameter to the password.

- TPM2_Create is used to create objects that can be loaded into the TPM. The authorization type, userWithAuth, and the authValue are configured by setting the same fields used by TPM2_CreatePrimary.

- TPM2_NV_DefineSpace is used to define an NV index. A password authorization can be used if the attributes TPMA_NV_AUTHREAD and/or TPMA_NV_AUTHWRITE are set. The input parameter, authValue (the password), is passed in as the auth parameter of the TPM2_NV_DefineSpace command.

Changing a Password Authorization for an Already Created Entity

To change the password of an entity, these commands are used:

- TPM2_ObjectChangeAuth: Can be used to change the authorization of objects that aren't primary objects.

- TPM2_HierarchyChangeAuth: Used to change the authorization for a hierarchy (platform, owner, or endorsement) or for the lockout authority.

- TPM2_NV_ChangeAuth: Changes the authorization value for an NV index.

---

[6]All of these commands have the ability to set the authorization to use an authValue and/or a policy, but only the use of authValue is described here.

Now let's look at step 2, authorizing actions using a password authorization.

Using a Password Authorization

A password authorization is the simplest authorization. To use a password authorization, no session needs to be started. The caller simply fills in the command authorization block as shown in Figure 13-8.

Type	Name	Description
TPMI_SH_AUTH_SESSION	authHandle	Required to be the reserved authorization session handle TPM_RS_PW
TPM2B_NONCE	nonce	Required to be an empty buffer
TPMA_SESSION	sessionAttributes	Only continueSession may be set[7]
TPM2B_AUTH	password	Authorization compared to the authValue of the TPM entity

Figure 13-8. *Password authorization command*[7]

The response authorization area looks like Figure 13-9.

Type	Name	Description
TPM2B_NONCE	nonceTPM	Zero-length for a password authorization
TPMA_SESSION	sessionAttributes	Copy of the flags from the password authorization in the command[8]
TPM2B_AUTH	hmac3	Zero-length buffer for a password authorization

Figure 13-9. *Password acknowledgement in response*[8, 9]

Code Example: Password Session

Listing 13-1 shows a code example of a password session using the password session test from the TSS SAPI test code. This code uses the TSS System API that was described in Chapter 7. Because you hadn't yet learned about authorizations and sessions, a description of the authorization-related structures and functions was deferred until this

---

[7]Because the password session is always available, continueSession has no effect.
[8]The continueSession flag is an exception to this. For password sessions, the continueSession flag is always set in the response.
[9]This field is called hmac in the specification, but it isn't really an HMAC. Actually it's not anything at all, because it's a zero-length buffer. Probably the specification writers called it hmac to keep it consistent with HMAC authorization areas.

chapter. In order to follow the code example, you need to understand these session and authorization related System API data structures:

- TSS2_SYS_CMD_AUTHS: Specifies the number of authorization areas for the command and the specific authorization areas to be used. The structure looks like this:

```
typedef struct {
    uint8_t cmdAuthsCount;
    TPMS_AUTH_COMMAND **cmdAuths;
} TSS2_SYS_CMD_AUTHS;
```

- TSS2_SYS_RSP_AUTHS: In a like manner, specifies the number of authorization areas in a response and the specific response authorization areas. The structure looks like this:

```
typedef struct {
    uint8_t rspAuthsCount;
    TPMS_AUTH_RESPONSE **rspAuths;
} TSS2_SYS_RSP_AUTHS;
```

■ **Note** The CheckPassed and CheckFailed functions used in the code example are the same as those described in the code example in the SAPI section of Chapter 7.

Now that you understand the new structures, let's look at the code. I've added notes for each major block of the code to help you follow it better.

Listing 13-1. Password Authorization: Code Example

```
// Password used to authorize access to the NV index.
char password[] = "test password";

// NV Index used for the password test.
#define TPM20_INDEX_PASSWORD_TEST        0x01500020

void PasswordTest()
{
    UINT32 rval;
    int i;
```

Create an authorization area for the command and response.

```
// Authorization structure for command.
TPMS_AUTH_COMMAND sessionData;

// Authorization structure for response.
TPMS_AUTH_RESPONSE sessionDataOut;

// Create and init authorization area for command:
// only 1 authorization area.
TPMS_AUTH_COMMAND *sessionDataArray[1] = { &sessionData };

// Create authorization area for response:
// only 1 authorization area.
TPMS_AUTH_RESPONSE *sessionDataOutArray[1] = { &sessionDataOut };

// Authorization array for command (only has one auth structure).
TSS2_SYS_CMD_AUTHS sessionsData = { 1, &sessionDataArray[0] };

// Authorization array for response (only has one auth structure).
TSS2_SYS_RSP_AUTHS sessionsDataOut = { 1, &sessionDataOutArray[0] };
TPM2B_MAX_NV_BUFFER nvWriteData;

printf( "\nPASSWORD TESTS:\n" );
```

Create an NV index.

```
// Create an NV index that will use password
// authorizations. The password will be
// "test password".
CreatePasswordTestNV( TPM20_INDEX_PASSWORD_TEST, password );

//
// Initialize the command authorization area.
//

// Init sessionHandle, nonce, session
// attributes, and hmac (password).
sessionData.sessionHandle = TPM_RS_PW;

// Set zero sized nonce.
sessionData.nonce.t.size = 0;

// sessionAttributes is a bit field. To initialize
// it to 0, cast to a pointer to UINT8 and
```

```
// write 0 to that pointer.
*( (UINT8 *)&sessionData.sessionAttributes ) = 0;

// Init password (HMAC field in authorization structure).
sessionData.hmac.t.size = strlen( password );
memcpy( &( sessionData.hmac.t.buffer[0] ),
        &( password[0] ), sessionData.hmac.t.size );
```

Do writes, one with the correct password and one with an incorrect one; then verify the results.

```
// Initialize write data.
nvWriteData.t.size = 4;
for( i = 0; i < nvWriteData.t.size; i++ )
    nvWriteData.t.buffer[i] = 0xff - i;

// Attempt write with the correct password.
// It should pass.
rval = Tss2_Sys_NV_Write( sysContext,
        TPM20_INDEX_PASSWORD_TEST,
        TPM20_INDEX_PASSWORD_TEST,
        &sessionsData, &nvWriteData, 0,
        &sessionsDataOut );
// Check that the function passed as
// expected. Otherwise, exit.
CheckPassed( rval );

// Alter the password so it's incorrect.
sessionData.hmac.t.buffer[4] = 0xff;
rval = Tss2_Sys_NV_Write( sysContext,
        TPM20_INDEX_PASSWORD_TEST,
        TPM20_INDEX_PASSWORD_TEST,
        &sessionsData, &nvWriteData, 0,
        &sessionsDataOut );
// Check that the function failed as expected,
// since password was incorrect. If wrong
// response code received, exit.
CheckFailed( rval,
        TPM_RC_S + TPM_RC_1 + TPM_RC_AUTH_FAIL );
```

Delete the NV index.

```
    // Change hmac to null one, since null auth is
    // used to undefine the index.
    sessionData.hmac.t.size = 0;

    // Now undefine the index.
    rval = Tss2_Sys_NV_UndefineSpace( sysContext, TPM_RH_PLATFORM,
            TPM20_INDEX_PASSWORD_TEST, &sessionsData, 0 );
    CheckPassed( rval );
}
```

A good understanding of password authorizations and the data structures used to enable them provides a foundation for understanding the other types of authorizations. Next I describe HMAC and policy authorizations: specifically, how to start them.

Starting HMAC and Policy Sessions

Both HMAC and policy sessions are started using the TPM2_StartAuthSession command. When a session is started, it must be one of the following session types: HMAC, policy, or trial policy. Earlier I described HMAC and policy sessions at a high level, but those descriptions didn't mention trial policy sessions. *Trial policy sessions* are neutered policy sessions: they can't authorize any actions, but they can be used to generate policy digests before creating entities (more on that later). For the purposes of this section, policy and trial policy sessions are grouped together.

When a session is started, basic characteristics of the session are determined. Specifically, whether the session is bound or unbound, whether the session is salted or unsalted, the strength of the session key, the strength of the anti-replay protections, the strength of parameter encryption and decryption, and the strength of the session HMACs are determined by the parameters used to call TPM2_StartAuthSession.

Some terms need to be understood before this section describes the process of starting HMAC and policy sessions:

- *KDFa*: The key-derivation function used to create session keys.[10] An HMAC function is used as the pseudo-random function for generating the key. The inputs to the KDFa are a hash algorithm; an HMAC key, K (described next); a 4-byte string used to identify the usage of the KDFa output; contextU and contextV (variable-length strings); and the number of bits in the output. These parameters are cryptographically combined by the KDFa function to create the session key, described below.

- *K*: The key used as input to the KDFa function. For session-key creation, K is the concatenation of the authValue (of the entity corresponding to the bind handle) and the salt parameter passed to the TPM2_StartAuthSession command.

---

[10]KDFa is used for many other things in the TPM, but this section only discusses its use in sessions.

- sessionKey: A key created when an HMAC or policy session is started.[11] For session key creation, the KDFa function takes the following as inputs:

  - sessionAlg (a hash algorithm)

  - K (the HMAC key used as input to the KDFa's HMAC function)

  - A unique 4 byte label, ATH (three characters plus the string terminator)

  - Two nonces, nonceTPM and nonceCaller (corresponding to contextU and contextV in the KDFa)

  - The number of bits in the resulting key

- nonceCaller: The nonce sent by the caller to the TPM2_StartAuthSession command.

- nonceTpm: The nonce generated by the TPM in response to the TPM2_StartAuthSession command and returned to the caller.

TPM2_StartAuthSession Command

As noted earlier, the parameters to the TPM2_StartAuthSession function determine many of the session's characteristics, including the session's security properties. The command schematic for this command is shown in Figure 13-10; the response is shown in Figure 13-11.

---

[11]It is important to avoid confusing terms here; specifically, sessionKey should not be confused with hmacKey. The hmacKey isn't determined at session creation time, but it's partially determined by the parameters used to start the session.

Type	Name	Description
TPMI_ST_COMMAND_TAG	Tag	TPM_ST_SESSIONS if an audit, decrypt, or encrypt session is present; otherwise, TPM_ST_NO_SESSIONS
UINT32	commandSize	
TPM_CC	commandCode	TPM_CC_StartAuthSession
TPMI_DH_OBJECT+	tpmKey	Handle of a loaded decrypt key used to encrypt salt May be TPM_RH_NULL Auth Index: None
TPMI_DH_ENTITY+	Bind	Entity providing the authValue May be TPM_RH_NULL Auth Index: None
TPM2B_NONCE	nonceCaller	Initial nonceCaller; sets the nonce size for the session Must be at least 16 octets
TPM2B_ENCRYPTED_SECRET	encryptedSalt	Value encrypted according to the type of tpmKey If tpmKey is TPM_RH_NULL, this must be the empty buffer.
TPM_SE	sessionType	Indicates the type of the session: simple HMAC or policy (including a trial policy)
TPMT_SYM_DEF+	Symmetric	Algorithm and key size for parameter encryption May select TPM_ALG_NULL
TPMI_ALG_HASH	authHash	Hash algorithm to use for the session Must be a hash algorithm supported by the TPM and not TPM_ALG_NULL

Figure 13-10. TPM2_StartAuthSession command

Type	Name	Description
TPM_ST	Tag	
UINT32	responseSize	
TPM_RC	responseCode	
TPMI_SH_AUTH_SESSION	sessionHandle	Handle for the newly created session
TPM2B_NONCE	nonceTPM	The initial nonce from the TPM, used in the computation of sessionKey

Figure 13-11. TPM2_StartAuthSession response

This command takes the following handles and parameters as inputs:

- Two handles:
  - If tpmKey is TPM_RH_NULL, the session is an unsalted session; otherwise, it's a salted session, and the encryptedSalt parameter is decrypted by the TPM to get the salt value used to add entropy. The TPM uses the loaded key pointed to by the tpmKey handle to do the decryption of encryptedSalt.
  - If bind is TPM_RH_NULL, the session is an unbound session. Otherwise, it's a bound session, and the authValue of the entity pointed to by the bind handle is concatenated with the salt value to form K, which is used in calculating the sessionKey.

- Five parameters:

  - `nonceCaller` is the first nonce set by the caller and sets the size for all subsequent nonces returned by the TPM.

  - `encryptedSalt` is used only if the session is salted as described earlier in the discussion of `tpmKey`. If the session is unsalted, this parameter must be a zero-sized buffer.

  - `sessionType` determines the type of the session: HMAC, policy, or trial policy.

  - `symmetric` determines the type of parameter encryption that will be used when the session is set for encrypt or decrypt.

  - `authHash` is the algorithm ID for the hash algorithm that will be used by the session for HMAC operations.

When a session is started, the TPM processes the command and generates a session handle, computes a `nonceTPM`, and calculates a session key. This key is used to generate HMACs, encrypt command parameters, and decrypt response parameters. After the session is created, the session key remains the same for the lifetime of the session. The session handle and the `nonceTPM` are returned by the command.

The session key is determined by these command parameters passed in to `TPM2_StartAuthSession`: `tpmKey`, `bind`, `encryptedSalt`, `nonceCaller`, and `authHash`. The response parameter, `nonceTPM`, also figures into the session key.[12] Use of the `nonceTPM` in creating the session key guarantees that using the same `authValue`, `salt`, and `nonceCaller` will generate a different session key.

Because the calling application also has to know the session key, it duplicates the TPM's calculations using the `nonceTPM` along with the input variables to perform this calculation. At this point, the session has started, and both the caller and the TPM know the session key.

Session Key and HMAC Key Details

Table 13-2 describes the variations of sessions and how the `sessionKey` and HMAC key are created for each case. Having all this information in a single table can be very helpful, which is why it's included here.

---

[12] The symmetric parameter to `TPM2_StartAuthSession` is only used for encryption and decryption of command and response parameters, so it isn't described in this chapter.

Table 13-2. Variations of Sessions and Session Key Creation

Session Variation	bind	tpmKey	K	sessionKey	HMAC key
Unbound/ Unsalted	TPM_RH_NULL	TPM_RH_NULL	Null	NULL key	Entity authorization value, authValue$_{entity}$
Bound	Not TPM_RH_NULL	TPM_RH_NULL	bind entity's authorization value, authValue$_{bind}$	KDFa(sessionAlg, authValue$_{bind}$, "ATH", nonceTPM, nonceCaller, bits)[13]	if entity == bind entity AND not a policy session: sessionKey; if entity!= bind entity OR session is a policy session[14]: sessionKey || authValue$_{entity}$
Salted	TPM_RH_NULL	Not TPM_RH_NULL	salt	KDFa(sessionAlg, salt, "ATH", nonceTPM, nonceCaller, bits)	sessionKey || authValue$_{entity}$
Bound/Salted	Not TPM_RH_NULL	Not TPM_RH_NULL	authValue$_{bind}$ || salt	KDFa(sessionAlg, (authValue$_{bind}$ || salt), "ATH", nonceTPM, nonceCaller, bits)	If(entity == bind entity AND not a policy session: sessionKey; if entity!= bind entity OR session is a policy session: sessionKey || authValue$_{entity}$

[13]Including the two nonces, nonceCaller and nonceTPM, in the session-key creation makes it statistically impossible to create two sessions with the same session key. This property of TPMs enables security analysis.

[14]A policy session always acts as if it's an unbound session.

Guidelines for TPM2_StartAuthSession Handles and Parameters

From the details in Table 13-2, we can deduce some guidelines for choosing the TPM2_ StartAuthSession parameters. The strength of the session key is determined by the combination of the bind and tpmKey handles, encryptedSalt, nonceCaller, and the hash algorithm used for the session.

The strongest possible session key is provided with the bind handle pointing to a TPM entity (bound session), the tpmKey handle pointing to a loaded key (salted session), and nonceCaller's size set to the size of the hash algorithm's output.

With bind and tpmKey set to TPM_RH_NULL, the result is a zero-length session key—a very weak session key. However, as long as the entity's authValue is strong, the HMAC key is still strong. As will be detailed in Chapter 17, the strength of the session key directly affects the strength of the encryption and decryption of the command and response parameters.

The length of the nonceCaller parameter determines the length of the nonceTPMs used in the session. The bigger the nonce, the better the protection against replay attacks.

The session key and the entity's authorization value are used in generating session HMACs, so again, a stronger session key and stronger authorization value result in greater security.

Programmers making calls to TPM2_StartAuthSession should consider carefully which properties are desired when selecting the parameters to use.

Session Variations

Now let's examine the meaning of bound vs. unbound sessions and salted vs. unsalted sessions in detail. I will also describe some use cases for them.

Salted vs. Unsalted

Both HMAC and policy sessions can be salted or unsalted. A salted session adds more entropy to the session key creation. Whether a session is salted or not is determined by the tpmKey parameter to the TPM2_StartAuthSession command. This decrypted salt is added into the session key creation process. If the authValue is weak, salting the session helps to prevent offline hammering attacks. An *offline hammering attack* consists of trying different values of authValue to see if the correct HMAC can be generated. If successful, the authValue has been discovered. Salting of sessions raises the bar for this type of attack.

Bound vs. Unbound

Similarly, both HMAC and policy sessions can be set to be either bound or unbound. A *bound* session means the session is "bound" to a particular entity, the "bind" entity; a session started this way is typically used to authorize multiple actions on the bind entity. The bind entity's authorization value is used to calculate the session key but isn't needed after that. This can be advantageous from a security perspective, because the calling application doesn't need to keep prompting for the authorization value (password) or maintain it in memory.

Bound sessions can also be used to authorize actions on other entities, and in that case, the bind entity's authValue adds entropy to the session key creation, resulting in stronger encryption of command and response parameters—sort of a poor man's salt. The authorization values for both the bind entity and the entity being authorized figure into the HMAC calculation.

An *unbound* session is used to authorize actions on many different entities. A policy session is most commonly configured as an unbound session. With the security offered by policy sessions, an HMAC isn't as important, and using policy sessions without having to calculate and insert HMACs is much easier.

Use Cases for Session Variations

Now let's answer the obvious question: what are the major use cases for bound/unbound and salted/unsalted sessions? There are many possibilities, but the most common ones are as follows:

- *Unbound sessions* are most commonly used for two cases:

    - If the session is also unsalted, this combination is often used for policy sessions that don't require an HMAC. This is okay because policy sessions use policy commands and HMAC authorization isn't really required in many cases. This simplifies the use of the policy session by eliminating the overhead of calculating the HMACs. The use case for this is any policy authorization that doesn't include the TPM2_PolicyAuthValue command.

    - They can also be used by HMAC sessions to authorize actions on many different entities.

- *Bound sessions* have two cases:

    - *Authorizing actions on the bind entity*: This HMAC authorization can be used to authorize many actions on the bind entity without prompting for the password each time. For example, an employee might want to view their personnel file many times; this type of authorization would work for that.

    - *Authorizing actions on an entity other than the bind entity*: In this case, both the bind entity's authValue and the authValue of the entity being authorized figure into the HMAC calculation. This results in a stronger session key and stronger encryption and decryption keys.

- *Unsalted session*: when the authValue of the bind entity is deemed strong enough to generate strong session and strong encryption and decryption keys. If a system administrator can enforce sufficient controls on the strength of a password, an unsalted session using that password may be sufficient.

- *Salted session*: when the authValue isn't considered strong enough for generating secure session and encryption/decryption keys. A web site could request two different passwords from a user: one to be used as the authorization value for use of an encryption key, and the other to be used for the salt. The combination of the two would be much stronger than using a single password, as long as a cryptographically strong salt was used.

Now that you have a foundation for starting sessions, let's see some differences between HMAC and policy sessions.

HMAC and Policy Sessions: Differences

HMAC and policy sessions differ primarily in how actions are authorized. Commands sent using HMAC sessions are successful only if the HMAC sent with the command is correct. In order to generate the correct HMAC, knowledge of a secret (authValue) that is shared between the caller and TPM is required. In other words, knowledge of the session key and authValue enable the calculation of the correct HMAC, effectively granting authorization to perform an action on the entity. An agent that doesn't know either the session key or the authValue can't calculate the correct HMAC, which causes the command to fail.

Policy sessions authorize actions based on the correct sequence of policy commands and, in many cases, conditions required by those commands. This is a very simple description of this rich and complicated type of authorization. The details are described in Chapter 14, but suffice it to say that policy sessions authorize actions using the following:

- A sequence of policy commands before the command whose action is being authorized. The presence of this sequence is proven by checking the policyDigest. Each policy command hash-extends policy command-specific data into the session's policyDigest. In the simplest case, a comparison between the session's policyDigest and that of the entity being accessed will determine whether the proper policy commands were performed beforehand.

- A set of conditions that must be met before and/or during the execution of the command whose action is being authorized. If these conditions aren't met, the policy commands fail or the command being authorized fails. This is described in detail later.

Interestingly enough, policy sessions can still have an HMAC in their authorization areas, even though the most common use of policy sessions doesn't, according to Part 1 of the TPM 2.0 specification. This most common use assumes that the session is unbound and unsalted. But when an HMAC is used in the authorization area (whether because the session is bound and/or salted or the TPM2_PolicyAuthValue command is used), contrary to HMAC sessions, the HMAC is always calculated as if the session isn't bound to any entity.[15] In policy sessions, the bind entity's authValue is only used for session key creation and never for HMAC calculation. Applications using the TPM need to account for this during HMAC calculation.

To summarize, HMAC authorizations are more secure than password authorizations, and policy authorizations are the most complex and rich authorizations. HMAC authorizations use a properly calculated HMAC as the means to prove knowledge of the authorization secret(s). Policy authorizations require a set of policy commands and a specific set of conditions required by those policy commands in order to authorize an action. In both HMAC and policy authorizations, HMACs can be used to guarantee command and response integrity.

Now let's look at HMAC authorization in detail.

HMAC Authorization

This section dives into the details of HMAC authorizations. It describes the high-level HMAC authorization lifetime and each of the steps in that lifetime: entity creation or alteration, HMAC session creation, and HMAC session use. The section ends with a description of the security properties of an HMAC session.

As you read this section, I recommend that you reference the example code section. The discussion refers to line numbers in the code where applicable. This section mainly focuses on describing the steps leading up to and including the NV index's write. The NV index's read code is very similar, and mapping of these steps to that code is left as a reader exercise.

HMAC Authorization Lifecycle

The steps for creating and authorizing actions on HMAC authorized entities are the following:

1. Create the entity that will use an authorization value, or change the authorization value for an existing entity. This step is typically performed once per entity.

2. Create an HMAC session.

3. Use the HMAC session to perform operations on the entity. This operation can occur any time after steps 1 and 2 and can occur multiple times. A single HMAC session can be used to authorize multiple actions.

---

[15]This is an optimization: the session context space normally used for the bind value is used for policy-specific parameters.

Altering or Creating an Entity That Requires HMAC Authorization

For the purposes of entity creation, the method of specifying the authValue is exactly the same as described earlier in the password authorization lifecycle. The same is true for altering the authValue for an existing entity. In both of these operations, the authValue is treated exactly the same for HMAC and password authorizations.

In the example code, lines 19-26, 42-44, and 55 set up the authValue and authPolicy for creating the NV index. Lines 101, 104-105, and 112 set up the NV attributes. And lines 115-117 create the NV index that we're going to authorize.

Creating an HMAC Session

An HMAC session is started with a TPM2_StartAuthSession command that has the sessionType field set to TPM_SE_HMAC. When the HMAC session is started, the TPM creates a session key using the formula described previously. This session key is created in the TPM. After TPM2StartAuthSession returns, the caller also recreates the session key, using the bind entity's authValue, the salt, and the nonceCaller parameters sent to the TPM by the TPM2StartAuthSession command, and the nonceTPM returned by the TPM.

Lines 140, 143, and 150 set up the parameters for starting the session, and lines 154-156 actually create the session.

Using an HMAC Session to Authorize a Single Command

The mechanics of a single command during an HMAC session are described in Figure 13-12.

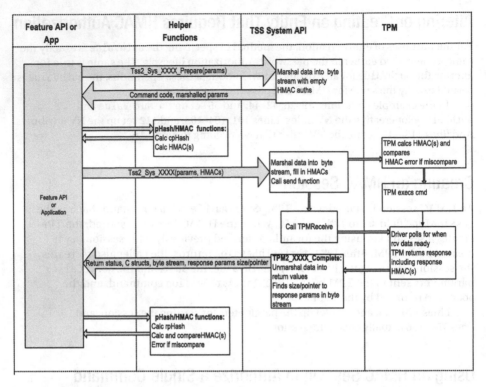

Figure 13-12. *HMAC session: single command. Note that this diagram assumes the use of the TSS SAPI layer. The TAB and resource manager layers are omitted for simplicity. Also, this diagram shows how HMAC sessions operate using the TSS SAPI Tss2_Sys_XXXX_Prepare and one-call interfaces*

To use an HMAC session for authorizing commands, the steps are as follows (see Figure 13-12 while reading the example code):

1.   The input parameters are marshalled and concatenated into a single sized byte buffer, cpParams. The Tss2_Sys_NV_Write_ Prepare call on lines 183–185 performs this task and puts the cpParams buffer into the sysContext structure.

2.   The caller calculates the cpHash, a hash of the marshalled command parameters contained in the cpParams buffer. This is done in the ComputeCommandHmacs call on lines 202–205.

3.   The caller calculates an HMAC for the command. The cpHash is one of the inputs to this calculation. This is done by the ComputeCommandHmacs call on lines 202–205.

4. The calculated HMAC is copied into the HMAC session's HMAC field. This is done automatically by the ComputeCommandHmacs call—-notice the pointer to nvCmdAuths being passed in on lines 202–205.

5. The complete command including header, sessions, and parameters must be marshalled into a byte stream and sent to the TPM. This is done in the one-call function call at lines 211–214.

6. The response must be read from the TPM. This is also done in the one-call function on lines 211–214.

7. After receiving the response, the caller calculates the rpHash, a hash of the marshalled response parameters in the byte stream. This is done in the CheckResponseHmacs call on lines 224–226.

8. The caller calculates the expected response HMAC. The rpHash is one of the inputs to this calculation. This is also done by the CheckResponseHmacs call on lines 224–226.

9. The caller compares this calculated response HMAC to the HMAC field of the response's HMAC session. If they aren't the same, the response parameters have been corrupted and none of the data can be trusted. If they are the same, then the response parameters have been received correctly. This is performed by CheckResponseHmacs, lines 224–226. It calculates what the response HMAC should be and compares it to the HMAC returned in nvRspAuths.

10. If the response HMAC is correct, the response parameters can be unmarshalled into C structures for use by the caller; this is performed by the one-call function on lines 211–214. Note that for the one-call, the code assumes that the HMAC is correct and unmarshals the response parameters. Later, if the response HMAC is proven incorrect, the unmarshalled response parameters can be ignored.

HMAC and Policy Session Code Example

Listing 13-2 presents a simple example of how to execute HMAC and policy sessions. This function is known to work, and all of its support routines are available in the TSS SAPI test code described in Chapter 7. To keep the code as simple as possible, it uses an unbound and unsalted session. If you'd like to see more complicated examples, all variations of bound/unbound and salted/unsalted are tested in the HmacSessionTest in the TSS SAPI test code.

■ **Note** Managing HMAC sessions and calculating HMAC authorizations are complicated tasks. Some of the functions called in Listing 13-2 are only explained at a high level. The goal was to demonstrate the high-level flow of an HMAC authorization without overwhelming you with low-level details. If you want to dig deeper, the source code for all the subroutines is available at the web site noted for the TSS SAPI test code in Chapter 7.

To help compare HMAC and policy sessions, this code does HMAC or policy authorizations, depending on the value of the hmacTest input parameter; if conditional statements using the hmacTest parameter are used for all the HMAC- or policy-specific code. For now, because this section is about HMAC authorizations, ignore all the parts of the code that only pertain to policy sessions (these areas are shaded).

Some notes about this code:

- The code does a write to an NV index followed by a read of the same NV index. Both the read and write are authorized using an HMAC authorization.

- To authorize the read and write operations, this code uses either an HMAC session or a policy session with a TPM2_ PolicyAuthValue command. This provides similar capability (both sessions use an HMAC for authorization), and thus provides a useful vehicle for comparing HMAC and policy sessions.

- The RollNonces function does what it says: it copies nonceNewer to nonceOlder and copies the new nonce to nonceNewer. The nonces must be rolled before each command and after each response. This is described more in the section "Using an HMAC Session to Send Multiple Commands (Rolling Nonces)." Here's the complete code for this function:

```
void RollNonces( SESSION *session, TPM2B_NONCE *newNonce  )
{
    session->nonceOlder = session->nonceNewer;
    session->nonceNewer = *newNonce;
}
```

This code example uses a single byte nonceCaller for both the NV write and read commands. This isn't a recommended usage—typically, to maximize replay protection, you would use a nonce that is the size of the session's selected hash algorithm, and you would use different randomly generated nonces for each command being authorized.

- This code relies heavily on an application-level structure, SESSION, that maintains all session state information including nonces. There are many ways this can be done—this just happens to be the implementation I chose. This structure looks like this:

```
typedef struct {
    // Inputs to StartAuthSession; these need to be saved
    // so that HMACs can be calculated.
    TPMI_DH_OBJECT tpmKey;
    TPMI_DH_ENTITY bind;
    TPM2B_ENCRYPTED_SECRET encryptedSalt;
    TPM2B_MAX_BUFFER salt;
    TPM_SE sessionType;
    TPMT_SYM_DEF symmetric;
    TPMI_ALG_HASH authHash;

    // Outputs from StartAuthSession; these also need
    // to be saved for calculating HMACs and
    // other session related functions.
    TPMI_SH_AUTH_SESSION sessionHandle;
    TPM2B_NONCE nonceTPM;

    // Internal state for the session
    TPM2B_DIGEST sessionKey;
    TPM2B_DIGEST authValueBind; // authValue of bind object
    TPM2B_NONCE nonceNewer;
    TPM2B_NONCE nonceOlder;
    TPM2B_NONCE nonceTpmDecrypt;
    TPM2B_NONCE nonceTpmEncrypt;
    TPM2B_NAME name;     // Name of the object the session handle
                         // points to. Used for computing HMAC for
                         // any HMAC sessions present.
                         //
    void *hmacPtr;       // Pointer to HMAC field in the marshalled
                         // data stream for the session.
                         // This allows the function to calculate
                         // and fill in the HMAC after marshalling
                         // of all the inputs is done.
                         //
                         // This is only used if the session is an
                         // HMAC session.
                         //
    UINT8 nvNameChanged;// Used for some special case code
                         // dealing with the NV written state.
} SESSION;
```

- StartAuthSessionWithParams starts the session, saves its state in a SESSION structure, and adds the SESSION structure to the application's list of open sessions.

- EndAuthSession is used to remove the SESSION structure from the application's list of open sessions after the session has ended.

Listing 13-2. Simple HMAC and Policy Code Example

```
1    void SimpleHmacOrPolicyTest( bool hmacTest )
2    {
3        UINT32 rval, sessionCmdRval;
4        TPM2B_AUTH  nvAuth;
5        SESSION nvSession, trialPolicySession;
6        TPMA_NV nvAttributes;
7        TPM2B_DIGEST authPolicy;
8        TPM2B_NAME nvName;
9        TPM2B_MAX_NV_BUFFER nvWriteData, nvReadData;
10       UINT8 dataToWrite[] = { 0x00, 0xff, 0x55, 0xaa };
11       char sharedSecret[] = "shared secret";
12       int i;
13       TPM2B_ENCRYPTED_SECRET encryptedSalt;
14       TPMT_SYM_DEF symmetric;
15       TPMA_SESSION sessionAttributes;
16       TPM_SE tpmSe;
17       char *testString;
```

Set up authorizations for NV index creation and deletion.

```
18       // Command authorization area: one password session.
19       TPMS_AUTH_COMMAND nvCmdAuth = { TPM_RS_PW, };
20       TPMS_AUTH_COMMAND *nvCmdAuthArray[1] = { &nvCmdAuth };
21       TSS2_SYS_CMD_AUTHS nvCmdAuths = { 1, &nvCmdAuthArray[0] };
22
23       // Response authorization area.
24       TPMS_AUTH_RESPONSE nvRspAuth;
25       TPMS_AUTH_RESPONSE *nvRspAuthArray[1] = { &nvRspAuth };
26       TSS2_SYS_RSP_AUTHS nvRspAuths = { 1, &nvRspAuthArray[0] };
27
28       if( hmacTest )
29               testString = "HMAC";
30       else
31               testString = "POLICY";
32
33       printf( "\nSIMPLE %s SESSION TEST:\n", testString );
34
```

```
35        // Create sysContext structure.
36        sysContext = InitSysContext( 1000, resMgrTctiContext, &abiVersion );
37        if( sysContext == 0 )
38        {
39            InitSysContextFailure();
40        }
```

Create the NV index, with either an HMAC or a policy authorization required.

```
41        // Setup the NV index's authorization value.
42        nvAuth.t.size = strlen( sharedSecret );
43        for( i = 0; i < nvAuth.t.size; i++ )
44            nvAuth.t.buffer[i] = sharedSecret[i];
45
46        //
47        // Create NV index.
48        //
49        if( hmacTest )
50        {
51            // Set NV index's authorization policy
52            // to zero sized policy since we won't be
53            // using policy to authorize.
54
55            authPolicy.t.size = 0;
56        }
57        else
58        {
59
60            // Zero sized encrypted salt, since the session
61            // is unsalted.
62
63            encryptedSalt.t.size = 0;
64
65            // No symmetric algorithm.
66            symmetric.algorithm = TPM_ALG_NULL;
67
68            //
69            // Create the NV index's authorization policy
70            // using a trial policy session.
71            //
72            rval = StartAuthSessionWithParams( &trialPolicySession,
73                    TPM_RH_NULL, TPM_RH_NULL, &encryptedSalt,
74                    TPM_SE_TRIAL,
75                    &symmetric, TPM_ALG_SHA256 );
76            CheckPassed( rval );
77
```

```
78          rval = Tss2_Sys_PolicyAuthValue( sysContext,
79                  trialPolicySession.sessionHandle, 0, 0 );
80          CheckPassed( rval );
81
82          // Get policy digest.
83          rval = Tss2_Sys_PolicyGetDigest( sysContext,
84                  trialPolicySession.sessionHandle,
85                  0, &authPolicy, 0 );
86          CheckPassed( rval );
87
88          // End the trial session by flushing it.
89          rval = Tss2_Sys_FlushContext( sysContext,
90                  trialPolicySession.sessionHandle );
91          CheckPassed( rval );
92
93          // And remove the trial policy session from
94          // sessions table.
95          rval = EndAuthSession( &trialPolicySession );
96          CheckPassed( rval );
97      }
98
99      // Now set the NV index's attributes:
100     // policyRead, authWrite, and platormCreate.
101     *(UINT32 *)( &nvAttributes ) = 0;
102     if( hmacTest )
103     {
104         nvAttributes.TPMA_NV_AUTHREAD = 1;
105         nvAttributes.TPMA_NV_AUTHWRITE = 1;
106     }
107     else
108     {
109         nvAttributes.TPMA_NV_POLICYREAD = 1;
110         nvAttributes.TPMA_NV_POLICYWRITE = 1;
111     }
112     nvAttributes.TPMA_NV_PLATFORMCREATE = 1;
113
114     // Create the NV index.
115     rval = DefineNvIndex( TPM_RH_PLATFORM, TPM_RS_PW,
116             &nvAuth, &authPolicy, TPM20_INDEX_PASSWORD_TEST,
117             TPM_ALG_SHA256, nvAttributes, 32  );
118     CheckPassed( rval );
119
120     // Add index and associated authorization value to
121     // entity table. This helps when we need
122     // to calculate HMACs.
123     AddEntity( TPM20_INDEX_PASSWORD_TEST, &nvAuth );
124     CheckPassed( rval );
```

```
125
126         // Get the name of the NV index.
127         rval = (*HandleToNameFunctionPtr)(
128                 TPM20_INDEX_PASSWORD_TEST,
129                 &nvName );
130         CheckPassed( rval );
```

Start the HMAC or policy session.

```
131         //
132         // Start HMAC or real (non-trial) policy authorization session:
133         // it's an unbound and unsalted session, no symmetric
134         // encryption algorithm, and SHA256 is the session's
135         // hash algorithm.
136         //
137
138         // Zero sized encrypted salt, since the session
139         // is unsalted.
140         encryptedSalt.t.size = 0;
141
142         // No symmetric algorithm.
143         symmetric.algorithm = TPM_ALG_NULL;
144
145         // Create the session, hmac or policy depending
146         // on hmacTest.
147         // Session state (session handle, nonces, etc.) gets
148         // saved into nvSession structure for later use.
149         if( hmacTest )
150             tpmSe = TPM_SE_HMAC;
151         else
152             tpmSe = TPM_SE_POLICY;
153
154         rval = StartAuthSessionWithParams( &nvSession, TPM_RH_NULL,
155                 TPM_RH_NULL, &encryptedSalt, tpmSe,
156                 &symmetric, TPM_ALG_SHA256 );
157         CheckPassed( rval );
158
159         // Get the name of the session and save it in
160         // the nvSession structure.
161         rval = (*HandleToNameFunctionPtr)( nvSession.sessionHandle,
162                 &nvSession.name );
163         CheckPassed( rval );
```

Do an NV write using either an HMAC or a policy authorization.

```
164        // Initialize NV write data.
165        nvWriteData.t.size = sizeof( dataToWrite );
166        for( i = 0; i < nvWriteData.t.size; i++ )
167        {
168            nvWriteData.t.buffer[i] = dataToWrite[i];
169        }
170
171        //
172        // Now setup for writing the NV index.
173        //
174        if( !hmacTest )
175        {
176            // Send policy command.
177            rval = Tss2_Sys_PolicyAuthValue( sysContext,
178                    nvSession.sessionHandle, 0, 0 );
179            CheckPassed( rval );
180        }
181
182        // First call prepare in order to create cpBuffer.
183        rval = Tss2_Sys_NV_Write_Prepare( sysContext,
184                TPM20_INDEX_PASSWORD_TEST,
185                TPM20_INDEX_PASSWORD_TEST, &nvWriteData, 0 );
186        CheckPassed( rval );
187
188        // Configure command authorization area, except for HMAC.
189        nvCmdAuths.cmdAuths[0]->sessionHandle =
190                nvSession.sessionHandle;
191        nvCmdAuths.cmdAuths[0]->nonce.t.size = 1;
192        nvCmdAuths.cmdAuths[0]->nonce.t.buffer[0] = 0xa5;
193        *( (UINT8 *)(&sessionAttributes ) ) = 0;
194        nvCmdAuths.cmdAuths[0]->sessionAttributes = sessionAttributes;
195        nvCmdAuths.cmdAuths[0]->sessionAttributes.continueSession = 1;
196
197        // Roll nonces for command
198        RollNonces( &nvSession, &nvCmdAuths.cmdAuths[0]->nonce );
199
200        // Complete command authorization area, by computing
201        // HMAC and setting it in nvCmdAuths.
202        rval = ComputeCommandHmacs( sysContext,
203                TPM20_INDEX_PASSWORD_TEST,
204                TPM20_INDEX_PASSWORD_TEST, &nvCmdAuths,
205                TPM_RC_FAILURE );
206        CheckPassed( rval );
207
208        // Finally!!  Write the data to the NV index.
209        // If the command is successful, the command
210        // HMAC was correct.
```

```
211        sessionCmdRval = Tss2_Sys_NV_Write( sysContext,
212                TPM20_INDEX_PASSWORD_TEST,
213                TPM20_INDEX_PASSWORD_TEST,
214                &nvCmdAuths, &nvWriteData, 0, &nvRspAuths );
215        CheckPassed( sessionCmdRval );
```

Get the response from the NV write. If it's an HMAC session, verify the response HMAC.

```
216        // Roll nonces for response
217        RollNonces( &nvSession, &nvRspAuths.rspAuths[0]->nonce );
218
219        if( sessionCmdRval == TPM_RC_SUCCESS )
220        {
221            // If the command was successful, check the
222            // response HMAC to make sure that the
223            // response was received correctly.
224            rval = CheckResponseHMACs( sysContext, sessionCmdRval,
225                    &nvCmdAuths, TPM20_INDEX_PASSWORD_TEST,
226                    TPM20_INDEX_PASSWORD_TEST, &nvRspAuths );
227            CheckPassed( rval );
228        }
229
230        if( !hmacTest )
231        {
232            // Send policy command.
233            rval = Tss2_Sys_PolicyAuthValue( sysContext,
234                    nvSession.sessionHandle, 0, 0 );
235            CheckPassed( rval );
236        }
```

Do an NV read, using an HMAC or a policy session. If it's an HMAC session, verify the response HMAC. Finally, test the read data against the write data to make sure they're equal.

```
237        // First call prepare in order to create cpBuffer.
238        rval = Tss2_Sys_NV_Read_Prepare( sysContext,
239                TPM20_INDEX_PASSWORD_TEST,
240                TPM20_INDEX_PASSWORD_TEST,
241                sizeof( dataToWrite ), 0 );
242        CheckPassed( rval );
243
244        // Roll nonces for command
245        RollNonces( &nvSession, &nvCmdAuths.cmdAuths[0]->nonce );
246
```

```
247        // End the session after next command.
248        nvCmdAuths.cmdAuths[0]->sessionAttributes.continueSession = 0;
249
250        // Complete command authorization area, by computing
251        // HMAC and setting it in nvCmdAuths.
252        rval = ComputeCommandHmacs( sysContext,
253               TPM20_INDEX_PASSWORD_TEST,
254               TPM20_INDEX_PASSWORD_TEST, &nvCmdAuths,
255               TPM_RC_FAILURE );
256        CheckPassed( rval );
257
258        // And now read the data back.
259        // If the command is successful, the command
260        // HMAC was correct.
261        sessionCmdRval = Tss2_Sys_NV_Read( sysContext,
262               TPM20_INDEX_PASSWORD_TEST,
263               TPM20_INDEX_PASSWORD_TEST,
264               &nvCmdAuths, sizeof( dataToWrite ), 0,
265               &nvReadData, &nvRspAuths );
266        CheckPassed( sessionCmdRval );
267
268        // Roll nonces for response
269        RollNonces( &nvSession, &nvRspAuths.rspAuths[0]->nonce );
270
271        if( sessionCmdRval == TPM_RC_SUCCESS )
272        {
273            // If the command was successful, check the
274            // response HMAC to make sure that the
275            // response was received correctly.
276            rval = CheckResponseHMACs( sysContext, sessionCmdRval,
277                   &nvCmdAuths, TPM20_INDEX_PASSWORD_TEST,
278                   TPM20_INDEX_PASSWORD_TEST, &nvRspAuths );
279            CheckPassed( rval );
280        }
281
282        // Check that write and read data are equal.
283        if( memcmp( (void *)&nvReadData.t.buffer[0],
284               (void *)&nvWriteData.t.buffer[0], nvReadData.t.size ) )
285        {
286            printf( "ERROR!! read data not equal to written data\n" );
287            Cleanup();
288        }
```

Cleanup: remove the NV index.

```
289
290      //
291      // Now cleanup:  undefine the NV index and delete
292      // the NV index's entity table entry.
293      //
294
295      // Setup authorization for undefining the NV index.
296      nvCmdAuths.cmdAuths[0]->sessionHandle = TPM_RS_PW;
297      nvCmdAuths.cmdAuths[0]->nonce.t.size = 0;
298      nvCmdAuths.cmdAuths[0]->hmac.t.size = 0;
299
300      // Undefine the NV index.
301      rval = Tss2_Sys_NV_UndefineSpace( sysContext,
302              TPM_RH_PLATFORM, TPM20_INDEX_PASSWORD_TEST,
303              &nvCmdAuths, 0 );
304      CheckPassed( rval );
305
306      // Delete the NV index's entry in the entity table.
307      rval = DeleteEntity( TPM20_INDEX_PASSWORD_TEST );
308      CheckPassed( rval );
309  }
```

I've demonstrated how to send single commands using an HMAC session. Now we need to consider multiple commands and how the nonces work.

Using an HMAC Session to Send Multiple Commands (Rolling Nonces)

The nonceTPM changes after every successful TPM command executed within a session. nonceCaller can be changed if the caller so desires. Because the nonces figure into the HMAC calculation, replay attacks are prevented. The HMAC calculation is as follows:

$$\text{authHMAC} := \text{HMAC}_{\text{sessionAlg}} \, ((\text{sessionKey} \, || \, \text{authValue}), \, (\text{pHash} \, || \, \text{nonceNewer} \, || \, \text{nonceOlder}$$
$$\{ \, || \, \text{nonceTPMdecrypt} \, \} \, \{ \, || \, \text{nonceTPMencrypt} \, \}$$
$$|| \, \text{sessionAttributes}))$$

In this equation, notice the nonceNewer and nonceOlder parameters. On a command, nonceNewer is the nonceCaller, and nonceOlder is the last nonceTPM. For a response, nonceNewer is the current nonceTPM, and nonceOlder is the nonceCaller from the command. For now, ignore the decrypt and encrypt nonces because they're only used for decrypt and encrypt sessions.[16] This section describes the mechanics of how the nonces are used in multiple commands in an HMAC session. A sequence of multiple commands in an HMAC session works like this (refer to Figure 13-13 and Listing 13-2):

1. When an HMAC session is started, nonceCaller1 is sent to the TPM and nonceTPM1 is received from the TPM. This happens in the StartAuthSessionWithParams call, lines 72–75 in Listing 13-2.

2. Every time a command is successfully authorized, a new nonceTPM is generated. This is called "rolling" the nonce. The caller can also change the nonceCaller before each command that is sent using the session, if desired. Look at the calls to RollNonces in Listing 13-2 on lines 198, 217, 245, and 269.

3. On the next session command:

    a. For the command HMAC, nonceTPM1 is used as the nonceOlder parameter. nonceCaller2, sent with this command in the authorization area for the session, is used as nonceNewer.

    b. For the response HMAC, nonceCaller2 is used as nonceOlder. nonceTPM2, sent with the response in the authorization area for the session, is used as nonceNewer.

4. For subsequent commands, this pattern repeats, with nonceCaller and nonceTPM flip-flopping between nonceNewer and nonceOlder in the HMAC calculation depending on whether the HMAC is being calculated on the command or response.

5. This pattern repeats until the session is closed. The nonces changing and the fact that they're used in command and response HMAC calculations prevent replay attacks.

---

[16]Because the nonceTPM figures into both the command and response HMACs, the obvious question is, what's the purpose of the nonceCaller? The answer (from the TPM specification writer) is that if the caller didn't trust the TPM to generate nonceTpm values with enough randomness, the caller could specify sufficiently random nonceCaller values to overcome this deficiency.

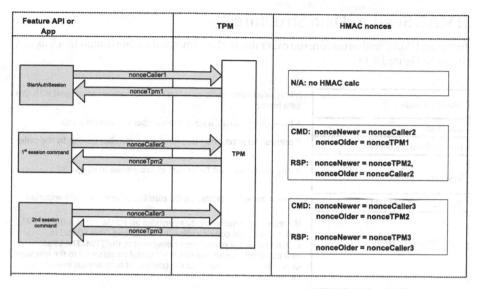

Figure 13-13. *Nonces used in an HMAC session to prevent replay attacks*

HMAC Session Security

What makes HMAC sessions secure? Basically, three aspects of HMAC sessions are used to secure commands:

- *Session key*: The bind authValue and salt are secrets that should be known only to the caller and the TPM. Both of these values are used in calculating the session key. An attacker who doesn't know these values can't calculate the session key. Because the session key is used to create the HMAC key, this means the attacker can't successfully send commands to or receive responses from the TPM. This this prevents man-in-the-middle attacks.

- *HMAC*: The session key and the entity's authValue are used to generate the HMAC key. The authValue of the entity being accessed is a secret that should only be known to the caller and the TPM. Again, this means the attacker can't successfully mount man-in-the-middle attacks.

- *Nonces*: The nonces are used to prevent replay attacks. The nonces figure into the HMAC calculation, which can't be properly performed without using the correct nonces. Since the nonces keep changing, a command byte stream can't be replayed.

As long as the secrecy of the bind authValue, salt, and entity authValue are maintained, attackers can't authorize actions on the entity, and the rolling nonces prevent replay of commands.

HMAC Session Data Structure

To use an HMAC authorization, the caller fills in the command authorization block as shown in Figure 13-14.

Session handle	A four-octet value indicating the session number associated with this data block.
Size field	A two-octet value indicating the number of octets in *nonce*.
Nonce (from the caller)	If present, an octet array that contains a number chosen by the caller.
Session attributes	A single octet with bit fields that indicate session usage.
Size field = `sizeof` HMAC	A two-octet value indicating the number of octets in *authorization*.
Authorization = HMAC	If present, an octet array that contains an HMAC. This is the HMAC generated by the code sending the command. This HMAC is calculated on the parameters being sent to the TPM. The TPM independently calculates this HMAC and compares it to the one sent down the wire to verify that the command byte stream wasn't corrupted.

Figure 13-14. Command HMAC authorization area

The code that fills in the command authorization blocks is in Listing 13-2 on lines 19–21, 150, 189–195, 198 (sets the tpmNonce), and 202–205 (sets the HMAC in the authorization area).

The response authorization area looks like Figure 13-15.

Size field	A two-octet value indicating the number of octets in *nonce*.
Nonce (from the TPM)	If present, an octet array that contains a number chosen by the TPM.
Session attributes	A single octet with bit fields that indicate session usage.
Size field	A two-octet value indicating the number of octets in *acknowledgment*.
Acknowledgment = HMAC	If present, an octet array that contains an HMAC. This HMAC is generated by the TPM over the response data returned by the command. The caller receives the response, independently calculates the HMAC of the response, and verifies it against the TPM-generated HMAC to verify that no data corruption has occurred.

Figure 13-15. Response HMAC authorization area

The code that sets up the response authorization blocks is in Listing 13-2 on lines 24–26. The call to the one-call function returns the authorization area from the TPM in nvRspAuths, and the call to CheckResponseHMACs on lines 224–226 verifies that the HMAC in the response authorization is correct.

This concludes the deep dive into HMAC sessions. Now the water gets even deeper with a discussion of the most feature-rich and complicated authorizations: policy or extended authorization.

Policy Authorization

Policy authorization, also known as Extended Authorization (EA), is the Swiss army knife of TPM authorizations. With the right expertise, you can do just about any kind of authorization with it. This section and the following chapter, Chapter 14, aim to give you the knowledge required to use the incredible power of EA. In this section, we describe how EA works at a high level, the high-level policy authorization lifetime, and each of the steps in that lifetime: policy hash creation, entity creation or alteration, policy session creation, and policy session use. We will also explore the security properties of EA. As much as possible, this section doesn't describe individual policy commands; the next chapter describes those in detail.

How Does EA Work?

At a high level, EA enables very expressive policies. EA, like HMAC and password authorizations, is used to authorize actions on a TPM entity. Some examples of the controls that can be enforced before authorizing an action are:

- Requiring certain values in a specified set of PCR registers

- Requiring a certain locality

- Requiring a certain value or range of values in an NV index

- Requiring a password

- Requiring physical presence

- Requiring sequences of conditions

And there are many more. These can be combined in AND and OR combinations that result in an infinite number of policy variations. Policy authorizations allow considerable complexity and creativity in authorizations. Policy authorizations are the "mother of all complex authorizations."

For a command to be authorized by a policy authorization, two things must be correct:

- Each policy command "asserts" that some condition(s) are true. If the specified conditions for each policy command aren't true, then the authorization fails. This failure can happen either:

  - *At the time of the policy command*: This is an *immediate* assertion, and this failure occurs before ever getting to the command to be authorized. This failure means the policyDigest for the session isn't hash-extended by the policy command. If the policy command is successful, the policyDigest is hash-extended with the proper values.

  - *At the time of the command being authorized*: This is a *deferred* assertion. In this case, the policyDigest is hash-extended with data that indicates that the particular policy command was executed. Testing of the conditions is deferred until the time of the action being authorized.

■ **Note** Some commands can be combined assertions, which means both immediate and deferred conditions must be valid for the assertion to pass.

- At authorization time:

  - Any deferred conditions are checked. If any of these fail, the command isn't authorized.

  - The entity's authPolicy is compared to the policy session's policyDigest. If they're equal, the command is authorized, and it executes. If they aren't equal, the authorization fails. Basically, if the authPolicy is equal to the policyDigest, this is proof that the required policy commands were executed, any immediate assertions generated by those commands passed, and that all this occurred in the correct sequence before the command being authorized.

Now you've seen two time-related terms: *policy command time* and *authorization time*. All the time intervals related to policy authorizations need to be defined precisely in order for you to understand policy authorizations.

Policy Authorization Time Intervals

In working with policy authorizations, four distinct time intervals must be considered. These are implied by various sections of the specification but not specifically delineated:

- *Build Entity Policy time*: The time interval when the authPolicy used to create an entity is built. There are two ways to create this authPolicy:

    - Software can replicate the policy calculations done by the TPM.

    - A trial policy session can be created. The policy commands used to generate the policyDigest are sent to the TPM. During a trial policy session, all assertions pass; the purpose of the trial policy session is to generate the policyDigest as if all the assertions passed. After all the policy commands are sent to the TPM, the policyDigest can be read from the TPM using the TPM2_GetPolicyDigest command.

■ **Note**   Policies may be, and often are, reused for creating multiple entities and for authorizing many actions.

- *Create Entity time*: The time when the entity is created. If the entity will use an authPolicy, the policy digest created at Build Entity Policy time is used to create the entity.

■ **Note**   Because an entity's name is created at Create Entity time, the policy digest input when creating the entity (for example, authDigest) can't include the entity's name.

- *Build Policy Digest time*: After a policy session is started, during this time interval, policy commands are sent to the TPM in preparation for a command to be authorized. These commands cause the session's policyDigest, which is maintained inside the TPM, to be hash-extended with policy command-specific values.

- *Authorization time*: The time when the command to be authorized is sent to the TPM. At this time the session's policyDigest must match the entity's authPolicy, and any deferred assertions must pass.

To summarize, a policy calculation is usually performed twice—once at Build Entity Policy time and once at Build Policy Digest time:[17]

- The first time is to create a policy hash used as the authPolicy when creating an entity.

- The second time occurs before authorizing an action on an entity: a policy hash is built up in the session context inside the TPM. When the command to be authorized is executed, the session's policy hash is compared to the authPolicy of the entity. If they match, the authorization is successful.

All policy commands do two or three things, and they do these things at the following time intervals:

- They check a condition or conditions (the *assertion*). This is done at Build Policy Digest time (immediate assertion) or Authorization time (deferred assertion), or some combination of the two (combined assertion).

- They hash-extend the current session policy digest with policy command-specific data. This is done at Build Entity Policy time and Build Policy Digest time.

- They *may* update other session state. This session state is used for deferred or combined assertions to indicate what deferred conditions should be tested at authorization time. These updates are done at Build Policy Digest time.

Now that you understand the various time intervals, let's look at a typical policy session lifetime.

Policy Authorization Lifecycle

The typical steps in a policy authorization lifecycle are very similar, with some additions, to the lifecycle steps used for password and HMAC sessions:

1. Build the entity policy.

2. Create the entity using the policy digest created in step 1.

---

[17]It should be noted that in some cases, a single real policy session can be used to generate the policy for both the creation of the entity and authorizing actions within the session; in this case, the policy digest is calculated only once. For instance, the following sequence would work: start a real policy session, send the TPM2_PolicyLocality command, get the policy digest, create the entity using the policy digest, and authorize a command using the policy session. This reverses the usual order of creating the entity and then starting the real policy session. It probably isn't very useful for most normal uses, but an understanding of this provides insight into how policy sessions operate. This only works for cases where the policy assertions can be can be satisfied before the entity is created.

■ **Note**   Steps 1 and 2 are typically performed long before the remaining steps. And the remaining steps can occur multiple times to authorize multiple actions on the entity.

---

3.   Start a policy session.

4.   Using the policy session, send policy commands to fulfill the required authorization.

5.   Perform the action on the entity that requires authorization.

Let's look at each of these steps in detail, with the applicable line numbers from Listing 13-2. For brevity's sake, line numbers are listed only for code that is unique to policy sessions.

Building the Entity's Policy Digest

The first task in using a policy session is to determine what the authorization policy will be: for example, what entities need to be protected, what actions on those entities need to be restricted, and the exact nature of those restrictions. Then, the policy digest must be created; this step corresponds to the Build Entity Policy time interval described previously. There are two ways to create a policy digest: use a trial policy session, or create the policy digest with software that emulates the actions of the TPM in creating a policy digest. I will describe both of these using a simple example; the code uses a trial policy session.

An example policy might allow an NV index of 0x01400001 to be written or read by someone who knows its authValue. In this case, building the entity policy using a trial policy session can be done as follows:

1.   Start a trial policy session using the TPM2_StartAuthSession command. The main inputs of concern for a policy session are:

   a.   sessionType = TPM_SE_TRIAL. This is what configures the session as a trial policy session.

   b.   authHash = TPM_ALG_SHA256. This sets the hashing algorithm used for generating the policyDigest. I chose SHA256, but any hashing algorithm supported by the TPM can be used here.

   This command returns a policy session handle, call it H_{ps}. Lines 63, 66, and 72–75 start the trial policy session.

2.   Send a TPM2_PolicyAuthValue command with the following inputs (see lines 78–79): policySession = H_{ps}.

   This command extends the session's policy digest as follows:

$$policyDigest_{new} := H_{policyAlg}(policyDigest_{old} \ || \ TPM\_CC\_PolicyAuthValue)$$

where policyAlg is the hash algorithm set by the TPM2_StartAuthSession command, and policyDigest$_{old}$ is the buffer of length equal to the size of the policy digest that corresponds to the policyAlg with all bytes set to 0.

3. Send a TPM2_GetPolicyDigest command (lines 83–85). This command returns the policy digest, digest$_{ps}$.

Alternatively, to calculate digest$_{ps}$ in software, the software needs to duplicate the policy digest calculation in step 2. Appropriate calls to a crypto library such as OpenSSL can be used to accomplish this.

Once the policyDigest has been calculated or created, the NV index can be created to use the policyDigest for authorization of write operations to the index. Unlike a password or HMAC authorization, after the NV index is created the policyDigest used to access an NV index or any other entity can't be directly changed. There are advanced policy commands that can accomplish this through a policy-specific method of indirection, but that topic is described in the next chapter.

Creating the Entity to Use the Policy Digest

Now we need to create the index in such a way as to allow writes with the policy authorization; this step corresponds to the Create Entity time interval described previously. This is done by sending a TPM2_NV_DefineSpace command with the following inputs (this is done by the call to the DefineNvIndex function):

- auth = TPM2B that contains the authValue used to access this NV index (lines 42-44).

- publicInfo.t.nvPublic.nvIndex = 0x01400001 (lines 115-117).

- publicInfo.t.nvPublic.nameAlg = TPM_ALG_SHA256. This is the hash algorithm used to calculate the index's name, and this algorithm must be the same as the policyAlg used to calculate the policyDigest, whether this was done by a trial session or by software. See lines 115-117.

- publicInfo.t.nvPublic.attributes.TPMA_NV_POLICYWRITE = 1 and publicInfo.t.nvPublic.attributes.TPMA_NV_POLICYREAD = 1. This configures the index to allow reads and writes only if the policy is satisfied. See lines 109–110.

- publicInfo.t.nvPublic.authPolicy = the TPM2B that contains the policyDigest, digest$_{ps}$. See lines 83-85 and 115-117.

- publicInfo.t.nvPublic.dataSize = 32. This indicates the size of the data contained in the NV index; in this case, the index is configured to be only 32 bytes wide. See lines 115-117.

- Set the NV index's auth value. See lines 42-44.

This command creates an NV index that can only be written if the policy is satisfied. The next step is to create a real—that is, non-trial—policy session and use it to authorize writes to the NV index.

Starting the Real Policy Session

Start a real policy session using the TPM2_StartAuthSession command. The main inputs of concern for a policy session are as follows (see lines 152 and 154-156):

- tpmKey = TPM_RH_NULL
- bind = TPM_RH_NULL

■ **Note** The tpmKey and bind settings mean this is an unbound and unsalted session. These settings were chosen in order to keep this example as simple as possible; they're also the most common way that policy sessions are used. The goal here is to understand the process and avoid low-level details as much as possible.

- sessionType = TPM_SE_POLICY. This is what configures the session as a real—that is, non-trial—policy session.

- authHash = TPM_ALG_SHA256. This sets the hashing algorithm used for generating the policyDigest. Because we used SHA256 when creating the policyDigest, we must use this same algorithm when starting the real policy session.

This command returns a policy session handle, H_{ps}. Now we can use this policy session to send commands to authorize actions on the NV index.

Sending Policy Commands to Fulfill the Policy

Using the policy session created in the previous step, the code now sends the same sequence of policy commands that it used to create the NV index's policyDigest at Build Entity Policy time; this step corresponds to the Build Policy Digest time interval described previously. In this case, the sequence is very simple, and we only need to send one policy command, a TPM2_PolicyAuthValue command with the following input (lines 177-179): policySession = H_{ps}.

In response to this command, the TPM does two things:

- It extends the policy session's policy digest just as it did for the trial session at Build Entity Policy time.

- Because TPM2_PolicyAuthValue is a deferred assertion, it saves some state information into the policy session's context so that it knows to check the HMAC at Authorization time.

At this point, the policy authorization is completely "locked and loaded" to authorize the action. The next thing that happens is that we attempt to write to the NV index.

Performing the Action That Requires Authorization

This step corresponds to the Authorization time interval described earlier. We write to the NV index, and, if it's been authorized correctly, the write completes successfully. To do this step, send the TPM2_NV_Write command with the following inputs:

- authHandle = 0x01400001. This handle indicates the source of the authorization. See lines 211-214.

- nvIndex = 0x01400001. This is the NV index to be authorized. See lines 211-214.

- The authorization area for authHandle must have the following settings:

  - authHandle = the policy session handle, H_{ps}. See lines 189-190.

  - nonceCaller = whatever nonce the caller wants to use. This can even be a zero-sized nonce. See lines 191-192.

  - sessionAttributes = 0. See lines 193-194.

  - hmac.t.buffer is set to the HMAC of the command. The HMAC key is the session key concatenated with the authValue of the NV index. See lines 202-205.

- data = 0xa5. See lines 166-169 and 211-214.

- offset = 0. See lines 211-214.

In response to this command, the TPM checks that policySession->policyDigest matches the authPolicy of the entity being accessed. Then it checks that the HMAC is correct. If both checks pass, the write proceeds and the command completes successfully.

■ **Note**   You may have noticed that in Listing 13-2, because the policy case uses a TPM2_PolicyAuthValue command, the HMAC and policy cases are very similar. The main difference is that the policy case requires more work. The obvious question is, if a policy session that uses TPM2_PolicyAuthValue requires more work, why wouldn't we just use an HMAC session? The answer, which is expanded in the next chapter, is that a policy session allows many other factors besides the authorization value to be combined, creating a much more configurable and, possibly, secure authorization.

You've now seen a complete policy authorization from cradle to grave. This was a very simple example, but it should form a good basis for understanding the more complex policy authorizations in the next chapter.

To finish this chapter, we unify the lifecycles for password, HMAC, and policy authorizations into one single lifecycle.

Combined Authorization Lifecycle

The typical steps in an authorization lifecycle are the following:

1. For HMAC or policy sessions, an authValue or authPolicy must be determined before creating the entity:

    a. If actions on the entity will be authorized using a policy session, precalculate the authPolicy policy hash.

    b. If actions on the entity will be authorized using a password or HMAC session, determine what the shared secret will be.

2. Create the entity to be accessed using an authorization value (authValue) and/or policy hash (authPolicy), or change the authValue value for an existing entity (changing the authPolicy for an entity is done by a different means and is described in the next chapter):

    a. The entity's authValue will be used for either password authorizations or HMAC authorizations. For password authorizations, the authValue will be used as a clear-text password. For HMAC authorizations, the authValue will be used to generate session HMACs.

    b. The entity's authPolicy is used to determine if the proper policy assertions have passed before the command to be authorized. This policy hash must be precalculated before creating the entity; hence step 1a.

3. Calculate the HMAC. For policy sessions that don't use an HMAC, this step can be skipped.

4. In the case of an HMAC or policy authorization, start the HMAC or policy session.

5. Do an authorized action using the authorization. The authorization passes if:

    a. The password sent during the command matches the entity's authValue.

    b. The HMAC sent during the command matches the HMAC calculated by the TPM. Both of these HMACs are derived, in part, from the authValue of the entity.

    c.   The policyDigest of the policy session at Authorization Time matches the authPolicy of the entity. This policy hash derives from a variety of factors determined by the policy command(s) used to create the policyDigest. Also, any deferred assertions must pass for the authorization to be successful.

6.   In the case of an HMAC session, calculate the expected response HMAC, and verify it against the one returned by the TPM.

These steps are represented in relative time order, but many other actions could occur between them. Also, a single policyDigest can be used to authorize multiple actions to multiple entities. Similarly, a single HMAC session can be used to authorize multiple actions to multiple entities. The exact mechanics of these steps vary with the authorization type, and these differences were described previously, but each of these steps must be performed for all authorizations with the following exceptions:

- Steps 3–4 aren't required for password authorizations.

- Step 6 isn't required for password or policy authorizations.

For more code examples of policy sessions, see the TestPolicy function in the TSS SAPI test code.

Summary

This concludes the discussion of authorizations and sessions. Congratulations on making it this far! If you understand this chapter, you're well on your way to becoming a TPM 2.0 master.

This chapter described the general concepts of authorizations and sessions and tried to clarify their differences. You looked at the command and response authorization areas, and lifecycles for password, HMAC, and policy authorizations. Then you saw an overall authorization lifecycle.

This may have felt like drinking from a fire hose, and that's because it was! This is one of the most difficult areas of the TPM to understand; good comprehension of this material will aid you immeasurably in understanding and using TPM 2.0 devices. The next chapter describes the most powerful of authorizations—policy authorizations—in detail, with a description of each of the policy authorization commands and use cases for them.

CHAPTER 14

■ ■ ■

Extended Authorization (EA) Policies

TPM 2.0 has unified the way that all entities controlled by the TPM may be authorized. Earlier chapters have discussed authorization data used for passwords and HMAC authorization. This chapter goes into detail about one of the most useful new forms of authorization in the TPM, starting with a description of why this feature was added to the TPM and then describing in broad brushstrokes the multifaceted approach that was taken.

This new approach for authorization has many capabilities. As a result, if a user wants to restrict an entity so it can be used only under specific circumstances, it's possible to do so. The sum total of restrictions on the use of an entity is called a *policy*. Extended authorization (EA) policies can become complex *very* quickly. Therefore this chapter's approach is incremental, first describing very simple policies and gradually adding complexity. This is done by examining how to build the following:

- Simple assertions

- Command-based assertions

- Multifactor authentication

- Multiuser/compound authorization

- Flexible policies that can be changed on the fly

Throughout this chapter, you see examples of practical policies like those used in most cases. It turns out that building policies is different than using them, so you learn how a user satisfies a policy; at that point it should become clear why policies are secure.

Finally, you consider some policies that can be used to solve certain special cases. This section may spur your creativity—you'll see that there are many more ways of using policies than you've thought of.

Let's begin by comparing EA policies to using passwords for authentication.

Policies and Passwords

All entities in the TPM can be authorized in two basic ways. The first is based on a password associated with the entity when it's created. The other is with a policy that is likewise associated with the entity when it's created. A policy is a means of authorizing a command that can consist of almost any approach to authorization that someone can think of. Some entities (hierarchies and dictionary attack reset handles) are created by the TPM and thus have default passwords and policies. The TPM-assigned *name* of these entities is fixed, not dependent on the policy that is used to authorize them. Such entities' policies can be changed.

All other entities—NVRAM indexes and keys—have their name calculated in part from the policy that is assigned when they're created. As a result, although their password can be changed, they have policies that are immutable. As you'll see, some policies can be made flexible so they can be easily managed in spite of this immutability.

Anything that can be done directly with a password can also be done with a policy, but the reverse isn't true. Some things (like duplicating a key) can only be authorized using a policy command. (However, making things more complicated, you can still use a password to authorize duplicating a key, by using a policy that describes a password authorization.)

A policy can be fine-tuned—everything is possible, from setting a policy to be the NULL policy that can never be satisfied, to having different authentication requirements for individual commands or for different users when applied to an entity. Thus EA is able to solve many issues that application developers need to deal with.

Why Extended Authorization?

EA in the TPM was created to solve the basic problem of manageability of TPM entity authorization. It makes it easier to learn how to use a TPM by having all TPM entities be authorized the same way, and it also allows a user to define authorization policies that can solve the following problems:

- Allow for multiple varieties of authentication (passwords, biometrics, and so on).

- Allow for multifactor authentication (requiring more than one type of authentication).

- Allow for creation of policies without the use of a TPM. Policies don't contain any secrets, so they can be created entirely in software. That doesn't mean secrets aren't needed to satisfy a policy.

- Allow attestation of the policy associated with an entity. It should be possible to prove what authorization is necessary in order to use an entity.

- Allow for multiple people or roles to satisfy a policy.

- Allow restriction of the capabilities of a particular role for an object to particular actions or users.

- Fix the PCR brittleness problem. In TPM 1.2, once an entity was locked to a set of PCRs that measured particular configurations, if the configurations ever had to be changed, the entity could no longer be used.

- Create a means to change how a policy behaves, providing flexibility.

Multiple Varieties of Authentication

Today, many different kinds of techniques and devices are used for authentication. Passwords are the oldest (and perhaps weakest) form of authentication. Biometrics such as fingerprints, iris scans, facial recognition, penned signatures, and even cardiac rhythm are used for authentication. Digital signatures and HMACs are forms of cryptographic authentication used in tokens or keys. Time clocks in banks use the time of day as a form of authentication and don't allow a vault to be opened except during business hours.

The TPM was designed so that objects can use almost any kind of authentication conceivable, although many forms require additional hardware. A policy can consist of a single type of authentication or multiple varieties.

Multifactor Authentication

Multifactor authentication is one of the most important forms of security and is popular today. It requires more than one means of authentication in order to provide authorization to execute a command. Those authentications may take many forms—smart cards, passwords, biometrics, and so on. The basic idea is that it's harder to defeat multiple authentication formats than it is to defeat a single one. Different forms of authentication have different strengths and weaknesses. For example, passwords can be easily supplied remotely—fingerprints less so, especially if the design is done correctly.

The TPM 2.0 design allows for many different forms of authentication and provides facilities to add even more using external hardware. Each mechanism that can be used for authentication is called an *assertion*. Assertions include the following:

- Passwords

- HMACs

- Smart cards providing digital signatures

- Physical presence

- State of the machine (Platform Configuration Register [PCR])

- State of the TPM (counters, time)

- State of external hardware (who has authenticated to a fingerprint reader, where a GPS is located, and so on)

A policy can require that any number of assertions be true in order to satisfy it. The innovation behind EA in the TPM is that it represents in a single hash value a complex policy consisting of many assertions.

How Extended Authorization Works

A policy is a hash that represents a set of authentications that together describe how to satisfy the policy. When an entity (for example, a key) is created, a policy may be associated with it. To use that entity, the user convinces the TPM that the policy has been satisfied.

This is done in three steps:

1. A policy session is created. When a policy session with the TPM is started, the TPM creates a session policy buffer for that session. (The size of the session policy buffer is the size of the hash algorithm chosen when the session was started, and it's initialized to all zeroes.)

2. The user provides one or more authentications to the TPM session, using TPM2_PolicyXXX commands. These change the value in that session policy buffer. They also may set flags in the session that represent checks that must be done when a command is executed.

3. When the entity is used in a command, the TPM compares the policy associated with the entity with the value in the session policy buffer. If they aren't the same, the command will not execute. (At this point, any session flags associated with policy authorizations are also checked. If they aren't also satisfied, this command isn't executed.)

Policies don't contain any secrets. As a result, all policies can be created purely in software outside a TPM. However, the TPM must be able to reproduce policies (in a session's policy digest) in order to use them. Because the TPM has this ability, it makes sense for the TPM to allow the user to use this facility to produce policies. This is done by using a *trial session*. A trial session can't be used to satisfy a policy, but it can be used to calculate one.

Policy sessions used to satisfy policies can be somewhat more complicated than the creation of a policy. Some policy commands are checked immediately and update a policy buffer stored in the session. Others set flags or variables in the session that must be checked when the session is used to authorize a command. Table 14-1 shows which policy commands require such checks.

Table 14-1. *Policy Commands that Set Flags*

Command	Sets Flag or Variable in Session Requiring the TPM to Check Something at Execution Time
TPM_PolicyAuthorize	No
TPM_PolicyAuthValue	Yes—sets a flag that requires an HMAC session to be used at command execution
TPM_PolicyCommandCode	Yes—checks that a particular command is being executed
TPM_PolicyCounterTimer	Yes—performs logical check against TPMS_TIME_INFO structured
TPM_PolicyCpHash	Yes—checks that the command and parameters have certain values
TPM_PolicyLocality	Yes—checks that the command is being executed from a particular locality
TPM_PolicyNameHash	Yes—identifies objects that will be checked to be sure they have specific values when the command is executed
TPM_PolicyOR	No
TPM_PolicyTicket	No
TPM_PolicyPCR	Yes—checks that PCRs have not changed when the command is executed
TPM_PolicySigned	No
TPM_PolicySecret	No
TPM_PolicyNV	No
TPM_PolicyDuplicationSelect	Yes—specifies where a key can be moved
TPM_PolicyPassword	Yes—sets a flag that requires a password at command execution

Creating Policies

Incredibly complicated policies are possible but are unlikely to be used in real life. In order to explain the creation of policies, this chapter introduces an artificial distinction between different kinds of policies, which are described in detail:

- *Simple assertion policy*: Uses a single authentication to create a policy. Examples include passwords, smart cards, biometrics, time of day, and so on.

- *Multi-assertion policy*: Combines several assertions, such as requiring both a biometric and a password; or a smart card and a PIN; or a password, a smart card, a biometric, and a GPS location. Such as policy is equivalent to using a logical AND between different assertions.

- *Compound policy*: Introduces a logical OR, such as "Bill can authorize with a smart card OR Sally can authorize with her password." Compound policies can be made from any other policies.

- *Flexible policy*: Uses a wild card or placeholder to be defined later. A policy can be created in which a specific term can be substituted with any other approved policy. It looks like a simple assertion, but any approved (simple or complicated) policy can be substituted for it.

As mentioned, a policy is a digest that represents the means of satisfying the policy. A policy starts out as a buffer that is the size of the hash algorithm associated with an entity, but set to all zeroes. As parts of the policy are satisfied, this buffer is extended with values representing what has happened. Extending a buffer is done by concatenating the current value with new data and hashing the resulting array with the designated hash algorithm. Let's demonstrate this with the simplest of all polices: those than require only one type of authorization to be satisfied.

Simple Assertion Policies

A simple Extended Authorization (EA) policy: the simple assertion policy, which consists of a single authentication, can be one of the following types:

- Password or HMAC (policies that require proof of knowledge of an object's password)

- Digital signatures (smart cards)

- Attestation of an external machine (a particular biometric reader attests that a particular user has matched, or a particular GPS attests that the machine is in a particular location)

- Physical presence (an indication such as a switch that proves a user is physically present at the TPM. While this is in the specification, it is not likely to be implemented, so we will ignore it in the following.)

- PCRs (state of the machine on which the TPM exists)

- Locality (the software layer that originated the TPM command)

- Internal state of the TPM (counter values, timer values, and so on)

Creating simple assertion policies can be done using the TPM itself, in three steps:

1. Create the trial session. This is as simple as executing the following command:

   TPM2_StartAuthSession

   It's passed a parameter TPM_SE_TRIAL to tell the TPM to start a trial session, and a hash algorithm to use for calculating the policy. This returns (among other things) the handle of a trial session. It's referred to as myTrialSessionHandle.

2. Execute TPM2 policy commands that describe the policy (described shortly).

3. Ask the TPM for the value of the policy created with the command by executing

   TPM2_PolicyGetDigest

   and passing it the handle of the trial session: myTrialSessionHandle).

4. End the session (or reset it if you want to use it again) by executing

   TPM2_FlushContext

   again passing it the name of the trial session: myTrialSessionHandle.

Because steps 1, 3, and 4 are common to all simple assertions, they aren't repeated in the following; we merely describe the second step for each command.

Passwords (Plaintext and HMAC) of the Object

Passwords are the most basic form of authentication used today, but they're far from the most secure. Nonetheless, because they're in use in so many devices, it was important that the TPM support them. (The TPM 1.2 did not support passwords in the clear—only proof of knowledge of the password using an HMAC. The TPM 2.0 supports both.) It's assumed that when a password is used, the device provides for a trusted path between the password entry and the TPM. If this doesn't exist, facilities are present in the TPM 2.0

architecture to allow for using a salted HMAC session to prove knowledge of a password without sending it in the clear, as seen in Chapter 13. When an object is loaded into a TPM, the TPM knows its associated password. Therefore, the policy doesn't need to include the password. Thus the same policy can be used with different entities that have different passwords.

Creating a simple assertion policy can be reduced to four steps:

1. Set the policy buffer to all zeroes, with the length equal to the size of the hash algorithm.

0x00000....0000

Figure 14-1. Initializing the Policy

2. Concatenate TPM_CC_PolicyAuthValue to this buffer.

0x00000....0000 TPM_CC_PolicyAuthValue

Figure 14-2. Concatenation of the buffer with the policy data per the Specification

3. Substitute the value of TPM_CC_PolicyAuthValue from its value in part 2 of the specification.

0x00000....0000 0000016B

Figure 14-3. Substituting the value of TPM_CC_PolicyAuthValue

4. Calculate the hash of this concatenation, and put the result in the buffer. This end result *is* the policy for a simple assertion.

0x8fcd2169ab92694.................1fc7ac1eddc1fddb0e

Figure 14-4. Hashing the result provides a new value for the buffer

When this policy command is executed, the policy buffer of the session is set to this final value. In addition, a flag is set in the TPM's session specifying that when a command with an object in it that requires authorization is used, a password session must be provided with that command and the password provided must match that of the object.

Similarly, when a policy is created to use the HMAC assertion (TPM2_PolicyAuthValue), two things happen

1.   The policy is extended with the value TPM_CC_PolicyAuthValue.

2.   A flag is set in the TPM's session indicating that when objects requiring authorization are used, a separate HMAC session is required. The TPM checks the password HMAC against the object's authorization data and allows access if they match (see Chapter 13.)

If you're using a trial session to create the policy, you accomplish this by executing the command TPM2_PolicyAuthValue and passing it the handle of the trial session.

This inherently means that when you're using passwords, either in plaintext or as an HMAC, either the plaintext password or the HMAC must be included to authorize a command with a policy session. The fact that TPM_CC_PolicyAuthValue appears twice in the previous explanation isn't a typo: the repetition means the choice of password or HMAC isn't decided when the policy is created, but rather when the non-policy command is executed. It's up to the user of the entity, not the creator of the entity, to decide how they will prove their knowledge of the password to the TPM.

Passwords aren't the most secure means of authentication. A much more secure approach is to use a digital signature, often implemented with a smart card such as a United States Department of Defense (DoD) Common Access Card (CAC card) or United States Federal Personal Identity Verification (PIV) card.

Passwords of a Different Object

A new (and very useful) assertion policy in TPM 2.0 is an assertion that the user knows the password of an entity *different from the one being used*. Although this might seem odd at first, it's particularly useful because of the difference in the behavior of NVRAM entities versus key objects. When the password of a key object is changed with TPM2_ChangeAuth, what is really happening is that a new copy of the key is being created that has a new password. There is no guarantee that the old copy is discarded. This is because key objects normally reside in files outside the TPM, and the TPM therefore can't guarantee that the old copy of the key file has been erased. However, NV entities reside entirely in the TPM: if their password is changed, it really is *changed*. The old copy can no longer be used.

This means if a key is created and a policy is created for it that requires the user to prove knowledge of an NV entity's password, it's possible to change the password necessary to use the key without worrying that the old password can still be used to authorize the key. In this case, changing the password of the NV entity effectively changes the password of the key. TPM 2.0 allows you to make authorization of a key dependent on knowing an NVRAM entity's password.

This further provides opportunities to manage the passwords of a large number of entities. Suppose you create a policy that points to a particular NV index's password, and then you associate that policy with a large number of keys. You can effectively change the password of all those keys by changing the password of the one NV index.

The TPM2_PolicySecret command requires you to pass in the name of the object whose password is required to satisfy the policy. It's perhaps not obvious, but when creating the policy for an object, you can't pass in the name of the object being created. This is because the name of the object depends on the policy, and if the policy depends on the name of the object, a vicious circle is created. This explains why the TPM2_PolicyAuthValue command is also needed. It provides a way of pointing to the authorization of the object being authorized.

To calculate the policy in a trial session, you execute the command TPM2_PolicySecret and pass it the handle of the trial session, as well as the handle of the object whose authorization will be used. Doing so extends the session policy buffer with TPM_CC_PolicySecret || authObject→Name || policyRef. The variable of note that is passed to the command is, of course, a handle for the object whose authorization will be used. As explained regarding names, although the handle of that object is passed to the TPM when executing TPM_CC_PolicySecret, the TPM internally uses the Name of the object in extending the session policy buffer. This prevents a change in the handle from causing a security exposure.

Technically, you need to include an authorization session for the handle of the object being authorized when executing this command. Although the specification indicates that it doesn't need to be satisfied in a trial session, most implementations require it. Therefore you must also include a correct password or HMAC session when executing this command. If you instead calculate the policy without using the TPM, this requirement isn't necessary.

Digital Signatures (such as Smart Cards)

It wasn't generally possible to authenticate use of a TPM 1.2 entity using a private key. In TPM 2.0, this has changed. It's now possible to require a digital signature as a form of access control. When a policy is formed using this assertion, the policy value is extended with three values: TPM_CC_PolicySigned, SHA256[1](publicKey) and a policyRef. (A policyRef is used to identify precisely how the signed assertion will be used. Often it will be left as an Empty Buffer, but if a person is asked to authorize an action remotely, that person may want to precisely identify what action is being authorized. If the policyRef is part of the policy, the authorizing party will have to sign that value when authorizing the action.)

This can be done using a trial session by using the TPM2_PolicySigned command; but before this can be done, the TPM must know the public key used to verify the signature. This is done by loading that public key into the TPM first. The easy way to do this is to use a TPM2_LoadExternal command and load the public key into the TPM_RH_NULL hierarchy. You do so with the command TPM2_LoadExternal, passing in the public key structure.

---

[1]SHA256 is used throughout this book as the hash algorithm for everything except PCRs. However, technically you can use any hash algorithm that matches that chosen when the policy is created.

This returns a handle to the loaded public key, for now called aPublicHandle. Then you execute the command TPM2_PolicySigned, passing in the handle of the trial session and the handle of the loaded public key.

Satisfying this policy is trickier. Proving to the TPM that the user has the smart card with the private key that corresponds to this public key is a bit more involved. This is done by using the private key to sign a nonce produced by the TPM. You see this in detail at the end of this chapter.

Another assertion can be required: that the TPM resides in a machine that is healthy. This is done with PCRs.

PCRs: State of the Machine

Platform Configuration Registers (PCRs) in a TPM are typically extended by preboot or postboot software to reflect the basic software running on a system. In the 1.2 design, only a few things could use this authorization. Further, because using PCRs to restrict use of TPM 1.2 keys is a brittle operation, the restriction made this feature difficult to use.

In the 2.0 design it's possible to require that PCRs contain particular values for authorizing any command or entity. The policy merely has to specify which PCRs are being referenced and the hash of their values. Additionally, TPM 2.0 includes multiple ways of handling the brittleness. Again, all policies begin as a variable of size equal to the hash algorithm and initialized to zero. To use the PCR assertion, the policy is extended with TPM_CC_PolicyPCR || PCRs selected || digest of the values to be in the PCRs selected.

If a trial session is being used to calculate this policy, the user first selects the PCRs they wish to have defined values and puts them into a TPML_PCR_SELECTION. The user then calculates the hash of the concatenation of the defined values, calling the result pcrDigest. Then the user executes the command TPM2_PolicyPCR, passing in again the handle of the trial session and the PCRs selected and the pcrDigest just calculated.

When a user wishes to use an entity locked to PCRs, they execute the TPM2_PolicyPCR command, passing it the list of PCRs selected and the expected value of pcrDigest. Internally the TPM calculates the digest of the then-current values of those PCRs, checks it against the passed in value, and, if they match, extends the session's digest with TPM_CC_PolicyPCR || PCRs selected || digest of the values currently in the PCRs selected.

This might leave a security hole—what if the PCR values change after the assertion is made? The TPM protects against this by recording its PCR-generation counter in the TPM session state as TPM_PolicyPCR is executed. Each time any PCR is extended, the TPM generation counter is incremented. When the policy session is used to authorize a command, the current state of the generation counter is matched against the recorded value. If they don't match, it indicates that one or more PCRs have changed, and the session is unable to authorize anything.

As added flexibility, the platform-specific specification can indicate that certain PCRs will not increment the TPM generation counter. Changes to those PCRs will not invalidate the session.

Locality of Command

The 1.2 design had a characteristic called *locality* that was used to designate which software stack originated a command when it was sent to the TPM. The main usage in 1.2 was to provide proof that a command originated when the CPU was in a peculiar mode caused by entering either the Intel TXT or AMD-V command (in Intel or AMD processors, respectively). These commands are used for the Dynamic Root of Trust Measurement (DRTM) when the machine is put into a vanilla trusted state while in the midst of operations, so that the state of the machine's software can be reported in a trusted manner.

In 2.0, just as PCR assertions are extended for use whenever authorization can be used, locality is extended to a general-purpose assertion. When locality is used as an assertion in a policy, the session policy digest is extended with TPM_CC_PolicyLocality || locality(ies).

When using the trial session to calculate the policy, you execute the command TPM2_PolicyLocality, passing in the handle of the trial session and the locality structure, TPMA_LOCALITY, found in part 2 of the specification.

When satisfying a locality for a session, the user uses TPM2_PolicyLocality to pass the localities to which the session is to be bound. Then two things happen:

1. The session digest is extended with TPM_CC_PolicyLocality || locality(ies).

2. A session variable is set, recording the locality passed in.

When a command is then executed with that session, the locality from which the command is coming is compared to the locality variable set in the session. If they don't match, the command will not execute.

In the 1.2 specification, there were five localities—0, 1, 2, 3, and 4—which were represented by a bitmap in a single byte. This allowed you to select several localities at a time: for example, 0b00011101 represented the selection of localities 0, 2, 3, and 4. In the 2.0 specification, this result can be easily achieved using the PolicyOr command; but to reduce the cognitive load on people moving from 1.2 to 2.0, the localities 0–4 are represented the same way as before.

The problem with this solution is that it limits the number of localities available. It was possible to add three more localities, represented by bits 5, 6, and 7. However, the mobile and virtualization workgroups in TCG wanted more. This resulted in a bit of a hack in the specification. To extend the number of localities, the byte values above the fifth bit are used to represent single localities. This results in localities of the form 0, 1, 2, 3, 4, 32, 33, 34, ...255. That is, there is no way to represent localities 5–31. This is shown in Table 14-2. Note the change that happens when the value is 32.

Table 14-2. *Locality Representations and the Locality(ies) They Represent*

Value	Binary Representation	Locality(ies) Represented
0	0b00000000	None
1	0b00000001	Locality 0
2	0b00000010	Locality 1
3	0b00000011	Localities 0, 1
4	0b00000100	Locality 2
5	0b00000101	Localities 0, 2
6	0b00000110	Localities 1, 2
7	0b00000111	Localities 0, 1, 2
8	0b00001000	Locality 3
9–30	…	…
31	0b00011111	Localities 0, 1, 2, 3, 4
32	0b00100000	Locality 32
33	0b00100001	Locality 33
34	0b00100010	Locality 34
35–254	…	…
255	0b11111111	Locality 255

Localities can be used in a number of places. They can represent the origin of a command used to create an entity. They can also be used to lock functions so they can be used only if the command originates from a certain location. In 1.2, the locality was used to allow the CPU to control resetting and extending certain PCRs (for example, 17 and 18) to record putting the PC in a known state before doing a DRTM. Trusted Boot (tboot) is a program available on SourceForge[2] that shows how this is used; Flicker,[3] a program from CMU, used tboot to do run security-sensitive operations in a memory space separate from the OS.

Localities therefore tell the TPM where a command originated. The TPM inherently knows the values of its internal data, and localities can also be used for authorization restrictions.

---

[2]http://sourceforge.net/projects/tboot/.
[3]http://flickertcb.sourceforge.net.

Internal State of the TPM (Boot Counter and Timers)

TPM 1.2 had both an internal timer that measured the amount of time elapsed since the TPM was last powered on (and that could be correlated with an external time) and internal monotonic counters. Neither could be used as authentication elements. TPM 2.0 has a timer, a clock, and boot counters, which can be used in complicated formulas to provide for new assertions. A *boot counter* counts the number of times the machine has been booted. The timer is the amount of time since the TPM started up this time. The clock is similar to a timer, except that it (mostly) can only go forward in time, can be set equal to an external time, and stops whenever the TPM loses power.

These can be used to restrict usage of a TPM entity to only work when a boot counter remained unchanged, or when the clock is read between certain times. The entity's use can also be restricted to daylight hours. The latter is the most likely use case—restricting a computer to accessing files only during business hours helps protect data if a hacker gets access to the network at night.

The TPM can always check the values stored in its internal clock and boot counter, so they're referred to as *internal states*. Internal state assertions require that a policy session be created before the command is executed and that the assertion be satisfied before the command is executed. They need not be true when the command is actually executed.

This is done by extending a policy with TPM_CC_PolicyCounterTimer || HASH(Time or Counter value || offset to either the internal clock or the boot counter || operation). The operation parameter indicates the comparison being performed. The table of operations is in part 2 of the specification: a set of two-byte values representing equality, non-equality, greater than, less than, and so on.

Using the trial session to create such a policy involves sending TPM2_PolicyCounterTimer with four parameters: the handle of the trial session; an indication as to whether the comparison is being done to the timer, the clock, or the boot counter; something to compare that value to; and the comparison being done.

Although these values are considered the TPM's internal state values, it's also true that the TPM can read values that are in any of its NV index locations. Those can also be used for policy commands.

Internal Value of an NV RAM Location

A new command for the TPM 2.0 specification allows the use of an entity based on the value stored in a particular NVRAM location. For example, if an NV index is associated with 32 bits of memory, you can gate access to a TPM entity based on whether one of those bits is a zero or a one. If each bit is assigned to a different user, a user's access to a particular entity can be revoked or enabled by simply changing a single bit in an NVRAM location. Of course, this means the person with authority to write to that NVRAM location has the ultimate authority for using the key.

This command is more powerful than that, because logical operations on the NVRAM location are allowed. So you could say that the entity could be used only if

6 <= NVRAM location <8 OR 9 < NVRAM location < 23

was a true statement.

NVRAM locations in a 2.0 TPM can be set to be counters. This means you can use them in clever manipulations in a policy that can make a counter useable only *n* time. An example of this is shown later in the chapter.

This works by extending the policy buffer with `TPM_CC_PolicyNV || calculated Value || name of NV location`. The calculated value is `HASH(value to compare to || offset into the NVRAM location || number that represents the operation)`, where the operation is one of the following:

- Equals.

- Not equal.

- Signed greater than.

- Unsigned greater than.

- Signed less than.

- Unsigned less than.

- Unsigned greater than or equal.

- Signed greater than or equal.

- Unsigned less than or equal.

- Signed greater than or equal.

- All bits match the challenge.

- If a bit is clear in the challenge, it's also clear in memory.

Using these functions, you can allow all values greater than 1 or less than 1,000. When you get to multifactor authentication, you can combine these to have a value that is between 1 and 1000, including or not including the endpoints.

You can use a trial session to create this policy by executing `TPM2_PolicyNV` with the same parameters used in the `TPM2_PolicyCounterTimer` command: the handle of the trial session, the index being compared (and the offset from the beginning of the index), the thing to compare against, and how it is to be compared.

If you consider an entity like a lock, the value of the NVRAM is like the tumblers. If their state is correct, the entity can be used. Locks open if their internal state is correct.

However, TPM 2.0 allows something more interesting: an entity can be used according to the state of a device *external* to the TPM.

State of the External Device (GPS, Fingerprint Reader, and So On)

Perhaps one of the most interesting new assertions in the TPM design is the ability to use an assertion that is dependent on the state of an external device. The device is represented by a public/private key pair. The state of the device may be anything the device can use its private key to sign (together with a nonce from the TPM). If the device is a biometric, it may be as simple as "Bob just authenticated himself to me." If it's a GPS unit, it may be "My current position is Baltimore." If it's a time service, it may be

"The current time is business hours." The assertion identifies both the public key that represents the external device and the value expected. The TPM does nothing more than compare the signature and the identified information with what it's expecting. It doesn't perform calculations on the resulting information, so the device making the representation needs to decide if its input matches the thing it's signing.

This provides flexibility for a biometric: if Bob has registered several fingerprints with the matcher, the TPM doesn't need to know which one was signed with—just that the match corresponds to "Bob." A GPS coordinate need not be exact—just in a specified area. The assertion need not specify an exact time, but rather an identifier for the range of times that are acceptable. However, the flexibility isn't entirely general. This doesn't say "Some fingerprint reader attests that Bob has authenticated to the device"; it says "This particular fingerprint reader (as demonstrated by a signature) attests that Bob has authenticated to the device." This allows the creator of the policy to determine which biometric (or other devices) it trusts to not be easily spoofed.

Once this policy is satisfied, there are no further checks, so it's possible for an assertion to no longer be satisfied when the TPM actually executes the command.

Creating the policy is done by starting with a variable of size equal to the hash algorithm and initialized to zero. This is then extended with `TPM_CC_PolicySigned || SHA256(publicKey) || stateOfRemoteDevice`, where `stateOfRemoteDevice` consists of two parts: the size of the description followed by the description.

If you're using a trial session to create this policy, you execute the command `TPM2_PolicySigned`. Again, you must pass the handle of the trial session, the handle of the public key that corresponds to the private key of the device, and the state of the remote device that it will sign when the policy is satisfied. For example, if the remote device is a fingerprint reader, the device may sign "Sally correctly authenticated."

Sometimes the object's creator doesn't really know under what circumstances they want a key to be used. Perhaps the key will be used in case of an emergency, and the creator doesn't know who will use the key or how. This is a use case for a wild card policy.

Flexible (Wild Card) Policy

One major problem with the TPM 1.2 design was the brittleness of PCRs. When an entity was locked to a PCR, it was not possible to change the required values of the PCR after it was so locked. PCR0 represents the BIOS firmware, which is security critical. If PCR0 changed, it could indicate a security breach. As a result, applications like Microsoft BitLocker use it for security. However, BIOS firmware may need to be upgraded. When it's upgraded, the value of PCR0 will change, which makes anything locked to that PCR no longer useable.

Programs got around this limitation by decrypting keys, upgrading the BIOS, and then re-encrypting the keys to the new value of PCR0. However, this process is messy and leaves keys exposed for a short period of time while the upgrade is taking place. As a result, it was important that EA be able to allow for changing of the values to which a PCR was locked without decrypting the locked data. But it needed to also be obvious to anyone who wished to check the policy under what circumstances the policy could be changed. A number of possibilities were considered, including having yet another authorization whose only use was to change the policy.

The solution chosen was clever and is given using the command TPM2_PolicyAuthorize, which I call a *wild card policy*. A wild card policy is owned by a private key whose public key is associated with the wild card. In poker, a wild card can substitute for any card the holder of the wild card wishes. A wild card policy can substitute for any policy the owner of wild card wishes. Any policy approved by the owner of a wild card can be used to satisfy the wild card policy. Policies also can be restricted with a wildCardName that can be given to the wild card when it's created. This allows the owner of the wild card to specify that only wild cards with a particular name can substitute for a particular policy. A wild card associated with an OEM's BIOS signing key could theoretically be used to approve any BIOS signed by the OEM.

The wild card policy is created in a way similar to the command used for the state of an external device, by extending a policy session with TPM_CC_PolicyAuthorize || keySign→nameAlg || keyName || wildCardName. Just as with the PolicySigned assertion, if you're using a trial session to create a wild card policy, you first have to load the public key into the TPM (using the TPM2_LoadExternal command) and then execute the PolicyAuthorize command.

TPM2_LoadExternal returns the handle of the loaded public key, here called aPublicHandle. Then you can execute TPM2_PolicyAuthorize, passing it the handle of the trial session, wildCardName, and aPublicHandle.

TPM2_PolicyAuthorize is one of the most useful policies in the TPM, because it's the only way to effectively change a policy after an object has been created. This means if objects have been locked to one set of PCR values (corresponding to a particular configuration), and the configuration has to change, the objects' policy can be effectively changed to match the new set of configuration values. You see a number of other uses as well in the "Examples" section.

Command-Based Assertions

Although not strictly an assertion, it's possible to restrict a policy so that it can only be used for a particular command. For example, you can restrict a key so that it can be used for signing but not to certify other keys. If this is done, then the policy can only be used to do that one particular command. Generally this isn't done as a single assertion, but it could be. By declaring in a key's policy that it can only be used for signing, the key is prevented either from certifying another key or from itself being certified. This is because when a key is certifying or being certified, it needs to provide an authorization that can't be provided.

To create such a policy assertion, you create a policy variable of size equal to the hash algorithm and initialize it to zero. It's then extended with the value TPM_CC_PolicyCommandCode || the command code to which the policy is to be restricted.[4] If you're using a trial session to create this policy, you execute TPM2_PolicyCommandCode, passing it the handle of the trial session and the command code.

Usually, if you're restricting a TPM entity like a key to only be used in a single command, you also want to authenticate use of that key for that command. This requires that more than one restriction be placed on the key, which is the subject of multifactor authentication.

---

[4]The TPM_CC listing table is found in part 2 of the specification.

Multifactor Authentication

The TPM knows how to authenticate using assertions. It also can be told to require more than one of them. For example, it may be asked to specify that both a fingerprint and a smart card be used to provide authentication to log in to a PC.

Policies, as you'll see, build together in a way similar to the way PCRs are extended. They start with an initial value of all zeroes (the number of zeroes depends on the size of the hash algorithm used to create the policy). When a policy command is invoked, the current policy value is extended by appending a new parameter to the old value, hashing the result, and then replacing the old value with the result of this calculation. This calculation is called *extending* in PCRs. A logical AND in a policy is accomplished by extending the new assertion into the policy. Just like a PCR, the policy is initialized to all zeroes before the first assertion, but later assertions build on the value created by the previous assertion.

This means if you're using a trial session to build this kind of policy, you start and end exactly the same way—you just add more commands in the middle to correspond to the various ANDed assertions.

Example 1: Smart card and Password

If you wish to require that both a smart card that signs with a key, whose public part is S, and a password be used in a policy, you create a policy by first extending

```
TPM_CC_PolicySigned || SHA256(publicKey) || 0x0000 = 0x0000060 || SHA256(S)
||0x0000⁵
```

into a buffer of all zeroes. You then extend a requirement for proving knowledge of a password by extending

```
TPM_CC_PolicyAuthValue=0x0000016B
```

into the result.

If you wish to also require that the command be executed in locality 4, you extend

```
TPM_CC_PolicyLocality || locality4
```

Extending a new requirement is equivalent to a logical AND.

Using a trial session, you first load the public key into the TPM and then execute the three commands used in each of the simple assertion policies: TPM2_PolicySigned, TPM2_PolicyAuthValue, and TPM2_PolicyLocality.

---

[5] In this case you don't assign a PolicyReference to this signature, so the last appended value is 0x0000, which is 2 bytes of 0, which means the value of the PolicyReference of the signature is EmptyBuffer.

Example 2: A Policy for a Key Used Only for Signing with a Password

In this example, Bob creates a key that requires a key *only* be used for signing, and only if a password is presented for the key. Start with a policy of all zeroes, and first extend it with

TPM_CC_PolicyCommandCode || TPM_CC_Sign = 0x0000016C || 0x0000015D

Then extend it again with

TPM_CC_PolicyAuthValue =0x000016B

Example 3: A PC state, a Password, and a Fingerprint

In this example, Bob creates a key which requires that PCR1 be equal to an approvedPCRdigest, a password, and a fingerprint. When crafting a policy that involves a PCR digest, it's generally good practice to start with that term first. This is because if it fails, there is no need to bother the user with a password and a fingerprint.

You use the TPM to create this policy value as follows:

1. Start a trial session.
2. Use TPM2_PolicyPCR to lock the policy to approvedPCRdigest.
3. Use TPM2_PolicyAuthValue (to require a password at execution).
4. Load the publicKey of the fingerprint reader.
5. Use TPM2_PolicySigned pointing to the public key and stateOfRemoteDevice (which is "Bob's finger").
6. Get the value of the policy from the TPM.
7. End the session.

Example 4: A Policy Good for One Boot Cycle

In this example, the IT administrator gives permission (for example, to a technician) for a previously created key to be used only during this boot cycle. First the administrator creates a key that has a policy controlled by a wild card. When the administrator wants to allow the technician to use the key, the admin reads the current boot counter value from the PC using TPM2_GetCapability and authorizes a policy for the key that states that the value of the boot counter must be its current value. The admin does this using their private key to sign this new policy, called newPolicy. If the key is in his own TPM, he can use the command TPM2_Sign to sign it. The admin sends this policy and signature to the technician.

The technician loads the public key into the TPM, using TPM2_LoadExternal, and then uses the TPM2_VerifySignature command to verify the signature of the new policy. This command returns a ticket to the technician.

The technician uses the key by starting a policy session and then executing TPM2_PolicyCounterTimer with an offset pointing to the boot counter. This satisfies the newPolicy. The technician then executes TPM2_PolicyAuthorize, feeding it the newPolicy and the ticket, and points to the admin's public key. The TPM verifies that the ticket is valid for the newPolicy, using the admin's public key, and then substitutes the current policy buffer with the wildCardPolicy. At this point, the technician can use the key during this boot cycle.

When the PC is rebooted, the boot counter is incremented. If the technician tries to use the policy again, they can never satisfy newPolicy, so they can't use the key.

Example 5: A Policy for Flexible PCRs

In this example, an IT administrator wants to lock a full-disk-encrypting software key to a set of PCRs that represent (among other things) the BIOS firmware. But the admin realizes that the BIOS might need to be updated and so uses TPM2_PolicyAuthorize to provide flexibility as to what PCR values are used to release the hard-disk encryption keys.

The admin's key is created with only TPM2_PolicyAuthorize, but the admin authorizes a new policy that requires the PCRs to be equal to the initial PCR values. The admin then uses TPM2_VerifySignature to create a ticket that can be used to validate use of that new policy.

When the disk-encryption key is to be decrypted, the machine needs to do the following:

1. Start a new policy session.

2. Use TPM2_PolicyPCR to replicate the new policy in the TPM.

3. Use TPM2_PolicyAuthorize (with the public administrator key, the new policy, and the policy ticket) to cause the TPM to change the internal policy buffer of its session to the original PolicyAuthorize policy.

4. Use the satisfied policy session to release the disk-encryption key.

If the admin ever needs to change the PCR values that are validated, the admin can send the user a newly signed policy corresponding to the new PCR values, and the user can use that to create a new ticket to use after the PCRs have changed.

Example 6: A Policy for Group Admission

In this example, a group of people are given access to use a department key. But as people come and go from the department, some people's access is removed and other people's access is granted. Each member of the department has access to a private key that represents them. You can do this with a clever use of TPM2_PolicyNV, TPM2_PolicyAuthorize, and TPM2_PolicySigned.

First you create a NV index that has 64 bits (assuming there will never be more than 64 people in your department). Write authority is given only to the IT administrator, using the admin's private key. The admin writes it with all zeroes, noting the value of the index name. The admin then creates the department key with only a `PolicyAuthorize` policy, with the public key corresponding to the IT administrator of the department.

The IT administrator assigns each member of the group a bit in the NV space. To give a user the right to use the key, the admin creates and approves a policy that requires the corresponding bit of the NVRAM index to be a 1 (using `PolicyNV`) and that the appropriate user use their private key for authentication, using `PolicySigned`. When the admin wants to remove a user's ability to use the key, the admin changes the bit in the NVIndex that corresponds to that user to a 0. The admin then signs each of these new policies and gives them to the appropriate user.

When a user wants to use the key, they do the following:

1. Start a policy session.

2. Executed a `PolicyNV` command to verify the user is still in the department.

3. Execute a `PolicySigned` command to prove the user is the corresponding person.

4. Execute a `PolicyAuthorize` command to change the TPM's internal policy buffer to the `PolicyAuthorize` policy.

5. Use the key.

Example 7: A Policy for NV RAM between 1 and 100

As noted earlier, this is as simple as executing two commands: one to say the NV RAM value is greater than 1 and another to say it's less than 100. This only allows values 2, 3, 4, ...99.

Compound Policies: Using Logical OR in a Policy

The `TPM2_PolicyOR` command completes the logical constructions that can be done with policies and makes it possible to create useful policies that will do anything logically feasible. It lets you join more than one policy in multiple branches, any of which can be taken in satisfying a compound policy, as shown in Figure 14-5.

Although `TPM2_PolicyOR` commands can be used in more complicated settings, it's easiest to create individual policies for specific means of authorizing use of an entity and then use `TPM2_PolicyOR` to create a compound policy. Usually this is done by creating simple policies by ANDing assertions together to represent either a person or a role, and then ORing the simple policies together.

Suppose the following things happen:

1.   Dave authorizes himself using a policy created by a fingerprint together with a password when at one machine.

2.   Dave authorizes himself using a password and smart card.

3.   Sally uses her smart card and an iris scanner to authorize herself.

4.   The IT administrator can only use his authorization to duplicate a key and must use a smart card when the system is in a state defined by PCR0-5 having specific values.

This can be represented pictorially using circuit diagrams as follows.

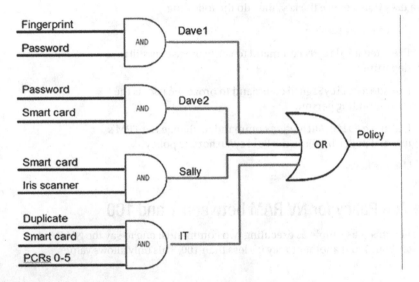

Figure 14-5. *A Compound Policy as a Circuit Diagram*

The easy way to create this compound policy is to start by creating four individual branch policies corresponding in the picture to Dave1, Dave2, Sally, and IT.

The first policy (Dave1) defines that Dave must authenticate himself with an external device (a fingerprint reader) and have it testify that Dave has authenticated himself. Dave must then present a password to the TPM. As you have seen, this is as simple as doing the following:

1.   Start a trial session.

2.   Use TPM2_PolicySigned (with the fingerprint reader's public key and appropriate policyRef).

3.   Use TPM2_PolicyAuthValue.

4.   Get the value of the policy from the TPM. Call this policyDave1.

5.   End the session.

The second policy (Dave2) has Dave present a password to the TPM and then use his smart card to sign a nonce from the TPM to prove his is the authorized owner of the smart card:

1.   Start a trial session.

2.   Use TPM2_PolicyAuthValue.

3.   Use TPM2_PolicySigned (with the smart card's public key).

4.   Get the value of the policy from the TPM. Call this policyDave2.

5.   End the session.

The third policy states that Sally must first use her smart card to sign a nonce from the TPM to prove she is the authorized owner of her smart card and then authorize herself to an external device, an iris scanner, and have the external device testify to the TPM that Sally has authenticated herself:

1.   Start a trial session.

2.   Use TPM2_PolicySigned (with the smart card's public key).

3.   Use TPM2_PolicySigned (with the iris scanner's public key and appropriate policyRef).

4.   Get the value of the policy from the TPM. Call this policySally.

5.   End the session.

Finally, the IT administrator's policy requires the administrator to use his smart card to sign a nonce produced by the TPM and then also check that PCRs 0–5 are in the expected state. Furthermore, the IT administrator can only use this authorization to duplicate the key:

1.   Start a trial session.

2.   Use TPM2_PolicySigned (with the smart card's public key).

3.   Use TPM2_PolicyPCR (with PCRs selected and their required digest).

4.   Use TPM2_PolicyCommandCode with TPM_CC_Duplicate.

5.   Get the value of the policy from the TPM. Call this policyIT.

6.   End the session.

Making a Compound Policy

Each of these policies, by itself, could be assigned to a TPM entity such as a key. However, you wish to allow any of the policies to be used to authenticate access to a key, and you do this using the TPM2_PolicyOR command:

1. Start a trial session.

2. Use TPM2_PolicyOR, giving it the list of policies to be allowed: policyDave1, policyDave2, policySally, and policyIT.

3. Get the value of the policy from the TPM. Call this policyOR.

4. End the session.

Policies created this way on one TPM will work fine on any TPM. One restriction on PolicyOr is that it can only be used to OR together up to eight policies. However, just as with electronic circuit design, PolicyORs can be compounded together to create the equivalent of an unlimited number of ORs. For example, if X is the result of 8 policies ORed together with TPM2_PolicyOR, and Y is the result of a different 8 policies ORed together with PolicyOR, you can apply TPM2_PolicyOR to X and Y to create the equivalent of a PolicyOr of 16 different policies.

Example: A Policy for Work or Home Computers

John has a home PC with a fingerprint reader and a work PC with a smart-card reader. He wants to authorize reading his cloud-based encrypted data from either computer. He does this by locking a key to a policy that requires a fingerprint reader from his home computer and his smart card (using his work PC's smart-card reader) for work.

He first creates a policy for his home computer. He gets the public key of the fingerprint reader and sets it up to sign "John's fingerprint" when he swipes his finger on that reader:

1. Start a trial session.

2. Use TPM2_LoadExternal to load the fingerprint reader's public key into the home computer's TPM.

3. Use TPM2_PolicySigned (with the fingerprint reader's public key and appropriate policyRef).

4. Get the value of the policy from the TPM. Call this HomeFingerprintPolicy.

5. End the session.

John now goes to his work computer:

1. Start a trial session.

2. Use TPM2_LoadExternal to load the smart card's public key into the work computer's TPM.

3. Use TPM2_PolicySigned (with the smart card's public key and NULL policyRef).

4. Get the value of the policy from the TPM. Call this policy WorkSmart cardPolicy.

5. End the session.

Now John can create the combined policy, which can be satisfied with both computers:

1. Start a trial session.

2. Use TPM2_PolicyOr with both HomeFingerprintPolicy and WorkSmart cardPolicy listed.

3. Get the value of the policy from the TPM. Call this policy WorkOrHomePolicy.

4. End the session.

This is the policy John uses when creating a key that he will use to identify himself to the cloud. He duplicates this key to his other computer, and then he can securely use this key on either computer.

Considerations in Creating Policies

In most cases, policies should be considered to represent roles when using TPM entities—and usually there are only a few possible roles.

End User Role

This represents the authentication that is satisfied for a user to use an entity. *Using an entity* means doing something like one of the following:

- Signing with a key

- Reading a NV location

- Writing an NV location

- Quoting with a key

- Creating keys

Administrator Role

An administrator of an entity may do different things for different entities. For NVRAM, they may be given the responsibility of managing the limited resource of available NVRAM. This would include the following:

- For NV:
  - Creating and destroying NV indexes
- For keys:
  - Authorizing duplication
  - Changing authorization with `PolicyAuthorize`

Understudy Role

In the event that the user of a key leaves the company or is unable to use a key necessary to obtain some enterprise data, it's important that another person (for example, the user's manager) be able to use the key. This is an *understudy role*.

Office Role

An office role consists of a combination (`PolicyOr`) of an enterprise administrator role and the user's role.

Home Role

A home role consists of a combination of a user acting as an administrator and acting as an end user. It may also include using different roles for using an entity on different machines, because different forms of authentication may be available on different machines. (For example, one machine may have a biometric reader and another may not.)

Once the roles are defined, policies can be created for them. Once the policies are created, they can be reused whenever entities are created, obviating the need to re-create the policies each time.

Using a Policy to Authorize a Command

You've seen how to satisfy a number of simpler policies. In order to satisfy any policy so that an object that requires the policy can be used, the steps are always the same:

1. Start a policy session.

2. Satisfy the policy for that session (this can require multiple steps).

3. Execute the command.

4. End the session.

This is very similar to the way policies are created, but satisfying a policy often requires additional steps. In a high-level API, most of the grunt work of satisfying a policy is done for you; but if you're talking directly to the TPM, some details are required to achieve this.

Starting the Policy

Starting the PolicySession is easy, as shown in Chapter 13. It's done with the command TPM2_StartAuthSession. This command returns a bunch of stuff, including a session handle, here called myPolicySessionHandle; and a nonce, created by the TPM, here called nonceTPM. You need both of these variables to satisfy the policy.

Satisfying a Policy

The considerations for satisfying the different kinds of policies—simple assertions, multifactor assertions, compound assertions, and flexible assertions—are slightly different, so let's consider them separately. It's important to remember that the order in which a policy is satisfied is important. A policy constructed with a TPM2_PolicyPCR followed by TPM2_PolicyPassword is different from a policy constructed with TPM2_PolicyPassword followed by TPM2_PolicyPCR. In general, policy commands aren't commutative.

Simple Assertions and Multifactor Assertions

Most simple assertions are easy to apply to a policy. Password, PCR, locality, TPM internal state, internal state of an NV RAM location, and command-based assertions are asserted in the same way as when the policy was created, except instead of using a trial policy, you use the policy handle myPolicySessionHandle. Other commands that require signature verification (the TPM2_PolicySigned command with or without a policyRef) require more work.

For example, if you're asserting that a password must be used to satisfy the policy, you execute the command TPM2_PolicyPassword. The password isn't actually passed at this time. This is just telling the session that when the command is finally executed with the object, the user must prove at that time that they know the password by passing it in either as a plaintext password or as an HMAC in the session.

To satisfy TPM2_PolicySigned, a signature is needed, and the signature is over a hash that is formed in part from the nonceTPM returned by the last use of the session. Additionally, the TPM must have the public key loaded so that it can verify the signature.

Loading the public key is done exactly the same way you did it to create the session, using the TPM2_LoadExternal command. This returns a handle to the loaded public key, here called aPublicHandle. You use this when calling the PolicySigned command, but first you have to pass in a signature. To do this, you first need to form a hash and sign it. The hash is formed by

aHash = HASH(nonceTPM || expiration =0 || cpHashA = NULL || policyRef = 0x0000) where nonceTPM was returned by the TPM when the session was created, expiration is all zeroes (no expiration), cpHashA = Empty Auth, and policyRef is emptyBuffer. (If you're using this for verification of a biometric reader, then policyRef is equal to the name of the person whose biometric was verified). The private key is used to sign this hash; and when signed, the result is called mySignature.

Next you execute the TPM2_PolicySigned command, passing in the handle of the session, APublicHandle, and mySignature. At this point, the TPM checks the signature internally using the public key, and if it's verified, extends its internal session policy buffer as desired. Now any command with an object whose policy that matches that policy buffer can be executed.

If the Policy Is Compound

If a policy is compound—that is, it's a logical OR of several branches—the user knows which branch they're going to try to satisfy. Once the user picks the branch, they satisfy that branch and then execute a TPM2_PolicyOR command with the TPM, which transforms the satisfied branch into the final policy, ready for execution. See Figure 14-6.

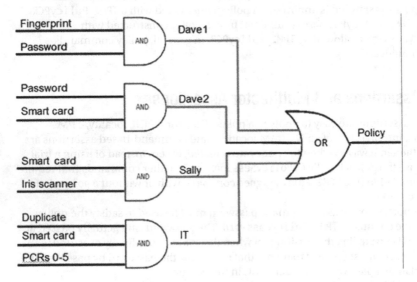

Figure 14-6. An example of using an OR policy

This figure shows that there are four different ways to satisfy this policy. You can satisfy it with the first branch, Dave1, by using a fingerprint reader and a password:

1. Start a policy session.

2. Satisfy the Dave1 branch of the policy:

    a. Satisfy the fingerprint assertion using TPM2_PolicySigned.

    b. Satisfy the password assertion using TPM2_PolicyPassword.

3. This sets a flag in the session, telling it that a password must be sent in when the final command is executed.

4. Transform the TPM's session policy buffer to the final session value using TPM2_PolicyOR.

5. Execute the command, including both the policy session and another session that satisfies the flag, by passing in the password (which can be done using the password [PWAP] permanent session).

   Note: As a side note, the policy session can be told to automatically close after this command is completed. Failing that, you can close the session manually.

In order to satisfy the first assertion in the policy, you have to get the fingerprint reader to attest to the TPM that Dave's fingerprint has been matched by the reader with the public key aPub. To do this, you need to pass a message to sign in to the fingerprint reader, which is calculated in part from nonceTPM, which the TPM returned when you created the policy. This value is sent to the fingerprint reader. Then Dave swipes his finger along the fingerprint reader, and when the fingerprint reader matches his fingerprint, it signs

```
aHash = SHA256(nonceTPM || expiration=0 || cpHashA=NULL || state Of
Remote Device)
```

using its private key aprivate. Note here the PolicyRef is the state of the remote device. In particular, the fingerprint reader needs to sign the fact that Dave has just swiped one of his fingerprints on the device and it has matched the template the device stored. The result is called fingerprint_Signature.

Next you have to load the fingerprint reader's public key into the TPM. Recall that this public key's handle is aPub.

Finally, the TPM is sent proof that the fingerprint reader successfully identified Dave using the command TPM2_PolicySigned, passing in aPub and fingerprint_Signature.

Next you execute the PolicyAuthValue command, which promises that when you eventually ask the TPM to perform a command with an object, that user will present evidence that they know the password associated with the object. This is done by executing TPM2_PolicyAuthValue.

Now that you've satisfied one of the branches of the policy, you can execute TPM2_PolicyOR to change the internal buffer of the session to equal the compound policy by passing it a list of the ORed policies.

If the Policy Is Flexible (Uses a Wild Card)

Satisfying a wild card policy is more complicated than creating one. For one thing, when the wild card policy is created, only the public key of the party who can authorize the eventually satisfied policy is identified. When one is used, an authorized policy must have been created, and a ticket proving that it's authorized must be produced. Then a user satisfies the approved policy and runs TPM2_PolicyAuthorize. The TPM checks that the policy buffer matches the approvedPolicy and that the approvedPolicy is indeed approved (by using the ticket), and if it is, changes the policy buffer to the flexible policy.

Preparing a policy to be used is then a two-step process. First, the authorizing party has to approve a policy by using their private key to sign Hash(approved Policy || wildCardName=policyRef). This is then sent to the user.

The user loads the public key of the authorizing party in their TPM and uses TPM2_VerifySignature against this signature, pointing to the handle of the public key. Upon verification, the TPM produces a ticket for this policy.

When the user wants to use this new approved policy, the user first satisfies the approved policy the way they ordinarily would and then gets the TPM to switch the approved policy to the flexible policy by calling TPM2_PolicyAuthorize, giving it as parameters the name of the session that has satisfied the approved policy, the approved policy, wildCardName, keyName, and the ticket. The TPM verifies that the ticket is correct and matches the approved policy in the session policy buffer. If so, it changes the session policy buffer to be the value of the flexible policy.

Thus creating a flexible policy is really a two part process.

Recapitulating: First the policy itself is created:

- Start a Trial Session

- Load the administrator's public key

- Use TPM2_PolicyAuthorize pointing to the administrator's public key

- Get the Value of the policy from the TPM. We call this policy workSmartcardPolicy

- End the session

Then an authorized policy is created using the administrator's private key

- Create a policy

- Load the administrator's private key

- Use the administrator's private key to sign the policy

- Use the TPM on which the approved policy is to be used to verify the signature (this produces a ticket)

Satisfying the Approved Policy

Satisfying the approved policy is done just as though it were the only policy you had to worry about. It doesn't matter if the approved policy is simple, compound, or flexible. After it's satisfied, it's then transformed.

Transforming the Approved Policy in the Flexible Policy

Now that the TPM's buffer is equal to the approved policy, you can transform it into the flexible policy by executing TPM2_PolicyAuthorize, passing the current value of the session policy buffer, PolicyTicket, and AdministratorPublicKeyHandle. The TPM checks that the policy buffer matches the approved policy and that the approved policy is indeed approved (by using the ticket) and, if it is, changes the policy buffer to the flexible policy. At this point, commands can be executed on an object that requires this particular flexible policy.

Although flexible policies were introduced to the TPM in order to provide a solution to the brittleness of PCRs, they can be used to solve many more conundrums than that. They allow an administrator to decide after an object is created how the policy for that object can be satisfied. Because the name of an object (or NV index) is calculated from its policy, it isn't possible to change the policy of an NV index or a key. However, using a flexible policy, you can change the way a policy is satisfied after the fact.

Suppose a key is given a flexible policy when it's created, and later the administrator of the flexible policy wants to make it be the policy in Figure 14-6. The admin can accomplish this by signing the policy represented by Figure 14-6 and sending it to the user. Someone must do the preparatory step of creating a ticket by running TPM2_VerifySignature, but after that the user only has to satisfy the policy given by Figure 14-6 and then run PolicyAuthorize to prove that the policy has been approved.

Certified Policies

One last thing you can do with policies is prove that a policy is bound to a particular entity. When ink is used to sign a contract, the signature that is formed is irrevocably tied to the person signing it via a biometric that represents the way the person's muscles and nerves are formed. That is what produces the characteristic swirls of a signature. Electronic signatures have never been tied to a person in the same way. Typically, electronic signatures have been tied to a password (something a person knows) or a smart card (something a person has), or sometimes (usually in addition to the others) a biometric. Biometric devices can break, so in most implementations, there is always a backup password that can be used if the biometric doesn't work. (Interestingly, the ink signature has a similar problem, because people can break their hands.)

With the TPM 2.0, it's possible to tie the use of a key directly to a biometric and prove that it's so tied. First a non-duplicatable key is created, with its authValue set so that a password isn't useful for authorization. This means only the policy can be used to authorize use of the key. The policy is set to only allow use of the key when authorized by a biometric reader, using TPM2_PolicySign and a policyRef that is produced and signed by the biometric reader when it matches the person. This produces a key that can only be used to sign something if the biometric reader is convinced the person is who it thinks the person is. We call this key A.

Next a credentialed non-duplicable restricted signing key is used with TPM2_Certify to produce a signature over the name of key A. This signature binds the public portion of key A (which is in the name), the authValue (which are in the name), and the policy (which is in the name). By checking the credential of the restricted signing key, an attesting agent can verify that the certificate produced by TPM2_Certify is valid. Then, by hashing the public data of the key, the agent can verify that the name is correct. This then validates that the only way the key could be used for signing is by satisfying the policy, not by a password. The policy is then examined and, using the public key of the biometric device, is validated to be satisfied only if the user swiped their finger over the reader.

In this way, the electronic signature with the key becomes tied to the fingerprint biometric. In a similar way, producing certificates binding policies to keys can be used to prove to an auditor that the policies being used for keys meet a corporate standard for security. This in turn satisfies the last of the problems that EA was created to solve.

Summary

This chapter has examined the new enhanced authorization in the TPM 2.0, which can be used to authorize any entity in the TPM. You have seen that EA policies can be used to create logical combinations (AND and OR) of multiple kinds of assertions—everything from passwords and smart cards to the state of the TPM or the state of a remote machine. You have looked at examples of using EA for multiple users, multifactor authorization, and the means to create policies that allow flexible management. Many examples demonstrated the ways these commands can be used to solve varied problems. Then you saw how such policies can be satisfied. Finally, you saw how a key can be bound to its policy. EA in the TPM 2.0 is one of the most complex but also most useful new capabilities in the TPM 2.0 design.

CHAPTER 15

■ ■ ■

Key Management

There are many considerations when designing a key-management system with a TPM. If keys are going to be used for critical operations, such as encryption or identification, it's vital that an architecture be used to provide a standard means of managing the key's lifetime and prepare for problems if hardware breaks. Such an architecture must be able to handle key generation, key distribution, key backup, and key destruction. The design of the TPM was architected with these things in mind. This chapter describes the various options possible for these steps in a key's life.

Key Generation

When generating a key, the most important thing the user has to consider is that the key be generated randomly. If a poor random number generator is chosen, the key that is picked won't be secure. The second most important thing to consider is keeping the key material confidential. TPMs are designed to be secure against software-based threats. Hardware threats can be protected against by the manufacturer, but that isn't part of the design per se. However, the design does allow for *key split* creation of keys, where entropy used to generate a key is stored in both in and outside the TPM, so that when the TPM isn't in use, keys remain secure even with physical access.

There are three ways that keys can come to reside in a TPM. They can be generated from a seed, generated using a random number generator in the TPM, or imported. Primary keys are generated using a seed that exists in the TPM. The seed used for generating the EK is associated with the Endorsement hierarchy and isn't likely to be one that the end user can change.

The seed associated with the storage hierarchy, on the other hand, changes whenever a TPM_Clear command is issued. This can be done either via the BIOS, which uses the platform hierarchy authorization, or by the end user using the dictionary-attack reset password.

As stated in Chapter 10, primary keys are generated using a FIPS-approved key derivation function (KDF), which hashes together the primary seed together with a key template. The template for key generation is in two parts. The first part is a description of the kind of key to generate—whether it's a signing key or an encryption key, asymmetric or symmetric, what type of signing scheme it uses if it's a signing key, the algorithm and key size, and so on. The other part is a place where entropy can be introduced to the command to be used in generating the key. In most cases, the second part is set to all zeros (as in the TCG Infrastructure Work Group's published EK template). However, if the user doesn't trust the entropy generator in the TPM, they can use this facility to provide a key split.

A key split is a cryptographic construct where two sets of entropy—each with as much entropy as the final key—are used to produce a key. Neither one alone is able to provide even a single bit of the final key's entropy—both are necessary. Thus, one can be held separate from the TPM, and one held inside the TPM.

In case of a primary key, one split of the key is the hierarchy's seed, inside the TPM. The other, which can be stored securely when not in use (for example, in a smart card or safe) is held outside the TPM in the template.

Primary storage keys have an associated symmetric key which is generated when the primary key is generated and is associated with it. This is also derived from the primary seed and introduces entropy. As long as the seed associated with a hierarchy isn't changed, using the same template will generate the same primary key and associated symmetric key. Because both the primary key and the symmetric key use the template in generation, if entropy is introduced there, the entropy in the template also acts as a key split for them.

Why would anyone split a key? The main reason is usually that the user is worried that it might be possible for someone to get hold of one of the two key splits. Either they're worried that the TPM's seed was squirted into the TPM at manufacturing time and someone still has a copy, or they're worried that someone will de-layer the TPM, as was done with an Infineon 1.2 chip years ago.[1] These attacks are mostly worries for the truly paranoid—the Infineon attack was successful only after destroying a handful of TPMs, and at a cost of over $200,000. But people in the security space tend to be paranoid types.

Generating a primary key can either take a relatively long time (if the key is an RSA key) or be virtually instantaneous (if it's an ECC key.) If the key takes a long time to generate (or if the secret entropy introduced in its generation isn't generally available), then the user may decide to store the key in the persistent memory of the TPM using the TPM2_EvictControl command, which requires the associated hierarchy's authorization. In this case, the key is given a persistent handle, and a power cycle doesn't affect the presence of the key in the TPM. It can be evicted with the same command. Depending on what attacks a user is worried about, the user may or may not decide to make their key persistent.

If a user is worried that the TPM seed has been compromised, then they're worried that primary keys may be compromised. If the primary key is compromised, all keys stored using the primary key are also compromised. In this case, the user can use a key split to introduce their own entropy into primary keys via the template, make the key persistent, and then escrow the key's template somewhere where an attacker can't get it. This prevents an attacker who knows the TPM's seed (generated at manufacturing time) from being able to determine the secrets of the primary key.

---

[1]William Jackson, "Engineer Shows How to Crack a 'Secure' TPM Chip," GCN, February 2, 2010, http://gcn.com/articles/2010/02/02/black-hat-chip-crack-020210.aspx.

Alternatively, a primary key can be generated and used only to create another storage key child of the primary key. The storage key is then loaded into the TPM under the primary key of the TPM. The new child storage key is then made persistent. This key behaves similarly to a TPM 1.2 SRK. It's generated by the TPM's random number generator, not from the seed. However, it exists in encrypted form for a short period of time outside the TPM after it's created, but before it's reloaded—which results in a slight risk of attack if the primary key were compromised.

If a user is worried about physical attacks against the TPM, they may wish to use entropy encoded into the key's template in a second factor and present that entropy each time the primary seed is to be generated, but *not* store the primary key in the TPM. (If the primary key is stored persistently, then a physical attack may be able to recover it.) In this case, each time the TPM is power cycled, all traces of the primary key disappear from the TPM. This is of course hard to manage, because the template must be kept secret (possibly in a USB key), separate from the TPM, and then introduced each time the key is to be loaded into the TPM.

Similarly, for the truly paranoid, who not only are worried about the TPM seed but also don't trust the TPM's random number generator, an external key can be generated by a trusted entropy source and then wrapped so that it can be imported into the TPM by a primary (or any storage) key (generated with entropy that is later discarded) and made persistent; and then the primary key is evicted. If additionally this person is worried about their system being stolen and the TPM de-layered to reveal its secrets, they should not make keys persistent in the TPM, but rather should redo this complicated loading of a key every time they power on the TPM.

USE CASE: CREATION OF DIFFERENT SRKS FOR DIFFERENT USERS

If a system has several users, they may want to have completely different sets of keys. If this is the case, they may all generate their own SRKs (individual primary restricted storage keys). This is easily possible if they each use different entropy in their template when creating their primary seed to use as their SRK. In order to make sure the same key isn't generated for each user, the templates used to generate the keys must be distinct. For example, they could use the hash of a user secret as entropy in the key's template. However, different users might pick the same user secret. It's probably better to have the TPM use its hardware random number generator to create a key under the SRK for each user.

THE RULE OF THUMB

There are only three reasons to make a key persistent. The key may be an RSA key and hence may take an unreasonably long time to re-generate, the key may be one created using a secret entropy source in the template that isn't always available, or there may not be enough (or any) persistent memory outside the TPM to store a key template. The last may be the case if the TPM is being used in a constrained environment, such as during a boot cycle. In any other case, a key should be generated as necessary. This is different from the 1.2 design, because in a 2.0 design, key loading is done with symmetric decryption and hence is very quick.

Templates

There are standard templates for creating keys, and generally it makes sense to use those rather than create your own. Templates typically use matched algorithm strengths. The one time you might *not* use matched algorithm strengths is when choosing the symmetric key. Because the symmetric key is used for loading other keys into the TPM rather than the asymmetric key, it's possible to design a system where a symmetric key with a higher strength than the asymmetric key is used for the primary key. Once this is done, no keys generated on the TPM are exposed to the weakness of the asymmetric key or algorithm.

Key Trees: Keeping Keys in a Tree with the Same Algorithm Set

Although it's technically possible to mix algorithms—make a key with one set of algorithms and then store it under a key with a different set of algorithms—it's a bad practice (and one, as you have seen, that the TSS Feature Application Programming Interface [FAPI] won't allow.) The problem is that the strength of a set of keys is dictated by the strength of the weakest key in a chain. This means not only should algorithm sets not be mixed, but chains of keys (with one key wrapping another one) should generally be kept fairly short. If any key in a chain is broken, then all keys below it are broken. So a key chain of four keys is four times weaker than a chain with one link when exposed to a brute force attack. (Of course, given a reasonable key size, a factor of 4 is unimportant.)

The reason you might decide to have a longer chain is manageability. A user may want to migrate their entire set of keys or a subset of those keys from one system to another system, or duplicate their set of keys among two or more computers. In order to make this easy, it's likely that the user will wish to rewrap only one key—at the top of a tree of keys—with the public key on a different system and then copy the encrypted blobs that represent their other keys to the appropriate location in the other system.

You might want to keep enterprise keys separate from personal keys, and different department keys separate in an enterprise, as shown in Figure 15-1. Nevertheless, it's best to keep key trees as short as possible.

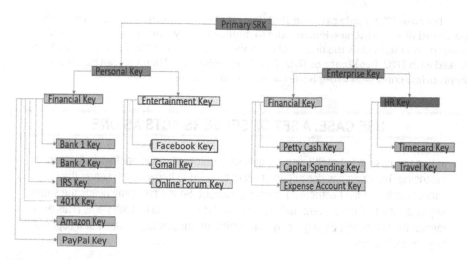

Figure 15-1. Example key tree

Duplication

In the key tree in Figure 15-1, the keys that might be duplicated are the Personal Key, the Enterprise Key, the Financial Keys (both Personal and Enterprise), the Entertainment Key, or the HR Key. In order to do this, all of these keys must be created to be duplicable, and they must have a policy created for them that has TPM2_Policy_CommandCode with TPM2_Duplicate selected (along with whatever restrictions are associated with duplicating a key). In most cases, a user creates two different duplication policies—one for personal keys and one for business keys—and associates those policies with a parent personal duplicable key (PDK) and a business duplicable key (BDK).

If a key isn't going to be duplicated, it can be made fixedParent. If a key under the SDK or UDK is going to be duplicated apart from the SDK or UDK, then it also must have a policy that allows for duplication.

With TPM 1.2, it wasn't possible to create a key that could be duplicated only to a few specified new parents and no others. With TPM 2.0, this is now possible using a command called TPM2_DuplicationSelect. This command allows you to specify exactly which parent (or parents) a key is targeted to be duplicated to. The main reason for using this command is in conjunction with PolicyAuthorize. By using PolicyAuthorize, an IT organization can change the target backup key for duplication. So if the organization normally backs up keys to a specified server, and that server dies, then by signing a TPM2_DuplicationSelect command that selects a new server, the organization can mail out a new signed policy to employees, knowing that they now are allowed to duplicate their keys to the new server. This allows the new duplication target without allowing employees to back up their keys to their home computers (which may not be trusted).

Because TPM2_Duplicate and TPM2_DuplicateSelect can't be authorized with a password or an HMAC session, in order to duplicate a key, you must first start a policy session and then satisfy the branch of the policy that has the TPM2_PolicyCommandCode linked with TPM2_Duplicate or TPM2_DuplicationSelect. Then you can execute the appropriate command to duplicate the key to a new parent.

USE CASE: A SET OF SERVERS ACTS AS ONE

In this use case, a set of SSL servers acts as a failover for one another or for load balancing. The company doesn't want users to need to know which server they're connected to—it isn't something users care about. So the company needs the same key to exist on all the servers that are being used to service its web page. (This also means the company has to get only one certificate for this key, instead of a separate key for each server.)

The company creates a duplicable key with a PolicyAuthorize command as the policy and then uses the private key associated with the PolicyAuthorize command to sign several TPM2_DuplicationSelect commands, each of which points to a different server. A user gets this key certified and puts a copy of the certificate on each server. The user then duplicates the key from the original server to all the other servers, and finally imports the key using TPM2_Import into each of the other servers. At this point, all the servers look identical to an outside user.

Steps

1. Create policy P using TPM2_PolicyAuthorize, an enterprise public signing key, and a policyRef of SSL.

2. Create a duplicable key using policy P on the initial SSL server.

3. Create restricted storage keys on all the other SSL servers using TPM2_Create, and call them SRK$_i$.

4. Use the enterprise private key to sign TPM2_PolicyDuplicateSelect, selecting the SRK$_{i\,public}$ as the target of duplication. Do this once for each SRK$_i$.

5. Use TPM2_VerifySignature on the initial SSL server to create a ticket for each signed policy. This allows that signed policy to be used by the initial SSL server for duplication.

6. For each policy, create a duplicated key that can be loaded by SRK_i by doing the following on the initial SSL server:

   a. Load the enterprise public signing key using TPM2_Load.

   b. Load the SRK_i public key into the initial SSL server using TPM2_LoadExternal.

   c. Use TPM2_StartAuthSession to start a policy session.

   d. Execute TPM2_PolicyDuplicationSelect, selecting the SRK_i of one of the target servers.

   e. Execute TPM2_PolicyAuthorize, using the policy, a policyRef of SSL, and the ticket corresponding to SRK_i.

   f. Execute TPM2_Duplicate, passing it the handle of the loaded SRK_i public and the handle of the enterprise signing key.

   g. The result of the TPM2_Duplicate command is an encrypted version of the enterprise signing key. Send it to the server with SRKi.

   h. Import the duplication blob into the server with SRKi.

7. Copy the certificate of the enterprise signing key to that server.

At this point, the key is the same on all the servers and can be used for SSL identification and communication.

Key Distribution

In some cases, keys need to be distributed long after a system is initially set up. Being able to distribute keys securely is very important in these cases. The TPM design makes this easy. When each system is set up, a non-duplicable storage key is generated on the system, and a central system keeps a record associating this key with the system name (or perhaps the system serial number). This can be done in an Active Directory or LDAP database. Additionally, at provisioning time, the local platform gets a public key of the central system that corresponds to a signing key. At some later point, if the central system wants to distribute an HMAC key to the system, the following takes place:

1. The central IT system creates an HMAC key using TPM2_GetRandom.

2. The central IT system encrypts the HMAC key with the public portion of the target client's storage key.

3. The central IT system signs the encrypted HMAC key with its private signing key. This is done so the local platform knows that what is being sent is authorized by IT.

4. The encrypted HMAC key is sent to the client along with a signature that proves it came from the central IT system.

5. The client verifies the signature on the encrypted key by loading the central server's public key. (This can be done with the TPM using TPM2_Load and then using TPM2_VerifySignature, if you like.)

6. The client imports the verified, encrypted HMAC key into its system using TPM2_Import, getting out a loadable, encrypted blob containing the HMAC key.

7. The client loads the HMAC key when the user wishes to use it, using TPM2_Load, and uses it as normal. At this point, the local platform has received an HMAC key from the IT central system that has never been decrypted in the local system's memory.

Key Activation

Because of the ability to create and re-create keys from the seed in the TPM, it's possible to use multiple key templates at provisioning time of a system and have a central IT system record the key template and corresponding public portion of the keys associated with the system. Central IT can then power cycle the TPM, destroying the system's copy of the key. Thus when the system is distributed to an end user, it doesn't have any of these keys available.

Later, when IT wants to activate those keys, it need only send the key template used to create the key to the end user and allow the system to re-generate the key from the template using TPM2_CreatePrimary. Note that the key template includes the policy of the key so generated, but not the password associated with it, which is chosen whenever the key is re-generated. If the central system wishes to avoid the use of that password when controlling the key, two bits in the template can be selected: userWithAuth and adminWithPolicy. These can be set in such a way as to make the password unable to control the key. If userWithAuth is set FALSE, and adminWithPolicy is set TRUE, then the password can't cause the key to perform any functions.[2]

In using this technique, the templates should be chosen in such a way as to include random entropy. Without the template, the key can't be re-created, so the central system can be sure the key isn't used until the template is received by the client.

---

[2]Because these flags are part of the template, if a user tries to change them, the user gets a different key.

There is another way to do key activation, similar to what was possible with TPM 1.2: using migratable keys. When a key is duplicated, you can doubly encrypt it: once using the parent key of the system to which it's being duplicated, and once using a symmetric key that is inserted when the duplication is done. The produces a key blob that is encrypted twice. The outside encryption is gated by the new parent's private key. The inner encryption is done with a symmetric key. In this case, when a TPM2_Import command is executed, the TPM must have the private asymmetric key already loaded; its handle is given to TPM2_Import, and a secret is passed into the TPM2_Import command as a parameter. The secret is used in calculating the symmetric key, which in turn is used to decrypt the inner encryption. The command flow is as follows:

1. A duplicable key is generated on a central system.

2. The key is duplicated to the client system using the symmetric key option. This parameter is called encryptionKeyIn in the TPM2_Duplicate function.

3. The key blob is signed by the central system and sent to the client, but the encryptionKeyIn parameter is kept safe by the IT administrator.

4. When the IT administrator wishes to allow the key be used, encryptionKeyIn is provided to the client system, allowing the client system to import it using the TPM2_Import command.

Key Destruction

Once a key has been created, it's sometimes important to be able to destroy it as well. One example is if a user is going to sell, surplus, or recycle a computer and wants to make sure data that was encrypted on that system with that key is no longer available. TPMs provide this facility in a number of easy ways.

If the key used is a primary key, the easiest way to destroy it is to ask the TPM to change its copy of the seed of the hierarchy on which it was created (usually the storage hierarchy). TPM2_Clear does this for the storage hierarchy. Clearing the TPM destroys all non-duplicable keys that are associated with the hierarchy, evicts all keys in the hierarchy from the TPM, and changes the seed, preventing any primary keys previously associated with that hierarchy from being re-generated. It also flushes the endorsement hierarchy, but it doesn't change that seed.[3] Duplicable keys can no longer be loaded into the system, although if they have been duplicated to a different system, they may not be destroyed.

---

[3]This way, the EK and TPM vendor certificates are still valid.

If such a drastic step isn't necessary (perhaps the machine is only going to be loaned for a time to a different employee, or multiple employees are using the machine), other things can be done, if preparations are made ahead of time. For example, if a primary key is generated with secret entropy in the template and then made into a persistent key, then the only thing that needs to be done to destroy the key is to destroy the copies of the template and evict the primary key from the persistent storage. Once this is done, the key is gone and can't be re-generated. Because there can be multiple trees underneath different primary keys, this provides a way to destroy a particular tree of keys without destroying all the trees of keys in a TPM. This may be important if multiple users are using the same TPM.

It's even possible to destroy keys that are generated outside the TPM, imported into the TPM, and then made persistent. If the copies outside the TPM are destroyed (which may be possible if the import was done in a controlled facility), then merely evicting the key from persistent memory also destroys the key.

Putting It All Together

This section provides two examples of how different types of businesses might decide to manage TPM entities. We start with a simple case, which might apply to a small business, and then consider a large enterprise.

Example 1: Simple Key Management

An end user is handling all of their own keys. The user has two systems: a primary system and a backup system for backing up keys. Here are the steps the user follows to manage the keys:

1. Create an SRK on each system using a standard non-duplicable key template. Set userWithAuth to TRUE, adminWithPolicy to FALSE, and the policy to a NULL policy. This means the policy is disabled and the password can be used to authorize use of the SRK. The user sets the password to a well-known password when using the TPM2_CreatePrimary command to create the SRKs.

2. Create a duplicable storage key (DSK) under the SRK on the primary system. Use TPM2_Create to create this key. It has userWithAuth set to TRUE and adminWithPolicy set to TRUE. This allows the password to authorize using the key and the policy for duplicating the key. (Remember that keys can only be duplicated using a policy.) It has a policy that specifically has a branch with TPM2_PolicyCommandCode with TPM2_Duplicate selected, together with TPM2_PolicyAuthValue. This policy requires the user to prove knowledge of the key's password in order to duplicate it.

3. Load the public key of the new SRK to which the key is to be duplicated.

4. Duplicate this storage key to the backup system by creating a policy session, executing TPM2_PolicyCommandCode with TPM2_PolicyDuplicate, and then executing TPM2_PolicyAuthValue. Then an HMAC session is started (using the DSK password). The two sessions are referenced when executing the TPM2_Duplicate command, passing it the handle of the DSK and the public key of the SRK of the backup system. This produces a blob that contains the duplicated key and is encrypted in a way that can be imported into the TPM, which knows the SRK private portion.

5. Move the blob to the backup system, and use TPM2_Import to import the key into the backup system. This produces another blob, which can be loaded into the backup system on demand.

6. As new keys are created under the DSK on the primary system, send copies of those key blobs to the backup system, where they can also be loaded using the copy of the DSK, and used.

7. To decommission the primary system, use TPM2_Clear, using the lockout password to clear the TPM's storage hierarchy.

8. To migrate all keys to a new system, create an SRK on the new primary system.

9. Repeat the process of duplication from step 4. This time, the new parent is the SRK of the new primary system.

10. Copy all other keys blobs onto the new primary system.

Example 2: An Enterprise IT Organization with Windows TPM 2.0 Enabled Systems

In this case, the enterprise doesn't want to use EKs that are potentially known outside the organization. The enterprise wants to use its own EKs after the machines are provisioned, but use the OEM EK to prove to itself that the system is genuine. The organization provisions each system as it comes in, as follows:

1. Generate the OEM EK using TPM2_CreatePrimary and the TCG Infrastructure Workgroup's standard EK template. Compare it to the vendor EK certificate that came with the system. Check the certificate as well, using the vendor's public key.

2. Run TPM2_Clear to wipe the TPM's storage and EK hierarchies.

3.   In a trusted location, evict the OEM EK, ask the TPM for a random number, repopulate the EK template with this entropy, and read out the EK public portion, making the enterprise's own certificate for this key.

4.   Change the storage hierarchy, endorsement hierarchy, and dictionary-attack authorization values to random values, storing them in an LDAP server.

5.   Create a restricted encryption key and make it persistent, for use as an SRK. This key has an authorization value of NULL and a policy of NULL. This allows anyone to use it who wishes to.

6.   Create a restricted signing key and make it persistent, for use as an AIK. This key also has an authorization value of NULL and a policy of NULL, so that TNC software can use it.

7.   Store a copy of the SRK's public key in the enterprise's LDAP associated with this machine.

8.   Create a certificate of the AIK that associates it with this machine. This certificate is stored both on the LDAP and on the system itself.

9.   Uses the AIK to quote the current PCR values, and check them against golden measurements that came with the system.

10.   Change the software load and configuration of the system to match the enterprise's own policies.

11.   Use the AIK to quote the current PCR values, and store them in the LDAP associated with this system. These are used as a new set of golden measurements.

12.   Create virtual smartcards on the machine using the TPM, and set up the Windows VPN server to accept the certificate of this key.

13.   Set up another virtual smartcard on the machine using the TPM, and set up a Radius server to accept it for connections to the enterprise's wireless network, using WPA2 in Enterprise mode.

14.   Create a 32-byte NV index, and store a hash of the enterprise's IT organization public key there. The policy of the key only allows this same key to be used to write to the index. This key will be used later to check software updates before they're installed, to see if they're approved by IT.

15. Install Wave software to report the PCR measurements on each boot, sending an alert to the IT organization if they aren't correct. (Alternatively, a StrongSwan VPN can be used, which doesn't grant access to the network unless the PCRs pass muster.)

16. Create a policy for allowing duplication of a key to the IT backup server's TPM, and store it on the system. This policy is signed with the IT private key.

17. The user's boss provides a policy that allows the boss to use the keys in their employee's absence.

18. When the user gets the system, the user creates a duplicable restricted decryption (storage) key, under which the user stores all their enterprise keys. The policy the user gives it is the OR of the policies in steps 16 and step 17. Before doing this, the user checks the policy's signature using the hash of the public key stored in step 14.

19. The user duplicates their duplicable storage key to the IT organization's backup server and then its wrapped keys in their normal backup.

20. If the user quits or the machine is to be recycled, use the stored owner authorization to send the system a notice that it should execute TPM2_Clear, thus wiping all the keys stored on the system. The OEM EK is used to restart the process.

21. If the user is moved to a new system or their motherboard dies, re-duplicate their backed-up key (stored in step 18) to their new system, and copy their other key blobs from backup to the new system. The user can then continue working.

Summary

You've seen that the facilities of the TPM allow for very sophisticated or very simple key management, depending on the needs of the end user. These needs can range from those of a paranoid enterprise worried about industrial espionage, including theft of machines, to those of a non-paranoid home user, who merely wishes to keep their keys safe on their home system. By crafting the key hierarchies and setting up authorizations and policies correctly, you can keep keys safe and usable.

CHAPTER 16

■ ■ ■

Auditing TPM Commands

As used in the TPM, *audit* is the process of logging TPM command and response parameters that pass between the host and the TPM. The host is responsible for maintaining the log, which may be in host memory or on disk. An auditor can later use the TPM to attest to the log's integrity (that it has not been altered) and authenticity (that it was logging TPM transactions).

The underlying audit concept is similar to that of attestation using PCRs. The TPM extends command and response parameter hashes into an audit digest. The auditor can later request a signed audit digest and verify the signature and certificate chain. The auditor can then walk their local copy of the audit log to validate its integrity.

Audit always records both command and response parameters and only audits a successful command. The latter requirement vastly simplifies an implementation.[1]

This chapter first gives a rationale as to why you may want to audit, then describes the audit types, and finally goes on to the details of the audit mechanism.

Why Audit

Why would an auditor want a certified list of command and response parameters? This section provides several use cases, from auditing a single command to auditing an atomic sequence of commands to auditing a continuous stream of commands.

In the simplest case, the TPM can audit one command. In a sense, this is a generalization of a TPM quote, which signs PCRs. In fact, you could do a quote using audit: start an audit log, read a set of PCRs, end the audit log, and request a signed audit digest. Although it's simpler to use TPM2_Quote for a PCR attestation, it can't be used to quote NV PCRs.[2] Audit is the only way to quote an NV PCR.

While there is already a TPM point solution for getting a signature over PCRs, audit provides a slightly more complicated but more flexible facility.

---

[1]Historically, TPM 1.2 did not at first have this requirement. This led to many corner cases where the failure was itself due to the audit, where the audit digest was partially updated but then the command failed, and so on. Late in TPM 1.2, the requirement was changed to "only audit successful commands," and this was carried forward to TPM 2.0.

[2]See Chapter 11 for an explanation of how to create an NV extend index PCR.

USE CASE: WHAT TPM AM I CONNECTED TO?

An auditor wants to know the precise TPM properties: manufacturer, firmware revision, and so on. The auditor starts an audit log, runs several TPM2_GetCapability commands to read the properties of interest, and then validates the audit log to ensure that the responses are legitimate.

The TPM commands are as follows:

- TPM_StartAuthSession: Start a session to be used for audit

- TPM2_GetCapability: Set the audit attribute, read the manufacturer and firmware version, and keep a log of the results

- TPM2_GetSessionAuditDigest: Get a signature over a digest of the log. The auditor uses the signature to verify that the log containing the capabilities has not been tampered with.

USE CASE: WHAT IS THE STATE OF AN NV INDEX, COUNTER, OR BIT-FIELD INDEX?

These indexes might be used to revoke the use of another entity through the entity's policy. That policy would use the TPM2_PolicyNV command, where the NV index is either a counter or a bit field. Chapter 14 explains the policy use case. Here, the caller is concerned that the NV index might not have been updated correctly. For example, the caller wants to ensure that a counter has been incremented or a bit set in a bit field. The caller can audit a read of this index to get a signed digest of its value. In some cases, where the index is authorized using an HMAC, the response HMAC itself provides response integrity. However, if the index is password or policy authorized, or if the caller doesn't have the HMAC key, audit provides the required integrity.

The TPM commands are as follows:

- TPM2_StartAuthSession: Start a session to be used for audit

- TPM2_NV_Read: Set the session attribute and read the index being used in the policy. The caller keeps an audit log.

- TPM2_GetSessionAuditDigest: Get a signature over a digest of the log. The caller uses the signature to verify that the audit log containing the NV read data has not been tampered with.

USE CASE: NV INDEX USED AS A PCR

As described in Chapter 11, a hybrid extend index can be used to implement PCRs beyond the platform-specified value. These can't be attested to using the TPM2_Quote command, but a signed audit gives equivalent integrity.

The TPM commands are as follows:

- TPM2_StartAuthSession: Start a session to be used for auditing.

- TPM2_NV_Read: Set the session attribute and read the index being used as a PCR. The caller keeps an audit log.

- TPM2_GetSessionAuditDigest: Get a signature over a digest of the log. The caller uses the signature to verify that the audit log containing the NV PCR value has not been tampered with.

Audit Commands

This is a summary of the TPM commands used for audit. See the TPM 2.0 specification Part 3 for the complete command set and API details:

- TPM2_StartAuthSession is used to start a session that can be used for audit.

- TPM2_GetSessionAuditDigest returns the session audit digest and optionally a signature over the digest.

- TPM2_GetCommandAuditDigest returns the command audit digest and optionally a signature over the digest.

- TPM2_SetCommandCodeAuditStatus determines which commands are included in a command audit digest.

Audit Types

The TPM library supports two audit types: command audit and session audit.

Command Audit

Command audit has two important traits, which it shares with TPM 1.2 audit.

First, it's on a per-command basis. Most commands include an attribute that, when set, indicates that the TPM should audit all instances of the command. There is a global, TPM-wide audit digest, and an auditor can request a signature over that digest.

Second, it's optional in the PC Client TPM specification. In TPM 1.2, to keep down development and test costs, vendors routinely ignored optional commands. Hardware 1.2 TPMs didn't implement command audits. Software can't rely on command audit being implemented in all TPM 2.0 devices.[3]

USE CASE: AUDITING THE TPM USED AS A CERTIFICATE AUTHORITY

A TPM can be used as a certificate authority (CA). As a hardware security module, it protects its private signing key far better than a software solution. A CA might want a verifiable list of all certificates that it signed. By setting a command audit of the TPM2_Sign command, the auditor can verify the list of signatures and detect any tampering of the list.

The TPM commands are as follows:

- TPM2_SetCommandCodeAuditStatus: Make TPM2_Sign be audited.

- TPM2_Sign: Uses the TPM as a CA to sign certificates. The caller keeps an audit log.

- TPM2_GetCommandAuditDigest: Gets a signature over a digest of the log containing the certificate hashes that were certified. The caller can use the signature to verify that the audit log has not been tampered with.

Session Audit

Session audit is new for TPM 2.0. It's mandatory in the PC platform specification, so it's likely to be widely available.

As the name suggests, session audit provides for an audit digest per session. An authorization session can additionally be used as an audit session by simply setting the audit attribute in each command to be audited. That is, a session doesn't become an audit session at the time it's started, but rather when it's used with the audit attribute set. For commands that don't require authorization, or to decouple audit from authorization, the audit session can be a separate session.

For example, TPM2_Create requires one authorization session to authorize the parent key. This session can also be marked as an audit session. Alternatively, a second session can be included with the command, this one marked for audit. TPM2_GetCapability requires no authorization and is normally used with no sessions. However, a session can be used for audit.

A command with multiple sessions can mark only one as an audit session.

---

[3]TPM2_GetCapability with the parameter TPM_CAP_COMMANDS retrieves a list of implemented commands.

Audit Log

The beginning of the chapter said that command and response parameter hashes are logged on the host, and the auditor can validate the signed log. This section outlines the required steps:

1. The auditor retrieves a list of command and response parameters from an audit log that the host stored as it executed the commands. From these, command parameter and response parameter hashes are calculated.

   a. Fortunately, the command-parameter and response-parameter hash calculations used for audit are exactly the same as those used for authorization. The command and response parameters are serialized (marshaled), and a digest over the resulting byte stream is calculated.

   b. For a command, the hash calculation, which requires marshaled parameters, should be straightforward. A TSS would naturally expose command-parameter marshaling to assist in the command-parameter authorization operation. Responses are trickier, because a TSS naturally unmarshals responses but doesn't marshal them. One approach is for the audit log to hold the marshaled response as well as the response parameters. The auditor can use the TSS to unmarshal and then validate those response parameters. If the TSS doesn't expose the unmarshal function, or if the audit log doesn't hold the marshaled response, the auditor has no choice but to write or obtain a marshaling function. Because a TPM naturally has this function, it's possible that it can be copied from a future open source TPM implementation.

   c. Either way, at the end of this step, the auditor should have command and response parameter hashes that are cryptographically validated against the command and response parameters.

2. The auditor performs the equivalent of an extend calculation, accumulating each command plus response parameter hash from step 1 into an audit digest.

3. The digital signature is verified. The calculated audit digest from step 2 is validated against the TPM signature and a public key.

4. The auditor walks a certificate chain back to a trusted root certificate, thereby establishing trust in the verification public key.

For continuous auditing, it's likely that the public key will be cached.

USE CASE: USING THE TPM TO SECURE AN APPLICATION AUDIT LOG

In addition to auditing TPM functions, the TPM audit facility can secure an application audit log. The application creates an NV extend index to record its events. Each time it records an event, it first extends that event into the NV index. It later gets a signature over the NV index data and uses it to verify that the event log has not been tampered with.

The TPM commands are as follows:

- `TPM2_NV_DefineSpace`: Define a hybrid extend index

- `TPM2_NV_Extend`: Extends the application event while also recording the event in the application event log.

When the application wishes to validate the audit log:

- `TPM2_StartAuthSession`: Starts the audit session

- `TPM2_NV_Read`: Reads the event digest

- `TPM2_GetSessionAuditDigest`: Gets a signature over the NV read data

If available, `TPM2_NV_Certify` can be used to get a signature over the NV read data, but that command may not be present on all TPMs.

Audit Data

The session audit digest is read using the `TPM2_GetSessionAuditDigest` command. In the typical use case, a signing key is supplied and the response is signed.

The digital signature isn't merely over the audit digest. As with other attestation functions, the TPM wraps the digest in a structure that includes other information. The TPM specification Part 2 describes this wrapping, where a `TPMS_ATTEST` wraps a `TPMU_ATTEST` union, which is a `TPMS_SESSION_AUDIT_INFO` structure.

The `TPMS_ATTEST` fields were covered in Chapter 12, including `TPM_GENERATED`, the qualified name of the signing key, the "extra data," the clock, and firmware information. Their security properties are the same here.

`TPMS_SESSION_AUDIT_INFO` includes, as expected, the session audit digest. It also includes a flag indicating the "exclusive" status of the session. See the following section.

Exclusive Audit

Exclusive audit permits an auditor to validate that a sequence of commands in an audit log was contiguous—that no other commands were interleaved with the exclusive sequence. A caller can designate only one session as an exclusive session. The caller sets the audit session `auditExclusive` attribute as part of a command. Assuming there was no exclusive session already in progress, this session becomes the exclusive session, and the attribute is echoed in the response.

Once a session becomes the exclusive session, it can be used for several commands. However, any intervening command not using this exclusive audit session causes it to no longer be the exclusive session. That is, an exclusive session in progress doesn't block another command but does record that another command intervened.

When the audit digest is returned, the structure includes a flag, exclusiveSession, which is true if there were no intervening commands.

USE CASE: ENSURE THAT PCRS DO NOT CHANGE DURING A COMMAND SEQUENCE

A user wants to run a sequence of commands at a specific trust state. PCR values indicate the trust state of the platform. The user therefore wants to ensure that PCR values don't change during a sequence of commands. The user runs the sequence in an exclusive session. If there was a PCR extend between two commands, it changes the current exclusive session. When the caller next tries to use the original exclusive session, the TPM returns an error, indicating an intervening command.

The TPM commands are as follows:

- TPM2_StartAuthSession: Starts a session to be used for the exclusive audit.

- TPM command sequence that should be run without an intervening PCR extend. Set the audit and auditExclusive session attributes.

- If there was an intervening command, the request for an exclusive audit session returns TPM_RC_EXCLUSIVE.

Summary

Audit in the TPM is the process of logging command and response parameters. The TPM logs these parameters with an extend operation, similar to that used for PCRs, while the host saves the actual parameters. Later, the TPM can return a signed digest of the audit log. The recipient can validate the signature and thus verify the integrity of the log.

The TPM offers two audit options. Command audit records all instances of a selected group of commands, regardless of the session. Session audit records all commands in a session, regardless of the command. An exclusive session permits the recipient to detect whether an audit session was interrupted by an intervening, non-audited command. It can also provide a guarantee that there was no intervening command.

CHAPTER 17

■ ■ ■

Decrypt/Encrypt Sessions

2B or not 2B, that is the question.

Dave Challener,
During TCG TSS Working Group discussion of
decrypt/encrypt sessions

Chapter 13 briefly touched on decrypt and encrypt sessions. As you may remember, these are per-command session modifiers. This chapter describes these two session modifiers in detail: what they do, practical uses of them, some limitations on them, how to set them up, and some code examples.

What Do Encrypt/Decrypt Sessions Do?

In a nutshell, decrypt and encrypt sessions protect secrets being transmitted over an insecure medium. A caller, to protect the confidentiality of data, can encrypt it with a command encryption key known only to the caller and the TPM. The encryption key is determined, in part, by the parameters used to start the session (more on that later). A decrypt session then informs the TPM that the first parameter is encrypted. This means after receiving the parameter, the TPM must decrypt it—hence the name, *decrypt session*. For a response, an encrypt session indicates that the TPM has encrypted the first response parameter before returning it to the caller, which is why it's called an *encrypt session*. After receiving the encrypted response parameter, the caller uses the response decryption key to decrypt the data.

Two different symmetric-key modes can be used for decrypt and encrypt sessions: XOR and CFB. CFB mode offers stronger encryption but requires that the TPM and the caller both have access to a hashing algorithm and an encryption algorithm. XOR requires only a hashing algorithm and is the right choice for very small code size, but it is less secure.

Practical Use Cases

So, what are these symmetric key modes good for? The quick answer is that there are many ways to use them; just look in Part 3 of the TPM 2.0 specification for every command that has a TPM2B as a first command and/or first response parameter. All of those parameters are possible candidates to be encrypted.

A small sampling of common use cases are as follows:

- Tpm2_Create: The first command parameter to this command, inSensitive, is a structure which contains the password (called userAuth in the structure description) in one of its fields. This should probably be sent to the TPM encrypted, which would require that the session be set up as a decrypt session.[1]

- Confidential data being written to or read from TPM NV indexes. Suppose you want to use the TPM NV indexes to save password information or personal credit card information. Encrypting this data before sending it to or receiving it from the TPM helps protect it.

- Use of decrypt and encrypt sessions becomes even more important when communicating with a remote TPM over the network. Suppose you want to store keys on a remote server and recover them from client machines. Sending these in the clear over the network is obviously insecure. SSL sessions can remedy the network snooping vulnerability, but the keys are still in the clear in multiple software layers on the client and server machines. Encrypt and decrypt sessions can vastly reduce the attack surface.

Decrypt/Encrypt Limitations

There are some limitations on which parameters can be encrypted and decrypted and the number of encrypt and decrypt sessions per command.

Only the first command parameter can be encrypted and only the first response parameter can be decrypted, and in both cases, only if that first parameter is a TPM2B as defined in Chapter 5. Commands that don't have a TPM2B as the first command parameter cannot be sent to the TPM using sessions set for decrypt; likewise, if a response's first parameter isn't a TPM2B, the response can't be received using an encrypt session.

As you learned in Chapter 13, commands can be sent with up to three sessions. But a maximum of one session per command can be set for decrypt and a maximum of one for encrypt. If a command allows the use of both decrypt and encrypt sessions, the same session can be used to set both attributes or separate sessions can be used, one for each attribute.

So how do you enable decrypt and encrypt sessions?

---

[1]There's an interesting wrinkle related to the first response parameter from Tpm2_Create: even though this parameter is a TPM2B and could be encrypted by setting the session as an encrypt session, it's always encrypted by the TPM. Encrypting it again would seem to be of little value.

Decrypt/Encrypt Setup

At first glance, configuring sessions as decrypt and/or encrypt sessions is very easy. For an open session, all you have to do is set either or both of the session attributes bits in the authorization area for the command: `sessionAttributes.decrypt` and/or `sessionAttributes.encrypt`.

Of course, things are rarely that simple, and it's certainly true here. For a decrypt session, the caller has to properly encrypt the first parameter. Likewise for an encrypt session, the caller has to properly decrypt the first response parameter after receiving it from the TPM; otherwise, it will be meaningless gibberish to the caller. Two modes of encryption are used for decrypt and encrypt sessions: XOR and CFB mode. These modes are set when the session is created. Both modes have the property that the plain text and ciphertext are the same length, so the byte stream lengths don't change. Session nonces figure into the encryption, which ensures that the encryption and decryption operations function as one-time pads.

For XOR mode, a *mask* (one-time pad) is generated and XORed with the data to be encrypted or decrypted. The mask is generated by passing the `hashAlg` (`authHash` parameter used when the session was started), the HMAC key, the string "XOR", `nonceNewer`, `nonceOlder`, and the message size to the key derivation function (KDFa). The output is a mask that is as long as the message to be decrypted or encrypted. A simple XOR of the mask with the data completes the encryption or decryption operation.

For CFB mode, the KDFa is used to generate the encryption key and initialization vector (IV). The inputs to the KDFa are `hashAlg` (the `authHash` parameter used when the session was started), `sessionKey`, the "CFB" string, `nonceNewer`, `nonceOlder`, and the number of bits (`bits`) needed for the symmetric key plus the IV. The output is a string of `bits` length, with the key in the upper octets and the IV in the lower octets. The IV size is determined by the block size of the encryption algorithm. The key and IV are used as inputs to the encryption algorithm to perform the required encryption or decryption operation.

For both XOR and CFB modes, `nonceNewer` and `nonceOlder` figure into the encryption. For XOR mode, because the nonces change, a different mask is generated for encryption of command parameters than the one used for response parameters. Likewise, for CFB mode, a different encryption key and IV are generated for commands and responses. In both XOR and CFB modes, because the nonces roll for every usage of the session, encrypt and decrypt sessions act as one-time pads.

Pseudocode Flow

As you may recall from Chapter 13, sessions can be one of three types: HMAC, policy, or trial policy sessions. HMAC and policy sessions can be used as decrypt or encrypt sessions; trial policy sessions cannot.

To keep things very simple, the following example uses an unbound, unsalted policy session that isn't being used for authorization.[2] The only use of this session is for decryption and encryption of command and response parameters. A separate password session is used for authorization. This means the test code doesn't need to calculate HMACs or manage the `policyDigest` for the encrypt and decrypt session.

---

[2]Unbound and unsalted sessions don't yield strong encryption keys and should not normally be used for decrypt or encrypt sessions. This was done to keep the example as simple as possible.

When a session is started, the TPM generates a session key. To use decrypt and encrypt sessions, the caller needs to independently generate that session key, just as he had to do in order to use HMAC and policy sessions.

To unify all this into a single flow, the steps in decrypt and encrypt session lifecycles are as follows:

1. Start the session using `Tpm2_StartAuthSession`, and set the symmetric parameter to

    - CFB mode:

      ```
      // AES encryption/decryption and CFB mode.
      symmetric.algorithm = TPM_ALG_AES;
      symmetric.keyBits.aes = 128;
      symmetric.mode.aes = TPM_ALG_CFB;
      ```

    - XOR mode:

      ```
      // XOR encryption/decryption.
      symmetric.algorithm = TPM_ALG_XOR;
      symmetric.keyBits.exclusiveOr = TPM_ALG_SHA256;
      ```

2. Generate the session key, and save it.

3. For a command that has a TPM2B as the first parameter, if you desire to encrypt that parameter, do the following:

    a. Generate the HMAC key for this use of the session. The session key figures into the generation of this key.

    b. For CFB mode:

        - Generate the encryption key and IV using the session hash algorithm, HMAC key, special label ("CFB"), nonceNewer, nonceOlder, and the number of bits to be encrypted.

        - Encrypt the first parameter, using the encryption key and IV.

    c. For XOR mode:

        - Generate the mask using the HMAC key, the session hash algorithm, nonceNewer, nonceOlder, and the number of bytes to be encrypted.

        - XOR the clear text data with the mask to generate the encrypted data.

    d. Set the `sessionAttributes.decrypt` bit.

4. If the first response parameter is a TPM2B and you want the TPM to send that parameter in encrypted format, set the sessionAttributes.encrypt bit.

5. Send the command to the TPM.

6. Receive the response from the TPM.

7. If the first response parameter is a TPM2B and the sessionAttributes.encrypt bit is set, do the following:

    a. Generate the HMAC key for this use of the session. The session key figures into the generation of this key.

    b. For CFB mode:

        • Generate the encryption key and IV using the session hash algorithm, HMAC key, special label ("CFB"), nonceNewer, nonceOlder, and the number of bits to be decrypted.

        • Decrypt the first parameter, using the encryption key and IV.

    c. For XOR mode:

        • Generate the mask using the HMAC key, the session hash algorithm, nonceNewer, nonceOlder, and the number of bytes to be decrypted.

        • XOR the encrypted data with the mask to generate the clear data.

For details on CFB and XOR decryption/encryption see the "Session-based encryption" section of Part 1 of the TPM 2.0 specification.

Sample Code

This section shows an example of actual working code for doing decrypt and encrypt sessions. First some notes about this code:

• This code does a write of encrypted data to an NV index (decrypt session attribute set) followed by two reads from the same NV index: a plain text read (encrypt attribute not set) and a ciphertext read (encrypt session attribute set). After both reads, the read data is compared to the plain text write data.

■ **Note**   The reason for doing the plain text read is to verify that the NV index was written with plain text, not encrypted data. If you didn't set the decrypt session attribute, encrypted data would be written to the NV index. But the test would still appear to be working because the encrypted data would be written to the TPM, read back, and decrypted by the calling application, and the test to verify the read and write data would pass. This was actually a mistake that I made on my first pass at writing this code.

To catch this issue, do a plain text read of the NV index and compare this to the unencrypted write data. They should be equal.

- This function tests both CFB and XOR mode encryption. CFB is done on the first pass and XOR on the second pass.
- The code demonstrates some new features of the TSS system API code that couldn't be discussed earlier:[3]
  - *Getting and setting of encrypt and decrypt parameters*: These calls enable the caller to get the plain text unencrypted command parameters (Tss2_Sys_GetDecryptParam), encrypt them, and then set the encrypted command parameters in the command byte stream (Tss2_Sys_SetDecryptParam) before sending the command. Likewise, Tss2_Sys_GetEncryptParam and Tss2_Sys_SetEncryptParam enable the caller to properly process response parameters that were encrypted by the TPM.
  - *Asynchronous execution* (Tss2_Sys_ExecuteAsync and Tss2_Sys_ExecuteFinish): This mode of execution allows the application to send the command (Tss2_Sys_ExecuteAsync), do some work while waiting for the response, and then get the response (Tss2_Sys_ExecuteFinish) with a configurable timeout.
  - *Synchronous execution calls* (Tss2_Sys_Execute): This function will wait forever for a response, so it assumes that the TPM eventually responds.

---

[3]For details on these system API calls, review the TSS System Level API and TPM Command Transmission Interface Specification at www.trustedcomputinggroup.org/developers/ software_stack.

- *Setting command authorizations* (Tss2_SetCmdAuths) *and getting response authorizations* (Tss2_GetRspAuths): These functions are used to set command authorization area parameters and get response area parameters, including nonces, session attributes, passwords (for password sessions), and command and response HMACs. In this example they will be used for nonces, session attributes, and the password. Access to the command and response HMACs isn't needed in this code since the code doesn't use HMACs.

- This code relies heavily on an application-level structure, SESSION, that maintains all session state information including nonces. There are many ways this can be done—this just happens to be the implementation I chose. This structure looks like this:

```
typedef struct {
    // Inputs to StartAuthSession; these need to be saved
    // so that HMACs can be calculated.
    TPMI_DH_OBJECT tpmKey;
    TPMI_DH_ENTITY bind;
    TPM2B_ENCRYPTED_SECRET encryptedSalt;
    TPM2B_MAX_BUFFER salt;
    TPM_SE sessionType;
    TPMT_SYM_DEF symmetric;
    TPMI_ALG_HASH authHash;

    // Outputs from StartAuthSession; these also need
    // to be saved for calculating HMACs and
    // other session related functions.
    TPMI_SH_AUTH_SESSION sessionHandle;
    TPM2B_NONCE nonceTPM;

    // Internal state for the session
    TPM2B_DIGEST sessionKey;
    TPM2B_DIGEST authValueBind; // authValue of bind object
    TPM2B_NONCE nonceNewer;
    TPM2B_NONCE nonceOlder;
    TPM2B_NONCE nonceTpmDecrypt;
    TPM2B_NONCE nonceTpmEncrypt;
    TPM2B_NAME name;        // Name of the object the session handle
                           // points to. Used for computing HMAC for
                           // any HMAC sessions present.
                           //
    void *hmacPtr;         // Pointer to HMAC field in the marshalled
                           // data stream for the session.
                           // This allows the function to calculate
```

```
                          // and fill in the HMAC after marshalling
                          // of all the inputs is done.
                          //
                          // This is only used if the session is an
                          // HMAC session.
                          //
    UINT8 nvNameChanged;// Used for some special case code
                        // dealing with the NV written state.
} SESSION;
```

- The RollNonces function does what it says: it copies nonceNewer to nonceOlder and copies the new nonce to nonceNewer. The nonces must be rolled before each command and after each response, as described in Chapter 13. Here's the complete code for this function:

```
void RollNonces( SESSION *session, TPM2B_NONCE *newNonce )
{
    session->nonceOlder = session->nonceNewer;
    session->nonceNewer = *newNonce;
}
```

- The StartAuthSessionWithParams function starts the session, saves its state in a SESSION structure, and adds the SESSION structure to a list of open sessions.

- The EndAuthSession function is used to remove the SESSION structure from the list of open sessions after the session has ended.

- EncryptCommandParam encrypts command parameters, and DecryptResponseParam decrypts response parameters. Both functions examine the authorization structures' TPMA_SESSION bits to determine if the decrypt and/or encrypt bits are set. This chapter doesn't describe the details of these functions, but they perform the encryption and decryption operations as explained in Part 1 of the TPM 2.0 specification.

- For some of the common routines and data structures that aren't described here, please refer to Chapters 7 and 13 as well as the TSS System API specification.

This working code can be downloaded in source form as part of the TSS System API library code and tests. Because the code is a bit long, to help you better understand the flow, notes are interspersed before each major block of functionality. And now for the actual code:

```
UINT32 writeDataString = 0xdeadbeef;

void TestEncryptDecryptSession()
{
    TSS2_RC                  rval = TSS2_RC_SUCCESS;
    SESSION                  encryptDecryptSession;
    TPMT_SYM_DEF             symmetric;
    TPM2B_MAX_NV_BUFFER      writeData, encryptedWriteData;
    TPM2B_MAX_NV_BUFFER      encryptedReadData, decryptedReadData,
                             readData;
    size_t                   decryptParamSize;
    uint8_t                  *decryptParamBuffer;
    size_t                   encryptParamSize;
    uint8_t                  *encryptParamBuffer;
    TPM2B_AUTH               nvAuth;
    TPM2B_DIGEST             authPolicy;
    TPMA_NV                  nvAttributes;
    int                      i;
    TPMA_SESSION             sessionAttributes;
```

The following lines set up the authorization used for the NV Undefine command.

```
// Authorization structure for undefine command.
TPMS_AUTH_COMMAND nvUndefineAuth;

// Create and init authorization area for undefine command:
// only 1 authorization area.
TPMS_AUTH_COMMAND *nvUndefineAuthArray[1] = { &nvUndefineAuth };

// Authorization array for command (only has one auth structure).
TSS2_SYS_CMD_AUTHS nvUndefineAuths = { 1, &nvUndefineAuthArray[0] };

printf( "\n\nDECRYPT/ENCRYPT SESSION TESTS:\n" );
```

Copy the write data array into a TPM2B structure.

```
writeData.t.size = sizeof( writeDataString );
memcpy( (void *)&writeData.t.buffer, (void *)&writeDataString,
        sizeof( writeDataString ) );
```

Create the NV index.

```
// Create NV index with empty auth value.
*(UINT32 *)( (void *)&nvAttributes ) = 0;
nvAttributes.TPMA_NV_AUTHREAD = 1;
nvAttributes.TPMA_NV_AUTHWRITE = 1;
nvAttributes.TPMA_NV_PLATFORMCREATE = 1;

// No authorization required.
authPolicy.t.size = 0;
nvAuth.t.size = 0;
rval = DefineNvIndex( TPM_RH_PLATFORM, TPM_RS_PW,
        &nvAuth, &authPolicy, TPM20_INDEX_TEST1,
        TPM_ALG_SHA1, nvAttributes,
        sizeof( writeDataString ) );

//
// 1st pass with CFB mode.
// 2nd pass with XOR mode.
//
for( i = 0; i < 2; i++ )
{
```

Set up authorization structures for NV read and write commands and responses.

```
// Authorization structure for NV
// read/write commands.
TPMS_AUTH_COMMAND nvRdWrCmdAuth;

// Authorization structure for
// encrypt/decrypt session.
TPMS_AUTH_COMMAND decryptEncryptSessionCmdAuth;
```

```
// Create and init authorization area for
// NV read/write commands:
// 2 authorization areas.
TPMS_AUTH_COMMAND *nvRdWrCmdAuthArray[2] =
        { &nvRdWrCmdAuth, &decryptEncryptSessionCmdAuth };

// Authorization array for commands
// (has two auth structures).
TSS2_SYS_CMD_AUTHS nvRdWrCmdAuths =
        { 2, &nvRdWrCmdAuthArray[0] };

// Authorization structure for NV read/write responses.
TPMS_AUTH_RESPONSE nvRdWrRspAuth;

// Authorization structure for decrypt/encrypt
// session responses.
TPMS_AUTH_RESPONSE decryptEncryptSessionRspAuth;

// Create and init authorization area for NV
// read/write responses:  2 authorization areas.
TPMS_AUTH_RESPONSE *nvRdWrRspAuthArray[2] =
        { &nvRdWrRspAuth, &decryptEncryptSessionRspAuth };

// Authorization array for responses
// (has two auth structures).
TSS2_SYS_RSP_AUTHS nvRdWrRspAuths =
        { 2, &nvRdWrRspAuthArray[0] };
```

Set the session for CFB or XOR mode encryption/decryption, depending on which pass through the code is being run. Then start the policy session.

```
// Setup session parameters.
if( i == 0 )
{
    // AES encryption/decryption and CFB mode.
    symmetric.algorithm = TPM_ALG_AES;
    symmetric.keyBits.aes = 128;
    symmetric.mode.aes = TPM_ALG_CFB;
}
else
{
    // XOR encryption/decryption.
    symmetric.algorithm = TPM_ALG_XOR;
    symmetric.keyBits.exclusiveOr = TPM_ALG_SHA256;
}
```

```
// Start policy session for decrypt/encrypt session.
rval = StartAuthSessionWithParams( &encryptDecryptSession,
        TPM_RH_NULL, TPM_RH_NULL, 0, TPM_SE_POLICY,
        &symmetric, TPM_ALG_SHA256 );
CheckPassed( rval );
```

Write the NV index using a password session for authorization and a policy session for encryption/decryption. First marshal the input parameters (Tss2_Sys_NV_Prepare).

```
//
// Write TPM index with encrypted parameter used
// as the data to write. Set session for encrypt.
// Use asynchronous APIs to do this.
//
// 1st time:  use null buffer, 2nd time use populated one;
// this tests different cases for SetDecryptParam function.
//

// Prepare the input parameters, using unencrypted
// write data. This will be encrypted before the
// command is sent to the TPM.
rval = Tss2_Sys_NV_Write_Prepare( sysContext,
        TPM20_INDEX_TEST1, TPM20_INDEX_TEST1,
        ( i == 0 ? (TPM2B_MAX_NV_BUFFER *)0 : &writeData ),
        0 );
CheckPassed( rval );
```

Set the authorization structures (Tss2_Sys_SetCmdAuths) for the command.

```
// Set up password authorization session structure.
nvRdWrCmdAuth.sessionHandle = TPM_RS_PW;
nvRdWrCmdAuth.nonce.t.size = 0;
*( (UINT8 *)((void *)&nvRdWrCmdAuth.sessionAttributes ) ) = 0;
nvRdWrCmdAuth.hmac.t.size = nvAuth.t.size;
memcpy( (void *)&nvRdWrCmdAuth.hmac.t.buffer[0],
        (void *)&nvAuth.t.buffer[0],
        nvRdWrCmdAuth.hmac.t.size );

// Set up encrypt/decrypt session structure.
decryptEncryptSessionCmdAuth.sessionHandle =
        encryptDecryptSession.sessionHandle;
decryptEncryptSessionCmdAuth.nonce.t.size = 0;
*( (UINT8 *)((void *)&sessionAttributes ) ) = 0;
```

```
decryptEncryptSessionCmdAuth.sessionAttributes =
        sessionAttributes;
decryptEncryptSessionCmdAuth.sessionAttributes.continueSession
        = 1;
decryptEncryptSessionCmdAuth.sessionAttributes.decrypt = 1;
decryptEncryptSessionCmdAuth.hmac.t.size = 0;

rval = Tss2_Sys_SetCmdAuths( sysContext, &nvRdWrCmdAuths );
CheckPassed( rval );
```

Get the location and size of the decrypt parameter in the byte stream
(Tss2_Sys_GetDecryptParam), encrypt the write data (EncryptCommandParam), and copy
the encrypted write data into the byte stream (Tss2_Sys_SetDecryptParam).

```
// Get decrypt parameter.
rval = Tss2_Sys_GetDecryptParam( sysContext,
        &decryptParamSize,
        (const uint8_t **)&decryptParamBuffer );
CheckPassed( rval );

if( i == 0 )
{
    // 1st pass:  test case of Prepare inputting a NULL decrypt
    // param; decryptParamSize should be 0.
    if( decryptParamSize != 0 )
    {
        printf( "ERROR!! decryptParamSize != 0\n" );
        Cleanup();
    }
}

// Roll nonces for command.
RollNonces( &encryptDecryptSession,
        &decryptEncryptSessionCmdAuth.nonce );

// Encrypt write data.
rval = EncryptCommandParam( &encryptDecryptSession,
        (TPM2B_MAX_BUFFER *)&encryptedWriteData,
        (TPM2B_MAX_BUFFER *)&writeData, &nvAuth );
CheckPassed( rval );

// Now set decrypt parameter.
rval = Tss2_Sys_SetDecryptParam( sysContext,
        (uint8_t )encryptedWriteData.t.size,
        (uint8_t *)&encryptedWriteData.t.buffer[0] );
CheckPassed( rval );
```

Write the NV data (Tss2_Sys_ExecuteAsync and Tss2_Sys_ExecuteFinish). The write uses asynchronous calls to illustrate this feature of the TSS System API.

```
// Now write the data to the NV index.
rval = Tss2_Sys_ExecuteAsync( sysContext );
CheckPassed( rval );

rval = Tss2_Sys_ExecuteFinish( sysContext, -1 );
CheckPassed( rval );
```

Get the response authorizations to set up for the next use of the sessions (Tss2_Sys_GetRspAuths).

```
rval = Tss2_Sys_GetRspAuths( sysContext, &nvRdWrRspAuths );
CheckPassed( rval );

// Roll the nonces for response
RollNonces( &encryptDecryptSession,
        &nvRdWrRspAuths.rspAuths[1]->nonce );

// Don't need nonces for anything else, so roll
// the nonces for next command.RollNonces( &encryptDecryptSession,
        &decryptEncryptSessionCmdAuth.nonce );
```

Read the data back as plain text to be sure the decrypt session worked correctly during the NV write operation.

```
// Now read the data without encrypt set.
nvRdWrCmdAuths.cmdAuthsCount = 1;
nvRdWrRspAuths.rspAuthsCount = 1;
rval = Tss2_Sys_NV_Read( sysContext, TPM20_INDEX_TEST1,
        TPM20_INDEX_TEST1, &nvRdWrCmdAuths,
        sizeof( writeDataString ), 0, &readData,
        &nvRdWrRspAuths );
CheckPassed( rval );
nvRdWrCmdAuths.cmdAuthsCount = 2;
nvRdWrRspAuths.rspAuthsCount = 2;
```

```
// Roll the nonces for response
RollNonces( &encryptDecryptSession,
        &nvRdWrRspAuths.rspAuths[1]->nonce );

// Check that write and read data are equal. This
// verifies that the decrypt session was set up correctly.
// If it wasn't, the data stored in the TPM would still
// be encrypted, and this test would fail.
if( memcmp( (void *)&readData.t.buffer[0],
        (void *)&writeData.t.buffer[0], readData.t.size ) )
{
    printf( "ERROR!! read data not equal to written data\n" );
    Cleanup();
}
```

Now read the NV data encrypted using an encrypt session. This time, use a synchronous call, Tss2_Sys_Execute. The reason is simply to demonstrate another method; you could use asynchronous calls similar to how the NV write was performed.

```
//
// Read TPM index with encrypt session; use
// synchronous APIs to do this.
//

rval = Tss2_Sys_NV_Read_Prepare( sysContext, TPM20_INDEX_TEST1,
        TPM20_INDEX_TEST1, sizeof( writeDataString ), 0 );
CheckPassed( rval );

// Roll the nonces for next command.
RollNonces( &encryptDecryptSession,
        &decryptEncryptSessionCmdAuth.nonce );

decryptEncryptSessionCmdAuth.sessionAttributes.decrypt = 0;
decryptEncryptSessionCmdAuth.sessionAttributes.encrypt = 1;
decryptEncryptSessionCmdAuth.sessionAttributes.continueSession = 1;

rval = Tss2_Sys_SetCmdAuths( sysContext, &nvRdWrCmdAuths );
CheckPassed( rval );

//
// Now Read the data.
//
rval = Tss2_Sys_Execute( sysContext );
CheckPassed( rval );
```

Use Tss2_Sys_GetEncryptParam and Tss2_Sys_SetEncryptParam combined with
DecryptResponseParam to decrypt the response data.

```
rval = Tss2_Sys_GetEncryptParam( sysContext, &encryptParamSize,
        (const uint8_t **)&encryptParamBuffer );
CheckPassed( rval );

rval = Tss2_Sys_GetRspAuths( sysContext, &nvRdWrRspAuths );
CheckPassed( rval );

// Roll the nonces for response
RollNonces( &encryptDecryptSession,
        &nvRdWrRspAuths.rspAuths[1]->nonce );

// Decrypt read data.
encryptedReadData.t.size = encryptParamSize;
memcpy( (void *)&encryptedReadData.t.buffer[0],
        (void *)encryptParamBuffer, encryptParamSize );

rval = DecryptResponseParam( &encryptDecryptSession,
        (TPM2B_MAX_BUFFER *)&decryptedReadData,
        (TPM2B_MAX_BUFFER *)&encryptedReadData, &nvAuth );
CheckPassed( rval );

// Roll the nonces.
RollNonces( &encryptDecryptSession,
        &nvRdWrRspAuths.rspAuths[1]->nonce );

rval = Tss2_Sys_SetEncryptParam( sysContext,
        (uint8_t)decryptedReadData.t.size,
        (uint8_t *)&decryptedReadData.t.buffer[0] );
CheckPassed( rval );

// Get the command results, in this case the read data.
rval = Tss2_Sys_NV_Read_Complete( sysContext, &readData );
CheckPassed( rval );

printf( "Decrypted read data = " );
DEBUG_PRINT_BUFFER( &readData.t.buffer[0], (UINT32 )readData.t.size );
```

```
// Check that write and read data are equal.
if( memcmp( (void *)&readData.t.buffer[0],
        (void *)&writeData.t.buffer[0], readData.t.size ) )
{
    printf( "ERROR!! read data not equal to written data\n" );
    Cleanup();
}


rval = Tss2_Sys_FlushContext( sysContext,
        encryptDecryptSession.sessionHandle );
CheckPassed( rval );


rval = EndAuthSession( &encryptDecryptSession );
CheckPassed( rval );
    }
```

Delete the NV index.

```
    // Set authorization for NV undefine command.
    nvUndefineAuth.sessionHandle = TPM_RS_PW;
    nvUndefineAuth.nonce.t.size = 0;
    *( (UINT8 *)((void *)&nvUndefineAuth.sessionAttributes ) ) = 0;
    nvUndefineAuth.hmac.t.size = 0;

    // Undefine NV index.
    rval = Tss2_Sys_NV_UndefineSpace( sysContext,
            TPM_RH_PLATFORM, TPM20_INDEX_TEST1, &nvUndefineAuths, 0 );
    CheckPassed( rval );
}
```

Summary

As you can see, there is a fair amount of work involved in using decrypt and encrypt sessions. Abstracting this work into well-designed functions or even using a higher-level API such as the Feature API helps to reduce this work.

Decrypt and encrypt sessions provide secrecy for sensitive information while in transit to and from the TPM. You've seen what they do, some use cases, and how to program them using the TSS System API, and you've learned about some new functionality in the System API.

The next chapter focuses on TPM context management.

CHAPTER 18

■ ■ ■

Context Management

In general, we don't prevent things unless there is a good reason for that.
Put another way, we try to allow anything that doesn't cause a security
problem.

David Wooten,
During an e-mail exchange about context management

TPMs, for all their tremendous capability, are very limited in their memory, largely to
reduce cost. This means objects, sessions, and sequences must be swapped in and out of
the TPM as needed, much like a virtual memory manager swaps memory pages to and
from disk drives. In both cases, the calling application thinks it has access to many more
objects and sessions (in the TPM case) or much more memory (in the virtual memory
case) than can actually be present at any given time.

For a system where only a single application sends commands to the TPM, these
swapping operations can be performed by the application itself.[1] However, when multiple
applications and/or processes are accessing the TPM, two components of the TSS stack
are required: the TPM Access Broker (TAB) and the resource manager (RM).

This chapter describes the high-level architecture of the TAB and RM. Then it
describes the features and commands of the TPM that support swapping objects,
sessions, and sequences in and out of TPM memory, the details of how different
swappable entities are handled by the related commands, and some special cases.

TAB and the Resource Manager: A High-Level Description

The TAB and RM were first described in Chapter 7 as layers in the TSS. This section
provides some insights into the internals of the TAB and RM.

The TAB and RM transparently isolate TPM applications and processes from the
messiness of arbitrating multiprocess access to the TPM and swapping objects, sessions,
and sequences in and out of TPM memory as needed. The TAB and RM are closely

---

[1]Even in this case, the use of an RM is advantageous because it relieves the application of the
burden of performing the swapping.

related and typically integrated into the same software module. Depending on system design, they may reside in the top layer of a TPM device-driver stack, or they may be integrated as a daemon process sandwiched between the TSS system API layer above and the TPM device driver below.

TAB

The TAB's responsibility is fairly simple: arbitrate multiple processes accessing the TPM. At a minimum, all processes must be guaranteed that, between the time their command byte stream begins to be transmitted to the TPM and the time the response byte stream is fully received from the TPM, no other processes communicate with the TPM. Some examples of multiprocess collisions that could occur in the absence of a TAB are as follows:

- Process A's command byte stream begins to be transmitted to the TPM, and before it's done, process B's command byte stream starts being transmitted. The byte stream sent to the TPM will be a mix of command bytes from both processes, and the TPM will probably return an error code.

- Process A sends a command, and Process B reads the response.

- Process A's command byte stream is transmitted, and then, while its response is being read, Process B's byte stream starts being transmitted.

- Process A creates and loads a key exclusively for its own use. Process B context saves (using the TPM2_ContextSave command) the key and then, sometime later, context loads it (using the TPM2_ContextLoad command) and uses it for its own purposes.

A TAB can be implemented in a couple of different ways: either with a TPM lock or without one.

In the lock architecture, a software method of sending a "lock" down to the TAB could be designed. This would signal the TAB that no other process would be allowed access to the TPM until the process that locked it is completes. This would have the advantage of allowing a TAB to complete multiple commands to the TPM without interruption. And interestingly enough, this architecture would eliminate the need for an RM, assuming you could make it work. An application could claim a lock on the TPM and send commands to the TPM while managing all TPM contexts itself (this management includes cleaning up after itself by evicting all objects, sequences, and sessions before releasing the lock). The Achilles heel of this architecture is that the application might fail to release the lock, starving all other applications. There could be some sort of timeout mechanism, but that would place artificial limits on the time that an application could exclusively use the TPM. This in turn would force applications to do some fairly complex management of corner cases related to TPM contexts since they couldn't depend on the lock being active long enough to complete their TPM operations. This approach was initially considered by the TCG TSS working group and rejected after some very wise advice from Paul England of Microsoft.

The simpler lock-less architecture allows the transmission of a TPM command and reception of its response atomically without interruption from any other processes' interactions with the TPM. This reduces the time that the process exclusively accesses the TPM to the time it takes to send a command and receive a response. This architecture requires an underlying RM because competing applications cannot be in the business of managing each other's objects, sessions, and sequences. For example:

1. Process A happens to be the only application accessing the TPM for a while, and during this time it starts three sessions and loads three keys.

2. Then process B decides it's ready to talk to the TPM and wants to create a session and a key. If the TPM has only three session slots and three object slots, process B must first unload at least one of process A's sessions and one of its objects.

3. This forces process B to manage process A's TPM contexts— an untenable position in terms of inter-process isolation (security) and software complexity. Without a central RM, applications must manage all TPM contexts themselves. It's almost impossible to make this work, and it guarantees that processes can mess with each other's TPM contexts.

Hence the need for an RM.

Resource Manager

The RM is responsible for transparently handling all the details of swapping objects, sessions, and sequences in and out of the TPM. Very highly embedded, single-user applications may choose to handle these tasks themselves, but, as discussed previously, most systems are multiuser and require an RM. As an analogy, imagine if all PC applications had to manage memory swapping in and out of memory and the hard disk themselves instead of relying on the operating system to do this. The RM performs a similar function for processes that access TPMs.

Resource Manager Operations

At the risk of stating the obvious, if a transient entity is used in a command, it must be loaded into TPM memory. This means that an RM must parse the command byte stream before the command is sent to the TPM and take any actions required to ensure that all transient objects used by that command are loaded into the TPM. This includes all sessions referenced in the authorization area and all objects, sessions, and sequences whose handles are in the command's handle area.

The basic operations that an RM must perform are as follows[2]:

- Virtualize all object and sequence handles sent to and received from the TPM. Because more of these can be active than can be in the TPM's internal memory, they must be virtualized.[3]

- Maintain tables to keep track of contexts for objects and sequences.

- Maintain a virtual-to-TPM handle mapping for objects and sequences that are loaded in the TPM.

- For commands being sent to the TPM:

  - Capture all command byte streams before they're sent to the TPM.

  - Check for any handles in the authorization area or handle area. If these handles represent objects, sequences, or sessions, ensure that the saved contexts for these are loaded into the TPM so that the command can successfully execute. For objects and sequences, replace the virtual handles in the command byte stream with the real handles returned from the load commands before sending the command to the TPM.

■ **Note**   Session handles do not need to be virtualized, because they are constant for the lifetime of the session: that is, when a session is reloaded, it keeps the same handle. The "why" of this is discussed later. For now, it's sufficient to understand the difference between objects and sequences, which get new handles every time they're context loaded, and sessions, which do not.

- For responses from the TPM:

  - Capture these responses before they are returned to higher layers of software.

  - Virtualize any object or sequence handles in the responses, and replace the handles returned by the TPM in the response byte stream with these virtualized handles.

- It must either proactively guarantee that commands will never fail due to being out of memory in the TPM or reactively fix the problem when the required contexts can't be loaded into the TPM.

---

[2]For a reference implementation of a resource manager see the Test/tpmclient/ResourceMgr directory in the SAPI library and test code. The location for this was described in Chapter 7.
[3]TPM handle virtualization is not to be confused with OS level virtualization of hardware or operating systems.

- There are two possible ways to implement the proactive approach:

  - The simplest proactive approach requires that, after completion of each TPM command from software layers above the RM, all objects, sessions, and sequences must be context saved and removed from TPM internal memory. This is inherently a simpler approach, but it does cause more commands to be sent to the TPM. For example, after a load command for an object, the object is unloaded even though it might be used in the next command.

  - The second proactive approach is to examine the command's handle and session area before executing it, to find all the objects, sequences, and sessions that must be loaded into the TPM. Next, enough of the objects, sequences, and sessions currently loaded into the TPM are evicted that the required ones can be context loaded. Then the required ones that aren't already loaded into the TPM are loaded.

■ **Note** A hardware-triggered command, _TPM_Hash_Start, is discussed later in this chapter. This command implicitly, and transparently to the RM, evicts an object or session. This imposes some special requirements on the second type of proactive approach.

- The reactive approach takes actions after a command fails when the response code indicates that the TPM was out of memory. When this type of error code is received, the RM must remove objects, sessions, or sequences until enough memory is freed to load the objects, sessions, and sequences required for the current command. Then the original command must be replayed.

■ **Note** From hard-earned experience, the reactive approach is extremely difficult to code and even harder to debug. I highly recommend one of the proactive approaches. I tried the reactive approach and it didn't end well, resulting in a recoding effort. Enough said.

- The RM must properly handle object, sequence, and session contexts across reset events, as described in the previous section.

The above covers the basic requirements. Others for handling corner cases and some more esoteric functionality are detailed in the "TSS TAB and Resource Manager Specification".

Now let's examine the TPM features that support RMs.

Management of Objects, Sessions, and Sequences

Because the TPM has limited internal memory, objects, sessions, and sequences need to be dynamically swapped in and out of memory. As an example, the reference implementation of a TPM 2.0 implemented by the Microsoft simulator only allows room for three object slots. An object slot is internal TPM memory for an object or sequence. There are also three session slots. Hence the need for virtualization of transient entities (here, the term *transient entities* describes transient objects, sessions, and sequences). This section describes the TPM capabilities and commands that are used to accomplish this virtualization.

TPM Context-Management Features

The TPM capabilities used to manage transient entities are capability properties that can be queried, special error codes, three TPM commands, and some special handling for TPM2_Startup and TPM2_Shutdown. These capabilities are used by the caller or, preferably, a dedicated RM to virtualize and manage transient entities.

TPM Internal Slots

TPM internal memory for transient entities consists of slots. A maximum number of slots are available for loaded objects and sequences (MAX_LOADED_OBJECTS), and a similar maximum for loaded sessions (MAX_LOADED_SESSIONS). Both of these maximums can be queried using the TPM2_GetCapability command. The RM can query these maximums and use them to manage the loaded contexts. Or it can rely on error codes returned by the TPM. Because of a special case related to _TPM_Hash_Start, some RMs require a combination of these.

Special Error Codes

Special error codes are used to tell the RM that the TPM is out of memory, meaning no slots are available, and the RM must do something: TPM_RC_OBJECT_MEMORY (out of memory for objects and sequences), TPM_RC_SESSION_MEMORY (out of session memory), or TPM_RC_MEMORY (out of memory in general).

These error codes are returned by commands that need to use object, sequence, or session slots in the TPM. For example the TPM2_Load command tries to load an object, and if there is no memory, TPM_RC_OBJECT_MEMORY or TPM_RC_MEMORY may be returned. The commands that explicitly use object or sequence slots are TPM2_CreatePrimary, TPM2_Load, TPM2_LoadExternal, TPM2_HashSequenceStart, TPM2_HMAC_Start, and TPM2_ContextLoad (when the context being loaded is an object or sequence context).

Additionally, three commands implicitly use an object slot. TPM2_Import uses one slot for scratchpad memory; the slot is freed after the command completes. Likewise, any command that operates on a persistent handle uses one slot for scratchpad operations and frees the slot after completion. Both types of commands return one of the above error codes if no slots are available. In response, the RM must evict a transient entity and retries the command.

The third command that implicitly uses an object slot is kind of strange: _TPM_Hash_Start. This command is typically triggered by hardware events, and it doesn't return an error code if no slots are available. Instead, it kicks an object out and provides no indication of which object was evicted. This means the RM and/or calling applications had better make sure one of the following is true during any time period when this command could be triggered by hardware:[4]

- One slot is available. The RM can use the TPM2_GetCapability command and query the MAX_LOADED_OBJECTS property. Based on the response, the RM can offload an object to free a slot. [5]

- The contexts for all objects or sequences that currently occupy the TPM's slots are saved. Otherwise, an object will be evicted with no ability to be reloaded.

- The contexts for all objects or sequences that currently occupy the TPM's slots are unneeded. In this case, it doesn't matter if one is evicted with no chance of being reloaded.[6]

The commands that explicitly use session slots are TPM2_StartAuthSession, TPM2_ContextLoad (when the context being loaded is a session context), and all commands that use sessions (except for those that use sessions for password authorization).

TPM Context-Management Commands

The TPM commands that enable transient entity management are TPM2_ContextSave, TPM2_ContextLoad, and TPM2_FlushContext. These commands have different effects depending on the type of transient entity being operated on.

TPM2_ContextSave saves the context of a transient entity and returns the entity's context. The returned context is encrypted and integrity protected. This is done in a manner that only allows the context to be loaded on the exact same TPM that saved it; a saved context can't be loaded into a different TPM. It is important to note that saving the context saves it into system memory, which may be volatile. Some other mechanism is required if the saved context needs to preserved across events that might erase memory contents, such as hibernation or sleep. For the PC, in the case of hibernation, the system saves all memory contents to some form of nonvolatile storage, such as a disk drive; for a sleep event, the memory remains powered on, which preserves the memory contents.

---

[4]This argues in favor of the simplest proactive approach to RM design, described earlier in this chapter. In that case, for the most part, none of these mitigations is required. There is still a small vulnerability: the time window from the time the RM completes the command to the time it is done evicting objects and sessions. If the _TPM_Hash_Start is triggered in this time window, an object or sequence context will be lost.

[5]The best way to do this would be for the process that's going to trigger the _TPM_Hash_Start command to send a request to the RM to free up an object slot.

[6]Since the RM really has no way to do this, the OS would have to have some way of ensuring this.

After the context is saved, if the entity is an object or a sequence, the entity still resides in the TPM and has the same handle. The saved context is a new copy of the object or sequence context.

A session, however, is handled differently. When a session's context is saved by the TPM2_ContextSave command, it is evicted from TPM memory. A session's context handling is unique: the context can either be evicted and in system memory, or it can be loaded on the TPM, but not both. Regardless of where the session's context resides, it always has the same handle and it's always "active" until its context is flushed by the TPM2_FlushContext command or a command is sent using the session with the continueSession flag cleared.

The reason for this special handling of sessions' handles is to prevent multiple copies of sessions and, hence, session replay attacks. A small piece of session context is retained inside the TPM after the context is saved.

For objects, sequences, and sessions, TPM2_FlushContext removes all of the transient entity's context from the TPM. In the case of an object or a sequence, the object—which still resides in the TPM after the TPM2_ContextSave command—is completely removed, but the saved context can still be reloaded. In the case of a session, the remaining session context is removed, which means the session is no longer active, the session context cannot be reloaded, and the session handle is freed for use by another session.

TPM2_ContextLoad is used to reload a saved context into the TPM.[7]

For an object or sequence, the context is loaded and a new handle is created for the object. An object or sequence context can be reloaded multiple times, returning a new handle each time. This means multiple copies of an object or sequence can reside in the TPM at any given time.[8]

For a session, the TPM2_ContextLoad command reloads the session and returns the same session handle. Also, a session's context can only be reloaded once after its context was saved in order to prevent session replay attacks.

Special Rules Related to Power and Shutdown Events

TPM Restart, TPM Reset, and TPM Resume are described in detail in Chapter 19. There are some special context-handling rules related to these events. This section describes the high-level "why" of these rules and then the details of the rules themselves.

A TPM Reset is like a cold power reboot, so session, object, and sequence contexts saved before a TPM Reset can't be reloaded afterward. Because TPM2_Shutdown(TPM_SU_CLEAR) was performed or no TPM2_Shutdown at all was executed, none of the information required to reload saved contexts was saved.

---

[7]It should be noted that although the names are similar, the TPM2_Load and TPM2_ContextLoad commands are quite different. TPM2_Load performs the initial load of an object after creation by TPM2_Create. This load command can't be used for sessions, nor can it be used to load an object's or sequence's saved context. TPM2_ContextLoad loads a transient entity after its context has been saved by the TPM2_ContextSave command. The similar names and overlap in functionality (in the case of objects) has tripped up many an unwary developer, including me at times.

[8]Having multiple copies of an object or a sequence loaded in the TPM serves no useful purpose and uses up more of the limited slots available in the TPM. The quote by David Wooten at the beginning of this chapter resulted from a discussion about this. Even though it serves no useful purpose, it doesn't pose a security risk, so the TPM allows it in the interest of internal TPM firmware simplicity.

A TPM Restart is used to boot after the system hibernated, and a TPM Resume is used to turn on your computer after a sleep state has been entered. For both of these cases, because TPM2_Shutdown(TPM_SU_STATE) was executed, saved session, object, and sequence contexts can be reloaded; the one exception is that objects with the stClear bit set cannot be reloaded after a TPM Restart.

The detailed rules are as follows:

- Any type of TPM reset removes transient entities from the TPM. If the transient entity's context wasn't saved, there is no way to reload the entity.

- As for the case of the context being previously saved, if:

  - *TPM Resume occurs:* Saved contexts can be context loaded.

  - *TPM Restart occurs and the object has the* stClear *bit cleared:* The object's saved context can be context loaded.

  - *TPM Reset or a TPM Restart occurs with the object's* stClear *bit set:* The saved object's context can't be context loaded.

- For a session, if the session's context was saved:

  - The context can be context loaded after a TPM Resume or TPM Restart.

  - The context can't be context loaded after a TPM Reset.

State Diagrams

Because of all these complicated rules, some diagrams may help to illustrate both the normal handling and the special rules related to TPM Reset, TPM Restart, and TPM Resume (see Figure 18-1).

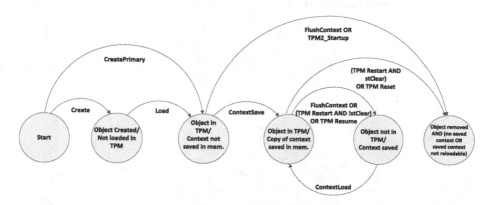

Figure 18-1. *TPM state diagram for objects and sequences*

Some notes about this diagram:

- Even though the word *objects* is used, this refers to both objects and sequences.

- The Load and ContextLoad arcs can be performed multiple times. Each instance results in a new copy of the object in the TPM with a new handle. Other than the handle, this object is identical to the other copies. Having multiple copies loaded in the TPM serves no useful purpose, as noted earlier.[8]

- The ContextSave arc can occur multiple times. Each instance results in a new copy of the object's context.

- For sequences, the diagram is the same except for the following: a sequence's context must be saved after each SequenceUpdate. Otherwise a ContextSave followed by a ContextLoad would result in a bad hash or HMAC computation.

The state diagram for sessions is relatively simple compared to objects and sequences (see Figure 18-2). The important differences to note are as follows:

- Objects and sequences can exist both on and off the TPM simultaneously, whereas sessions can't.

- Objects can be flushed and then reloaded. Sessions, when flushed, are terminated, and their saved contexts can't be reloaded.

- Unlike objects and sequences, active sessions always keep the same handle.

- Sessions can be "active" whether loaded in the TPM or not. They only become inactive when they are terminated (Session Ended state).

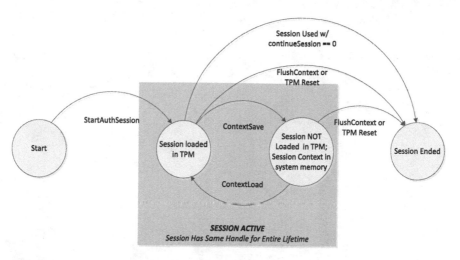

Figure 18-2. *TPM state diagram for sessions*

Summary

This concludes the discussion of context management. The TPM provides all the functionality needed to implement a resource manager. Although there are probably many ways to design a resource manager, at a high level, the simplest proactive approach is recommended.

CHAPTER 19

■ ■ ■

Startup, Shutdown, and Provisioning

Startup here is defined as software operations that occur each time a platform boots. The boot can be a cold boot, or it can be what in PC terms is called a *resume from suspend* or a *boot from hibernate*. The TPM holds several classes of volatile state, including PCR values, loaded sessions and keys, enables, authorization and policy values, hybrid NV indexes, and clock state. Based on the type of power cycle, this volatile state must either persist or be initialized. The TPM provides two commands that, in various combinations, permit external software to manage the power-cycle requirements.

Provisioning, on the other hand, is a rare occurrence. It might happen only once over the lifetime of the platform. A TPM vendor, platform manufacturer, IT department, or end user generates keys and other secrets, inserts certificates, and enables or disables certain TPM features. The other side of provisioning is deprovisioning: what the parties do before they repurpose, surplus, or discard a platform to ensure that secrets are erased.

This chapter discusses startup first, followed by the TPM provisioning tasks that various parties may perform. Those parties may include the TPM manufacturer, the platform manufacturer (also called the OEM), and the end user (either an individual or an IT department).

Startup and Shutdown

Startup (and shutdown as well) is handled by low-level software. On a PC platform, this is the BIOS and operating system. The intent is that state is reset or restored as required so that resuming applications are unaware of these events. For example, an application doesn't expect loaded keys or sessions to suddenly disappear. It may not be able to reload keys, and it may not want to rerun a policy evaluation because a session vanished. The TPM, with support from the operating system and boot code, makes power cycling transparent to applications by saving volatile state to its nonvolatile memory on power down and restoring state on power up.

The TPM specification defines three startup events: *TPM Reset*, *TPM Resume*, and *TPM Restart*. They follow a signal called *TPM Init* during a platform reset. In a typical hardware TPM, Italicize is assertion of the TPM reset pin, possibly preceded by a power cycle. At this time, it's assumed the TPM's volatile state is lost, and only the saved (if any) nonvolatile state remains.

TPM Reset normally occurs when the platform is booting after a power on or rebooting without a power cycle. The TPM receives a startup command to reset the TPM volatile state. *Reset* in this case can mean either setting state to a specified initial value or generating new random values for nonces. *TPM Reset* establishes a new trusted platform state. All required software components are measured into the set of reset PCRs. All the TPM's resources are reset to their default provisioned state.

TPM Resume typically occurs when the platform resumes from suspend, sometimes also called a *sleep state* or *low-power state*. Because the platform is continuing rather than rebooting, all state, including PCR values, is restored. *TPM Resume* restores the TPM's state to that before the power loss or reset, because the platform trust state has not changed since the reset or power off.

TPM Restart typically occurs when the platform comes out of hibernation. Before the power cycle, the TPM receives a command to save state, and most of the state is restored at startup. The exception is PCR values, which are initialized, not restored. This permits a booting platform to extend new measurements to the TPM, while the TPM state used by the operating system and applications are restored. *TPM Restart* is a special case where the platform reestablishes its trusted state (by creating new measurements), but the user's state (operating system and applications) is restored.

The TPM provides two commands to support these startup events: TPM2_Shutdown and TPM2_Startup. Shutdown is typically performed by the operating system just before transitioning to a platform reset or power down. TPM2_Shutdown has two options: CLEAR and STATE. Startup is executed by the root of trust for measurement (RTM) in the initialization firmware (for example, BIOS on the PC). TPM2_Startup also has two options: CLEAR and STATE.

Here are the commands in combination:

- TPM Reset (reboot) is TPM2_Shutdown with the CLEAR option (or no shutdown command) followed by TPM2_Startup with the CLEAR option.

- TPM Restart (hibernate) is TPM2_Shutdown with the STATE option followed by TPM2_Startup with the CLEAR option.

- TPM Resume (suspend, sleep) is TPM2_Shutdown with the STATE option followed by TPM2_Startup with the STATE option.

The following is a brief overview of the command behaviors. There are many details surrounding the clock and time counters, session context, hybrid NV indexes, and more. These are discussed in other parts of the book as the concepts are introduced:

- TPM2_Shutdown with the CLEAR option is an orderly shutdown before the platform powers down or reboots. The TPM saves certain volatile values to nonvolatile memory: the clock and NV indexes with the orderly attribute that are normally shadowed in volatile memory.

- TPM2_Shutdown with the STATE option is a shutdown typically due to hibernation or suspend. The TPM stores the previously listed items plus tracking for session contexts, PCRs that the platform specification mandates should be saved, certain NV index flags, and state associated with audit.

- TPM2_Startup with the CLEAR option initializes TPM volatile state, including PCR and NV volatile state; enables the three hierarchies; and clears the platform authorization and policy.

- TPM2_Startup with the STATE option is only permitted after TPM2_Shutdown with the STATE option. PCRs are restored or initialized based on the platform specific specification.[1]

For example, the detailed behavior and rationale for PCRs though the three power-cycle types are as follows:[2]

- On a reboot, *TPM Reset*, all PCRs must be initialized. The TPM2_Startup with the CLEAR option always initializes PCRs, regardless of the type of shutdown.

- On a resume from hibernation, *TPM Restart*, the platform is rerunning BIOS code and doing its measurements, so the PCRs must be initialized. TPM2_Startup with the CLEAR option again initializes PCRs, even though they were saved during the power-down sequence.

- On a resume from suspend, *TPM Resume*, the PCR values may be lost on power down. However, the platform resumes without rerunning BIOS, boot, or OS initialization code. PCR values must therefore be restored. TPM2_Shutdown with the STATE option saves volatile PCRs as the platform suspends. TPM2_Startup with the STATE option restores those values.[3]

Startup Initialization

The TPM has several parameters that must be initialized at each startup. In TPM 1.2, there was one hierarchy with one owner authorization, and that authorization was persistent. It had one disabled and one deactivated flag. As described in Chapter 9, TPM 2.0 has three hierarchies, each with an authorization secret, a policy, and an enable flag.

TPM 2.0 has a platform hierarchy with a volatile authorization value and policy, which are reset on *TPM Reset* or *TPM Restart*. Software early in the boot cycle is expected to set these values. It also has a hierarchy enable flag, enabled at startup. We expect that platform OEMs will not provide a means for the operating system or applications to disable the platform hierarchy, because OEMs may use the platform hierarchy for runtime functions.

---

[1]The PC Client specification mandates restoring PCRs 0-15 and initializing PCRs 16-23.
[2]Chapter 18 discusses the management of objects and sessions in detail.
[3]The platform-specific specification indicates which PCR indexes must be restored and which must be initialized.

Platform policy is straightforward. If it isn't set, it's *empty*: a policy that can never be satisfied. If the platform OEM has a policy for platform-hierarchy control, its boot software sets the policy value using TPM2_SetPrimaryPolicy. The policy contains no secrets, but its value must be protected from tampering while in the boot software. If the OEM has no such policy, it leaves the platform policy empty, so the policy can't be satisfied.

Platform authorization (HMAC shared secret–style authorization) works differently. The TPM architecture expects the platform to set the platform authorization value to a strong secret using TPM2_HierarchyChangeAuth and make this value inaccessible to the operating system or applications. Alternatively, if the OEM has no need for the platform authorization, it can set it to a random value and then "forget" the value by erasing it from system memory. The platform hierarchy is still enabled, but it can't be authorized using a password or HMAC.

The specification designers first considered a persistent value, similar to the TPM 1.2 owner authorization. This raised two questions: how would the platform software remember the shared secret through boot cycles, and how would the platform ensure that a strong secret is used? The solution was to use a volatile value: a large, random number set at startup. The random number can even be obtained from the TPM random number generator. Now the platform software doesn't have to remember the value through power cycles. It's stored in platform volatile memory that's accessible only to the platform software.

We expect that the platform authorization value may not be set immediately. Because the platform software trusts itself, it may leave the value empty, a very easy value to remember, and set it later, before exiting to option ROMs or other untrusted software, to protect the platform hierarchy from other software.

Other hierarchies are persistent and need not be initialized at startup. These include the (storage hierarchy) owner authorization and policy, endorsement authorization and policy, and the lockout authorization and policy.

The storage and endorsement hierarchy enables are set at *TPM Reset* and *TPM Restart*. The platform is expected to remember the owner's and privacy administrator's requested state and disable them if required.

Provisioning

Here, *provisioning* includes all TPM setup that occurs less frequently than once per boot cycle. In a typical TPM lifetime, these actions may be performed only once.

This book divides the provisioning operations among three parties: the TPM manufacturer, the platform manufacturer (often referred to as the OEM), and the end user. Although this is a typical partition, the TPM doesn't enforce it, and enterprises may deviate from this pattern based on their trust model. For example, a platform in a large enterprise may further partition end-user provisioning between an actual user and an IT department administrator. A high security use case may replace a TPM vendor-supplied endorsement primary key or certificate with its own.

In TPM 1.2, certain provisioning steps could only be performed once. For example, although it had the concept of a *revocable* endorsement key that could be deleted and regenerated with a different value, this was optional and not implemented in commercial hardware TPMs.

In the TPM 2.0 architecture, there are no once-per-lifetime values. However, a platform specification may, for example, make TPM2_ChangeEPS optional, and a vendor may not implement it. In that case, an endorsement key created with a known template (see Chapter 15 for details) could not be permanently destroyed, although it could be flushed from the TPM. TPM 2.0 can also provision additional endorsement keys.

TPM Manufacturer Provisioning

The TPM manufacturer is uniquely qualified to certify that its hardware is authentic. Once the TPM part enters the supply chain, most purchasers don't have the expertise to distinguish a counterfeit from a genuine part.

The TPM generates[4] a primary seed in the endorsement hierarchy when it's first powered on. The TPM manufacturer then uses TPM2_CreatePrimary one or more times to create endorsement primary keys—the ones at the root of the endorsement hierarchy.[5] This command returns the public key, which the manufacturer uses to create a certificate.

The certificate, typically in X.509 format, asserts that the public key belongs to a genuine vendor TPM. It typically includes manufacturer identification. There is no security-related reason for the vendor to store either the primary key or its certificate on the TPM. Practical concerns drive the decision.

The primary key is generated from the primary seed and a caller-supplied template. The template contains the key algorithm and size, and possibly other entropy. If the seed isn't changed, the same template will always generate the same key. Thus, the vendor need not ship the TPM with the key stored in persistent memory. The user can re-create it at any time. This avoids consuming valuable NV memory in cases where the TPM vendor generates many primary keys for different templates, or when the key is likely to be used infrequently.

Why does the TPM use seeds? TPM 1.2 generated the endorsement key directly, but there was one algorithm (RSA) and one key size (2,048 bits). TPM 2.0 can have many algorithms and key sizes. If the TPM 1.2 pattern was used, each key would have to be stored on the TPM, consuming valuable NV memory. The TPM 2.0 design requires only a single persistent seed. The derived keys can be generated (and then discarded) as needed.

The advantage of shipping the TPM with a primary endorsement key is performance. Why have the user create the primary key when the vendor has already created it?

In practice, the TCG platform working groups are expected to specify one or more standard templates based on anticipated application needs. The TPM vendor will generate multiple keys but only provision one for a commonly used algorithm and size on the part before shipment.

---

[4]The manufacturer is permitted to create the endorsement primary seed externally and "squirt" it into the TPM in a vendor-specific process. This potentially saves manufacturing time, because the primary keys can also be calculated external to the TPM.

[5]Chapter 10 explains the general process of creating primary keys, and Chapter 15 goes into even more detail.

A similar practical concern determines whether the TPM ships with certificates. Although it's true that a user can usually ask the TPM manufacturer for a certificate corresponding to their public key, it's certainly more convenient to read it from TPM NV storage. There may be use cases where the platform isn't connected to a public network, making certificate retrieval even more inconvenient. In practice, we expect the TPM vendor to provision a certificate corresponding to the one or more primary keys. The certificate likely resides in the TPM's NV storage.

There can be use cases where the user doesn't completely trust the TPM vendor processes. Other use cases require an end user such as a government agency to prevent any link in the supply chain from tracking which machines are used by that agency. They want to remove any unique key that may aid in that tracking. This user can use TPM2_ChangeEPS to change the endorsement primary seed;[6] generate new, different primary keys;[7] and sign their own certificates. The user can also change the template to include a random number, which is unknown to the vendor, thus generating an endorsement primary key unknown to the vendor without invalidating existing primary key certificates.

In summary, the four differences from TPM 1.2 that contribute to these scenarios are as follows:

- Primary endorsement keys can be re-created at any time as long as the primary seed doesn't change and the template is known.

- Because primary endorsement keys can be re-created, they need not be stored long term in the TPM.

- Because TPM 2.0 supports multiple algorithms and added template entropy, there can be more than one primary endorsement key.

- If rolling the EPS is supported, endorsement keys can be deleted, and thus the certificates invalidated.

Platform OEM Provisioning

Platform OEM provisioning has two concerns:

- Authenticity

- Control

As with the TPM manufacturer, a platform manufacturer certificate[8] (typically in X.509 format) asserts that the hardware is authentic. It asserts that the TPM is attached to the OEM's platform. It further asserts that the platform software meets certain TCG recommended standards. For a PC client, this includes a CRTM that performs measurements of software and extends those measurements to PCRs.

---

[6]Rolling the EPS also deletes any primary or descendent keys in the hierarchy.
[7]Keys generated using the new EPS are cryptographically unrelated to those generated using the old EPS.
[8]We know of no OEM that currently is provisioning platform certificates.

Although an attacker could physically remove a TPM from the OEM platform and put it in a counterfeit, the TCG technology doesn't defend against physical attacks. Further, this would compromise only one platform per attack. On the other hand, a successful attack that extracts a primary seed from a TPM would permit the attacker to manufacture an unlimited number of counterfeits.

Platform certification typically begins with an endorsement primary key generated by the TPM at the TPM manufacturer. The OEM wants to verify that the TPM is authentic before asserting that its platform is authentic. It reads the TPM certificate and validates it; it may go further, reading the public key and verifying that it matches, or even use the private key to prove that the key pair is present.

As with the TPM vendor endorsement key certificate, there is no security-related reason to store the platform certificates on the TPM before shipping the platform. Practical considerations will likely drive the OEM to include a certificate in the TPM's persistent memory, corresponding to the vendor TPM certificate.

TPM 2.0 specifies a platform hierarchy. The platform OEM may optionally provision that hierarchy with a platform policy. As explained earlier, the TPM initializes this policy to empty: a policy that can never be satisfied. The OEM must provision it at startup using TPM2_SetPrimaryPolicy.

Where does the platform policy value (a hash) come from? We expect that the value will be embedded in early platform boot software, protected by the same OEM mechanism that protects the CRTM. So, this value is provisioned during platform manufacturing not into the TPM, but into the platform CRTM. It's inserted into the TPM at startup.

End User Provisioning

The term *end user* is used loosely here. For a home computer, the end user is typically the literal user of the computer. For an enterprise, centrally managed platform, the end user may be the actual user or support personnel.

The end user must provision the endorsement and storage hierarchies. This is a case where an IT organization may decide to provision the endorsement hierarchy and/or the dictionary-attack reset authorizations, and leave the provisioning of the storage hierarchy to the person who is actually using the platform.

The first consideration is whether to disable the hierarchies (always enabled at startup) using TPM2_HierarchyControl. The method of disabling a hierarchy is platform specific. We expect something equivalent to a BIOS screen, with a means of disabling a hierarchy for the remainder of a boot cycle or having it persist through boot cycles. (We hope to present enough valuable use cases that you will never dream of disabling the TPM.)

Next, the end user must provision the endorsement and storage hierarchy, and the dictionary-attack protection policies and authorization values. Owner authorization is initially empty (no authorization required), as is owner policy (no policy is present). TPM2_HierarchyChangeAuth and TPM2_SetPrimaryPolicy change these values, which persist until cleared. The endorsement authorization and policy are set and changed using the same commands. The owner authorization and endorsement authorization should be set to high-entropy values, because they aren't guarded by the dictionary-attack protection.

The dictionary-attack logic has both a policy and an authorization value. The same party may provision all policies and authorization values, but they may choose different logic and values. It's particularly important to provision the dictionary-attack reset policy. If triggered, the dictionary-attack password can be used only once before a large wait is enforced. However, the policy can be used to reset the dictionary-attack counter even when the dictionary-attack password has been locked out.

The endorsement primary seed is generated during TPM vendor manufacturing. The end user doesn't typically change this value.

The storage primary seed is similarly generated during TPM vendor manufacturing. The end user can either use this value or generate a new one. Generating a new one invalidates all objects in the storage and endorsement hierarchies except the endorsement hierarchy primary keys. Thus, the endorsement primary key certificate is still useful.

Deprovisioning

Deprovisioning is primarily the process of removing secrets from the TPM, although a user may wish to remove public but unique data as well. A user typically deprovisions before surplusing a platform in an enterprise, selling used equipment, or scrapping the system.

What secrets aren't touched? Those in the platform hierarchy (if any) are controlled by the platform manufacturer. The endorsement hierarchy primary seed is typically fixed for the lifetime of the TPM. Changing this seed would invalidate endorsement primary keys and thus make their certificates useless.

A platform OEM may be tempted to use NV space to store end-user settings. For example, consider the BIOS configuration. Such an index could have a policy permitting the end user to write a value and anyone (specifically, the BIOS) to read it. Such use is discouraged if any value is even remotely secret or privacy sensitive, because end-user deprovisioning is easy to overlook.

Deprovisioning uses the TPM2_Clear command. Note that the authorization for this command is not, as you may expect, TPM_RH_OWNER, the role that controls the storage hierarchy. Rather, it's either TPM_RH_LOCKOUT (the dictionary-attack reset authorization) or TPM_RH_PLATFORM (platform authorization).

Lockout authorization is a reasonable choice. It's likely that the user knows this authorization. The TPM probably uses this value rather than owner authorization because, in some situations, the owner authorization may be more widely known. Because deprovisioning has wide-ranging effects, it's better to assign it to a more restrictive role.

Platform authorization is trickier, because it's available only early in the boot cycle, not at the OS level. This poses two problems. First, none but the most tech-savvy users can be expected to do *any* operation at the BIOS-screen level. Second, BIOS screens preclude remote deprovisioning, which is a requirement for cloud-type data centers. The solution to this dilemma is a platform policy, the alternative to a simple platform HMAC or password-based authorization. For example, suppose the platform owner wishes to allow a user to run the TPM2_Clear command with owner authorization. A platform policy includes an OR term that says, "command code = TPM2_Clear AND Policy Secret's handle == TPM_RH_OWNER". This policy permits owner authorization to be used, and the user can apply this authorization at the OS level.

What does TPM2_Clear do? Quite a lot. First, shProof and ehProof are changed. These proofs serve as HMAC keys for saved (nonresident) contexts. Once the proof changes, contexts in the storage and endorsement hierarchies can no longer be loaded. Next, any TPM-resident objects in either the storage or platform hierarchy are flushed. The storage primary seed is changed; this prevents primary storage keys from being regenerated, and thus, any object created under these keys can no longer be loaded. Finally, any NV index created by the owner is deleted. This is an improvement over TPM 1.2, where some indexes have to be individually deleted.

TPM2_Clear also prepares the TPM for the next owner. It resets authorization values. The lockout authorization is cleared (to a zero-length password), and the policy is cleared (to no policy in effect). The owner and endorsement authorization and policy are similarly reset. The storage and endorsement hierarchies are enabled; this is a departure from TPM 1.2, which required a reboot after an owner clear before a new owner could be installed.

The dictionary-attack mechanism count of failed authorization tries is reset. The clock is reset so that the new owner can accurately set it as desired. (The clock can't normally go back in time.) Reset count and restart count, which track boot cycles, are reset.

Summary

There are three startup cases, roughly corresponding to a PC cold boot, resume from suspend, and power up after hibernate. The TPM provides startup commands to reset or restore its state as appropriate for these cases.

So that startup authorization secrets need not be saved in the clear off the TPM or be accessible during boot, the TPM resets certain values and expects them to be provisioned during startup. Before it reaches the end user, the TPM may be provisioned with keys and certificates. These include TPM manufacturer-provisioned endorsement primary keys and corresponding certificates, and perhaps another set created by the platform manufacturer. The end-user provisioning steps include initialization of the storage hierarchy and installing endorsement and storage hierarchy authorization keys or policies.

Finally, deprovisioning through TPM2_Clear removes secrets and NV-defined indexes, resets authorizations and policies, and resets other values in preparation for the new owner.

CHAPTER 20

■ ■ ■

Debugging

> *"I still remember my early days of Z80 assembly language programming: a couple of times, just to get a reaction, I bragged that I could write bug free code the first time. Just write, assemble, link and voila, a perfectly working program! I was scoffed at and justifiably so—truthfully, in over 30 years of experience, I've never achieved that and probably never will."*

Will Arthur, reflecting while writing this chapter

It is possible that somebody somewhere has written a significant program that ran without bugs the first time, but if so, it's in the noise, statistically speaking. Because the process of programming seems to also be the process of inserting bugs, the need for debugging is an inexorable law of the programming world.

This chapter aims to educate you about some specific tools and methods for debugging TPM 2.0 programs as well as debugging common bug areas. We will discuss two major areas of debugging: lower-level applications that communicate with the TPM and higher-level applications that use the Feature API to communicate with the TPM. Lower-level applications include applications that use the ESAPI and SAPI, as well as implementations of specialized TSS layers such as the SAPI library, TPM Access Broker (TAB) and Resource Manager (RM). Most of the text for the lower-level applications flows directly from the experience of that section's author in developing the System API, TAB, RM, and TPM 2.0 device driver, all very low-level pieces of software. Because of the current lack of implementations for the Feature API and Enhanced System API layers of the TSS stack, no TSS 2.0–specific tribal knowledge is available for debugging those areas. For this reason, the chapter relies on debugging experiences from TSS 1.2, because we expect that many of the issues are similar.

Low-Level Application Debugging

Because low-level applications are the only ones we have actual experience debugging for TPM 2.0, we discuss them first.

The Problem

When a TPM command has an error, an error code is returned. The TPM 2.0 specification writers worked very hard to design error codes that facilitate debugging. Many times, the error code tells you exactly what's wrong, but due to lack of familiarity with the specification, you're left scratching your head. And in a few cases, the error code only indicates an area to look for the error, without the granularity needed to identify the exact cause. Either way, whether due to knowledge or specification deficiencies, you, the poor programmer, are left wondering what to do.

This section describes a few different error conditions and illustrates a hierarchy of techniques used to debug these types of problems, from simplest to more complex:

- *Error code analysis:* Many simple errors can be completely debugged this way.

- *Debug trace analysis:* This requires instrumenting the low-level driver to spit out the command byte stream being sent to the TPM and the response byte stream received from the TPM. Quite often, comparing known good debug trace data to bad data quickly highlights the problem.

- *More complicated errors:* These take more work to debug. An HMAC authorization error is quickly spotted by the error code, but debugging it requires detailed examination of all the steps that were used to generate the HMAC.

- *The hardest errors to debug:* These require stepping through the TPM 2.0 simulator with a debugger in order to understand what the TPM is unhappy about. Often, after debugging through the simulator code, the answer becomes obvious. A better understanding of the specification would have uncovered the problem. Human nature being what it is, we often get distracted by the forest and fail to see the particular tree that needs to be eradicated. Hence, this technique is often needed. The author of this section has debugged many errors this way both for himself and for others within Intel developing TPM 2.0 code.

Analyze the Error Code

The first step when you get an error is decoding the error code. This decoding is described in the "Response Code Details" section of Part 1 of the TPM 2.0 specification. The "Response Code Evaluation" flowchart in that section is particularly helpful.

The first example error involves the TPM2_Startup command. The following code snippet generates an error (this is a slight modification of the TPM2_Startup test described in Chapter 7:

```
rval = Tss2_Sys_Startup( sysContext, 03 )¹;
CheckPassed(rval);
```

The call to CheckPassed fails because an error code of 0x000001c4 was returned instead of 0 (TPM2_RC_SUCCESS). Following the flowchart mentioned previously, you can decode this error as follows:

```
Bit 8: 1
Bit 7: 1
Bit 6: 1
```

These bits indicate that the error code is in bits 5:0 and the parameter number is in bits 11:8.² So, parameter #1 is bad, and the specific error is TPM_RC_VALUE from the "TPM_RC Values" section of Part 1 of the TPM 2.0 specification. The text description for this error is, "value is out of range or isn't correct for the context." This means parameter #1 was bad for this command. In looking at the description of the TPM2_Startup command, it's easy to see that the only values allowed for this parameter are TPM_SU_CLEAR(0x0000) and TPM_SU_STATE (0x0001). Obviously, using 0x3 for the parameter is the source of our error.

We strongly encourage the use of a tool for decoding errors, because hand-decoding errors can become burdensome for repeated debug sessions. Sample output of such a tool looks like this³:

```
>tpm2decoderring /e 1c4

ERROR:  PARAM #1, TPM_RC_VALUE: value is out of range or is not correct for
the context
```

Debug Trace Analysis

Quite often, due to lack of TPM knowledge or, in some cases, obscurity of the error, error-code analysis is insufficient. Additionally, if a program was previously working, a comparison to the output from the previously working program can highlight the error much more quickly. For this reason, we highly recommend instrumenting

---

¹Experienced programmers will immediately notice the use of a "magic" number in this line of code. There is no constant defined in the TPM specification for a bad parameter to the startup command. Although not generally a good programming practice, in this case hardcoding the number seems better than defining a special value for use here.

²In some cases, the error code may indicate a parameter, session, or handle number of 0. This indicates an error with a parameter, session, or handle, but the TPM isn't giving any indication of which one.

³This is the output from an Intel internal tool. This tool hasn't been released publicly, but development of such a tool for public use is strongly encouraged.

the TPM device driver with code that displays the command bytes sent to the TPM and the response bytes received from the TPM. This feature has saved many weeks of debugging time over the past two years of TPM 2.0 development work.

In the case of the previous program, the trace dump from the command from a good program looks like this:

```
Cmd sent: TPM2_Startup
Locality = 3
80 01 00 00 00 0c 00 00 01 44 00 00

Response Received:
80 01 00 00 00 0a 00 00 00 00
    passing case:        PASSED!
```

The trace dump from the bad program, with the differences highlighted, looks like this:

```
cmd sent: TPM2_Startup
Locality = 3
80 01 00 00 00 0c 00 00 01 44 00 03

Response Received:
80 01 00 00 00 0a 00 00 01 c4
    passing case:        FAILED!  TPM Error -- TPM Error: 0x1c4
```

Use of a good compare utility quickly highlights the bad value, 00 03, in the bad command.

One caveat in this method is that much of the TPM output is randomized, and often these randomized outputs are fed back as inputs to other commands. This means these randomized parts of your trace data need to be ignored when you visually compare output. Experience will help you quickly learn which areas to ignore and which differences to focus on. It's not nearly as hard as it sounds.

Another good way to use trace dumps is when comparing multiple traces coming from different layers in the stack. For instance, you might have a trace dump from the ESAPI layer, one from the driver layer, and maybe even one from the TPM simulator. It can be challenging to synchronize these trace dumps. Session nonces, because they are random, unique, and the same no matter where in the stack they appear, can be used to synchronize these trace dumps. Find a nonce being returned in a session in one trace dump, and then search for where that same nonce is returned in the other trace dumps.

More Complex Errors

An example of a more complex error is an HMAC authorization error. This error is indicated by the error code, TPM_RC_AUTH_FAIL. The description of this error is, "the authorization HMAC check failed and DA counter incremented," and high-order bits in the error code tell which session is seeing the HMAC error.

Unfortunately, it isn't nearly so easy to debug this error. Many steps go into calculating the HMAC: key generation, hashing of input and/or output parameters, and the HMAC calculation. There are also many input parameters that feed into these steps: nonces, keys, and the type of authorization session. Any error in the data or steps used to generate the HMAC will result in a bad HMAC.

The only effective way we've found to debug these errors is to enhance the debug trace capabilities to display all the inputs and outputs for the key generation, hashing, and HMAC calculation steps. A very careful analysis of these inputs while carefully comparing to the TPM specification usually pinpoints the failure. This type of debugging requires very detailed knowledge of the TPM 2.0 specification—in particular, all the nuances of how HMACs are calculated.

Last Resort

The last category of errors consists of those that resist all other attempts at debugging. Typically these occur when implementing new TPM commands or features. There's no debug trace data from a previously working program to compare to, and error-code analysis doesn't pinpoint the problem. Fortunately, the situation isn't at all desperate; with the simulator, these errors can be easily debugged.

A common error in this category is a *scheme error*, TPM_RC_SCHEME. This error indicates something wrong with the scheme for a key, either when creating it or when using it. Schemes are typically unions of structures, each of which contains multiple fields. Much of the understanding of how to set up schemes is non-intuitive, especially to newcomers to TPM 2.0.

Often, the best way to debug these errors or any other errors that have resisted easier debugging techniques is to run the code against the TPM 2.0 simulator and single-step through the simulator. This provides an inside view of what the TPM is expecting to receive and why it's returning an error. Of course, this assumes that you have access to the source code of the simulator.[4] With the TPM source code, you can step into the TPM 2.0 simulator and figure out exactly why the TPM is complaining.

---

[4]Currently all TCG members have access to this source code.

The steps to debug this way are as follows:

1. Build and start the TPM 2.0 simulator on a Windows system[5] in Visual Studio. Review the instructions in Chapter 6 that describe how to do this. Select the "Debug" pull-down tab, and select "Start Debugging" to start the simulator running in debug mode.

2. Port your failing program to run against the simulator. The easiest way to do this is to create a subroutine using the System API functions and then add that subroutine to the list of test routines called by the System API test code. This way, because the System API test code, by default, communicates with the simulator, you don't have to develop a TPM 2.0 driver to talk to the simulator or deal with the simulator-specific platform commands to turn on the simulator, set the locality, and so on. You also get a TAB and resource manager for free. If you don't go this route, you must do all this work yourself.

3. Start your failing program in the debugger of your choice,[6] step to the place where it sends the failing command, and stop. Use a combination of single-stepping and breakpoints to get to this place.

4. Pause the simulator in its instance of Visual Studio by selecting the "Debug" pull-down and selecting "Break All".

5. Set a breakpoint in the simulator at an entry point that you know you'll hit. If you're new to the simulator, set a breakpoint at the _rpc__Send_Command function in the TPMCmdp.c source file.

6. Start the simulator running again, by selecting the Debug pull-down and selecting Continue.

7. In the test program's debugger, select the proper command to cause the test program to continue running from the breakpoint where it was stopped.

8. The simulator stops at the breakpoint you selected in the simulator code. From here you can debug into various subroutines and eventually figure out why the TPM is generating the error.

---

[5]Currently, only one TPM 2.0 simulator is available, and it only runs under Microsoft Visual Studio. If and when this changes, all steps related to debugging through the simulator will need to be altered accordingly.

[6]Because communication with the TPM 2.0 simulator is via sockets, the test program can be built and debugged on a remote system running any operating system. This means any debugger can be used to debug the test program. Chapter 6 describes how to run the test program on a remote system.

Common Bugs

Now that we've discussed debugging techniques for TPM 2.0 programs, we'll briefly describe some of the common bug areas. Again, keep in mind that these are all based on our experience with fairly low-level programming. These bugs are the types of issues that low-level TPM 2.0 programmers are likely to encounter. These bugs fall into the following categories: endianness, marshalling/unmarshalling errors, bad parameters (including the scheme errors mentioned earlier), and authorization errors.

When programming on a little-endian system such as an x86 system, endianness has to be properly altered during marshalling and marshalling of data. This is a very common source of errors, and it can typically be spotted by a careful analysis of the TPM trace data.

Marshalling and unmarshalling errors are closely related to endianness errors and in a similar manner can be easily debugged by looking at the trace data. This requires understanding the details of the TPM 2.0 specification, specifically Parts 2 and 3.

Bad parameters, including bad fields in schemes, are sometimes harder to spot. They require a very detailed understanding of all three parts of the TPM 2.0 specification in order to diagnose from the trace data. For this reason, debugging these often requires stepping into the simulator.

The last category of errors—authorization errors, whether HMAC or policy— requires a detailed analysis of the whole software stack that was used to generate the authorization. As mentioned earlier, this can be accelerated by enhanced trace messages that display the inputs and outputs to all the operations leading up to the command being authorized.

Debugging High-level Applications

Debugging applications, specifically those using the Feature API of the TSS, requires a different approach than debugging low-level software such as the TSS itself. This is because the expected errors are different. An application developer using a TSS shouldn't have to deal with bugs caused by parameter marshalling or unmarshalling, command and response packet parsing, and malformed byte stream errors. The reason is simple: the TSS libraries already perform those steps. Thus there should hopefully be no need to trace or decompose the command and response byte streams.

Our experience with TPM 1.2 applications—which we expect to carry forward to TPM 2.0—suggests that you should begin with the simulator. And we don't mean, "begin with the simulator after you hit a bug," but rather, start your developing using the simulator instead of a hardware TPM device. This approach offers several advantages:

- At least initially, hardware TPM 2.0 platforms may be scarce. The simulator is always available.

- A simulator should be faster than a hardware TPM, which is important when you start running regression tests. This becomes apparent when a test loop may generate a large number of RSA keys, or when NV space is rapidly written and a hardware TPM would throttle the writes to prevent wear-out.

- The simulator and TSS connect through a TCP/IP socket interface. This permits you to develop an application on one operating system (that might not yet have a TPM driver) while running the simulator on its supported platform.

- It's easy to restore a simulated TPM to its factory state by simply deleting its state file. A hardware TPM is harder to de-provision: you would have to write (and debug) a de-provisioning application.

- The normal TPM security protections (such as limited or no access to the platform hierarchy) don't get in the way.

- It's easy to "reboot" a simulated TPM without rebooting the platform. This eases tests for persistence issues and power management (suspend, hibernate) problems. It also speeds debugging.

- Finally, when it's time to debug, you already have the simulator environment set up.

Our experience with TPM 1.2 is that, once an application works with the simulator, it works unmodified with the hardware TPM.

Debug Process

Unlike the IBM TPM 1.2 simulator, the current Microsoft TPM 2.0 simulator, available to TCG members, has no tracing facility. You can't simply run the application and read the simulator's output. It's also unclear whether the TSS implementation will have a tracing capability. Trousers, the TPM 1.2 TSS, had little beyond command and response packet dumps.

However, the simulator source is available. The process is thus the same for nearly any application bug:

1. Run the application to failure, and determine which TPM command failed.

2. Run the simulator in a debugger, and set a breakpoint at the command. Each TPM 2.0 command has a C function call that has exactly the same name as the Part 3 command.

3. Step through the command until the error is detected.

4. It may be necessary to run again, stepping into the Part 4 subroutines, but our experience is that this is often unnecessary.

Typical Bugs

This section presents some TPM 1.2 application bugs in the hope that they may carry over to 2.0. We also list a few new anticipated error possibilities for TPM 2.0.

Authorization

TPM 2.0 plain text password authorization should be straightforward. However, HMAC authorization failures are common. The approach is the usual "divide and conquer." Trace the command (or response) parameter hash, the HMAC key, and the HMAC value. If the hash differs, the parameters that were used in the calculation were different from those sent to the TPM. If the HMAC keys differ, most likely the wrong password was used or the wrong entity was specified. If the HMAC value differs, either it was passed in differently or the salt or bind value was wrong.

Disabled Function

Perhaps the most common TPM 1.2 error we've seen is trying to use a disabled function. TPM 1.2 had disabled and deactivated flags, and TPM 2.0 has the corresponding hierarchy enabled.

TPM 2.0 has an additional HMAC error case: the entity may have been created in a way that disallows HMAC authorization. See the attributes userWithAuth and adminWithPolicy in Part 1 of the TPM 2.0 specification.

Missing Objects

A typical TPM 1.2 misunderstanding was that creating a key simply returned the key wrapped with the parent—that is, encrypted with the parent's key. It doesn't actually load the key into the TPM; a separate command is required to do that.

TPM 2.0 has an additional case. The TPM 1.2 SRK was inherently persistent. TPM 2.0 primary keys are transient and must be made persistent. Thus, primary keys may be missing after a reboot.

Finally, an object may have been loaded but is no longer there. You can break at the flush call (or add a printf to the flush call) and the failing command to determine when the object was flushed.

Similarly, a common error for TSS 1.2 was a *resource leak*—objects (or sessions) were loaded and not flushed, so the TPM eventually filled all its slots. Tracking the load and flush pairs should expose the missing flush, and this will also be true for TSS 2.0.

Wrong Type

In TPM 1.2, keys are basically signing keys or decryption/storage keys. Stepping through the function that performs the type check should uncover the error.

TPM 2.0 adds the concept of restricted keys, which introduce two new error cases. First a restricted key might may be used where only a nonrestricted key is permitted. Second, the user may try to change an algorithm, but restricted keys are created with an algorithm set that can't be changed at time of use.

There is also far more variability with respect to algorithms than TPM 1.2 has, where there were just a few padding schemes. Even PCRs have variable algorithms, which may lead to failures during an extend operation.

In addition, TPM 2.0 NV space has four types (ordinary, bit field, extend, and counter). This will undoubtedly lead to errors such as trying to write ordinary data into a bit-field index.

Bad Size

Asymmetric key operations are limited in the data size they can operate on. A common bug is trying to sign or decrypt (unseal) data that exceeds the capacity of the key and algorithm. For example, an RSA 2,048-bit key can operate on somewhat less than 256 bytes. The "somewhat" accounts for prepended data that includes padding and perhaps an object identifier (OID).

Policy

TPM 2.0 introduces policy authorization, which is very flexible but may prove hard to debug. Fortunately, the TPM itself has a debug aid, TPM2_PolicyGetDigest. Although you can't normally look inside the TPM or dump the contents of internal structures, this command is an exception and does exactly that.

Recall that an entity requiring authorization has a policy digest, which was precalculated and specified when the key was created. The value is computed by extending each policy statement. At policy-evaluation time, a policy session starts with a zero session digest. As policy commands are executed, the session digest is extended. If all goes well, the session digest eventually matches the policy digest, and the key is authorized for use.

However, in this chapter, the presupposition is that all isn't well. The digests don't match, and the authorization fails. We anticipate that the debug process will again consist of "divide and conquer." First determine which policy command failed, and then determine why.

Some policy commands, such as TPM2_PolicySecret, are straightforward, because they return an error immediately if authorization fails. Others—deferred authorizations like TPM2_PolicyCommandCode—are harder to debug because failure is only detected at time of use.

To determine which policy command failed, we suggest that you save the calculations used to calculate the policy hash. That is, the first hash value is all zeroes, there is an intermediate hash value for each policy statement, and there is a final value (the policy hash). Then, at policy-evaluation time, after each policy command, use TPM2_PolicyGetDigest to get the TPM's intermediate result. Compare the expected value (from the policy precalculation) to the actual value (from the TPM). The first miscompare isolates the bug to that policy statement.

One author's dream is that a premium TSS Feature API (FAPI) implementation will perform these steps. It has the policy, an XML document, so it can recalculate the intermediate hashes (or even cache them in the XML policy). It could implicitly send a TPM2_PolicyGetDigest after each policy evaluation step. This way, the evaluation could abort with an error message at the first failure rather than waiting until time of use, where it can only return a generic, "it failed, but I'm not sure where" message.

Determining why it failed strongly depends on the policy statement. Debugging the "why" is left as an exercise for you, the reader.

Summary

This chapter has described many of the best-known methods we've found for debugging TPM applications. Hopefully these will give you a good start in debugging, and you'll go on to discover even better techniques.

CHAPTER 21

■ ■ ■

Solving Bigger Problems with the TPM 2.0

Throughout this book, we have described examples of how you can use particular TPM commands in programs. This chapter looks at how some of those commands can be combined to create programs that use multiple features of the TPM. These ideas couldn't be implemented easily with TPM 1.2, but TPM 2.0 has added features that make it easy to solve these problems.

Remote Provisioning of PCs with IDevIDs Using the EK

Each client's TPM comes with an endorsement key (EK). This is a storage key, and it comes with a certificate indicating that it's from an authentic TPM. An enterprise may also have a list of EK certificates, corresponding to client machines it has bought. Enterprises would like to have a unique signing key on each system (usually called a device identity [IDevID]), which can be used to initiate a VPN connection. But, being a storage key, the EK can't be used as a VPN key. TPM 1.2 had a complicated protocol that could be used to create a certificate for a signing key created in the TPM, which proved that the key was generated in a TPM. However, no commercially available CAs followed that protocol.

TPM 2.0 has an EK that is slightly more robust than the 1.2 EK. A 2.0 EK can be used to wrap other keys. In particular, it's possible for an enterprise to create a restricted signing key and encrypt it such in a way that only the TPM that has that EK can import it. This is similar to (although more secure than) the "send a PKCS #12 file" technique used today to provision keys. Using this approach, PKCS #12 files that contain the private key are created and sent to clients. Clients are then given a password through a side channel, which they use to decrypt the PK12 file; they then store the private portion in a (hopefully) secure place. This technique exposes the private key at some point and is only as secure as the password. The TPM protocols are much more secure.

There are basically three ways you can name the signing key that is being created as an IDevID:

- *Technique 1*: Create the IDevID in a server-side TPM or TPM emulator, and use the standard CA to create a certificate for it. Then duplicate this key so that it can be imported into a system that has the client's EK resident. This is called *duplicating* the key so that its new parent is the EK.

- *Technique 2*: Create the IDevID and certify it. Wrap it up so that it looks like a duplicated TPM key and can be imported into the client's EK.

- *Technique 3*: Create the IDevID and certify it. Import it locally into a TPM or TPM emulator, and then duplicate it to have its new parent be the client TPM's EK.

These three techniques are implemented slightly differently, as discussed in the following sections.

Technique 1

In this case, because the key is to be duplicated by the TPM, several things must be true. First, the key must be duplicable. This means it isn't a fixedTPM key, and it isn't a fixedParent key. Further, it must have a policy, because only keys with a policy can be duplicated. One of the following must be true for that policy:

- Use TPM2_PolicyCommandCode with TPM2_Duplicate as a parameter

- Use TPM2_PolicyDuplicateSelect

Either of these must be in at least one branch of the policy. You don't want the key to be duplicated beyond the target TPM, so if you use the first option, you have to add a further restriction to that policy branch—perhaps a TPM2_PolicySigned. In this case, the second solution is better: you simply fix the target of duplication (the new parent of the key) to be the EK public key.

Further, for the IDevID key to act like an AIK, it must be a restricted signing key. Use TPM2_Create to create the key on the server.

Next you have to use your enterprise CA to make a certificate for this key. Before this is done, the EK's certificate is checked to make certain it's valid. Then the certificate can say that the IDevID belongs to the PC with that EK. Because the key is a signing key, this shouldn't be difficult—a normal CA protocol should work.

To duplicate the key, you now create three files, each of which represents a parameter that will be used to import the IDevID key into the target PC with the specified EK. You use the TPM (or emulator) with TPM2_Duplicate command to do this. (Of course, you first have to start and satisfy the branch of the policy that allows duplication.) This command has three outputs, which will be put into three different files:

- TPM2B_PUBLIC: This structure is a description of the IDevID key, including its public part

- TPM2B_PRIVATE: This structure contains the private portion of the IDevID, symmetrically encrypted; and an HMAC value that binds it to the public portion

- An encrypted value that allows a TPM with the correct EK to regenerate a seed

These three outputs are inputs to the TPM2_Import command. The seed is used by the TPM to generate an AES key, which is used to decrypt the private key, and an HMAC key, which is used to verify that the public and private portions of the key haven't been meddled with.

Finally, you send the three files to the target PC. There, if the EK isn't currently resident, it's regenerated using TPM2_CreatePrimary. Then you use TPM2_Import, passing it the three files that were given to the PC as parameters. The TPM2_Import command returns a normal TPM-encrypted blob, which can be used to load the IDEVID key into the TPM using the TPM2_Load command whenever the EK is present in the TPM.

The advantage of this technique is that the TPM (or emulator) does much of the work. The disadvantage is that the end user has to create a policy and also has to rely on the random number generator of the TPM or emulator. A hardware random number generator may be too slow, and a software one may not be high enough quality.

Technique 2

If you want to use a TPM to do duplication, you have to use a policy. But you can create the key entirely outside a TPM and wrap it up like a duplicated key, ready to be imported into the TPM with the referenced EK. If you do this, you don't need to associate a policy (other than the empty buffer) with the key. In this case, you need to write software that creates the three files to be used as parameters in the TPM2_Import command.

The first file contains the public data of the IDevID; the second holds the private data of the IDevID, encrypted with an AES key, together with an HMAC of both the public and private portions of the IDevID; and the third allows the TPM with the referenced EK to calculate a seed from which the AES key and the HMAC key are derived. If the EK is an RSA key, the third file is merely the seed, encrypted with the public EK. A number of details must be determined to create these files; they're described well in the specification, particularly in parts 1 and 2.

If the IDevID is an RSA public key, it uses the TPM2B_PUBLIC structure (defined in Part 2, section 12.2.5.) This structure refers to a TPMT_PUBLIC structure, which is defined in section 12.2.4. The TPMT_PUBLIC structure in turn refers to a number of other structures and parameters:

- The TPMI_ALG_PUBLIC, which is TPM_ALG_RSA
- The TPMI_ALG_HASH, which is TPM_ALG_SHA256
- A TPMA_OBJECT bitmap, which describes the kind of key (you specify whether it's a signing key, duplicable, and so on, just as though you were creating the key)

The next two parameters in the TPMT_PUBLIC structure are unions:

- TPMU_PUBLIC_PARMS (see section 12.2.3.7). Given that your key is TPM_ALG_RSA, it becomes TPMS_RSA_PARMS. (12.2.3.5)
- TPMU_PUBLIC_ID (12.2.3.2). Given that your key is TPM_ALG_RSA, it becomes TPMS_PUBLIC_KEY_RSA (the length and contents of the RSA public key).

We create the third file before the second one, though logically the public and private files go together. This is because we will need the third file to encrypt the second one. The third file is a seed encrypted with the new parent object. The seed can be generated using any random number generator (the TPM has a good one), and it should be the size of the hash—in this case, 256 bits long. Once you have this seed, you can use it to calculate two keys: an HMAC key to be used to prove the integrity of the linkage between the public and private sections of the key, and a symmetric encryption key to encrypt the private section. The HMAC key is found using equation 37, in section 22.5 of Part 1:

HMACkey := KDFa (pNameAlg, seedValue, "INTEGRITY", NULL, NULL, bits)

The encryption key you use is found in equation 35, just above the previous one:

symKey := KDFa (pNameAlg, seedValue, "STORAGE", name, NULL, bits)

You now must encrypt the seed with the EK public key. This is done in accordance with the annexes in Part 1. In particular for RSA, B.10.3 indicates that Optimal Asymmetric Encryption Padding (OAEP) using the RSA public key is used (as described in more detail in B.4, using DUPLICATE as the L parameter).

The private data is a TPM2B_PRIVATE structure, found in Part 2 12.3.7. It consists of a size and an encrypted private area. The encrypted private area consists of two pieces: an integrity area and a sensitive area. The sensitive area is calculated first.

The sensitive area consists of a TPMT_SENSITIVE area found in table 188 of 12.3.2.4. This is the TPMU_SENSITIVE_COMPOSITE, which table 187 says (for a TPM_ALG_RSA key) is a TPM2B_PRIVATE_KEY_RSAj. Table 160 specifies that this is one of the two primes, preceded by a 2-byte field containing the number of bits in the prime. It's encrypted using AES in cipher-feedback mode, where the IV is zero. This is found in equation 36, section 22.4, Part 1.

The integrity digest is an HMAC over the public and encrypted private data using the HMAC key calculated from the seed. This is calculated using the following equation:

```
outerHMAC := SHA256 (HMACkey, encrypted Sensitive area || TPM2B_PUBLIC)
```

The integrity digest is prepended to the sensitive area, and a size of the result (2 bytes) is prepended to this, to create the final private data structure. Once this is done, these three files can be sent to the remote client PC, where they are imported using TPM2_Import and the EK as the new parent.

This technique is somewhat complicated, but it lets you create the key in any manner the administrator wishes and is the only way to create a duplicated key that has a null policy. This approach guarantees that it isn't possible to duplicate the key from the target PC's TPM to any other TPM, because the TPM always requires a policy to duplicate a key.

Technique 3

If you would like to generate your IDevID key yourself, perhaps because you have a trusted random number generator, but you don't wish to do the hard part of generating the three files, you can import the key directly into a local TPM (or emulator) and let it do the hard work of duplicating the key. This still requires the end user to generate the public data of the key in TPM format, including having a policy that allows for duplication. But the generation of the seed—deriving an AES key from the seed and encrypting the private portion, generating the HMAC from the seed, and calculating the HMAC of the public and private portions of the data—is left to the TPM to accomplish.

This approach uses the TPM2_LoadExternal command, which doesn't require that the private key be encrypted when it's loaded. At this point the user continues using the same steps in as Technique 1 after the key was created. Then the user loads the public portion of the EK, satisfies the policy for duplication, and duplicates the key to the EK. Doing so produces the three files, which the user can load into the TPM once the user is assured that the EK is indeed loaded on their system.

Data Backups

Most PCs today have a lot of extra space on their hard drives. Most enterprises have many PCs with data that should be periodically backed up. It would be ideal if those PCs could back up their data on other PCs in the business. That way, as an enterprise expands with more PCs, the need to back up data and the available space on which to back up the data grow at the same rate. There are algorithms for backing up data in m copies, so that only n of the m copies need to be present to recover the data, and these algorithms can be made space efficient. However, this book doesn't describe those techniques, because we're concerned with another problem with this approach: how do you keep this backed-up data secure?

First, of course, the data must be encrypted in a way that only allows the owner of the data to access it. This can be done by having the TPM create an HMAC key and loading it in the TPM's persistent storage using TPM2_EvictControl. The filename can be HMACed to create a derived AES key that can then be used to encrypt the file before it's backed up.

(This provides a different key for each file and makes it easy to recover the AES key for those with access to use the HMAC key.) Alternatively, you can ask the TPM to generate an AES key (using its random number generator, so the key is unique for each file); that key can be encrypted with a public key whose private key is known to the TPM, and that AES key is used to encrypt the file. In either case, the HMAC key or private key should be backed up to another system's TPM in case of TPM failure.

Separation of Privilege

The end user today has to select and set authorization values for the storage hierarchy (owner authorization) for security, endorsement hierarchy (for privacy administration), and dictionary attack reset parameter (for TPM administration). This splits control of the TPM for different type of administrators. But finer control of these commands (particularly the owner authorization) may be required.

Chapter 10 gave a number of examples of different policies, but didn't examine how a policy for the storage hierarchy can be split. The owner of the storage hierarchy can create NV indexes, create primary storage hierarchies, and make keys persistent (and evict them from persistency), among other things. An administrator may very well want to allow an end user to create primary keys but not make them persistent, or make NV indexes but not evict persistent keys in the storage hierarchy.

If a storage root key (SRK) is made by an administrator and made persistent, then without owner authorization, it isn't possible to change the authorization value associated with this key. This is important, because that authorization is usually the empty buffer, in order to allow any software to use the SRK value stored in the TPM. If malicious code were to evict this key and then re-create it with a different authorization, it would be a type of denial of service attack.

But the end user may wish to allow software to use different algorithms than the default algorithm set chosen for the SRK. In this case, the owner may wish to allow the creation of SRK-like keys with different algorithm sets. As a result, the owner may wish software to be able to use keys created with TPM2_CreatePrimary. However, the owner may not wish to allow those keys to become persistent, because that uses precious resources in the TPM—another form of denial of service.

Finally, the owner may wish to allow software to create some NV RAM indexes that have a limited amount of space. But not all of these things can be done by choosing a correct policy.

To separate privilege, the owner first creates a long, random password for the owner-authorization value and then makes sure it's held secure. This requires that the end user use the policy to accomplish their goals. Next, branches of that policy are created for each command code that the owner wishes the end user to be able to use. To allow use of TPM2_CreatePrimary, one branch can be TPM2_PolicyCommandCode with TPM2_CreatePrimary as a parameter. To allow only the creation of certain NVRAM indexes, the TPM2_PolicyCpHash command is used, with parameters for TPM2_NV_DefineSpace and specific parameters indicating the index to be created and the public parameters of that index, for each index that the owner wishes the end user to be able to create. (This is similar to opening a port in a firewall—just because it's there doesn't mean it will be used.)

Securing a Server's Logon

Passwords are weak. Originally, usernames and passwords were stored on servers. That approach was vulnerable if someone got hold of the list. So, a shadow file system was set up to make it harder to get to the real list. But that was still too weak. Instead of storing passwords, the hashes of the passwords were stored. However, dictionary attacks and rainbow tables made this technique also vulnerable. Next, salted hashes (concatenating a random number before a password was hashed) were tried, but the salt itself had to be available for the computer to use to verify the password. In this case, very fast computers could do dictionary attacks against a salted list of passwords. So the server started doing many iterations of a hash—hashing the hash of the hash of the password, perhaps 1,000 times—to try to make dictionary attacks more expensive while not doing so many hashes that verifying a password took too long. Then cloud computing came along, making even this defense insufficient.

The TPM can be used to solve this problem. Instead of having the salt in the clear, a keyed hash can be used with the key stored in the TPM. The HMAC is over the user ID and password. If this is done, then even if the entire list of HMACed passwords were published, it wouldn't do an attacker any good—not having the key, they would have to rely on the TPM to do the HMACing. This reduces the risk of parallelization attacks or offline attacks using very fast computers.

Implementing this is relatively easy. In Linux, authentication is done using pluggable authentication modules (PAMs); they're designed specifically to allow different forms of authentication to be added to Linux.

First a large random number is created—say, a 256-bit number—which you use as your HMAC key. This is created with the TPM2_GetRandom command of the TPM or the Tpm2_GetRandom function in the FAPI. These commands ask how many bytes you want: in this case, you ask for 32 bytes. You call this result M and store it in a safe in case your TPM ever dies or the motherboard is replaced.

Next you need to load M into the TPM. You can do this with the TPM2_Load command. You choose an empty buffer password for M, because you want to use it without authorization. (You want to store M persistently, so you can't use the TPM2_LoadExternal command.) You load it into the storage hierarchy using the owner authorization. Then you use TPM2_EvictControl to make M persist in the TPM. This call also gives it a persistent handle, which can thereafter be used to identify M in the TPM.

Now you need to write a PAM (which is outside the scope of this book). When given a new password, it uses the TPM2_HMAC command to HMAC the user ID and password with M. When a user ID and password are passed in for authorization, the PAM likewise HMACs them with M and then compares the result with what is in the user ID / HMAC list.

The HMAC command is relatively fast, so this shouldn't delay the authentication procedure significantly, but it should be a good defense against attacks that steal the password file and try to reverse-engineer it with offline attacks of any sort.

Locking Firmware in an Embedded System, but Allowing for Upgrades

Healthcare systems need to be secure. Unfortunately, there has been a lot of research showing that devices such as pacemakers and glucose-control systems aren't terribly secure. One way of making a system more secure is to be certain the firmware used to run the device is approved by the manufacturer. This means a public key has to be available to the device, to verify that the firmware that is being loaded has been correctly signed by the manufacturer. But where can you store the key?

The obvious solution is to store the key in the TPM. This public key can be loaded using the TPM2_LoadExternal command and then made persistent using the TPM2_EvictControl command. Now commands that are used to update the firmware can use the certified TPM2_VerifySignature command to verify that the new firmware is indeed signed by the manufacturer before it's loaded. Writing cryptographic code isn't easy to do without making mistakes, so having certified code to do the cryptographic calculations is a real advantage.

As a side note, a similar approach could be used for documents: passports or even currency could come with signatures. A portable scanner with a TPM in it could have public keys preloaded that match the authority that made the documents and could be quickly used to verify the signature. If a counterfeiter started producing large numbers of fake bills, they would first require a large number of real bills from which to copy the signatures. If they copied only a few bills, once found, those certificates could be easily revoked.

Summary

TPM 2.0 is more than just a collection of algorithms that can be performed in hardware. It's an enabler of new functionality. The examples in this chapter haven't (to our knowledge) been attempted in commercial or open source software yet, but we're excited to see that happen. Even if only the solution for strengthening the storage of passwords were implemented, it would be a big win for the community. Security problems are everywhere, and TPM 2.0 can be used as a tool to provide solutions for those problems.

CHAPTER 22

■ ■ ■

Platform Security Technologies That Use TPM 2.0

Okay, we've written a whole book on TPMs, and you've apparently read the whole thing. Perhaps our attempts to keep the book interesting were successful. . .or you're extraordinarily persistent. . .or maybe you just cheated and skipped to the conclusion.

Either way, we've reached the end of the matter. TPMs are great and awesome, the security equivalent of sliced bread, no doubt about it. And TPMs by themselves offer a good level of security. For instance, an application like Microsoft's BitLocker can use a TPM to securely store a hard disk encryption key and control access to the key.

But there are also platform-level technologies that combine TPMs with other platform- and vendor-specific security features to produce even stronger solutions. The goal of this chapter is to describe three of those technologies and how they integrate with TPMs.

The Three Technologies

Three major platform technologies use TPMs. This chapter describes these three technologies at a high level, how they make use of TPM 2.0 devices, and how they empower applications to use TPMs. This chapter aims to be non-partisan and, for that reason, steers clear of comparisons of these three technologies and avoids marketing-oriented statements.[1] This is a TPM 2.0 book, so the focus is on how TPMs are used in each of these environments. In the interests of maintaining neutrality and accuracy, the sections on the technologies were written by experienced current and former representatives of the companies mentioned.

---

[1]It should be noted that Intel sponsored the publishing of this book, including the publishing costs. Intel seeks to advance the adoption of TPM 2.0 devices for the betterment of the computing security ecosystem.

Some Terms

Before we go any further, we need to define some terms:

- *Trusted computing base (TCB)*: Everything in a computer system that provides a secure environment. Basically, it's the set of hardware and software components that must trusted in order to provide security to the system.

- *Measured boot*: A boot method where each component is measured by its predecessor before being executed. Typically these measurements are accumulated in PCRs via extend operations.

- *Chain of trust*: A chain of operations that comprise a measured boot.

- *Root of trust for measurement (RTM)*: The base component of a chain of trust that is implicitly trusted. As such, it must be small and immutable (in ROM or protected by hardware).

- *Static root of trust (SRTM)*: The base component of the chain of trust that starts at power-on and extends to sometime before the OS boots. In the server version of Intel TXT, the SRTM is the CPU microcode. In other architectures, the SRTM is a ROM image.

- *Dynamic root of trust (DRTM)*: The chain of trust that starts after the OS has booted in non-secure mode. This allows the dynamic establishment of a measured boot environment. In Intel TXT, the CPU microcode is also the DRTM. DRTM is sometimes called *delayed launch*.

- *Authenticated code module (ACM)*: ACMs are Intel TXT digitally signed code modules that are invoked by the special Intel TXT GETSEC instruction. ACMs are the next components to execute after the SRTM and DRTM components execute. Which ACM is invoked and which sub-functionality is invoked is determined by a register setting when the GETSEC instruction is executed.

- *Unified extensible firmware interface (UEFI)*: A standardized version of BIOS that is CPU independent and standardizes boot and runtime services.

- *SEC phase*: The security phase of the UEFI BIOS. This is the first code to execute after reset.

- *PEI phase*: The pre-EFI phase of UEFI BIOS. This is the next phase after the SEC phase. The SEC and PEI phases together comprise what used to be called the BIOS *boot block*.

Intel® Trusted Execution Technology (Intel® TXT)

Intel TXT has been shipping since 2002 in client machines and since 2010 in servers. Intel TXT provides a chain of trust that is rooted in the microprocessor's hardware and is extended in stages to the OS and even to applications, depending on how higher levels of software make use of it.

This section describes Intel TXT at a high level first, including its features that offer advantages over a TPM-only solution, and then delves into the details of how it uses TPM 2.0's capabilities. At a high level, the advantages of Intel TXT over a TPM-only solution are a hardware-based root of trust, a smaller TCB, and specific checks of the hardware and software configuration performed by the ACMs. This section highlights how these advantages are implemented.

Other Intel technologies use TPMs, including Intel Boot Guard. This chapter doesn't describe these technologies or how they use TPM 2.0 devices, because Intel TXT is currently the most prevalent technology and a representative example of how TPM 2.0 devices are used. Also note that there are two flavors of Intel TXT: one for client platforms and one for server platforms. Many of the principles of operation are shared, but we focus on the server version, because it uses a superset of TPM functionality.

High-Level Description

Intel TXT for servers can defend against BIOS attacks, reset attacks, rootkits, and software attacks and allows the system integrator and user many options for configuring the level of protection. Although it does prevent or mitigate some attacks, its primary purpose is to notify the user and system software of the presence of a possible attack and prevent a verified launch if an attack is detected. Intel TXT hardware and software and the TPM are tightly integrated in a way that protects both the TPM and the TXT registers from unauthorized access. Critical measurements stored in the TPM cannot be spoofed, and the TPM protects OEM and user policies from unauthorized alteration.

How does it do this? A short description is that a chain of trust is extended from the Intel processor and/or chipset hardware through the BIOS. Then, after the OS has booted, if the user desires to enter secure mode at the OS level, a measured launch sequence is initiated by the OS or a software program running on top of the OS (DRTM). This measured launch ensures that there are no security holes in the system before launching the OS and entering secure mode. Basically, a chain of trust may be extended from the hardware all the way up to the highest levels of software, enabling a system administrator or user to create and use security policies. This chain of trust always measures components before actually executing them.

Intel TXT Platform Components

There are many components to Intel TXT:

- *CPU and chipset hardware*: The chipset contains special Intel TXT registers, many of which are readable and/or writeable only by Authenticated Code Modules and CPU microcode.

- *CPU microcode*: This is hardwired firmware inside the microprocessor for executing groups of micro-operations that are combined to perform assembly language instructions as well as other internal CPU functions.

- *Intel Authenticated Code Modules (ACMs)*: These ACMs can only be created by Intel and are digitally signed with a private key that is only known to Intel. The public key is hardwired into hardware registers in the chipset, and only a module signed with the matching private key is allowed to execute. ACMs are invoked by Intel microcode, and they function as extensions of microcode. For server Intel TXT, there are two ACMs, the BIOS ACM and the SINIT (measured launch initialization) ACM:

  - The BIOS ACM contains several sub-functions (calls), two of which are:

    - The *Startup ACM*[2] call is called by CPU microcode at power-on to start the SRTM. It typically measures the BIOS boot block, or, as it's called in UEFI, the SEC and PEI phases of BIOS.

    - The *Lock Config* call is made by the BIOS just before it exits the part of the BIOS measured by the Startup ACM. This performs some bookkeeping and locks some registers to prevent hostile software or firmware from changing critical hardware settings.

  - The SINIT ACM contains only one call and is called by the OS or applications running under the OS in order to perform a measured launch (DRTM).

  Both ACMs always run in a special internal CPU memory that prevents DMA accesses to the memory and any snooping of the ACM code and data.

---

[2]The Startup ACM isn't a separate ACM, but a function contained in the BIOS ACM. The misleading name has historical roots.

- GETSEC: This is a special Intel TXT assembly language instruction that invokes a function determined by a register setting. These functions invoke microcode flows used to enter, launch, and exit ACMs and exit the measured launch environment (MLE).[3] Which sub-functionality *(leaf[4])* is invoked by the GETSEC instruction is determined by a register setting. This is how the BIOS ACM *Lock Config* and SINIT ACM calls are invoked.

- *BIOS enabling for Intel TXT*: There is a table inside the BIOS, the firmware interface table (FIT), that tells the microcode and ACM whether Intel TXT is enabled, where the BIOS ACM is located, and which sections of BIOS to measure.

- *TPM*:

  - PCRs in the TPM are used to store measurements of components involved in the boot process. Some of these PCRs can only be extended by microcode, and some are only extended by ACMs.

  - NV indices are used to track some state information required by the verified launch process.

  The specifics of PC-compatible TPMs are described in detail in the TCG PC Client Platform TPM Profile (PTP) Specification. That specification describes the accessibility and number of the PCRs, special interfaces for measuring BIOS boot code, and other special TPM features used to support PC platforms.

- *OS/middleware enabling for Intel TXT*: The OS or middleware has to start the measured launch. In some cases, this might be an application or module running under the OS; in others, it might be a commercial virtual machine manager (VMM) software package.

- *High level applications that use Intel TXT to make security decisions:* Intel's Mount Wilson software is an example of this. For more examples and a much more detailed explanation of such high-level descriptions, read the book *Building the Infrastructure for Cloud Security: A Solutions View* (Apress, 2014).

All of these components work together to enable Intel TXT.

---

[3]For a full description of this instruction and its leaves, see the "Safer Mode Extensions" chapter in the *Intel 64 and IA-32 Architectures Software Developer's Manual*, Volume 2B. This manual can be downloaded from www.intel.com.
[4]*Leaf* is TXT jargon for a sub-function within an ACM.

Intel TXT Boot Sequence

Let's look at one possible boot sequence at a medium level of detail. If you desire more details, see the book *Intel Trusted Execution Technology for Server Platforms* (Apress, 2013).

One quick note about error handling so that we don't have to describe it repeatedly in the following sequence: if a failure occurs at any point in the sequence, a chipset register is written with an error indication. This chipset register, TXT.ERRORCODE, is only writable by ACMs and microcode to prevent less privileged and possibly hostile code from clearing it. An error value in this register prevents a measured launch later in the boot cycle, as described shortly.

Figure 22-1 and Figure 22-2 illustrate the Intel measured launch process and how various components interact with the TPM. Figure 22-1 is a complete timeline from power-on through launching a trusted OS. This includes the SRTM before OS boot and the DRTM initiated by the OS. Figure 22-2 provides more detail about the secure launch sequence, specifically the steps taken to verify that both the platform and the system software are trusted.

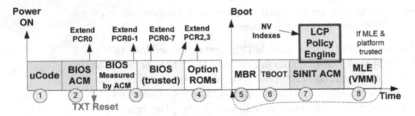

Figure 22-1. Intel TXT boot timeline

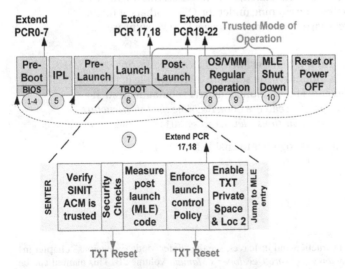

Figure 22-2. Breakout of measured launch details

336

The boot sequence is illustrated by Figure 22-1 and consists of two stages: the SRTM stage and the DRTM stage. The SRTM stage starts with the CPU microcode and extends up to OS boot. The DRTM stage starts when the SINIT ACM is invoked and extends through OS boot.

The first part of the sequence (SRTM) starts at power-on and protects against BIOS and reset attacks:

1. *Microcode*: When reset is de-asserted, the microcode checks the BIOS FIT to determine where the BIOS ACM is located in the BIOS image. The microcode verifies the signature of the BIOS ACM and does some other sanity checks on the ACM. If all is well—the ACM is uncorrupted, and it's the correct ACM—then the microcode starts the ACM running in protected CPU internal memory.

2. *Startup ACM*: The BIOS ACM contains a few different entry points that can be invoked by microcode or the BIOS. The Startup ACM call is invoked by microcode when the platform is powered-on or reset. This call's main function is to measure certain portions of the BIOS that must be trusted to operate correctly in order to guarantee system integrity, as well as to extend those BIOS measurements into PCR0. The regions of BIOS to be measured are specified by entries in the FIT table which are configured by the BIOS OEM. Some critical regions of the FIT table itself as well as the reset vector and some other regions of BIOS are required to be measured, and the BIOS ACM ensures that this is the case. Other regions of BIOS can be optionally measured, and it's up to the BIOS developer to properly configure the table to measure the correct regions of BIOS. The whole BIOS image doesn't need to be measured, and any regions of flash memory that can change under normal boot situations aren't measured, because this will cause false failures. At a minimum, to guarantee system integrity, the boot block of the BIOS must be measured—this block includes the basic system and memory initialization code. If the Startup ACM detects an error (probably indicating some sort of security issue), it sets an error code in TXT.ERRORCODE register and resets the CPU, and then the microcode directs the CPU to the reset vector. In this case, only a non-verified launch is possible. If the Startup ACM code completes successfully, the BIOS is executed.

3. *BIOS continues the static chain of trust*: The BIOS continues the chain of trust by measuring any additional BIOS code to PCR0 and measures other platform components to other PCRs. BIOS also creates a log of everything measured to the PCRs. All code in the BIOS trust boundary must be measured before that module executes. And before the BIOS executes any unmeasured code (code outside the BIOS trust boundary), it calls the BIOS ACM to lock the platform configuration to prevent untrusted code from altering the platform configuration. These calls to the BIOS ACM also test and perform security checks to ensure system integrity.

4. *Option ROMs*: Unless provided by the OEM, option ROMs are outside the trust boundary and option ROM code is measured into PCR2 while any option ROM configuration is measured into PCR3.

5. *OS boot*: When the BIOS completes, it boots to the OS loaded on the system. The OS is running in normal, non-verified boot mode, but it's locked and loaded to perform the DRTM phase of booting.

The second part of the sequence (DRTM) starts at the GETSEC(SENTER) leaf, which is invoked by the OS or a software component running in the OS. This provides a dynamic root of trust for measurement that measures the SINIT ACM and the MLE, which is sometimes the VMM.

6. *Measured launch*: When the OS wants to boot into trusted mode, it executes the GETSEC(SENTER) instruction. This causes a microcode flow that verifies the SINIT ACM in a manner similar to the BIOS ACM (see steps 1 and 2), loads it, and starts executing it.

7. *SINIT ACM*: The SINIT ACM verifies that no other security issues have occurred by checking the TXT.ERRORCODE register. It does some hardware configuration checks for certain security issues. It then measures the trusted OS code. The ACM also includes a Launch Control Policy (LCP) engine that performs policy checks, which includes checking the measured OS code and PCRs against lists of known good values. If any checks fail in the SINIT ACM, a platform reset is performed. If all is well, the ACM performs the measured launch and the OS enters secure mode. This is referred to as the *Measured Launch Environment (MLE)*. Measurements of the SINIT ACM, policies, and measured OS code are extended into PCR17 and 18.

8.   *Trusted mode*: At this point, the trusted environment has been enabled, and the OS has access to Locality 2 and thus the dynamic PCRs. The trusted OS continues the dynamic chain of trust by measuring additional OS components and configuration into PCRs 18–22.

9.   *Applications*: Local applications can use the values in PCRs to seal secrets that can only be unsealed when the platform is in that same trusted environment. For example, the OS can seal an encryption key it uses to encrypt private and privileged information. Only when the platform successfully performs the measured launch can the OS recover the key and decrypt the data. This is sometimes referred to as *local attestation*. *Remote attestation* is where external agents use the PCR values to make a trust decision—perhaps quarantining an untrusted platform while connecting trusted platforms to the production network.

10. *Termination*: The final stage is when the OS terminates the trusted environment. This can either shut down the platform (power-off or restart) or just exit the trusted mode, in which case the OS can re-enter it by performing another measured launch without the need to reset the platform. After the MLE shutdown, the OS no longer has Locality 2 access to the TPM.

This seems like a lot of detail, but we've actually skipped the low-level details of the Intel TXT policy, the security checks performed by the ACMs, the details of how TPM NV indices are used for communicating TXT status, and the BIOS enabling and provisioning of TXT.

How TPM 2.0 Devices Are Used

So, how do TPMs fit in this picture? Intel TXT uses PCRs and NV indices, primarily. Other TPM 2.0 features figure into how PCRs and NV indices are accessed and used: special hardware-triggered TPM commands, policy commands, and localities. These are described at a high level here.[5]

---

[5]TPM 1.2 also had PCRs, NV indices, hardware-triggered TPM commands, and localities. Policies and algorithm agility are the new TPM 2.0 features used by TXT.

NV Indices

NV Indices play an important role in Intel TXT. They are used to do the following:

- Securely pass information and states between ACMs

- Securely maintain state between platform resets and power cycles

- Allow OEM and platform owner to provide hashes of two policy lists, platform supplier and platform owner, of known good platform configurations

- Protect OEM and user policies from malicious alteration

Access to these indices is controlled by index attributes and a combination of password and index policy authorizations as described in Chapters 13 and 14 of this book. The ACM verifies that the attributes are correct before trusting their content.

PCRs

PCRs are used by both ACMs. Because TPM 2.0 supports algorithm agility, Intel TXT supports this agility at all levels from ACMs through Intel TXT launch-measured policies and BIOS trust policies. The details of this agility support are described in detail in the *Measured Launched Environment Developer's Guide*, which you can download from Intel's web site, and the *Intel TXT BIOS Writer's Guide*, which is available to OEMs.

The BIOS ACM extends the BIOS measurements and other early initialization values into PCR0. BIOS extends measurements of other platform configuration components into PCR0-7.

When doing a measured launch, the GETSEC(SENTER) instruction microcode performs the special hardware-triggered _TPM_Hash_Start, _TPM_Hash_Data, and _TPM_Hash_End commands. These commands are triggered by writing to special TPM interface registers that can only be written from Locality 4. Chipset hardware restricts access to these Locality 4 registers to hardware or, in this case, microcode. The special hash commands extend PCR17 with measured launch measurements during the microcode's execution of the GETSEC(SENTER) instruction.

After entering the SINIT ACM, this ACM extends other dynamic launch measurements into PCR17 and PCR18. If the Intel TXT measured launch policies are satisfied, then the OS is trusted and has access to PCRs 17-22; the OS uses these to measure additional OS code and OS configuration. Later, when higher-level software makes decisions about levels of trust, these measurements are used.

Conclusion: Intel TXT

This completes a high-level view of how Intel TXT uses TPM 2.0 devices. If you're interested, you can dive into the details by accessing the Intel documents referenced earlier.

ARM® TrustZone®

ARM TrustZone has been a feature of the ARM processor architecture since 2002 and first appeared in real processors—specifically the 1176JZF™—shortly afterward in 2003. Since then, not much has changed with TrustZone itself, but many additional features, technologies and use cases have grown up around it.

It's not uncommon for TrustZone and Intel TXT to be compared and/or lumped together as each architecture's 'security extension', but below a rather superficial level the two aren't particularly similar and such comparison doesn't aid understanding. This section explores a little of what TrustZone is, how it works, and how it relates to TPM technology. At a high level, TrustZone provides a safe place for a software TPM implementation to execute.

High-Level Description

At the simplest level, TrustZone provides a facility to create a virtual second processor inside a single system on chip (SoC). Through the implementation of a special operating mode, the SoC is able to create two separate parallel software stacks (or *'worlds'*): the Normal World (NWd), which runs the main OS and user interface, and the Secure World[6] (SWd), which runs a trusted software stack implementing security features. The two worlds are kept separate by the SoC hardware so that the main OS can't interfere with programs or data in the SWd. This enables users to retain trust in the integrity and confidentiality of SWd data even when they can't trust the state of the device as a whole.

Typically, a system designer doesn't want to impact the user experience of the device and so keeps the SWd hidden away, often using it to create a virtual security processor that the main OS calls when needed. For the most part, this idea of a virtual security processor is useful, but one very important detail must be made clear: while the SWd is completely protected from direct access by untrusted NWd code, the reverse isn't true. SWd code can, in principle, access *any* memory or device in the system. This asymmetric setup has many positive implications—high-speed data transfer and the ability to integrity-check NWd memory among them—but it also gives the SWd control over the entire device, not just the security module it implements.

TrustZone Is an Architectural Feature

The first thing to understand about TrustZone is that it's an architectural feature of ARM. And to understand that, you need to remember how the ARM partner ecosystem works.

---

[6]Note a slight problem of terminology here. The original naming of these architectural features follows a *secure* vs. *non-secure* theme, but as we all know, there is no such thing as absolute security: every protection system has its limits. In recent years, this terminology has given way to the more subjective *trusted* vs. *normal* concept, but remnants of the *secure* naming remain in the names of various components. This chapter uses the *(non-)secure* and *(un-)trusted* terms interchangeably.

ARM (the company) doesn't make chips itself: it designs processors and subsystems and controls an architecture specification that other companies take as the blueprint for their own chips. An architectural feature is something that is baked into the architecture specification and is implemented through standard mechanisms and signals (not as software or an auxiliary module/IP block) and is promised to be compatible on any ARM-based SoC regardless of any differentiating features they may implement. ARM-based SoCs are required to conform to the architecture specification (and pass a conformance test), so by specifying it in the architecture, it's assured that all such SoCs[7] have TrustZone.[8]

Another principal driver for implementing TrustZone as an architectural feature is that the security separation is then enforced by the chip hardware and doesn't rely on software or logical access control systems (which always fall to bugs in the end). This benefit is realized in ideal conditions and makes TrustZone extremely elegant and robust, although there are practical limitations on how much device makers can rely on this in the real world.

Protection Target

TrustZone is designed primarily to defeat software-borne attacks[9] such as those coming from rogue websites, errant downloads, root kits, and the like. It isn't designed to protect against concerted, targeted hardware penetration or lab attacks (like a smartcard might be). This makes sense when we consider the evolution of computing devices over the past decade or so: they have become increasingly networked, connected, and dynamic. Bulk data transfer is the norm, and data and applications flow seamlessly from one device to another with limited checks and balances. In such an environment, the growth in potential for scalable indiscriminate software attacks far outstrips those for targeted physical intrusion.

To be clear, in the TrustZone threat model, all software in the NWd is considered potentially hostile (either by rootkit infection or by deliberate replacement of kernel or similar). So while the SWd and NWd kernel often work together to provide overall device and application security, the SWd should never rely on information it receives from the NWd when making security decisions. This is important when considering TPM-like use cases.

---

[7]Specifically Cortex™-A class (or *application*) processors. ARM also designs R (*realtime*) and M (*microcontroller*) class processors, which don't have the kind of TrustZone feature described here.
[8]As you'll see later, simply having TrustZone isn't necessarily useful. It does have to be implemented correctly, something that requires skill and care.
[9]The term *shack attack* is sometimes used in association with TrustZone to describe a low-value, low-skill type of physical attack somewhere between the all-software hack attack and the high-end, skilled, and expensive lab attack. An example of a shack attack might be nondestructive bus probing on exposed wires. The degree to which an SoC can protect against shack attacks depends on the chip hardware design and isn't inherent to the TrustZone system.

System-Wide Security

ARM often describes TrustZone as *system security*,[10] but what does that mean? In this case, the *system* refers to everything in the SoC connected to the central processor by the AMBA®[11] AXI™ bus.[12] So in addition to providing simple memory and process separation for the two-worlds model, it also extends protection to data and interrupts handled by peripherals.[13]

Bus masters can be marked *secure*, meaning they're controlled by software running in the SWd, or *insecure*, meaning they can be accessed by either world.[14] When a secure peripheral interacts with the system, nothing in the untrusted world can see it or directly interfere with it: not even kernel code. Typical use cases for such a thing would be a Secure Element chip (cryptographic key storage device not accessible to normal code) or a touchscreen UI (trusted user interaction).

Implementation of TrustZone

The successful implementation of TrustZone in an SoC and system depends on many aspects of design but there are three major pieces to consider: the *NS bit*, the *Monitor*, and *secure interrupt handling*.

The NS bit

The NS (or 'Non-Secure') bit is the central manifestation of TrustZone in the ARM processor architecture. It's a control signal that accompanies all read and write transactions to system bus masters, including memory devices. As the name suggests, the NS bit must be set low in order to access SWd resources.

To understand how something so simple can reliably achieve world separation, it's sometimes useful to think of NS as an extra address bit[15] that effectively partitions the memory space into two parallel logical regions: 32-bit space plus NS. This analogy makes TrustZone isolation and error behavior intuitive: attempts from NWd to access SWd memory will fail, even if it knows the exact 32-bit address it wishes to attack, because the 33rd bit is different and so doesn't map to the desired memory location.

---

[10]www.arm.com/products/processors/technologies/trustzone/index.php.

[11]Advanced Microcontroller Bus Architecture. See http://en.wikipedia.org/wiki/Advanced_Microcontroller_Bus_Architecture for further definitions and acronyms.

[12]Technical note: Only AXI masters are able to correctly preserve TrustZone signals. Work is required to securely integrate AHB™ or APB™ devices.

[13]Again, *peripheral* here refers to masters connected directly to the AMBA AXI bus inside the SoC. It doesn't mean external devices like VDUs or printers.

[14]Remember the asymmetrical nature of TrustZone: SWd can access everything.

[15]The "33rd (or 41st or 65th) address bit" analogy can fail when you look at certain deep details, but it's close enough to be useful.

Clearly the security of the system would break down if NWd code were somehow able to set the NS bit in resource requests directly, so it's set, maintained, and checked by processor registers and bus components such as the memory controller and address space controller. Returning to the 33rd bit analogy for a moment, code makes a normal 32-bit request; and the processor hardware, knowing that the code is executing in insecure mode, adds NS=1 to the transaction.

The Monitor

Of course, nothing is ever quite as simple as a single bit in the architecture. A small amount of firmware is required to coordinate the two worlds, facilitate switching, and so on. This firmware[16] component is called the *Monitor*.

Alongside the two explicit operating modes (Secure and Non-Secure), there is a third processor mode called *Monitor mode* that runs a third separate software stack. In order to transition from NWd to SWd (or vice versa), requests must transition through Monitor mode and the Monitor firmware ensures that the transition is allowed, orderly, and secure.

The Monitor is able to access all the crucial security data in the system, so its quality and integrity are paramount. The code should be as small as possible and tested and reviewed[17] regularly in order to be, if such a thing is possible, bug-free.

World Switching

When NWd software wishes to contact SWd, it must issue a Secure Monitor Call (SMC) instruction. This invokes the Monitor, which must set the state of the NS bit in the Secure Configuration Register in the System Control Processor (CP15) (so that bus and memory devices know which world is executing and therefore calling them) and bank-sensitive registers to keep the system secure and consistent.

SMC calls are very simple: they take a single 4-byte immediate value that indicates to the software in the SWd what service is being requested, and the SWd runs that service. It's the responsibility of the system designer(s) to agree on conventional numbering and meanings for each value.[18]

---

[16]Note a coming confusion: from ARM V8, there is an official definition of *firmware* for Exception Level 3 (high privilege level) that is more than just the Monitor components. This text only refers to the code responsible for coordinating world switching, not any other firmware duties such as power management.

[17]The Monitor may even be a legitimate target for formally proven code.

[18]To help with this, ARM publishes various recommended calling conventions, but the system isn't required to follow them.

Interrupts

Earlier we introduced the idea that interrupts from secure peripherals can be routed directly to the SWd without ever passing through any untrusted code at any privilege level. At this point, it's important to introduce another configuration for peripherals: not secure or insecure, but *switchable*. Some peripherals (a touchscreen, for example) only need to be secured part of the time: when executing sensitive transactions. At all other times, it's acceptable, even required, for the NWd to have control.

To police this and ensure that the correct software stack has control at the correct time, all such interrupts are actually caught by the Monitor, and the Monitor decides (based on a configuration table) which driver (SWd or NWd) should receive the interrupt. When entering a secure transaction, the SWd can reserve the peripheral, meaning it receives all the interrupts. When it has finished, it can release the peripheral, informing the Monitor that it should send interrupts on to the NWd driver instead.

To deal with the various practical issues of performance, potential conflicts, and so on, a typical ARM system reserves the two interrupt signals for separate purposes: IRQ[19] for normal interrupts and FIQ[20] for secure.[21] This allows certain efficiencies such as static routing tables for certain events.

Relationship to TPMs

Historically, ARM SoCs have been most prevalent in mobile devices: smartphones, tablets, and the like. As such, TrustZone systems haven't typically *used* a *separate* hardware TPM, but rather have used TrustZone *as the TPM*.

Starting around a decade ago with the Mobile Trusted Module specification, and continuing today with the TPM 2.0 Mobile and PC Client specifications, the trusted computing community has developed the concept of a *firmware TPM*. With fTPM, rather than relying on separate hardware chips, the TPM functionality is implemented in a protected firmware execution space such as TrustZone and then called by the NWd OS for measurements, sealing, and so on in the normal way.

While no hard-and-fast requirements or architecture are specified for the precise implementation of the fTPM (beyond conformance to the TPM 2.0 library specification of course), the operating environment is required to provide some fundamental protection for the TPM roots of trust and PCRs. In keeping with the TrustZone protection target, no software outside of the TPM implementation should be able to modify or access roots of trust directly, or manipulate PCRs except though the authorized interfaces.

A well-implemented TrustZone system is able to provide these guarantees (and, indeed, several implementations are commercially available).

---

[19]An interrupt request (IRQ) is a signal sent from a hardware peripheral to alert the processor to an event.
[20]A fast interrupt request (FIQ) is an additional signal like IRQ but is (supposedly) handled faster.
[21]Although not actually required, there are two reasons for this recommendation: compatibility (existing NWd software makes much more use of IRQ than FIQ) and security (the ARM architecture allows for masking control of FIQ in CP-15 but not IRQ).

AMD Secure Technology™

The AMD Secure Processor™ (formerly known as the Platform Security Processor [PSP]) is a dedicated hardware security subsystem that runs independently from the platform's main core processors and is integrated into the SoC. It provides an isolated environment in which security-sensitive components can run without being affected by the software running as the main system workload. The PSP can execute system workloads as well as workloads provided by trusted third parties. Although system workloads are preinstalled and provide SoC-specific security services, the system administrator has complete control over whether and which third-party workloads are installed on the PSP. The PSP is made up of the following components:

- Dedicated 32-bit microcontroller (ARM with TrustZone technology)

- Isolated on-chip ROM and SRAM

- DRAM carved out via hardware barrier and encrypted

- Access to system memory and resources

- Secure off-chip NV storage access for firmware and data

- Platform-unique key material

- Hardware logic for secure control of CPU core boot

- Cryptographic coprocessor (CCP)

The PSP uses the ARM TrustZone architecture, as described in the section on ARM TrustZone, but there are some differences: rather than being a virtual core, the PSP is a physically disparate core integrated into the SoC that has dedicated SRAM and dedicated access to the CCP. The PSP provides the immutable hardware root of trust that can be used as the basis for optionally providing the chain of trust from the hardware up to the OS.

The CCP is made up of a random number generator (RNG), several engines to process standard cryptographic algorithms (AES, RSA, and others depending on processor model), and a key storage block. The key storage block contains two key storage areas: one dedicated to storing system keys that can be used by privileged software but that are never readable; and the other into which keys can be loaded, used, and evicted during normal operation by software running either on the PSP or on the main OS. During boot, SoC-unique e-fused keys are distributed to the CCP system key storage block.

Hardware Validated Boot

Hardware Validated Boot (HVB) is an AMD-specific form of secure boot that roots the trust to hardware in an immutable PSP on-chip ROM and verifies the integrity of the system ROM firmware (BIOS). The PSP ROM contains the initial immutable PSP code. The PSP ROM validates a secure boot key and then uses the key to validate the PSP firmware, which it reads from system flash. The PSP firmware loads and starts the system application execution. The system manufacturer can choose whether the PSP validates the BIOS platform-initialization code. The PSP then initiates BIOS execution. The PSP completes its own initialization and enters steady state while the BIOS and OS finish booting on the x86. The platform manufacturer decides whether to implement UEFI secure boot. The platform manufacturer also decides what interfaces are provided for the user to select whether UEFI secure boot is enforced. In this way, the platform manufacturer decides when to terminate the chain of trust that was rooted in the immutable hardware.

Figure 22-3 shows the scope of HVB as it relates to the UEFI secure boot.

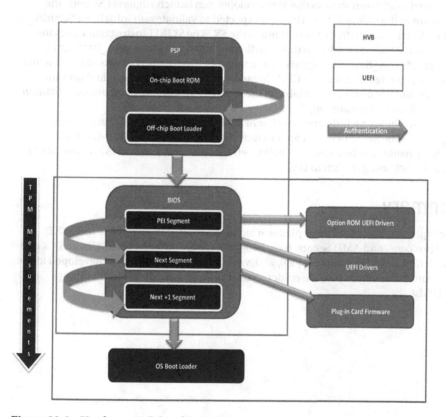

Figure 22-3. *Hardware Validated Boot Overview*

TPM on an AMD Platform

As a founding member of the Trusted Computing Group, AMD strives to support a wide range of options for the OEM and platform owner. To this end, platform manufacturers have several choices when integrating TPMs into AMD-based platforms. Platform manufacturers can continue to choose among the discrete TPM hardware options that are widely available; or the platform manufacturer can choose to integrate an AMD-provided TPM application as one of the system applications running on the PSP SWd. This firmware TPM utilizes the CCP for cryptographic processing.

SKINIT

SKINIT is the instruction that initiates the late launch CPU reinitialization to start the DRTM. SKINIT takes one parameter: the address of the Security Loader (SL) code. The SL must fit within 64KB of memory known as the Security Loader Block (SLB), which is protected from tampering and snooping. CPU microcode ensures that the CPU is reinitialized to a known state so that the developer can launch whatever SL code they need to run in the secured state. The SL is expected to validate and initialize a Security Kernel (SK) and then to transition control to the SK. The SKINIT instruction writes the contents of the SLB to an address that is redirected into the TPM via the _Hash_Init, _Hash_Start, and _Hash_End signals. These signals measure the contents of the SLB into PCR 17. Further details about the CPU characteristics that are validated and how the SKINIT instruction works are available in the *AMD64 Architecture Programmer's Manual Volume 2: System Programming.*[22]

This concludes a whirlwind overview of AMD Secure Technology™ that covers the high points of the introduction of an on-chip hardware root of trust into AMD SoCs. More information can be found on AMD's web site: www.amd.com/en-us/innovations/ software-technologies/security.

Summary

This chapter has discussed three platform technologies that use TPM 2.0: Intel TXT, ARM TrustZone, and AMD Secure Technology. There are other technologies on PCs and other platforms that also use TPM 2.0, and, we hope, many more will be developed in the future. And this is where you, the reader, come in. Go out and do wonderful things with TPMs!

---

[22]http://developer.amd.com/resources/documentation-articles/developer-guides-manuals/.

Index

■ C

■ D